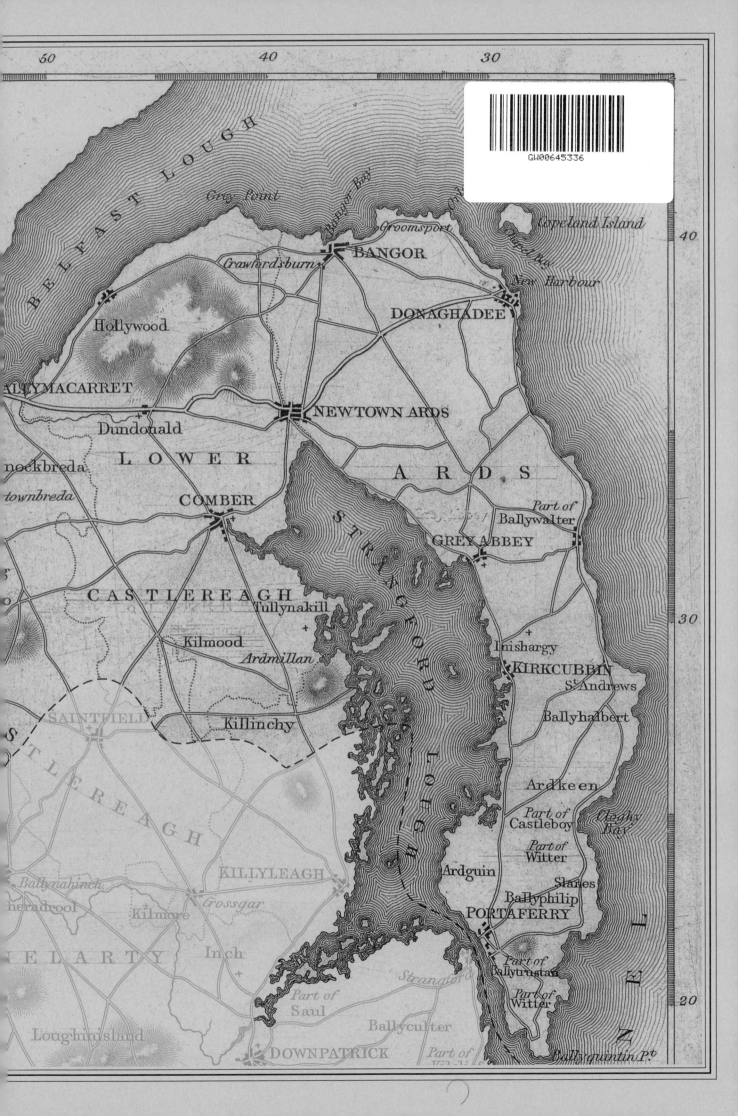

BUILDINGS OF
NORTH
COUNTY DOWN

by

C E B BRETT

with photographs by

ANTHONY C W MERRICK

A publication of the
ULSTER ARCHITECTURAL HERITAGE SOCIETY

BELFAST
2002

First published 2002
by the
Ulster Architectural Heritage Society
66 Donegall Pass, Belfast BT7 1BU

Edited by Gordon Wheeler
Designed by Della Varilly
Printed by Nicholson & Bass, Ltd

ISBN 0 900457 57 0

A catalogue record for this book
is available from the British Library

Frontispiece: Quintin Castle (58) from the shore
Photograph: Patrick Rossmore, courtesy of the Irish Architectural Archive
End-papers: Part of map of County Down, 1837 (from S Lewis: *Topographical dictionary*)

DEDICATED

to

Jennifer Jenkins

who has done so much in the cause of conservation
for the Historic Buildings Council of England (now English Heritage),
and the National Trust, of both of which she has been chairman;
and not only in England and Wales, but in Ireland too

CONTENTS

UP, DOWN !

(war-cry of the supporters of the Down County team of the Gaelic Athletic Association)

ACKNOWLEDGEMENTS

I am most grateful to the many people who have helped me in the compilation of this book, in particular, to the five who have driven me, or accompanied me on my travels, around the countryside: Harvey Bicker, of the Spa, Ballynahinch; Tanya Greenfield, of Ballyhalbert in the Ards; Karen Latimer, of Ballynahatty in Castlereagh; Brian Boyd, of Bangor; and Dorinda Dunleath, of Ballywalter. I must also thank John and Linda Mahon of Waringstown for good advice and information about buildings in that locality Between them, they have contributed a notable corpus of local knowledge to this book.

Then, I am grateful to the staff and committee of the Ulster Architectural Heritage Society; to Gerry Healey, John Killen, and Bernadette Kane, of the Linen Hall Library, Belfast; to Dr Valerie Adams of the Public Record Office of Northern Ireland, and her staff; to Terence Reeves-Smyth of the Monuments and Buildings Record; to Peter and Belinda Jupp; to Karen Latimer of the Architecture Library of the Queen's University of Belfast; to Trevor Parkhill of the Ulster Museum; to Roger Dixon and Sally Skilling of the Ulster Folk and Transport Museum; to Peter Marlow of the National Trust; to Ian Wilson of the North Down Heritage Centre; to Lola Armstrong of the Dufferin and Ava archive at Clandeboye; to Brian Mackey of the Lisburn Museum; to Fred Rankin for help with matters ecclesiastical; to Jill Lever of London; to David Walker and John Knight of Edinburgh; to Ann-Martha Rowan and David Griffin, of the Irish Architectural Archive; to Edward McParland; and to Maurice Craig; all of Dublin.

As to the preparation and production of the text, Gordon Wheeler has excelled himself in the diligence of his comments, corrections, and suggestions; exasperating as his niggling comments sometimes may have been, but eminently salutary. And I owe him a great debt for his labours on the Bibliography and the Index. I am very grateful to Della Varilly for all her hard work on the preparation and layout; and to Dianne and Gareth Williams for coming to my rescue when, as so frequently happened, the abilities of my computer outstripped my own. And I am grateful to Maurice Hayes for elucidating for me the history of my epigraph: which, he tells me, probably stems from the old Irish tradition of faction-fights.

Whilst I am very sorry that, by reason of family commitments, Michael O'Connell was unable to undertake the photography for this volume (as he did for its earlier companions), yet his advice and assistance have been of value both to me and to Anthony Merrick who has so conscientiously, and successfully, taken his place: to the latter I owe an enormous debt of gratitude: all the photographs, both black and white and in colour, are his work, unless otherwise stated; and, so impressive were his colour transparencies, that they warranted a whole extra section of colour illustrations.

I owe thanks to the following copyright-holders for permission to make use of illustrations: Patrick Rossmore, and the Irish Architectural Archive, for the photograph employed as frontispiece, and the detail on page 110; Barry Hartwell of the Department of Archaeology, QUB for the aerial photograph on page 2, and Gail Pollock for that on page 4; Museums and Galleries of Northern Ireland, and the Ulster Folk and Transport Museum, for the illustrations on pages 5, 13, 18, 199, and 237, and to the Ulster Museum for those on pages 17, 123, 142, 146 and 255; to the Monuments and Buildings Record of Northern Ireland for those on pages xiv, 25, 26, 38, 65, 74, 92, 93, 147, 209, 230, 255, 261, 268, 271, 277 and 284; to the Public Record Office of Northern Ireland for those on pages 28, 83, 84, 90-91, 230 and 262; to the National Trust, for those on pages 75, 263, and 266; to the North Down Heritage Centre for those on pages 56 and 122; to Mrs Dorothy Russell for that on page 44; to Mr Michael Harnett for that on page 79; to Mr and Mrs Day of Donaghadee for those on pages 86 and 132; to Mr Tughan of Portavo for that on page 125; to the Reverend C W Bell for that on page 135; to Mr Marcus Patton for that on page 148; to Mr Allan Anderson for those on page 155; to the Lisburn Museum for those on pages 158 and 248; to Mr Robert McKinstry for the plan on page 159; to Mr D Monteith of Beech Park for the illustration on page 185; to Mr G D Hunter for that on page 205; and to the Northern Ireland Housing Executive for the aerial view on page 223. All the illustrations in colour were specially taken for this book by Anthony Merrick, save for the George Dance drawing reproduced as Illustration 12, and in black and white on page 99, which appears by kind permission of the Trustees of Sir John Soane's Museum; and the water-colour of Donaghadee Harbour at Illustration 35, and detail at page 225, which is from the collection of a private owner.

I must also acknowledge the courtesy of those who have allowed me to quote from documents deposited by them, or their forbears, in the Public Record Office of Northern Ireland: in particular, the Duke of Abercorn; the late Sir Roland and Lady Nugent, and the late Mrs Elizabeth Cooke.

I express my thanks and appreciation to the charities, local authorities, and others who have provided financial support for this publication; and, in particular:

The Belfast Society
The British Academy
Craigavon Borough Council
The Dufferin Foundation
Environment and Heritage Service, Department of the Environment
The Esme Mitchell Trust
J Paul Getty Jr Charitable Trust
Lisburn Borough Council
Marc Fitch Fund
Paul Mellon Centre for Studies in British Art
The School of Irish Studies Foundation
Ulster Garden Villages

Finally, I must thank all those people in County Down who so generously helped me in one way or another, by volunteering information, by showing me their buildings, or by turning up old pictures, old documents, title-deeds, or other records which enabled me to put flesh on the bare bones of an inspection on the ground.

C E B B

INTRODUCTION

Although it deals with only half a county, this book is intended as a companion for my two previous volumes, Buildings of County Antrim and Buildings of County Armagh, and adopts the same arrangement of entries. North County Down is thickly populated and contains a very large number of buildings, of all dates, and of many styles; that is my justification for cutting the county in half. I had some difficulty, however, in finding a logically defensible boundary. In the end, I decided to include the whole of the District Council areas of North Down, Ards, and Castlereagh, and those parts of the District Council areas of Lisburn and Craigavon which lie within the old boundaries of the county. The rest of the county must await another day, or another author.

I must emphasise that, like its predecessors, this book is to be regarded as an anthology rather than as an inventory: I have been highly selective in the choice of buildings for inclusion; especially so, amongst the dozens of fine Victorian and Edwardian mansions of the North Down coast. And, once again, my selection has been a very subjective one, plainly reflecting my personal tastes, preferences, and prejudices: for which I make no apology.

As before, my primary purpose has been to help plug gaps. Down is indeed fortunate to have the benefit of the magisterial Archaeological Survey published in 1966, and its companion volume, Industrial Archaeology of County Down, published three years earlier in 1963. I gratefully acknowledge my debt to the authors, the late Martin Jope, Dudley Waterman, A E P Collins, and Rodney Green. But their labours were concentrated on the earlier periods of Irish history, and they touch on only a small number of buildings later than 1800, and practically none later than 1850. There is still no word of the promised Pevsner Architectural Guide for Antrim, Down and Belfast. There is no equivalent to the English volumes in the Victoria County History series; Alexander Knox's county history of 1875, and the various earlier books mentioned below, are all useful in their different ways; but, as in so much of Ireland, a good modern county history is sadly lacking. Naturally, no such history is primarily concerned with buildings or architecture. There are, of course, useful handbooks to many of the towns and villages, including in particular the relevant books and booklets published by the Ulster Architectural Heritage Society[1]; but, within my chosen boundaries, only the towns of Bangor (Marcus Patton), Donaghadee (Hugh Dixon), Holywood (Tony Merrick), Hillsborough (myself), and a handful of individual big houses, have received systematic attention from architectural historians.

The physical landscape of the county, apart from Slieve Croob and the Mournes, is endearingly described by the compilers of the Parliamentary Gazetteer: "The remainder of the county's surface, with comparatively inconsiderable exceptions, is a continuous tumulated expanse, - an almost uninterrupted congeries of swells and hillocks and hills, - a rolling and tumbling sea of verdure, mellowness, and wood ... Fondness for system, aided by an irregular fancy, may draw out the hills in ranges, or agglomerate them in determinate groups; but a sober inspection will pronounce them little otherwise collocated or connected than the tempest billows of what mariners technically call 'a short sea'"[2]. That is as good a description as I know of for the drumlin country of which most of north County Down is composed.

The Lagan is the principal river, and it is spanned by stone bridges of some antiquity. There are the broad expanses of Strangford Lough, with its innumerable islands (drumlins gone paddling); the narrower waters of Belfast Lough; the rocky and dangerous outer coast of the Ards; a minimal coastline to Lough Neagh; and many small lakes. To quote the Parliamentary Gazetteer again: "Most of the streams, from the largest to very nearly the smallest, have fine water-falls for machinery: they would be valued beyond all price by such sound English economists as those who have contrived to work such wonders with the rivulets of Sheffield: and, even as they exist, they drive innumerable mills, and are, in hundreds of places, rendered cheerful by the industrious hum of the corn-miller, the flax-dresser, or the linen-bleacher"[3]. Alas, no longer, though these activities have left river-side ruins in many places. (For good measure, seeing that I am on the subject of water, though it has nothing to do with architecture, I cannot forbear to quote from Samuel Lewis, writing in 1837: "This county is remarkable as being the first place in Ireland in which frogs were seen: they appeared first near Moira, in a western and inland district, but the cause or manner of their introduction is wholly unknown"[4].

As to styles of building, there is a very clear distinction between the eastern part of my area, and the western. The Scottish influence is strong and plain throughout the Ards peninsula, and gradually diminishes as one goes inland; the influence of the English settlers, and to a lesser extent of the Huguenot refugees, is strong and plain in the Lagan valley, and gradually diminishes as one travels eastward from Lough Neagh. Examples of both styles will be found in the pages which follow.

A very large part of my territory is now Belfast commuter-land: even places such as Moira and Waringstown serve this function, thanks to the M1 motorway; and the cohesion of many of the towns and villages has suffered. The centres of Moira and Hillsborough are still pretty and ornamental, if sometimes a little precious; Waringstown has been largely spoiled, except for its church and big house; enormous growth of new speculative housing has engulfed Bangor, Donaghadee, all too much of the Ards peninsula, Comber, Dundonald, and Castlereagh; and the threat continues unabated, thanks to lax planning controls and the disinterest of the politicians (of all parties). Holywood, Cultra, Helen's Bay, Crawfordsburn, and the rest of what is cynically known as 'the Gold Coast', on the south-east shore of Belfast Lough, are now much over-developed. Particularly worrying has been the tendency to 'restore' a building of some note as apartments, then to destroy its environment by surrounding it with closely-packed modern villas: as has happened to, amongst others, Crawfordsburn House, and Groomsport House. Both of these, which might otherwise (just) have earned a mention in this book, have been omitted, as has Rockport, a once-decent old house, spoiled by over-ambitious additions.

All over the county, houses of a certain age and presence are being subjected to the indignities of plastic window-frames, doors, and guttering. Only in exceptional circumstances have I admitted houses so altered to my pages: though I think the Environment Service is perhaps too quick to de-list buildings so afflicted, for the damage done is seldom irreversible. On the other hand, I point also to a number of instances where, to my mind, the listers of the Environment Service have greatly under-estimated the merits of buildings which seem to me of the first rank.

I may be accused, not entirely without justification, of including a disproportionately large number of isolated rural houses, not all of great distinction; and a disproportionately small number of town and village houses. My defence is, that any Ulsterman with any interest at all in the subject will already be acquainted with the numerous pleasing late-Georgian and early-Victorian houses which adorn the street frontages of towns and villages such as Newtownards, Greyabbey, Donaghadee, Portaferry, Kircubbin, Killinchy, Comber, Hillsborough, and Moira; but comparatively few are acquainted with the many pleasing buildings scattered throughout the countryside, many of them invisible from the roads, tucked away amidst trees at the end of long lanes. And these have been my particular quarry: the length of my chapter on middling-sized houses, which certainly includes many buildings whose existence I had never dreamed of, will provide some evidence of my success in tracking them down - though I do not assert that many of them were previously unknown to the Environment Service's listers, whose lists, available for inspection but not unfortunately for purchase, have been my starting-point.

The arrangement of the eight chapters, and of the entries within each chapter, are broadly consistent with my previous volumes. Within each section, buildings are mostly arranged in approximate order of date, unless considerations of contrast, comparison, or layout, suggest otherwise. (The exception is the chapter on churches where Gothic revival buildings and neo-classical buildings are generally grouped together). But it must be noted that the dating of Irish buildings is still a somewhat inexact science: documentary evidence is rare, except in the case of the more important (or more recent) buildings. In the absence of documentary evidence, it is almost impossible to date with confidence a vernacular building within a local tradition that lasted, with surprisingly few changes, from around 1720 until around 1870. There are some helpful details - banisters and rails, glazing bars, panelled doors, window-shutters - but, so far as my experience goes, every one of them can lead to delusive conclusions. Where the building history of a house seems to cover a wide span, I have endeavoured to assess its, so to speak, centre of gravity: but the process has often been an arbitrary one. And documentary evidence is not always so helpful as might be supposed.

It still requires a stroke of luck to uncover clear evidence of the name of the architect of most Ulster buildings. I have striven to be as scholarly as possible in my researches, but there is still a lot of guesswork in this book, as in its predecessors; and inevitably some of my guesses will turn out to have been wrong. I shall welcome corrections.

I have tried to provide the basic information on address, townland, District Council area, and grid reference, which a researcher is likely to need; but it should be remembered that boundaries can be moved over the years: and a review of local government seems to be impending at the time of writing. I started, but abandoned, the attempt to record parishes: the number of changes over the years, and the absence of reliable maps showing parish boundaries, defeated me. The grid references mostly represent my own estimates, based on the 1:50,000 Ordnance Survey maps. I am afraid that some mistakes will inevitably have crept into these particulars: I can but hope that they are not too many.

I have sought to indicate whether a building is listed and, if so, in which category (some seem still to be uncategorised); and whether a building falls within the boundary of a conservation area. But buildings are, with increasing frequency, re-listed or (worse) de-listed. The ward-by-ward Second Survey, at present apparently making very slow progress, may well invalidate some of my entries. Any reader with an interest in a particular building would be wise to check its current status with the Environment Service. The system of grading employed by the Service differs from that used in England, Scotland, and Wales; and is moreover far from transparent; I very much hope that, before the Second Survey is completed, the Service will publish a clear, plain and definitive guide to its system of classification, and its implications; and that a coherent and consistent method of publishing the revised lists, on a ward basis, will be adopted.

My primary concern has been, throughout, with the external appearance of the buildings recorded; my next concern with their history, owners and occupiers, and associations. I have, of course, recorded internal features of particular interest when I have come across them, but I have not gone out of my way to seek them out. I have not, however, in general recorded too-easily-portable items such as chimney-pieces. Because of the understandable security-consciousness of some householders, I had some difficulties with access. (In a few cases, I suspect that fear of the tax inspector rather than fear of burglars was the underlying reason). There are accordingly, once again, few modern interior photographs or ground plans in this book. I succeeded in getting inside around two-thirds of the buildings described, but where I was evidently unwelcome, I preferred not to insist. I was flatly refused access in four cases. Another problem was posed by the foot-and-mouth disease restrictions on access in force during much of the period when this book was in gestation. But most people, however suspicious at first, became friendly and helpful once they understood the purpose and nature of the book. On the other hand, I accept that people are well entitled to privacy inside their own homes. Of course, buildings form an important part of our common heritage; and it is certainly right that the public should have access to information about them. The vast majority of owners have shown me every kindness and courtesy, and I owe it to them to urge readers of this book not to intrude where they are not wanted, but to content themselves with visits to houses, castles, monuments and churches which are open to the public.

Amongst the earliest sources are maps: for County Down, Moll's map of 1728; Sloane's, of 1739 and 1743; Kennedy's, of 1755 and 1767; Williamson's, of 1810. Unfortunately, these are almost uniformly unhelpful, save for the sites of bridges, roads, and churches: and even then, it is not possible to tell how often the structures existing today have been rebuilt, or even completely replaced. The same holds largely true for Taylor and Skinner's maps of 1777 in their Roads of Ireland, and for the topographical information in William Wilson's Post-Chaise Companion, of 1784, with later editions; my own copy is of 1803, so that is the one from which I have mostly quoted.

A number of useful books were published in the early years of the 19th century, though James Dubourdieu's Statistical Survey of 1802 is a dry work, bearing no comparison with Walter Harris's much chattier Antient and present State of County Down of 1744. The most useful source for County Down, however, is the first volume of the obscure A Atkinson's Ireland exhibited to England, published in 1823 but based on a visit six years earlier, which contains an invaluable list of gentlemen's seats: though as usual, there is no way of being sure whether the building listed is the same as that standing today.

The next group of essential source material comprises the first Ordnance Survey maps, the Ordnance Survey memoirs, and the first set of Valuation books, all dating from the 1830s. The value of the maps is self evident; but a map does not tell the inquirer whether a building denoted is a cottage or a skyscraper. The usefulness of these maps is greatly enhanced by the possibility of collating them with the memoirs, prepared at much the same time, and now all admirably edited and published by the Institute of Irish Studies at the Queen's University of Belfast. The volumes for County Down are not quite as informative as those for County Antrim, although much more so than the scanty volumes for County Armagh. We must be thankful for what we have inherited.

A number of scholars made use of these important memoirs whilst they were still unpublished; but, as yet, not very many have made good use of the almost contemporary Valuation books in the Public Record office[5]. The exceptions are, on the whole, the industrial archaeologists, such as Rodney Green and Fred Hamond: and it is the case that these records, appropriately, have brought much grist to the their mills. But, though they are now being much more used, these books may be difficult to work with: the researcher needs to know beforehand much information which may not readily be available. So he may all too often draw a maddening blank. Nevertheless, once again, I believe that, by collating information derived from the first valuation with information from the Ordnance Survey maps and memoirs, I may have been able to assemble a worth-while quantity of hitherto unknown facts.

The later, so-called 'Griffith' valuation of 1859 - 1862, and the subsequent series running on into the 1930s,

have also provided some interesting information. But the valuations are more helpful for the larger houses; less helpful for the smaller ones, where the identification is a constant problem. In the interval between the valuations, a number of useful books appeared, in particular Samuel Lewis's Topographical Dictionary of Ireland, in editions of 1837, 1840, and 1847; and the Parliamentary Gazetteer of Ireland, of 1845-6. Both are informative, and in general (though not quite always) reliable.

As before, I have of course made use when possible of family papers, title-deeds, and newspaper cuttings. I fear I may have missed a considerable number of local history articles and leaflets: it would be helpful if the authors or publishers could make a habit of sending copies to the Belfast Central Library, the Linen Hall Library, the Queen's University Library, and the local history collections of the relevant library boards.

As I have previously remarked, this book is an anthology not an inventory, though I have tried hard to ensure that each entry is as complete and free-standing as possible. For this reason, the references are collected together at the end of each entry, not relegated to separate footnotes at the end of the volume. I greatly hope that, once again, it may provide a useful groundwork upon which others can build.

I started this book on New Year's Day 2000, and finished it in November 2001. Changes will of course have taken place between the date of writing this, and the date of actual publication. Not only may there be changes on the ground, there may also be mistakes which I could and should have avoided: for these, I accept full responsibility; but as in previous volumes I shall welcome corrections, in the hope that, if there should ever be another edition of this book, it may prove possible to incorporate them.

I should like to end on a personal note. I was born in north County Down; my home was there during my boyhood; I spent long summer holidays on a farm in the Ards peninsula. As will be evident (perhaps too evident? - have I been too self-indulgent?) to attentive readers of this book, I regard it as very much home ground, even though I have not lived in north Down for some fifty years. It has been a considerable pleasure to revisit so many scenes of my childhood and adolescence; it has also been a considerable pleasure to discover buildings I never knew existed. As always, my expeditions of exploration were not without surprises: some very pleasant, some rather less so. But I should like to express my gratitude and appreciation to the many people of north Down who made me welcome, showed me their buildings, and recounted their histories. It is a good place to be; and a good place to write about.

C E B B
December, 2001

References: 1. UAHS Lists and Surveys, 'Portaferry and Strangford', 1969; 'Craigavon', 1971; 'East Down', 1973; 'Mid Down', 1974; 'Donaghadee and Portpatrick', 1977; 2. PG, II, 1846, p 51. 3. ibid, p 52. 4. Lewis, TD, 1837, I, p 489. 5. T Parkhill, 'Valuation records in the Public Record Office of Northern Ireland', in 'Ulster local studies', XVI, 1994, pp 45-58.

ABBREVIATIONS

AAI	Architectural Association of Ireland
APSD	*Dictionary of architecture* (Architectural Publication Society)
ASCD	*Archaeological Survey of County Down*
BAR	*Buildings at risk*
BCDR	Belfast and County Down Railway
BELB	Belfast Education and Library Board
BL	British Library
BNL	*Belfast Newsletter*
CL	*Country life*
C of I	Church of Ireland
CSPI	*Calendar of State papers relating to Ireland*
DB	*Dublin builder*
DNB	*Dictionary of national biography*
DoENI	Department of the Environment, Northern Ireland
Hearth	Hearth Housing Association and Revolving Fund
HMNI	*Historic monuments of Northern Ireland*
HMSO	Her Majesty's Stationery Office
IAA	Irish Architectural Archive
IB	*Irish builder*
IGS	Irish Georgian Society
JRSAI	*Journal of the Royal Society of Antiquaries of Ireland*
JUAHS	*Journal of the Upper Ards Historical Society*
MBR	Monuments and Buildings Record of Northern Ireland
nd	no date
NIHE	Northern Ireland Housing Executive
NT	National Trust
OS	Ordnance Survey
OSM	*Ordnance Survey memoirs*
PBNHPS	*Proceedings of the Belfast Natural History and Philosophical Society*
PG	*Parliamentary gazetteer of Ireland*
PRO	Public Record Office, Kew
PRONI	Public Record Office of Northern Ireland
PSAMNI	*Preliminary survey of the ancient monuments of Northern Ireland*
QUB	Queen's University, Belfast
RC	Roman Catholic
RHA	Royal Hibernian Academy
RIAI	Royal Institute of the Architects of Ireland
RIBA	Royal Institute of British Architects
RSUA	Royal Society of Ulster Architects
td	townland
TD	Lewis's *Topographical dictionary of Ireland*
UA	*Ulster architect*
UAHS	Ulster Architectural Heritage Society
UFTM	Ulster Folk and Transport Museum
UM	Ulster Museum
UJA	*Ulster journal of archaeology*
VAL	Valuation books

Throughout the text, figures appearing in parentheses
refer to the entry numbers for other buildings discussed

Schoolgirls at Nendrum (2). Photograph: MBR

CHAPTER ONE

ANTIQUITIES, FORTIFICATIONS AND RUINS

The antiquities, fortifications and ruins of all County Down, up to a cut-off date of "about 1780", have been completely and definitively inventoried in that most authoritative volume, The Archaeological Survey of County Down, published in 1966: which fully deserves comparison with the Royal Commission volumes for England, Scotland and Wales. Alas, it stands alone in Northern Ireland: no comparable volume for any other county in the province has since appeared, or seems likely to appear.

Accordingly, it has not seemed necessary for me to treat at any great length of the antiquities: I have limited my selection to a few of the more visible (and, in most cases, visitable) sites. The northern half of the county is densely populated and has been extensively built over, so that many antiquities, which might otherwise in open country have survived, have disappeared. However, there remain several monastic sites, with the stumps of two round towers, at Mahee (2), and Drumbo, neither very exciting compared to Antrim or Devenish; many raths and ring-forts, few of especial interest; a handful of early churches and sites of priories; a generous sprinkling of mottes from the period of Norman occupation; and a clutch of tower-houses, of which in this area by far the best-preserved is that at Kirkistown (9), though many fewer than on the southern and western shores of Strangford Lough. Unhappily, Portaferry tower-house is a roofless ruin, and there is scarcely a trace of the tower-house at Ardkeen where, on the night of 8 January 1574, a certain Lieutenant Jerome Brett was obliged to report to his superiors the escape of "a notorios treytor & a murderer", who after midnight "soudenly slypt patricke hazard his ffote owte of Irons & lept out of the Castell off Arkyne such a lepe as yff he had ben condemned, I had ffor his dethe as leve have given hem that lepe as the gallows; yet he ded yt"[1].

I have included one 18th-century fort, and one 20th-century fort, for good measure: both now in pretty good health and repair, though neither incapable of further improvement in presentation.

Reference: 1. Savage-Armstrong, 'Savage family in Ulster', 1906, p 188.

The Giant's Ring, Ballylesson, Drumbo

1. Very crisply described by Miss Gaffikin and Estyn Evans, following Lawlor, who (although not a trained archaeologist) had excavated it in 1917: "This remarkable monument consists of a great circular rampart averaging 590 ft. in internal diameter, and about 15 ft. in height, enclosing a space of some 7 acres near the centre of which is a megalithic chamber. The rampart, now grass-grown, is composed of small stones: its base is some 80 ft. in width. It is divided into seven unequal segments by depressions; but it is not clear if all seven gaps are original: at least two may be more recent. Mr Lawlor's excavations in 1917 showed that there is no ditch, and revealed hardly any traces of habitation within the ring" (PSAMNI).

The Archaeological Survey of County Down says "A large circular banked enclosure ... over 600 ft. in diameter,

crest to crest of bank. The bank averages about 60 ft. in width and has a height of about 12 ft. ... Much flaking of flint had been carried out in the shelter of the bank soon after its completion. A dolmen ... built of basalt boulders lies just south-east of the centre of this banked enclosure. Five uprights enclose a polygonal chamber roofed by a single capstone. A slipped stone, now lying on edge, may have been a second capstone ... Abundant traces of cremated bone were found within it." The authors add, in their Introduction, "flint was ... readily obtainable from the chalk exposures high on the scarp of the Antrim plateau, overlooking Belfast, and one is tempted to regard the isolated enclosure of the Giant's Ring, with its megalithic chamber, near the first easy crossing of the River Lagan south of Belfast ... as a site connected with trade in

Antrim flint and roughed-out stone axes".

Mallory and McNeill consider it to be probably a henge, that is "a large circular enclosure with one or more entrances and where an earthen bank forms the outer perimeter of the monument while a ditch is found to the inside ... On what little evidence is available to us, they would appear to be ceremonial enclosures erected towards the end of the Neolithic period": and say "A ... spectacular henge candidate is the Giant's Ring just south of Belfast ... As to which came first - the megalith or the bank - archaeologists have generally assumed the tomb was earlier ... it would appear that the ring was laid out essentially centred on the megalith, perhaps by a cord, measuring c. 200 metres long." "It is part of a ritual complex in this area, including cists, barrows and a huge timber enclosure with structures and burials to the north-west" (MBR). Hartwell considers that the passage grave came first; that the timber circles should be regarded as later mortuary enclosures: "This phase ends with the deliberate firing of the structures" - charcoal samples come up with the surprisingly early dating of 3018 - 2788 BC. The henge came last.

The site is extraordinarily impressive: on a sunny winter day, a broad, silent, saucer of prehistory on the edge of a traffic-rumbling city. Harris says "About the middle of the *Giants-Ring*, is ... [an] ancient *Altar*, ... and consisting of a huge rude upper Stone unwrought, almost circular, being seven Feet and an Inch one way, and six Feet eleven Inches the other, near two Feet, at a medium, thick, but swelling both in the upper and under Surface. Two Ranges of rude Pillars support this monstrous Stone, each consisting of seven, and round it, at about four Feet Distance, are several fixed Stones yet remaining, not above two Feet high from the Earth". And: "The *Giant's Ring*, an artificial *Rath* so called, stands Northward of the Tower of *Drumboe* near two Miles, and is regularly thrown up, encompassing many Acres; but it has no Advantage of Height ... The Ground about it is often used as a Race Course, round which Horses run six times in each Heat, which makes two Miles, and it is consequently judged to be a Third of a Mile in Circumference. But this conjectural Manner of Admeasurement is not so certain, as that the the Circuit of it takes up 842 Paces".

Views about its purpose and function vary widely. Benn thought it a site for sun-worshippers (1823). Atkinson, on a visit in 1817, took a more romantic view of it: " ... the person who enters to inspect it, finds himself precluded, by an immense rampart, from the observation of every object in the universe, save the great altar of sacrifice, and those visible heavens, to which the smoke of the victim ascended as a cloud of incense, to avert its wrath, and propitiate the favour of the gods". Borlase, the Victorian authority on dolmens, thought it a "centre of sepulchral and it may be sacrificial rites ... which were essentially and ultimately associated with the Dead" (1897). Professor MacAlister thought "The unusual size of the Giant's Ring may be confidently taken as an indication of the great and important rank which the person commemorated by it held amongst his contemporaries. He was most likely deified after his death" (1918). Hartwell thinks that it "should be seen as a focus of community ceremony and death rituals in the Late Neolithic and Early Bronze Age Lagan Valley" (1998).

It is surrounded by a circular stone wall, erected by Lord Ranfurly in 1861, with a sympathetic inscription beside the gate. On the whole very well cared for, and surprisingly little used, though the Heritage Service might be justly criticised for allowing the access ways to be so deeply puddled by the grazing cattle used to keep the grass down. I recall visiting it in the company of Professor Estyn Evans, and seeking elucidation from him as to its purpose and history. Even that most learned of men could offer me little guidance: he advised me that perhaps it could best be regarded as a large prehistoric fair-ground, or marketplace. Perish the thought, and heaven forbid, but, if access and parking could be improved, it would surely provide a remarkable setting for a pop concert.

Photographs: B Hartwell, QUB, Department of Archaeology, QAD/13-7-89/V/27; central dolmen, from south, A C W Merrick.
Situation: Just outside south Belfast city boundary; td, Ballynahatty; District Council, Lisburn; Grid ref. J 327 677.
References: Monument in state care. Harris, 'County of Down', 1744, pp 200, 218; Atkinson, 'Ireland exhibited', 1823, I, p 284; UJA, 1st series, III, 1855, p 358; Borlase, 'Dolmens', I, 1897, p 275; H C Lawlor and RAS MacAlister, in PBNHPS, 1917-18, pp 13-28; PSAMNI, 1940, p 86; A E P Collins, in UJA, 3rd Series, XX, 1957, p 44-50; ASCD, 1966, pp x, 89-91; Mallory and McNeill, 'Archaeology of Ulster', 1991, pp 74-77; Rice, 'Giant's Ring', 1996, passim; B Hartwell, in 'Prehistoric ritual and religion", 1998, pp 32-44.

Monastic Buildings and Tide Mills, Nendrum, Mahee Island, Tullynakill

2. This remarkable site has been the subject of see-saw speculation for over 150 years. It must be said at the outset that this, a grassy drumlin on a former (now causeway-connected) island on the western shores of Strangford Lough, is a place of singular beauty. The grass is mown by the Environment Service; the trees sway in the wind; the lough's waters glitter; the ancient stones are elegantly disposed; but, just how old are they? Early Christian, or 1920s? And what, in truth, was their purpose? Was this in fact originally a monastic site; or a secular one? "By the 11th century the tradition was crystallised in Annals and other writings that Nendrum was a monastic establishment of Mochaoi where Finian of Movilla and Colmán of Dromore had received their early training in the 6th century. Though their writers no doubt drew upon some earlier material, none of our sources come closer than within four centuries of Mochaoi's alleged foundation".

"The last recorded of the pre-Norman abbots was 'burned in his own house' in 974, presumably in a Viking raid" (Archaeological Survey of County Down). Thereafter, Mochaoi's foundation disappears from history for almost a thousand years, until 1844 when the Rev. and learned William Reeves, searching for the churches listed in the papal taxation of 1302, found just what he was looking for, and identified Mahee island as the site of St Mochaoi's Nendrum, partly because, rightly or wrongly, he identified a limekiln as a monastic round tower. There matters rested for another eighty years, when H C Lawlor, a Belfast linen merchant and amateur archaeologist, "carried out large-scale excavations and restoration", with the rather unskilled aid of the members of the excellent Belfast Natural History and Philosophical Society (of which I

declare an interest as a member). By the time he and they had finished, the 'round tower' had been rebuilt to a height of several feet; the church, of which only the foundations had remained, had likewise been rebuilt to a height of several feet; and the great triple circle or oval of dry-stone cashel protective walls had been extensively rebuilt. In his enthusiastic (though very readable) book on the subject of 1925, Lawlor made a great many claims which later scholars have doubted. In particular, the late Dudley Waterman - for whose integrity and scholarship I have always had great respect - writing in 1966, in the magisterial Archaeological Survey, threw many buckets of cold water over Lawlor's finds and findings. "Lawlor's identification ... rests on most slender grounds ... It is, in fact, extremely difficult to determine the extent of the reconstruction carried out at the conclusion of the work of 1922-4 and, indeed, to assess the evidence which warranted such rebuilding". Even the much more sanguine Ann Hamlin acknowledges that both excavations and restorations "were poorly recorded and present us today with difficult problems of interpretation".

However, a number of interesting finds were made, or reconstructed; including an early sun-dial marking the hours of terce, sext, and none; round foundations for huts; a supposed school-house or scriptorium; sundry inscribed stones; "knives, nails and pottery ... crucibles and moulds ... brooches and pins"; and the iron bell, coated in bronze, now in the Ulster Museum. There is no doubt at all that the site was a monastic one after the Anglo-Norman Benedictine resettlement of 1179 by John de Courcy, who imported monks from Cumberland. The awkward question is, just how much earlier was it in fact settled? As

Waterman pithily put the argument, as it stood in 1966: "From the extensive digging of this site has come no object which carries us back beyond the 8th or 7th centuries to the supposed period of foundation in the 5th century, let alone to a pre-monastic secular occupation; this does not disprove the latter, but there is no evidence for it, and it is not profitable to postulate it".

The equivalent of the US Marines, however, have now arrived, in the persons of the archaeologists Tom McErlean and Norman Crothers, who discovered in 1999 that a bay on the east of the island had not been, as previously thought, used as a fish-pond or fish-trap; nor as Waterman had supposed, a harbour; but had contained a sequence of highly sophisticated, and very early, tide-mills. To quote from their summary notes "Excavation revealed that a sequence of three horizontal mills of the Early Christian period had been constructed on the site. The first phase mill, dated by dendrochronolgy to AD 619 and currently the earliest dated horizontal mill in western Europe, proved to be a very sophisticated and complex structure". The phase two mill-house or wheel-house, possibly of the late seventh or early eighth century, was largely destroyed in the building of the third mill. Remains of the third mill on the site have been dated, again by dendrochronology, to late AD 788 - early 799. "This site differs from the majority of other horizontal mills in that it is a tide-mill which uses the flow of the tide to fill the mill-pond and the water released from the mill-pond to drive the wheel when the tide had receded. Only one other tide-mill of this period has so far been found in Ireland". And, of the third mill: "Drystone-built wheelhouses are not uncommon in Ireland but the stone" (chiselled sandstone) "flume at the time of writing is unique ... Two" (Mourne granite) "mill-stones and three horizontal paddles were also recovered" ... "It is interesting to note that" (the dendrochronological date of AD 619 for the first phase) "immediately pre-dates the first secure annual entry relating to Nendrum, the death of bishop Cridan recorded in the Annals of Ulster in AD 639".

All this is interesting, indeed exciting, but leaves open the question whether the tide-mills were secular or ecclesiastical. Since very skilled artificers must have been imported, and a substantial investment made, perhaps the latter is marginally the more likely. It is unfortunate that, for reasons of safety if no other, the excavations have had to be back-filled: and, for practical purposes, nothing is now visible except the dam in the tidal mill-pond. Accordingly, this fascinating site is, for all practical purposes, today quite invisible; quite inscrutable; indeed, on the face of it, quite incomprehensible, without lengthy exegesis.

Archaeology is an occupation for which only optimists are suited.

In the aerial photograph, the 7th-century dam for the tide-mills is situated in the bay on the middle left. The photograph below was taken by W A Green on 29 July 1922, and shows (I think) the youthful Mr H C Lawlor, then Hon. Secretary of the Archaeological Section of the Belfast Natural History and Philosophical Society, lecturing at Mahee to a joint excursion of the members of that Society, and of the Belfast Naturalists' Field Club, come to admire his excavations and reconstructions. By a happy coincidence, the chairman of the Section in that year is given as Sir Charles Brett, LL D; though I cannot see him in the photograph. However, he was quite a small man: and, for that matter, then aged 83; and it looks as if rain was rather expected; so he may have stayed at home.

Photographs: Gail Pollock, MBR; W A Green, UFTM, WAG 3049.
Situation: Above and below the car-park on Mahee Island; td, Mahee Island; District Council, Ards; Grid ref. J 524 636.
References: Monument in state care. Reeves, 'Ecclesiastical antiquities', 1847, pp 65, 194; Lawlor, 'Monastery of St Mochaoi', 1925, passim; ASCD, 1966, pp 292ff.; Gwynn and Hadcock,'Medieval religious houses', 1970, pp 42, 107; HMNI, 1983, pp 95,96; T McErlean and N Crothers, in 'Archaeology Ireland', XV, No. 2, 2001, pp 10-14; excavation notes in MBR.

Donaghadee Motte and Powder Magazine

3. A surprising, but dramatic, combination of Norman motte and romantic 19th-century powder magazine, lending much additional character to this already attractive harbour village. A great contrast to an inland Lagan-valley-settlement such as Waringstown; not the less to be treasured. The silhouette of the fortified walls lends much drama to the harbour and lighthouse down below.

"A massive motte ... overlooking the harbour, set on the edge of the natural cliff scarp of the ancient shoreline. It is 32 ft. high at maximum and has an oval summit 80 ft. x 46 ft., the longer axis being aligned parallel to the natural scarp. The mound is enclosed by a ditch much obscured on the N. by recent filling, but preserved to a depth of about 4¹/₂ ft. on the S.W. A sloping berm at the base of the mound on the E. and the natural cliff scarp may indicate the continuation of the ditch on this side. The castellated tower on the mound was built in 1821" (Archaeological Survey of County Down). H C Lawlor, in PSAMNI, suggests that "From the names of the Copeland Islands and Ballycopeland, both close to Donaghadee, it is probable that here was the manor of William De Coupland, one of John De Courcy's knights."

Dixon writes, "A large Anglo-Norman motte, or earthen mound, thrown up probably in the 13th century to dominate the natural haven which was later to become the town harbour ... Lawson, giving its height as 140 feet, includes the cliff. 'The Compleat Irish Traveller' (1788) noted its position 'on a natural hill of tolerable height, which has been by art formed and shaped round, so that the mount appears as if placed on another of the same sort. On the top of it a hollow is cut from east to west, the

earth of which thrown up has raised part of the mount higher than the rest, and seems to have been intended as a place for a watch to discover better the approaches of an enemy; it is encompassed by a large dry foss, 33 feet broad in some places' ... From Moat Street a path leads to a stout stone bridge across the ditch. and then spirals to the summit. On clear days there are spectacular views to the harbour, the Copeland Islands, Scotland, the Isle of Man, and beyond. The Moat was presented to the town by George Delacherois in 1945".

Kertland in the Ordnance Survey memoir of 1837 writes, "The powder magazine, situated on a high and ancient moat, is a great ornament to the town. It was constructed for containing the powder used in the blasting necessary for the building of the new harbour. It is built in the form of a miniature castle". Lewis and Bassett give their own accounts, but add little more to the picture.

Dixon says "Built c. 1821, of rendered brick and rubble masonry ... Styled as a picturesque castle it is massed with effective sculptural simplicity; a cube, surmounted by a cylinder, is connected on one side to a lower cube, and shielded by a part curtain-wall on the other. This foundation is embellished with corner towers, turrets, battlements, and a flagstaff, all combining to create exciting silhouettes in distant views. On closer inspection the castle is disappointing. Its dull grey rendering is peeling off, and its openings have been crudely blocked. Only the door merits close attention; in the Regency style it has six moulded panels and a semi-circular 'fanlight', all of solid bronze. Like the rest of the building it deserves more loving attention". The listers, a bit grumpily, just say "castellated building with towers" and give the date as 1818, citing an "inscription plate on building", now not easy to find. It is now in pretty good order, the grass cut, the steps and paths well looked after by the District Council. I did not at all share Hugh Dixon's sense of disappointment, greatly enjoying my visit on a brisk March morning. But I should certainly deprecate any attempts to 'improve' it or its surroundings; it seems to me fine as it is.

Photograph: A C W Merrick.
Situation: Off Moat Street, Donaghadee; td, Donaghadee; District Council, Ards; Grid ref. J 588 801.
References: Motte, scheduled monument; Powder magazine, listed B (24/6/2). 'Compleat Irish traveller', 1788, p 235; M M Kertland, OSM, 1837, 'Down', II, p 49; Lewis, TD, 1837, I, p 466; Lawson, 'Gazetteer', 1842, p 320; Bassett, 'County Down', 1886, p 307; PSAMNI, 1940, p 82; ASCD, 1966, p 193; Dixon, 'Donaghadee and Portpatrick', UAHS, 1977, p 9.

Holywood Motte

4. "This small but impressive site ... is backed to the SE by higher ground but has commanding views to the N over Belfast Lough. It also commands the narrow coastal strip between the high ground and the shore through which, even today, both main rail and road routes pass ... A small oval mound 30m NE - SW x 25m NW - SE. It varies in height 3.5m at SE to 5m at NW in response to the natural slope. The flat-topped summit is 12m in diameter" (MBR). Merrick says "part of a chain of such defensive forts erected by the Anglo-Normans ... in the late twelfth century. It was usual for the top of a motte to be ringed with a stout wooden palisade with a small timber residence in the middle, and this was certainly the case with Holywood, for excavations carried out in 1915 revealed the darkened traces of the post-holes". The Archaeological Survey of County Down says "King John stayed at Holywood in 1210, but there is no actual evidence to connect this

with the motte. Holywood Castle is mentioned in 1234".

O'Laverty piously thought that this, like other mottes, was a "sepulchral mound ... erected to cover the remains of some mighty chief ... the recognised place for the religious and deliberative assemblies of the neighbourhood". At some time in the mid-19th century, the motte was treated as a garden ornament for the adjacent Riverston House, when the spiral path to the top was made, and forest trees planted. Although modest in size, it is now a most attractive enclave near the heart of Holywood.

Photograph: A C W Merrick (see also colour illus. 2).
Situation: Off Brook Street, Holywood; td, Ballykeel; District Council, North Down; Grid ref. J 401 792.
References: Monument in state care; in conservation area. King John's itinerary, in CSPI, 1171-1251, 1875, p 64; O'Laverty, 'Down and Connor', II, 1880, p 192; PSAMNI, 1940, p 81; ASCD, 1966, p 194; Merrick, 'Buildings of Holywood', 1986, p 10.

Grey Abbey, Greyabbey

5. One of the most impressive, and attractive, historic monuments in Ulster. In 1683, William Montgomery wrote: "Neare and in view of Rosemount house" (his home, 47) "are ye walls of a large abby of curious work (ruinated in Tireowen's rebellion); it is called in inquisitions and patents Abathium de fugo Dei; in Irish, Monestrelea, in English, Gray (or Hoare) Abby, from the order of fryars who enjoyed it; and had, in ancient times, belonging thereunto, all its own parish, both in Spiritualibus et temporalibus conferred by De Courcy at ye inshanes of his wife, the King of the Isle of Man's daughter ... To this abby belonged also diverse lands and tithes in ye county of Antrim, viz. out of Ballymena. And also, tithes in the Lower Ards and Lecahill ... and also, (as tradition reports) in ye Isle of Man (likely by ye sd De Courcy's wives gift) and in the High Lands of Scotland ... The church thereof was in part roofed and slated and re-edifyed, and a yeard thereunto and walled about, and a competent stipend given for that by ye sd first Lord Montgomery;" and, added in 1701, "and in Anno Dni 1685 it was new roofed again by ye heirs of Wm Montgomery, and by contributions of gent. concerned therein."

It was visited on 2 May 1769 by James Boswell, who wrote - "We went to Grey Abbey, where is one of the finest Gothic ruins I ever saw, though there are but small remains of it. There has been a noble church and a large convent. Of the convent little is left. But there is a good part of the church standing; in particular there is an end window with three divisions in it, exceedingly Gothic, and covered with a thicker ivy than I ever saw, which adds greatly to its appearance. There is also standing a side window just adjoining to this end. It is a lofty arch eight yards or more wide at the bottom, I measured seven

lengths and a third of my cane". G Scott, writing up the Ordnance Survey memoir in the 1830s, remarks somewhat laconically "(The abbey is worthy of the antiquarian's notice)".

Roger Stalley says "Founded in 1193 by Affreca, wife of John de Courcy, Grey was colonised from the English monastery of Holm Cultram (Cumberland) with which it retained close ties in the early years. In 1222 and again in 1237 abbots of Grey went on to become abbots of Holm Cultram". (Stalley and the Archaeological Survey of County Down are by far the most important authorities amongst a very large number: though his use of the name "Grey" is highly disconcerting to one accustomed to the local usage: it is as though he were intimately referring to the Earl of Gowrie, lately Irish chairman of the Arts Council of England). In fact this is a very English group of buildings, evidently largely built by English stonemasons (some of whom left their masons' marks) and other craftsmen, occupied largely by English monks (and perhaps a few Burgundians from Clairvaux), its lands farmed largely by English lay brothers; and the style, with aisle-less nave, crossing tower, and pointed lancet windows, is very English too. At the same time, it is very much in the international Cistercian tradition of simplicity, austerity, and absence of ornament, save for the great ornate doorway of the church.

As Stalley remarks "Cistercian monasticism played a vital part in bringing Ireland into the mainstream of western Christianity, and within a few decades the buildings of the order had transformed the character of the country's architecture ... Grey Abbey has a good claim to be considered the first Gothic building in Ireland ... To the frontiers of European civilisation, to Brittany, Sweden, Poland, Wales and Ireland, the Cistercians brought the basic elements of Romanesque and Gothic design: clear principles of planning, well-proportioned, well-buttressed structures, along with excellent standards of construction. If not pioneers of Gothic, there is no doubt that the white monks were active 'missionaries' of the style". It seems paradoxical, none the less, that it was the Anglo-Norman incomers who here substituted the pointed Gothic for the round-headed Norman style.

The Cistercian *train-de-vie* was, or was supposed to be, austere and ascetic in the extreme. As Ailred of Rievaulx wrote, "Our food is scanty, our garments rough; our drink is from the stream and our sleep often upon our book. Under our tired limbs there is but a hard mat; when sleep is sweetest, we must rise at bell's bidding". And: Stephen of Lexington in 1228: "It is strictly forbidden for any variety of paintings, or other marble objects to be allowed in the church or other chambers, but the simplicity of the Order is to be observed. Otherwise the prior, cellarer, sacristan, and keeper of the works are to be on bread and water every Friday from the time of this presumptuous behaviour until the next visitation at which time they will be punished more severely". "The stone dormitories and refectories of a Cistercian monastery may have been cold and spartan, but compared with the fragile buildings outside they aspired to luxury. Nevertheless, there were occasions when Cistercian monks themselves preferred the traditional Irish mode of living. In 1227 the Pope was informed that groups of monks had reverted to dwelling outside their monasteries in 'miserably constructed' houses of wattle" (Stalley). However, "in the abbeys of Ireland the severity of Cistercian discipline and order is observed in scarcely anything except the habit, in that there is neither observance of choir service nor of silence in the cloister nor of the discipline of the chapter meetings nor use of the common table in the refectory nor of monastic quiet in the dormitory according to the manner of our order" (Stephen of Lexington again). Later, the abbey passed through many vicissitudes, and it is likely that both the numbers and the morals of the monks and lay brothers varied considerably, though it was still wealthy enough to undertake building works in the 15th century. However, by 1452, it seems that the Cistercians had mislaid some of their austerity: "Richard Seymour, the worldly abbott of Abington" (Limerick) "admitted that he had been negligent in carrying out the liturgy, and administering the sacraments, and that he had carried arms into the monastery. He confessed to a charge of alienating the property of the house, also to simony and fornication: 'overcome by the frailty of the flesh, he knew carnally many women through the act of fornication and from some of them produced offspring'. Nevertheless, after doing penance, he was confirmed in office by the Pope" (Stalley again).

The abbey was dissolved in 1541, and no doubt stripped of anything of value; and in 1572 its remains were burned by Sir Brian O'Neill to prevent their use by the English invaders of the Ards. The nave was re-roofed in the 17th century, and used as parish church until 1778, when a small Georgian church was built close by, the latter (except for its tower) replaced in 1869 by an indifferent but larger Victorian one designed by Henry Chappell of Newtownards.

Grey Abbey is neither as extensive nor as impressive as Fountains Abbey or Rievaulx, but it is in the same league: delightfully set in its parkland of lawns and ancient trees, between the stream which provided its indispensable water supply, Rosemount, the Victorian church, and the village of Greyabbey, it is one of the most pleasing antiquities of Ireland, and well presented and cared for. Entry is through the last cottage in the village, which has been converted into a kind of reception centre: the model and explanatory panels are excellent; the somewhat garish illustrative murals rather less so; and the stuffed stonemason appalling; but on the whole, high marks. Then comes an attractive and quite plausible "monastic" physick garden, laid out in 1993 by the late Gwen Buchanan; then a little

stone bridge over the stream; then the pathway to the stunning front entrance doorway to the abbey, probably one of the last elements to be built, perhaps between 1230 and 1250. Stalley says that "With its arch of four orders, decorated with dog-tooth ornament, this was one of the most elaborate Cistercian doorways in Ireland". Beyond this is the aisle-less nave, with transepts, whose walls still stand to a considerable height; and the east wall with its impressive series of pointed windows.

Only the lower parts survive of the chapter house (which must have been very impressive), and of the cloister. However, the refectory (the Archaeological Survey calls it the frater) stands nearly as tall as the church, and is exceedingly impressive with its three tall pointed windows, and its pulpit for readings during meals. Stalley says that it is the longest in Ireland: it appears to have been built to accommodate greater numbers than ever actually inhabited the abbey. The whole complex is built of local rubble, with sandstone trim and quoins. As Stalley remarks, "the Irish monasteries follow a pattern found in the more remote parts of Europe, where building traditions were less sophisticated and large quarries had yet to be developed. The Swedish abbeys use rubble extensively, as do some of the

monasteries of Wales and Brittany. From a visual point of view, this rather rough method of construction would not have been particularly noticeable, at least not from inside the buildings. Once plastered, whitewashed and marked out with false masonry joints, as was Cistercian custom, there would be little to show that the walls were not built of ashlar".

It is sobering for an Irishman to compare the present state of the 12th-century Norman abbey with that of the almost exactly contemporary 12th-century Norman cathedral of Cefalu in Sicily, built by the Norman King Roger II between 1133 and 1148 in fulfilment of a vow, which still retains all its original roof.

Photograph: A C W Merrick. Lithograph: from Doyle, 'Tours in Ulster', 1854. Wood-engraving: from 'Twenty-one views in Belfast', 1836.
Situation: Off Ballywalter Road, Greyabbey; td, Rosemount; District Council, Ards; Grid ref. J 583 682.
References: Monument in state care. Montgomery, 'Description of the ... Ards', 1701, in his 'Montgomery manuscripts', 1830, p 308; Boswell, journals, 2 May 1769, in 'Boswell in search of a wife', 1957, p 212; G Scott, OSM, nd, Down, II, p 71; ASCD, 1966, pp 128, 275ff; DoENI guide-card, 1979; HMNI, 1983, pp 50, 102; Stalley, 'Cistercian monasteries of Ireland', 1987, passim.

Priory, Holywood

6. An important landmark at the east end of Holywood's main street, in an extensive graveyard (where I hope to end up myself), believed to have been a holy site of great antiquity, going back at least to the first half of the 7th century. Built as a parish church in about 1200, but in the later Middle Ages this was a Third Order Franciscan friary. Today a roofless ruin, but was in use again as parish church from its restoration by Sir James Hamilton in 1615 until the mid 19th century: unroofed in 1845, when the new church above the town was completed. The Parliamentary Gazetteer of 1846 says "The church is a curious old structure, 78 feet by 24 in the clear, and about 20 feet high, with a remodelled square tower of about 10 feet on each side. The whole structure was originally built in an early variety of the pointed style, but has been so greatly mutilated and modernized as to have become bereft of its honours before all eyes except those of peering antiquaries"!

The peering antiquaries of the Archaeological Survey, however, provide a very clear ground plan; and write: "The original building, of Cultra stone ashlar with some red sandstone, is of the early 13th century and was entered on the S. In the 15th century the W. end of the nave was rebuilt in red sandstone rubble with reused ashlars, and quoins and dressings of similar material; a W. door was

provided, the E. window was rebuilt in Scrabo stone and the E. gable reconstructed ... In the 17th century a number of windows, all now blocked, were opened out in the S. wall and the tower was added c 1800".

The continuous nave and chancel of this surprisingly small church are now inaccessible - the east window is barred, and the door in the tower is kept locked. But it is possible to see through the east window that both nave and chancel are quite covered with funerary memorials, some of them evidently of considerable interest - burials inside the walls of the church having been permitted after 1846. Those interred there include the town's benefactor, Mr Robert Sullivan (see 150). G Scott of the Ordnance Survey endearingly observes "In the burial ground there are some showy tombstones". Mine will not be.

Photograph: A C W Merrick.
Situation: At junction of Main Street and Bangor Road, Holywood.; td, Ballykeel; District Council, North Down; Grid ref. J401 794.
References: Scheduled monument. G Scott, OSM, 1834, Down, II, p 81; PG, II, 1846, p 300; O'Laverty, 'Down and Connor', II, 1880, pp 190-191; PSAMNI, 1940, p 81; ASCD, 1966, pp 282-3; Gwynn and Hadcock, 'Medieval religious houses', 1970, pp 271, 386; HMNI, 1983, p 54; Merrick, 'Buildings of Holywood', 1986, p 91; J F Rankin, in 'Clergy of Down and Dromore', 1996, pp 125-126 .

St Columba's Dominican Priory, Newtownards

7. Founded in 1244, possibly by the Savage family of the Ards. "These are the only substantial remains in Northern Ireland of a Dominican (Black) Friary, founded in the mid 13th century. The lower parts of the nave are of the 13th century, with two blocked doors in the S wall leading to the now-vanished cloister. Extensive 14th-century remodelling involved rebuilding the upper parts of the nave, extending it westwards and adding a N aisle reached through the surviving arcade. The friary was suppressed in 1541 and burned in 1572, but after the Plantation it was granted to Hugh, first Viscount Montgomery, who refurbished the church, rebuilding the N aisle and adding the tower" (HMNI). The Newtownards property passed in 1605 from Con O'Neill to Hugh Montgomery of Ayrshire, who proceeded to convert the cloisters and out-buildings into a quite grand dwelling-house with extensive grounds and gardens - William Montgomery writes, in 1701, "some of the priory walls were roofed and fitted for Sir Hugh and his family to dwell in; but the rest of these walls, and other large additions of a gate house and office-houses, which made three sides of a quadrangle, (the south side of the church, being contiguous, made the 4th side) with coins and window frames, and chimney-pieces, and funnels of freestone, all covered; and the floors beamed with main oak timber, and clad with boards; the roof with oak plank from his Lordship's own woods, and slated with slates out of Scotland; and the floors laid with fir deals out of Norway, the windows were fitly glazed and the edifice thoroly furnished within ... the whole work was done many months before Sir Hugh ... went to London Ao. 1618".

According to a footnote by George Hill in his edition of the Montgomery manuscripts, "The conversion of the old Dominican priory into Newtown House drew the following bitter remark from a Franciscan friar, named Father Edmund MacCana, who journeyed through that district about the year 1643 ... 'there was even in my day, a monastery of St. Dominic, which some years ago, Mogumrius the Scotchman converted into a secular dwelling; such is the propensity of impious heretics to obliterate all memory of what has been deemed sacred'". This house was destroyed in a disastrous fire in 1664; in 1675 the estate was sold for £10,640 to Captain Robert Colvill of Galgorm, near Ballymena; in 1744, Robert Colville sold the manors of Newtown and Mount Alexander for £42,000 to Alexander Stewart, forbear of the Marquesses of Londonderry. So much is fairly clear: but there is a certain amount of confusion as to who built what.

The present buildings seem to date mostly from the 17th century (1607/8 onwards): they are rather unimpressive from the street, apart from the square five-storey tower with its much-worn carved doorcase, but the interior space is very much more rewarding, if seldom seen. It has a wall, dividing nave from north aisle, with very large and tall pointed arches carried on circular stone columns, with plain capitals: very unusually, the columns have been incised with memorial lettering, most notably that proclaiming "Here ly's the Body of R Robt Russall Stone Cutter who died Decmr 29 1771 Aged 27". There are thumping great mausolea of the Montgomery, Colville and Londonderry families, juxtaposed with curious small carved 18th-century human faces. A modern replica of the original ornate doorcase has been erected in a later exterior wall: it is dated 1988, and seems to be intended either to show what the 17th- century doorcase looked like before the Scrabo stone became so severely weathered; or to show the skill of the Heritage Service's stone masons; or, perhaps, both. Anyhow, it is a most curious exercise, causing the sensitive passer-by to stop and blink. The interior is only opened to the public on rare occasions; there are no explanatory notices or signboards outside; it is a matter of no mean difficulty to track down the claviger and his key.

Walter Harris, in 1744, writes: "The old Church of *Newtown* is a large Building, divided into Isles by four handsome stone Arches of the Dorick Order. It was finished, or at least repaired and adorned in 1632, as appears by an Inscription on the Pulpit. Another Inscription on a Stone over the North Entrance shews that the Steeple was finished in the Year 1636. The Door, which affords an Entrance under the Steeple, is an Arch curiously ornamented with carved Work in Stone, where may be seen the Arms of the *Mountgomerys*, under which, over the Portal, are these Letters in Cypher NA" (*sed qu:* HLM?). "The Steeple is but moderately high, yet neatly built, and a Spire of hewn Stone erected lately on it" (but long since gone) "gives it a handsome Appearance. A large Tomb of the *Colville* family (to a Descendant of which the Town now belongs) stands in the North Isle, raised five or six Feet above the Floor, but naked of any Inscription. This Church is only kept roofed, but is entirely out of Repair within side, and the Seats, except a few, destroyed". An excellent description of the Priory in 1879, with plan and illustrations, was published in that year by the distinguished architect R M Young, of Young & Mackenzie.

Somewhat mystifyingly, Harris adds to his account: "Divine Service is" (now) " performed in a Chappel adjoining to it, built by Sir *Robert Colville* for his Family

Since the Revolution; the Entrance into which is by a large stone Door Case, curiously adorned with Sculpture. This Chappel is the neatest Piece of Church Building within side that is to be met with in Ulster. The Pulpit is finely Carved and Guilded, and so are two large Seats of the *Colville's* placed on each side the great Door, over which are the King's Arms ... The other Seats are regularly placed and painted, the Floor well flagged, the compass Cieling divided into nine Pannels, and curiously adorned with Stucco Work in Plaister of Paris, well executed in various Wreaths, Foliages, and the Figures of Angels. The Communion Table is raised and wainscotted, and encompassed with twisted Pillars carved and guilded. These Ornaments, and much more of the same kind, added to the well lighting of the Room, have a fine Effect".

Some forty years earlier William Montgomery had written: "Here is also a fair long church, part whereof were ye walls of a priory, but new walls were erected, and a new church (wh hath a square tower five storeys high, and a great bell in it) joyned without any partition, but large free-stone pillars and arches; all wh now roofed, sclated, and made by ye sd first Lord Montgomery, (in his life-time and by his order and legacys after his death) and Sr Robert Colvil hath made a beautifull large chappell at ye eastmost end of the sd church, wh formerly was not used for divine service; but there ly the bones of the three first Lords Montgomerys, the two first Ladys, and many of their familys. The sd Sr Robt hath built a large burial place, wherein himself and his third lady are layd above ground ... Contiguous to ye sd old church walls (where stood ye Lord's house, accidentally burned, Ao Dmi 1664) the sd Sr Robert hath (from ye foundation) built up one double roofed house, stables, coach houses, and all other

necessary or convenient edifices, for brewing, bakeing, washing, hunting, hawking, pleasure-rooms, and pigeon-houses, &c. with inner, outer, and back courts: and a spacious well planted olitory, fruit and pleasant flower gardens, wh have a fish pond, spring wells, (thence conveyed in conduit pipes to ye kitchen court) long broad sanded without as well as within, and a bowling green; all thereof walled about, and set about with trees, and adorned wth diverse curious hewn stone gates, and balls uniformally placed in a regular comely manner. And hath also built a great and neat dairy house, lofted in ye fields near unto ye premises. The whole considered, there are few such or so much work to be seen, about any one dwelling in Ireland, nor any so great done by a gentn, at his own expence ..."

What a lot of questions this raises! The Montgomerys lacked money, the Colvilles had lots; just who built just what? Where exactly was this "Chappel"? When was it built, and did it have an architect? How did all this complex, save the bones of the priory, come to vanish so completely? Some clue, at least as to location, may be offered by the modest contribution of G Scott of the Ordnance Survey, who says, "Divine service was performed most recently in an addition made by Sir Robert Colville for his family since the Revolution. The walls of the church have recently been repaired and additions made. It now" (1835) "serves as a court house, the dimensions 63 feet by 46. In this church are the remains of the 3 first Lords and 2 first Ladies Montgomeries". And Samuel Lewis says "near the old church, now the court-house, are the ruins of a private chapel, built by Sir Robert Colville. In that church were interred the remains of the earls and others of the family of Mount-Alexander, of several of the Colville family; of the first Marquess of Londonderry; and of his father". The church continued to be used as a court house until 1850, after which it once again lost its roof. (The priory now stands in Court Street, presumably named from the makeshift court house).

Was the Colville chapel, perhaps, on the site of the now-lost chancel of the priory, or in an eastern extension of the aisle, also now gone? Dr McParland says that he has "speculated that this was one of a group of important examples of late C 17 plasterwork (including the chancel of Kilkenny cathedral, ?c.1684, Boyle's private chapel in Blessington, 1672, perhaps one of the interiors in the Dublin Tholsel, 1680s, and Marsh's chapel in TCD, early 1680s), which were siblings of the chapel in the Royal Hospital, Kilmainham, 1687 (at least as far as its plaster ceiling is concerned)".

Photographs: A C W Merrick; WA Green, UFTM, WAG 944. Engraving: RM Young, in JRSAI.

Situation: Court Street, Newtownards; td, Corporation South; District Council, Ards; Grid ref. J 493 738.

References: Monument in state care. Harris, 'County of Down', 1744, pp 57-58; Montgomery, 'Montgomery manuscripts', 1830, pp 65-66, 271, 316-318; ibid, 1869 ed, p 87; G Scott, OSM, nd (? 1835), Down, II, p 107; Lewis, TD, 1837, II, p 436; R M Young, in JRSAI, XV, 1879-1882, pp 144-152; H C Lawlor, in PSAMNI, 1940, pp 85-86; ASCD, 1966, pp 284-287; Gwynn and Hadcock, 'Medieval religious houses', 1970, p 228; HMNI, 1983, p 106; McCavery, 'Newtown', 1994, passim; letter from Dr E McParland to author, 12 April 2001.

Old Church, Magheralin

8. A most appealing ruin, in an extensive graveyard of considerable age; just across the road from its Victorian, and somewhat harsh, successor, which Rankin says is by Sir Thomas Drew; though Hugh Dixon thinks it is by Joseph Welland; but, for once, I disagree with both: it seems to me quite lacking on the one hand in Welland's flair and originality, and on the other hand, in Drew's sophistication, though I must acknowledge that I have no documentary grounds for my scepticism.

H C Lawlor, in PSAMNI, gives a pleasantly crisp account of the buildings: " About the year 1400, the larger church was built, incorporating the old one" (according to Lawlor, of the 10th century) "as a side chapel communicating through two semicircular-topped archways, with square pier of rubble between. At the W. end was built in 1442 a tower of four storeys serving as a porch over the main entrance and storeys above for the residence and 'a safe repository for his books and valuables' of the rector, John McGynd, canon of Dromore. In the inquisition of 1657, the church is stated to be ruinous. It was repaired shortly after the Restoration, and the large pointed E. window may date from this period. Bishop Pullen (1695-1713) built a see-house or episcopal palace near the church and used the latter as the cathedral or pro-cathedral of the diocese of Dromore. Bishop the Hon. William Beresford (1780-81) began, and his successor Bishop Percy completed the" (no longer) "existing episcopal palace of Dromore, when the see-house at Magheralin was dismantled, and the church surrendered its pro-cathedral status to the newly-built cathedral on the old site at Dromore. Magheralin Church continued as the parish church until 1845, when an entirely new church on a neighbouring site was built, and the venerable and historic church was dismantled". The Ordnance Survey memoir of 1837 describes the building in its final years as "plain ... with a tower and very low spire ... The inside ... plain ... It has an antique appearance ... the church is a very old one."

The Archaeological Survey of County Down, whilst not disputing a late mediaeval origin, is sceptical of Lawlor's interpretation. It says that "the present churchyard wall ... incorporates a length of thick old walling, presumably the N. wall of a building conjoined to the transept. It has a small recess towards the W. which may have been part of a stair, and this walling might possibly be the remains of the building '*parte in ecclesia et parte in cemeteno*'" (*sic: recte* cemetero?) "which John McGynd put up in 1442 as a safe repository for his books and valuables". As to "the W. tower of 4 stages (the upper one perhaps an addition) ... While it is not structurally impossible that this could be the tower erected" by John McGynd (or Maginn) in 1442, "it shows no medieval features whatever, and its character is more acceptable as part of a 17th century rebuilding (though no reused medieval stone can be found in it, as can be seen in 17th century reconstruction elsewhere in the building)." It seems that the north wall of the church was broken through when the transept was added, probably in the 16th or early 17th century, "to make an arcade of two pointed arches of rubble, carried on a square sectioned pier with chamfered angles on the S."

Whatever about its antiquity, this is an uncommonly attractive ruin.

Photograph: A C W Merrick.

Situation: Lurgan Road, Magheralin; td, Ballymakeonan; District Council, Craigavon; Grid ref. J 128 589.

References. Listed B (14/7/14). J R Ward and Thomas McIlroy, OSM, 1837, Down III, p 109; Atkinson, 'Dromore', 1925, pp 63-64, 137-138, 210-215; PSAMNI, 1940, p 91; ASCD, 1966, pp 307-8, pl 105; Oram, 'Craigavon', UAHS, 1971, pt II, p 9; HMNI, 1983, p 57; J F Rankin, in 'Clergy of Down and Dromore', 1996, pp 215-217.

Kirkistown Castle, Cloghy

9. "Tower-house and bawn, built by Roland Savage in 1622, situated on flat land about ¹/₃ of a mile from the E. coast of the Ards peninsula", says the Archaeological Survey of County Down. Described by Lewis in 1847 as "a heavy pile of building", this is an attractive and romantic-looking three-storey square tower topped by Irish crenellations, with a different pattern of openings to each face, somewhat altered about 1800 and later, set in the remains of a bawn, of which two round flankers linked by a wall, all very recently re-pointed, still stand. HMNI says "this remains a particularly fine example of a tower-house in its bawn ... it post-dates the Plantation but is fully in the late medieval tower-house tradition. The entrance to the tower on its SE side is protected by a corbelled machicolation at roof level ... Quoins, door and window dressings are in fine hard limestone". The rest of the walls are of split-stone rubble, roughly coursed. It is a pity that its surroundings are so miserable - caravan parks, motor-racing circuit, golf course, bungalows, adjacent farmhouse and unfriendly farmer, his piebald horse and Alsatian dog, and assorted agricultural rubbish; much of this mess brought into existence by the nearby war-time aerodrome, and about to be made even worse by housing development all over the airfield site.

Though much less thorough than the painstaking description in the Archaeological Survey, H C Lawlor's account of Kirkistown is more entertaining: "This castle, itself in plan 27 ft. N. to S. by 30 ft., was surrounded by a bawn some 150 ft. to 160 ft. square with a circular turret at each corner ... What strikes one on inspecting both castle and bawn is that both were built by a hopelessly incompetent architect; the ground is somewhat marshy, and he failed entirely to sink his foundations on to a solid base. Hence the castle is disfigured by an ugly buttress on the S. front around the entrance, and great iron clamps with screw-bolts at the corners trying their best, but failing, to keep the walls from bulging out owing to sinking foundation. The side walls of the bawn have almost entirely fallen notwithstanding numerous buttresses ..." And: "In the wall of the castle itself are carved several grotesque heads or faces which, with other cut-stone mouldings in the stair light, suggest that part at least of the stones for building the castle were formerly in a more ancient building, probably a church. It is said locally that a quantity of stone from the ruin of Black Abbey ... was brought here to build the castle, which is very probable, if difficult to prove". However, the Archaeological Survey would appear to accept the mouldings as dating from 1622.

William Montgomery, in 1683, says "Kirkestown Castle ... which with B.galgott and Quintin Bay, are the only ones in repair in this half barrony whose garden walls are washed with a pleasant fresh lough near the sea" (now dried up?). "James McGill of Ballymonestragh, Esqr improved this place very much, by building garden walls, and houses, and repairing in and about". Harris says "an English Castle, surrounded by a high Wall, strongly built, and containing within the Circuit of it a good Dwelling House of Mrs. Lucy Magil, now the Widow Savage". M M Kertland of the Ordnance Survey, in 1837, writes "There is an old castle in the townland of Kirkistown called Kirkistown Castle. Some attempt has been made to put it in a state of repair and a good deal of expense gone to for that purpose. It is, however, now left with a half-finished roof and broken windows and time and the weather are gradually bringing it back to its former state of ruin. The cause of this is that the present owner, Mr Montgomery of Grey Abbey, is a minor". It seems that windows were cut through the walls at either side of the entrance around 1800; but "The heads of these inserted openings have been concealed on the outside by the subsequent addition of a porch ..." (a very odd affair indeed framed in two massive buttresses). "About 1800, windows were cut through the S.E. wall flanking the entrance, large pointed openings, with sash windows, were inserted in the N.W. and N.E. walls of the main chambers, fireplaces were added at ground and first floor and these lower storeys were plastered and decorated in pseudo-Gothic style. At the same time, the original spiral stair to the first floor was replaced by a stone stair in two straight flights" (ASCD).

Knox, in 1873, says "When recently paying a visit to the place, I found the castle in wonderfully good condition, repairs having been effected from time to time by the Montgomery family ... Part of what appears to have been the original stone roof is still remaining, as well as the floors, which are, however, of subsequent construction. The doors are gothic or pointed, and there are small side rooms off the main apartments. Winding flights of stone stairs, still entire, lead to the summit of the building, the last occupant of which was a Colonel Johnston". Major Savage-Armstrong says "Kirkistone Castle is now" (1906) "the property of the Montgomerys of Grey Abbey, and it was occupied within the recollection of persons still living by some ladies of the Montgomery family. The fine old Keep is bound round with vamps of iron, and its walls bulge dangerously. But it is preserved with great care by its present owner, Lieut.-General Montgomery. On each side of it, high up, there is a carved human face. In the rooms are some handsome old mantelpieces ... The ruins are amongst the most imposing in the Ards, and are often visited by travellers from distant lands". More than one passer-by, in more recent times, has been tempted by the idea of seeking to rent it and bring it back into use as a holiday house: the plumbing and sewerage arrangements, as well as the immediate surroundings, tend to discourage any such idea, even if the Historic Monuments people would for a moment countenance it.

This little castle has been, on the whole, well restored, 1998-2001: the exterior must be considered really very successful indeed, despite the unfortunate dilapidation of its surroundings; the sensitivity of the handling of the re-pointing might be thought to atone for the stark restoration of Hillsborough Fort (12). The restoration of the interior is, though on the whole good, a bit more disputable. It was always going to be difficult to decide how best to restore a building occupied at so many disparate dates: the result is interesting, but perhaps a little bit of a muddle. There is a blessed freedom from the stuffed dummies of Carrickfergus Castle in County Antrim: instead, it is somewhat disconcerting to find, on the ground floor, triangular shelves displaying sea-shells and birds'-eggs; and blue-tinted-glass windows. The twisting and irregular staircase, with its numerous (very necessary) warnings "Mind your head", constitute a salutary reminder of the discomforts, in all periods, of tower-house life. It is perhaps a pity, if understandable, that access to the roof and battlements is firmly denied by an iron-barred gate. The variety of colours and textures, of rugs, furs, furnishings, textiles, and stained woodwork, employed in the refurbishment, is at times a little distracting. Perhaps, over the years, better examples of contemporary tower-house furnishings (but of which period?) may be found. In the meanwhile, this is a stimulating and rather unusual example of this kind of restoration.

Photographs: A C W Merrick (see also colour illus. 4); R J Welch, UM, W05/07/1.

Situation: At the end of a lane off the Portavogie-Cloghy road; td, Kirkistown; Parish, Ardkeen; District Council, Ards; Grid ref. J 644 580.

References: Monument in state care. Montgomery, Description of the ... Ards, 1701, in his 'Montgomery manuscripts, 1830, p 304; Harris, 'County of Down', 1744, p 67; M M Kertland, OSM, 1837, Down, II, p 2; Lewis, TD, 1847, I, p 25; Knox, 'Down', 1875, p 464; Savage-Armstrong, 'Savage family in Ulster', 1906, p 287; H C Lawlor, in PSAMNI, 1940, pp 100,101; ASCD, 1966, pp 238-241; HMNI, 1983, p 112; E J C Lyttle, in JUAHS VII, 1983, pp 18,19.

Market Cross, Newtownards

10. Originally, the Market Cross (erected in 1636, probably, the Archaeological Survey of County Down suggests, from a pattern-book), had a tall pillar standing in the centre, topped by a stone lion; very different from its present appearance. Over the years, it has aroused much commentary, of various kinds. The earliest, as transcribed by Harris, is the inscription on it, now indecipherable, which read:

*Theis Arms, which Rebels threw down and defac'd
- 1653 Are by this Loyal Burrowgh now replac'd - 1666
W.B. Prowest - Deus nobis haec otia fecit.*

In 1683, William Montgomery observed "The town hath in it an excellent piece of freestone work of eight squares, called the cross, with a door behind, within are stairs mounting to the towers, over which is a high stone pillar, and proclamations are made thereon; on the floor whereof at each square is an antique spout which vented claret, King Charles the 2nd being proclaimed our King of Great Britain, France, and Ireland, & Ao. Do. 1649". And: " ... a faire, neate, circular, octagonal building, (all hewn freestone) carved, painted, and guilded it was in diverse parts thereof, with a smal doore and stairs within it, ascending to a batlement, which is brest high from ye vault, and from ye pavement of ye sd vault issue severall spouts carved wth antique heads, wh at ye coronation and nativity days of our kings have dissembogued wine to ye glad and merry multitude. In ye middle of this fabric, upon ye vault aforesd, stands a pillar of hewn stones of eight squares, about twenty foot high, with a lyon seyant on the topp. This whole piece of work is called ye mercat

cross: whence are made publiq (with ye town solemnitys) all proclamations that come from our chief governor, and their own town business which needs an outcry". (An early predecessor of Downtown Radio, perhaps?).

Since then, the doorway had been blocked; a modern plinth had been added; all but one of the animal-head gargoyles had been removed; the pillar and lion had been long since abolished to be replaced by a pyramidal stone roof: all very sad. It is hard, now, to envisage the claret dissemboguing from the spouts: but, according to the Archaeological Survey it "must have been very similar in appearance to the Mercat Cross at Preston, Haddington-shire" in Scotland: which the late Colin McWilliam describes as "the most handsome in Scotland". (See illustration on following page).

In Harris's time, there was a fine 17th-century market house opposite. He writes: "before it stands a neat Octagon Building of hewn Stone, adorned with a slender Stone Pillar at top of the same form, which serves the Town for a Market Cross. In each side of the Octagon ... is a Niche curiously wrought, and adorned with an Escallop Shell. It is ten Feet ten Inches high from the Pedestal to the Cornish, and a Belt of Stone in an Architrave runs round it, through which, at every Angle, a stone Spout projects itself, consisting each of one entire Stone a Foot and a half long, to convey the water from the Roof; and all of these Spouts are set off with a variety of carved Work, some of them terminating in a Dog's Head, and others in those of other Animals. On the top of the Pillar springing out of the Roof a Lion, carved in Stone, is placed in a sitting Posture. The Room within serves as a Watch-house for the Town. On every Face of this Octagon are different Fancies or Arms carved in Stone, as namely, on one a Rose, on another a Helmet within the Horns of a Half Moon, and on it a Flower de Lys encompassed with a Wreath of Lawrel; on another a Cross within a Coronet; on another the Arms of Mountgomery, Earl of Mount-Alexander; on another the Arms (as we believe) of one Shaw, being a Star in the middle of three Cups, and the Crest of a Phoenix ... On the sixth face of this Octagon is a Harp for the Arms of Ireland; on the face next to the Market-house is inscribed, 1636, being the Date of this Building". (These armorial panels are now, for the most part, much worn, and barely decipherable).

Very different is the description given by G Scott of the Ordnance Survey, in the early 1830s: "At the eastern end of the town there is rather a singular building of hewn stone ... It is now perfectly useless from its prominent situation and unpleasant state in which it is kept. It is rather a nuisance than an ornament to the town although there is not the least doubt of it having been a decided ornament to the place when it served for what it was originally intended, viz. a fountain. Even yet the rude architecture is to be much admired". Samuel Lewis, in 1837, just says "A handsome stone cross of octagonal form, decorated with canopied niches, was built by the corporation in the centre of the town, to replace the ancient cross destroyed by the insurgents in 1641". The Parliamentary Gazetteer says, "Nearly in the centre of the town stands the lofty and sumptuous pedestal of an ancient cross - a handsome octagonal structure of hewn stone, decorated with canopied niches, and bearing inscriptions that the structure was erected in 1636 ...". Bassett, who evidently could not tell an octagon from a hexagon, remarks "At the junction of High-street, Castle-street and Movilla-street stands the Cross of Newtownards, or to be more correct, the pedestal of the cross. It is hexagonal in form, with deeply recessed panels. The Montgomery arms are visible, also the date, 1636, but the inscriptions have almost disappeared". H C Lawlor says in PSAMNI "The interior has been used as a prison for the drunk or disorderly".

The stonework was by degrees consolidated between 1979 and 1984; seven of the gargoyles were recarved, though there is nothing to tell the visitor which, or by whom, or on what models; the doorway was unblocked, and the opportunity taken to clear the interior, now again filled with rubbish, since the base of the monument is well below the present street-level, and detritus blows in between the railings. I do not think this is one of the success stories of the Environment and Heritage Service.

Photographs: WA Green, UFTM, WAG 945; Mercat Cross, Preston, John Knight, Edinburgh.

Situation: At the east end of High Street, Newtownards; td, Corporation South; Parish, Newtownards; District Council, Ards; Grid ref. J 492 741.

References: Scheduled monument ... Datestone; Harris, 'County of Down', 1744, p 58; Montgomery, Description of the ... Ards, 1701, in his

'Montgomery manuscripts', 1830, p 314; Montgomery, 'Montgomery manuscripts', 1869, p 68; G Scott, OSM, nd (?1837), Down, II, p 107; Lewis, TD, 1837, II, p 435; PG, III, 1846, p 31; Bassett, 'County Down', 1886, p 333; PSAMNI, 1940, p 84; ASCD, 1966, p 260; McWilliam, 'Lothian', 1978, p 390; HMNI, 1983, pp 57, 152.; notes in MBR.

Custom House, Bangor

11. "This split-stone rubble building with limestone dressings to openings and quoins is the only tower house in the province now to occupy an urban site" (Patton). (What about the tower-houses at Ardglass, Strangford, Portaferry?) In 1637, Charles Moncke, Surveyor-General of the Customs, saw "a fair customhouse built but not finished by the Lord of Clanneboye, who hath received between two and three hundred pounds of the King towards it, and hath bestowed at least six hundred pounds already and two hundred pounds more will hardly finish it: it is a large pile of stone made with flankers, and might serve as well for defence of the harbour. There are very large store-houses, lodging-chambers for officers, with chimneys, studies and places to lay all sorts of commodities in . . ." In the late 17th century, William Montgomery notices that

"At ye end of ye town is a small bay for barques, and on it a large slated house double lofted, intended at first for a custom-house, both built by ye said Lord Claneboye, from hence is a usual passage to Carrickfergus". In one of these lodging-chambers, it seems, my great-great-grandfather Charles Brett was born in 1752, his father, likewise Charles Brett, being then agent to his cousin, Bernard Ward.

"It ... comprises a rectangular house, of two storeys with an attic, and a tower, of four storeys, at the N.W. angle. The house ... with walls 4 ft. in thickness, has been considerably altered in recent times; it terminates on the N. in a crow-stepped gable, rising from a roll-and-hollow moulded skew-corbel ... The tower, semi-circular towards the N., is entered on the S. by a door the jambs of which, with quirked arris-roll, are original ... Commencing at first floor level of the tower, and originally accessible from the upper floors of the house, was a stair, apparently of timber construction, contained in a quarter-round projection in the re-entrant angle ... The tower and stair turret have a a battlemented parapet at roof level, rising to a greater height at the S.W. angle of the tower; the parapet has been rebuilt throughout" (Archaeological Survey of County Down).

"This is unique in Bangor and rare in Ulster. The style is early Scottish Baronial, distinctive Scottish features being the crow-stepped gable on the Northern side of the Tower, and the quarter-round turret ... The turret and Tower have a battlemented parapet, but it is likely that this was a later addition, with the original roof being conical like other Scottish towers of the period. Perhaps during the Napoleonic Wars, when flat-roofed Martello Towers were being built around the coast for defence and signalling, the Bangor building was converted to its present appearance" (Borough Council leaflet, unsigned and undated).

The Custom House seems never to have been properly completed, or to have been used for its intended purpose. Harris says that it was in ruins in 1744, which must have been uncomfortable for my great-great-great-grandmother, if true. It seems to have been let for lodgings; then, in the 1880s, a photographic studio; presented by Maude Ward, Lady Clanmorris, to the Bangor Urban Council in 1923; converted by the Council to Hot Sea Water Baths and opened as such in 1933; but closed in 1954, when the place was leased by the Council to Angus Macdonald, a well-known antique dealer. In 1982 the buildings were refurbished, and then re-opened as Tourist Information Centre below, and offices above: as they still are.

The group is not as handsome as it could and should be: the four-storey stone tower looks fine, though there is no access to it; and the stone back of the two-storey-and-attic block is likewise fine; but the front of the latter has at some date been roughcast, modern windows have been inserted, and the façade painted custard-colour, so that it bears no logical relationship to the stone tower. It is perhaps not too late to strip off the roughcast, restore the window-openings to more appropriate proportions, and open up the entire building - perhaps even transfer here the North Down Heritage Centre, which is not very happily sited in the stable-yard of Bangor Castle (64)?

Photograph: A C W Merrick. Lithograph: from Doyle, 'Tours in Ulster', 1854.
Situation: 34, Quay Street, Bangor; td, Corporation; Parish, Bangor; District Council, North Down; Grid ref. J 505 821.
References: Listed A (23/5/12). Charles Moncke, Report on the Customs, 1637, BL, Harleian Ms 2138; Montgomery, Description of the ... Ards, 1701, in his 'Montgomery manuscripts', 1830, p 313; Harris, 'County of Down', 1744, p 61; Lewis, TD, 1837, I, p 183; ASCD, 1966, pp 227-228; Patton, 'Bangor', UAHS, 1999, p 173; 'History of the old custom house and tower house', [ca 1985], passim.

Hillsborough Fort

12. First on this site, an Early Christian period hill-top rath or ring-fort; next, a star-shaped artillery fort and gate-house characteristic of the mid-17th century, "the earliest real artillery fortification in Co. Down" (Archaeological Survey of County Down). Then, and still, "the castellated garden house built by the first Earl of Hillsborough in the centre of the North West rampart of Hillsborough Fort ... typical of a type of building that was much more common in the Home Counties than round the Dublin Pale ... The details ... are typical of English eighteenth century Gothic but for Ireland they are handled with unusual conviction" (Rowan). "The fort is laid out as a 270 ft. square with spear-shaped bastions at each corner. The defences consist of an earthen rampart about 8 ft. high, sloped on the inside at about 45°, with a wall-walk 8-10 ft. wide, and retained on the outside by a stone facing" (ASCD). It is approached, either from the church (20) or from the market square, by a tree-lined avenue, the 'church walk', with attractive 18th-century pillars and wrought-iron gates and overthrow opposite the court house (146) in the square.

Four days before Christmas, 1660 ("in the 12th year of our reign", reckoned from the death of Charles I), King Charles II appointed Arthur Hill to be Hereditary Constable of Hillsborough Fort, "a considerable place of strength ... fortifyed with fower Bastions or Flankiers which commaunds the chiefest roade ... leading from Dublin to the townes of Belfast and Carrickfergus" and which Arthur Hill had "within thiese few yeares built att his own charges and upon his owne land". (But Canon Barry, rightly or wrongly, gives the date of building as 1630; and the name of the builder as Peter Hill; though he does not cite his authority. Lewis, too, says that the fort was built in the reign of Charles I). This was the artillery fort whose ramparts still overlook the lake, the church, the town, the forest, and the old road: not, however, the new

motorway, rumbling just out of sight in the background.

By 1758, Wills Hill, Earl of Hillsborough, had undertaken the reconstruction of its gatehouse. Mrs Delany visited it in September of that year, and wrote: "the old castle is fallen to decay, but as it is a testimony of the antiquity of his family," (Lord Hillsborough) "is determined to keep it up. The castle consists of one very large room, with small ones in the turrets; the court behind it measures just an English acre, and is laid out in a bowling-green, and round it is a raised high terrace, at each corner of which is a square of about fifty feet, which are to make four gardens, one for roses only, the other for all sorts of flowers - these on each side of the castle; the other two for evergreens and flowering shrubs".

As to this, Rowan exhibits scepticism; "If the work were carried out in 1758, it is very odd that Lord Hillsborough did not apply for the revival of his rights as hereditary Constable until twenty years later. It therefore seems more probable that it was his intention to restore the Fort in 1758, and that this was set aside, or interrupted, when he began to enlarge the parish church a few years later". I do not myself find this argument persuasive. But Alistair Rowan is, to me, more persuasive when he argues for the involvement at Hillsborough of the English gentleman-architect Sanderson Miller, on the basis of a letter written by Lord Barrington to Miller in June 1763: "My friend Lord Hillsborough has determined to make a considerable building in Ireland, but he wants some English advice concerning it. I have told him that you can give him the very best, and he is earnestly desirous to receive it" - this from an undeservedly neglected article of 1964 in the Irish Georgian Society's Bulletin. Rowan would also attribute to Miller the delightful two-storey Gothick gazebo on the centre of the north-east rampart of the enclosure. The whole complex seems to have served as "a pleasure ground for the Hill family" (HMNI) for many years: there are attractive records or representations of at least three great *alfresco* feasts there, in 1809, 1833 and 1837, and it must have been used informally for parties and junketings on many other occasions.

The fort seems always to have been rather a flimsy building: "a charming mock-castle with pointed windows, paper-thin walls, and snap-off battlements" (Dixon). In 1798, it "was used as a depository for arms, but ... 'there being no Warders at the time, the Rebels got through the old sally port and stole them'" (Barry). In 1802, he adds, the fort was described as "ruinous" and the warders as "dormant". By 1836, it had been appropriated as an armoury for the yeomanry of the town, according to Twenty-one Views in Belfast, which contains a fine wood-engraving showing the state of the fort in that year: stonework partly concealed by roughcast or limewash, ladder propped against the front wall, and wheelbarrow handy. Later in the century, the exposed walls and towers were hung with slates in a not wholly successful attempt to keep out wet and weather. Thereafter, its condition gradually deteriorated, especially after the sale by the Downshires of Hillsborough Castle (51) in 1925 to provide a Government House.

So matters went on - gradually downhill - until 1959, when the seventh Marquis leased the fort, with nine acres of land including the Fort Field running down to the lake, to the Ministry of Finance, for a term of 294 years from 21st December 1954: "being the same number of years as had then elapsed since the said Letters of His Late Majesty King Charles II were made patent": at a rent of one white rose payable each year to the Constable on his birthday. I enjoyed drafting that lease, which included one or two unusual provisions; including one, "that if there shall at any time be no Government of Northern Ireland ... then these presents shall ... be null and void ... and the fort and premises shall revert to Mr Hill his executors administrators

and assigns or if there be none such shall pass to and vest in the Crown of England and none other": a slightly mischievous piece of draftsmanship as I now, with hindsight, admit.

Captain Terence O'Neill, the minister then responsible, "putting aesthetics before practicalities, refused to contemplate the retention or replacement of the slate hangings. A compromise was reached, under which most of the stonework was carefully pointed or joint-harled, but left uncovered; whilst only the most vulnerable panels of the upper walls were rendered, using, in the fashion of the day, a cement render, with a fairly fine gravel, or pebble-dash. In the result, the public (informed and uninformed alike) developed a considerable affection for this little stone fort, in its charming setting, with all the irregularities and the contrasting textures so characteristic of the Picturesque" (Brett, 1995).

But the endemic damp returned. In the 1990s, "a trial section of one of the towers was coated in an inch-thick layer of a hard cement-based pebble render." By the autumn of 1994, despite protests from both local residents and conservationists, "both walls and towers had been encased completely in pebble rendering; instead of the agreeably irregular stonework, all surfaces were geometrically flat, and the corner arrises were (and are) as sharp and straight as the knife-edge crease of a bank manager's trousers. The glowing golden colour of the stonework has been replaced by a uniform grey. The Fort now appears, to some at least, rather dreary, suburban, and charmless". Matters have by no means improved; indeed, five years after the foregoing words were written, the fort looks drearier still, because of the constant staining at the battered feet of its walls.

In 1974 I wrote, "Public lavatories, and a residence for a caretaker, have been inserted in the ground floor of the gatehouse. The large room on the first floor is firmly locked; some day it is supposed to be opened as an architectural

museum. The former bowling green is disfigured by a half-moon-shaped excavation, from which nothing of any significance was extracted; but the authorities are too fond of it to fill it in. The public is grudgingly allowed in, but is far from being made welcome". Twenty-five years later, much of this, though not all, remains true. What is more, there is now a deplorably inappropriate railing around the slopes beside the little gazebo atop the side gate; and there seem to be semi-permanent hutments and containers, very possibly in breach of the covenants in the lease, where the flower-beds ought to be in the corner angles of the ramparts. Altogether, in this instance, a poor advertisement for the sensitivity of the Historic Buildings Service.

Photograph: A C W Merrick (see also colour illus. 3). Wood-engraving: from 'Twenty-one views in Belfast'.
Situation: Between St Malachy's church and the Courthouse, Hillsborough; td. Hillsborough; District Council, Lisburn; Grid ref. J 245 586.
References: Surprisingly, not a listed building but rather a monument in state care; in conservation area. Delany, 'Letters from Georgian Ireland', 1991, p 147, letter of 1 October, 1758; letter from Lord Barrington to Sanderson Miller, June 1763, in Warwick County Record Office, Ms 1253, L. 774; G F W Bordes, OSM, 1834, and J R Ward, T C McIlroy and J C Innes, 1837, Down III, pp 88, 91-92; 'Twenty-one views in Belfast', 1836; A J Rowan, in 'Quarterly bulletin of the IGS', VII, 1964, pp 9-11, 28; ASCD, 1966, pp 408-410; Brett, 'Mid Down', UAHS, 1974, p 12; Dixon, 'Introduction', UAHS, 1975, p 41; C Gaskell-Brown and N Brannon, in UJA, 3rd series, XLI, 1978, pp 78-87; Barry, 'Hillsborough', 1982, pp 41-45; HMNI, 1983, p 111; J Cornforth, in CL, 28 July, 1994, p 66; Brett, in 'UA', April/May 1995, pp 8,9.

Grey Point Fort, Helen's Bay

13. Grotesquely, this is neither a listed building nor a scheduled monument: it is a Wildlife Site within a Country Park. Thus, as Chairman Mao remarked, do flowers sprout from the muzzle of a gun!

Grey Point is a hilly headland which juts out into the south shore of Belfast Lough where the coastline turns the corner between Bangor Bay and Craigavad. From the 1858 Ordnance Survey map, it seems clear that the headland had formed part of James Fraser's 1840s scheme for the landscaping of the Clandeboye demesne. However, in 1904, it was considered necessary to strengthen the coastal defences of the British Isles: defensive gun emplacemants were established at Grey Point; just opposite, at Kilroot; and at Orlock, Larne, and Magilligan. The site was acquired in that year for £8,400 from the Clandeboye estate, and Fraser's plantings were cut down to establish

clear fields of fire to east, north, and west. Between 1904 and 1907, the fort was built by W J Campbell & Son for £10,000. This seems to have been the quintessential *éminence grise*. Two six-inch naval guns with a range of about six miles were mounted there, and first fired in 1907. They were initially manned by the Antrim Royal Garrison Artillery, during the first World War; from 1937 onwards, by territorial units of 188 (Antrim) Heavy Battery, Royal Artillery (TA). None of them seem to have been very good shots: there is no record that they ever hit anything, despite numerous test firings against towed targets. (It was perhaps as well that they never faced the same challenge as their colleagues in Norway in 1940 - who succeeded in sinking the German cruiser *Blucher* in Oslo fjord). The coast artillery was disbanded, and the fort closed, in 1956-7. Much of the land was sold off for housing, so the present site is much smaller than it used to be; and scrubby woodland was allowed to sprout again all around the carefully-cleared glacis.

In May, 1987, thirty years after its closure, the central part of the Fort - that is, the hexagonal enclosure containing the principal buildings - was re-opened by the Department of the Environment as an element (though somewhat isolated from the rest) of the Crawfordsburn Country Park. The original guns - two six-inch; two 4.5 inch howitzers for defence against shore-based attack; machine-guns; and searchlights - had long since been removed and sold off. However, in 1993 a six-inch gun from Spike Island, County Cork, on the same pattern, was successfully acquired after much arduous cross-border negotiation, and installed at Grey Point for the edification of visitors; and in 1999, a second, similar, gun, also from the Cork harbour defences (but this time from Fort Carlisle) was installed. The earlier gun is inscribed, on the barrel, with the date 1899, on the breech-block, 1903; its later companion has 1899 on the barrel also, but 1917 on the breech-block. Gun-houses to provide a (very limited) degree of protection from air attack were installed only in 1940. During the second World War, this was the Northern Ireland headquarters of the Royal Artillery Regiment, with command and control of all the guns here, at Kilroot, and at Orlock.

The Point now bears some semblance of its original appearance as I remember it, before and during the early years of the war (it was, naturally, inaccessible thereafter). It is, in general, very well presented and displayed. But, unfortunately, its dominating position, marvellous views to seaward, and splendid field of fire, have in recent years been almost entirely obscured by the growth of trees and foliage all around the perimeter; whilst paying due regard to the importance of the wildlife functions of the Department, in

this case, I think that they have plainly been allowed to go too far: and a drastic programme of pruning and cutting back of greenery - in the immediate vicinity of the Fort, only - is clearly long overdue. Having hammered its swords into ploughshares, the Department of the Environment now concentrates its publicity material on the birds, flowers and insects - as their guide to the Fort remarks, "Insects are the most numerous organisms on the earth and are everywhere. It is worth looking for the different types: moths, beetles, flies - see how many you can find." I do not really disagree; but it seems an odd twist of fate, that the Fort, after so much conservation effort on the part of so many parties, should neither be as visible from seaward as it might be, nor enjoy the seaward views which it used to. I doubt if the birds, flowers or insects would object to their restoration.

I recall being taken to Grey Point, when aged I suppose seven or eight, for some kind of military sports day or parade or tattoo; and being offered a mug of tea by a squaddie; which I declined, and asked for milk, my accustomed tipple; and being (as I thought and still think) most unjustly berated for rudeness, was told I would, in punishment, not be allowed to visit the battleships *Nelson* and *Rodney*, of the Home Fleet, due to be open to the public in Bangor Bay the following week. How I cried! Fortunately, the authorities relented. I have not much cared for Grey Point Fort, scene of my infantile humiliation, ever since.

Photograph: A C W Merrick. Plan: DoENI, redrawn by D Varilly.
Situation: Off Fort Road, Helen's Bay; td, Ballygrot; District Council, North Down; Grid ref. J 458 532.
References: Remarkably, neither listed nor scheduled, although in public ownership. OS map, 1858. Ian Gailey and Hugh Dixon, 'Grey Point Fort, County Down', HMSO, 1987, passim; successive undated guides, Environment and Heritage Service.

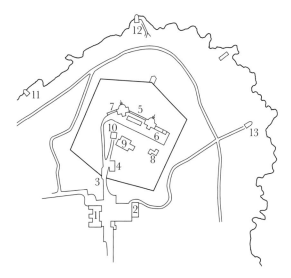

Key to plan: 1. Quarters, 2. Engine room, 3. Entrance to fort, 4. Store for magazine guns, 5. Battery, 6. Magazine, 7. Shelters, 8. Battery observation post, 9. Fire command, 10. Radar platform, 11. Searchlight emplacement 1936, 12. Searchlight emplacement 1940, 13. Searchlight emplacement 1936.

Pulpit, St Malachi's Church, Hillsborough (20). Photograph: MBR

CHAPTER TWO

CHURCHES AND CHAPELS

The churches and chapels of North County Down are a somewhat variegated lot, conforming to few clear architectural patterns; perhaps this is hardly surprising, since my arbitrary boundary cuts off the two Church of Ireland cathedrals - Downpatrick, and Dromore - both in the middle of the county; as also, the predominantly Roman Catholic areas of South Down. Moreover, unlike County Armagh, the dioceses of Down and Dromore have seldom enjoyed the direct patronage of any ecclesiastic so wealthy and powerful as Archbishop Robinson; nor the attentions of diocesan architects of the calibre of Thomas Cooley or Francis Johnston. However, there are some interesting observations to be made on church buildings in general within the area.

First, the principal architectural set-pieces, at any rate of the earlier years, result from the patronage of aristocratic Protestant landowners. St John's, Moira (19), of 1723, an early and rather rough-hewn Georgian church, "was built at the Expence of the late and present Sir *John Rawdon*".[1] Knockbreda parish church (18), of 1737, somewhat more ambitious architecturally, "was executed under the Direction of Mr. Castell," (the distinguished architect Richard Cassels) "at the sole Expence of the Right Honourable the Lady Viscountess Dowager *Middleton*".[2] St Mark's, Newtownards (22), a very much more sophisticated building of 1817, was built partly at the expense of the Board of First Fruits: but at the instigation, and partly at the cost, of "Lord Castlereagh, Prime Minister" (*recte* Foreign Secretary) "of England, afterwards Marquis of Londonderry, at a cost of £7000".[3] By far the best of this group, intended to be promoted to cathedral status though this never happened, is unquestionably St Malachi's parish church at Hillsborough (20), "supposed to have been begun in 1760 and finished in 1772",[4] at the expense of Wills Hill, Earl of Hillsborough, by an unknown but highly skilled architect, probably English: the names of Sanderson Miller, and of Thomas Wright of Durham, have been put forward.

Along with these quite grand earlier church buildings, there survive unspoiled two very simple and charming little churches, one Roman Catholic, one of the then established church, both as it happens in the Ards peninsula: Lisbane (17), of 1777, and Balligan (16), even earlier, of 1704: with many similarities between them.

The two next most important churches, architecturally, are both examples of the work in the classical style of that extraordinary and eccentric paragon, John Millar: Castlereagh Presbyterian Church (34), of 1834; and Portaferry

Presbyterian Church(37), of 1841. Son (or possibly grandson) of the owner of the quarries at Scrabo, he served his apprenticeship in London with the major architect Thomas Hopper (author of Gosford Castle in County Armagh, and Penrhyn in Caernarvonshire); built a remarkable series of highly original non-conformist churches in Belfast and County Antrim; fell into financial difficulties; and emigrated to Australia, then New Zealand, where he lived out a turbulent career. It is arguable that the two Presbyterian churches at Castlereagh and Portaferry are his very finest works. Alas, neither of these masterpieces is, at the time of writing, in the best state of preservation. The church at Portaferry is suffering from a sharp decline in the Presbyterian population of that town, and from various forms of decay: the congregation simply cannot afford the cost of setting things to rights; despite the self-evident merits of its architecture, it has received little help or support from those charged with the protection of historic buildings. The case of Castlereagh Presbyterian Church is the converse. Here, a headstrong minister and session, and a wealthy congregation, have determined to add a highly inappropriate extension in the contemporary style at the rear of the church, where it looks out over the Lagan valley; no remonstrances from Members of Parliament, members of the public, or the Environment and Heritage Service prevailed; the latter have weakly given in, and permitted the work to proceed. In fact, the desired new accommodation could easily have been added to the large church hall in the ample car-park on the opposite side of the road. The kirk has taken the high-handed line that the building is nobody's business but its own. Would the Castlereagh minister and elders not think that the public had a legitimate interest in proposals for modern additions to St Paul's Cathedral; Westminster Abbey; or for that matter even the Tron Kirk in Edinburgh? Probably not, for there is no debating aesthetics with those who do not wish to listen. And, might not the quarter-million pounds or so spent on the extension have gone a long way to solve the problems of the deserving sister congregation in Portaferry?

There are a few not particularly outstanding churches in the tradition of the Board of First Fruits, including those at Comber (23), and at Kilmood (21). There are a surprisingly large number of churches in the neo-classical tradition, mostly, but not all, non-conformist. The non-subscribers built new churches, after Dr Henry Montgomery had led seventeen Arian congregations out of the mainstream Presbyterian Synod of Ulster, in 1830, to form the Remonstrant Synod: at Ravara, 1838 (30); Comber, 1838 (35); Killinchy, 1846 (38); and Holywood, 1849 (40). These are all in a restrained, stylised, neo-classical style of considerable merit. The mainstream Presbyterian church, which long adhered to classicism, had earlier built churches in this style at Donaghadee, 1824 (31); and Bangor, 1831 (33). Somewhat surprisingly, there are quite late examples of the same style both in the Church of Ireland, and also in the Roman Catholic Church: the Doric Kircubbin parish church, 1843 (39), attributed to Charles Lanyon, is the best of these; but St Patrick's Roman Catholic Church, Magheralin, of the same year (32) is likewise not without interest.

One bizarre oddity is the episcopalian church at Waringstown (15), originally of 1681, its core undoubtedly authentic Jacobean; externally, all but the tower now hemmed in by later Victorian accretions; its interior, converted into a riot of carved 19th-century Jacobethan ornament due to the wood-working skills of the Rev. Holt Waring, the local squarson, proprietor but not rector of the parish.

There are two modest examples of the activity of the Down and Connor Church Accommodation Society, both to designs by Sir Charles Lanyon: St John's, 1840 (24) and St James's, 1841 (25), Kilwarlin. There is no great wealth, in any denomination, of High Victorian Gothic. The most successful of the late 19th- and early 20th-century churches in north County Down are, for the Church of Ireland, All Saints', Eglantine, 1875 (42), a very happy example of the work of Sir Thomas Drew at his best; St Patrick's Roman Catholic Church, Newtownards, 1877 (43), a particularly fine building internally, if a little mediocre externally, the work of the English architect J A Hansom; and Hillhall Presbyterian Church, 1902 (44), a striking example of the Arts and Crafts style by Vincent Craig, a younger brother of Lord Craigavon.

I fear there are no more recent churches in north County Down which much commend themselves to me: with the possible exception of the new Roman Catholic church at Holywood, 1993 (45), built after the disgraceful destruction, apparently by arson, of Timothy Hevey's church of 1874; of which the later spire of 1891 still stands, just a little uncomfortably, beside the modern circular church with its conical roof.

References: 1. Harris, 'County of Down', 1744, p 104; 2. ibid., p 73. 3. Ewart, 'Down & Connor & Dromore', 1886, p 54. 4. J Cornforth, in CL, 28 July, 1994, pp 66-67.

Entrance screen, St Malachi's Church, Hillsborough (20). Engraving: PRONI, T3793/1/32/24

Bangor Abbey (C of I) Church

14. On a site of great antiquity and holiness, the abbey here was, according to the Annals of Ulster, founded in the 550s by Saint Comgall. However, the tower of the present church seems to be 15th-century; its octagonal spire, and curious two-storey external staircase to the left of the tower, 17th-century; nave, transepts and chancel of the 19th century. Samuel Lewis says "The old church was built" (by Sir James Hamilton) "near the site of the old abbey, in 1623, and a very neat tower and spire were subsequently added to it ... In attempting to enlarge it, in 1832, the foundation was so much disturbed by injudicious excavations that it was found necessary to take the whole down, with the exception of the tower; and a spacious and handsome structure, in the later style of English architecture, was erected in the following year, at an expense of £935, which was defrayed by the parishioners, aided by subscriptions to a considerable amount from some of the landed proprietors". The chancel and transepts were added in 1844.

The church stands in the middle of a very extensive, and somewhat overgrown, graveyard, containing "many good 18th and 19th century slate headstones with beautiful naïve

lettering" (Patton), faithfully recorded by Tony Merrick, but some not now easily accessible or decipherable.

Harris reports: "The church of *Bangor* was built within the Precincts of the old Abby about the Year 1617, and was not finished till the Year 1623; both which particulars appear from Dates on a stone in the South Walks, and on an old oak Pulpit, now lying in a corner of the Church. The Steeple of it," (i.e. the tower) " through which the entrance is into the Church, is supported by an Arch of nine Strings or Beads, not centring in a point, as many others do, but springing at equal Distances round the Arch from side to side; and an Inscription thereon declares it was raised in 1693". According to the Archaeological Survey of County Down, "In 1469, the abbey having fallen into ruin, the Augustinian community was forced to accept Nicholas O'Hegarty, a priest of the Third Order of St. Francis, as abbot. The tower of the present church is probably a structure of about this date". The spire was added, along with the external staircase, in 1693; an inscription inside under the tower says "This steepel was raised anno 1693 Jo Blackwood Jo Cleeland Church wardens". There is also a monument to William

Stennors, master mason, 1626, displaying the tools of his trade, who may have been responsible for the building of Hamilton's church.

Internally, a spacious T-shaped church with a rather peculiar Tudoresque roof and a screen in similar style between the nave and the porch in the base of the tower. Replacing the 19th-century east window of the chancel, there is a somewhat garish side-lit mural of 1960 by Kenneth Webb, depicting the Ascending Christ adjuring Saints Comgall, Columbanus and Gall to go into all the world and preach the gospel. There are a number of memorials of considerable interest, all the best of them in the base of the tower. Aesthetically, much the most important of these is that by Scheemakers to James Hamilton and his wife Sophia Mordaunt, erected "in accordance with the will of their eldest daughter, Ann, who died May 17, 1760" (Archaeological Survey). Potterton says it "is of a type often repeated by Scheemakers, with a seated female figure of Religion holding an open book, and medallion portraits of the deceased".

In 1882, the newly built St Comgall's in Castle Street became the parish church, and the Abbey was "forsaken"

(Rankin); though Lavens Ewart noted in 1886 "The old church is carefully preserved, and is used as a mortuary chapel, and for occasional children's services" - a curious combination of functions. Due to the growth of Bangor, the Abbey was brought back into use in 1917, and was reconstituted a parish church in 1941. Various renovations and alterations took place in 1960; again in 1995, under the supervision of Hobart & Heron.

Interesting, but considering its associations - especially with St Malachi and his "noble institution, inhabited by many thousands of monks, ... a place truly sanctified and so fruitful in saints" - a bit disappointing.

Photograph: A C W Merrick.
Situation: Abbey Street, Bangor; td, Corporation; District Council, North Down; Grid ref. J 501 811.
References: Listed A (23/7/4). Harris, 'County of Down', 1744, p 61; Ewart, 'Down & Connor & Dromore', 1886, p 39; ASCD, 1966, p 265; Potterton, 'Irish church monuments', UAHS, 1975, pp 59, 77; Merrick, in 'Gravestone inscriptions', Down, XVII, 1978, pp 4 - 193; A C W Merrick, in 'North Down Mail', July, 1987; J F Rankin, in 'Clergy of Down and Dromore', 1996, pp 52-53; Patton, 'Bangor', UAHS, 1999, p 1; parish magazine, February 2000.

Holy Trinity (C of I) Church, Waringstown

15. "A small Walk from the House is a well finished Church, roofed with *Irish Oak*, and remarkable for the Workmanship of it. *William Waring* Esq;, who first settled here, gave the Ground for this Use, and obtained an Act of Parliament for changing the Site of the old Parish Church from *Donoghcloney* Bridge. After which, in the year 1681, he built this Church at his own expence, which encouraged Protestants to settle in the Village, at that Time thin of Inhabitants, and overgrown with Woods. Money is now raised by Subscription for erecting a Steeple

at the West End of the Church" (Harris).

This is in many ways a most deceptive church. Externally, it is 19th-century in appearance; triple round-headed windows with lattices, inset in blackstone walls - mostly random but one transept of squared stones with galleting and brick window-heads. Apart from the tower, which has a respectably 18th-century air, the exterior is now almost all in fact Victorian; yet the core of the building, the roof of the nave, is genuinely original Jacobean - though not one of its walls remains; and the ornate black-oak ornamentation of pulpit and uprights is, contrary to appearances, early 19th-century Jacobethan, from the skilled hand of the Rev. Holt Waring, squarson, though apparently never incumbent, of the village, whose workshop, and treadle lathe, survive in the out-buildings of Waringstown House (46). He was an odd fish: born 1766, died at Waringstown 1850 in his 85th year; curate of Hillsborough, rector of Shankill, Lurgan, later Dean of Dromore. "In his younger days, 1793, he was Chaplain of the Royal Downshire Militia, and even acted as Commanding Officer of the 3rd Iveagh Yeomanry Infantry - an anomalous mixture of characters which led to his on several occasions officiating in regimentals, thinly covered by his surplice" (Atkinson). However that may be, he was unquestionably a very skilful wood-carver, as well as good at drawing.

Mr Ward of the Ordnance Survey, whose researches do not seem to have been very thorough-going, says "It is a plain, stone building with a tower and low spire. The total height is 81 feet ... The accommodation is for   persons and the average attendance is   . The inside of the church is very neat. The roof is not ceiled. The supports rest on jambs jutting out of the top of the side walls. They are of oak and some of them look like bog timber, which gives the inside an antique appearance. The side windows are rectangular but those at the gable ends are Gothic. The church was built in   . The north wing was added in   ."

Lewis, in 1837, comments - "It is a large and handsome edifice in the Elizabethan style, to which a tower and spire were added in 1748; the interior is very elegantly fitted up, but is most remarkable for its roof of carved oak, resting on 18 carved corbels of the same material; the pulpit, communion-table, railings, and pews are all of oak. In 1832, the church, being found too small for the congregation, was enlarged by the addition of a northern transept, which is finished in its roof and all other parts to correspond with the original building, at which time the pulpit and communion-table were richly ornamented with carvings and pierced work of wreaths, festoons, and other similar embellishments, executed by the hand of the Rev. Holt Waring, proprietor of the estate, and by him presented to the parish".

Lavens Ewart, in 1886, says "the church at present consists of the original nave, built in the Jacobean style, with a curious oak roof; a western tower, with shingle steeple, built in 1748; and a north transept and south aisle, added during the present century. The east end is enriched by a quantity of well-executed carving by the hand of the late Dean Waring, to whom also is due the elaborate ornamentation of the pulpit".

The Archaeological Survey of County Down gives the following description: "said to have been supervised by James Robb, chief mason to the King's Works in Ireland" (who was, however, an invention of the late Colin Johnson Robb; see 79). "The W. tower was commenced c. 1745, and completed, after a partial collapse, in 1750." (A very full description of the building of the tower, its collapse on 15th August 1747, and the detailed expenses incurred, is given by Atkinson). "The church was enlarged at various times in the 19th century: a N. transept was added c. 1830, a S. aisle and porch in 1858 and the chancel was rebuilt, or extended, in 1880 by Sir Thomas Drew. The church is of rubble masonry throughout, the 19th century work with wrought quoins and dressings; the roofs are of slate and the tower spire is shingle-covered; the original church was also roofed with shingles ... The pulpit is of 17th century character but this, with other enrichments in the same style, is apparently 19th century work attributed to the Rev. Holt Waring in 1832."

Photographs: A C W Merrick (see also colour illus. 8).
Situation: Off Main Street, Waringstown; td, Magherana; District Council, Craigavon; Grid ref. J 103 552.
References: Listed B+ (14/16/2). Harris, 'County of Down', 1744, p 105; J R Ward, OSM, nd (? 1837), Down, III, p 60; Lewis, TD, 1837, II, p 674-5; Ewart, 'Down & Connor & Dromore', 1886, p 111; Atkinson, 'Ulster parish', 1898, passim; ASCD, 1966, pp 336-8, pl 118; Walker, 'Historic Ulster churches', 2000, pp 26-27.

St Andrew's (C of I) Church, Inishargy, Balligan

16. A charming little rustic church, set in a very pleasant stone-walled grassy graveyard, with overthrow and lantern at the gate. Smooth quoins, but roughcast walls, all painted cream, but not for some time; all the windows latticed, that at the porch pointed, those in the side walls rectangular, and the triple east window round-headed like a kind of Diocletian window. Inside the (later) porch, a lovely carved stone pointed doorway, with branches of leaves in the spandrels, and above the arch the legend 'B T AD 1704'. The interior very simple and delightful: Scrabo-stone-flagged floor; A-frame beams supporting the roof; simple benches (some less simple, concoctions of Denis O'D Hanna, architect); excellent furnishings; and a good sculpted memorial in the nave wall, to Alexander Allen of Dunover who died in 1821 (unsigned, alas), with grieving maiden of great charm, and an effusive inscription saying that he was "Eminently useful in Society. The suavity and

urbanity of his manners conciliated the respect and esteem of all who knew him" - just what I should wish to have said of myself!

M M Kertland of the Ordnance Survey just says: "The parish church in the townland of Balliggan measures 52 feet by 22 feet. It was built in the year 1704 and is capable of accommodating 200". The listers say "Simple single-storey gabled church of steep roof pitch with front belfry pinnacle and lower gabled porch".

Rankin gives a pretty full account: "On the dissolution of the Parish of Saint Andrew in 1844, this little church of 1704 found itself without a parish! It was, however, restored in 1844 by the Montgomery family of Greyabbey, who also installed a Walker organ. In 1932, it was further restored by Mr and Mrs Hawthorne of Rubane; a new ceiling was inserted along with oak panelling and floor tiling. Two chairs were donated from the chapel at

Mountstewart. The font came from Bangor Abbey, when its contents were dispersed in the 1880s. The latest restoration took place in 1966 under the supervision of Denis O'D Hanna; it was re-dedicated on 19 August of that year, the old organ was restored by" (the late) "Lord Dunleath. Balligan church is under the care of Ballywalter parish and services are held there on a regular basis. It is also used for festive concerts and recitals". There had been an earlier restoration in 1886, recorded by a plaque in the nave: most of this Victorian work was removed, and great efforts were made to restore the early Georgian character, by Denis Hanna. Some might think he somewhat over-restored it, but on the whole the effect is fine. Unhappily, not now in the best of order, and in some need of further expenditure before too long.

There is, as well as a useful leaflet, an unusually charming parish history, published in 1966, edited by Frances Jackson of Ballywalter, sister of the Rev Cecil Jackson (Rector 1937-1974), who contributes his piece, the main text being by the late Professor J C Beckett of Queen's University, with a specialist contribution on the organ from Lord Dunleath (every one of them, late good friends of mine) and woodcut (or perhaps, more probably, scraper-board) illustrations of much charm by the architect Denis O'D Hanna. From this we learn that "the oak roof-timbers, with tree-nails still in evidence, may be older than the building itself; possibly they were transferred from the church of Ballyhalbert, which was now no longer required and was thus allowed to fall into ruin" (Jim Beckett); that "in 1966, first the barrel-shaped ceiling, erected in 1749, was taken down revealing the old oak-timbered roof, thought to be one of the best in the province ... The porch,

also built in 1749, had been ceiled to provide a vestry at first-floor level reached by a staircase. Both ceiling and staircase were removed so that the fine old carved stone doorway with date-stone, 1704, can now be seen ... In the porch is a font of uncertain date ... Also in the porch is ... a thirteenth century coffin lid of sandstone, the upper surface of which bears a foliated cross and part of its shaft is in relief, the edge being moulded and enriched by a nail-head ornament" (Cecil Jackson). And, as to the organ, "probably a Gray built between 1770 and 1780. Its first written mention is in Messrs J W Walker's records, where it is described as having been removed from the parish of Kegworth in Leicestershire, rebuilt, and despatched to Kircubbin in 1861". (How delighted my great-great-grandfather must have been! He was very musical - see Kircubbin church and rectory, 39 and 75). In 1899 "Kircubbin parish took delivery of their new ... organ, and with the greatest good taste transferred their existing organ to Balligan ... There is no doubt that in so doing, they moved the old organ to an environment to which it was far more appropriate both in tone and appearance ... This small organ is a remarkably authentic example of late 18th century work" (Henry Dunleath).

Photographs: A C W Merrick (see also colour illus. 9).

Situation: At a cross-roads settlement, between Ballywalter and Kircubbin; td, Balligan; District Council, Ards; Grid ref. J 620 657.

References: Listed B+ (24/3/20). M M Kertland, OSM, nd (? 1836), Down II, p 85; 'St Andrew's, Inishargy, Balligan', 1966, passim; D O'D Hanna, in 'Church of Ireland Gazette', 19/8/1966, J F Rankin, in 'Clergy of Down and Dromore', 1996, p 48; Walker, 'Historic Ulster churches', 2000, p 30.

Lisbane (RC) Chapel, "Sal Wather Briggs", Ardkeen

17. The Sal Wather Briggs (I unrepentantly reproduce the pronunciation I knew in my boyhood) mark the boundary between the, perversely named, Upper Ards and the Lower Ards. The local historical society expounds, if it does not altogether explain, this oddity: "The Upper Ards is that part of the Ards Peninsula lying to the south of the

mid-Ards depression, which lies across the peninsula from mid-way between Kircubbin and Portaferry on one side to Portavogie on the other. In pre-historic times this area was an island, and until a Century or two ago was just as much cut off by the marshes in this depression as it had been when an island". It also marks out approximately the religious divide: predominantly Scots Presbyterian to the north of Kircubbin, predominantly Roman Catholic to the south of Portavogie.

Until very recently, there was a charming and unusual group of buildings, in a remote rural loughside area, at the Sal Wather Briggs: bridge, pub, and chapel. The bridge, which seems never to have been listed or noticed by industrial archaeologists, was a most unusual one, over a tidal inlet of Strangford Lough: because it had no feeder of substance, it could be almost level, unlike the hump-backs usual in bridges which had to cater for intermittent freshets or floods. I have no idea of its date, and know of no evidence: perhaps mid-18th-century? For unfortunately, any evidence there may have been has now been swept away by a regrettable 'refurbishment'. The same has happened to the little pub: it has recently been tarted up, and its unspoiled character quite lost.

As the Upper Ards Historical Society's Guide to Portaferry and District puts it, "This lovely little church in the townland of Lisbane is on the west side of the road between Kircubbin and Portaferry in the parish of Ardkeen, beside the Salt Water Bridge. The church is roofed with Tullycavey slates. A cross-shaped tablet in the inner side of the gable above the door reads 'Lord I have loved the beauty of Thy house and the place where Thy glory dwelleth. This house was erected AD 1777 Daniel O'Dornan PP.' When the new church in Ballycranbeg was opened in 1874 Lisbane Church was reduced to the status of a Mortuary Chapel ... Mass is celebrated on All Souls Day each year when those who are interred in the cemetery are remembered".

This is a delightful, simple, white-washed chapel, with sashed round-headed Georgian-glazed windows, four in the east wall, two at the west, and three smaller latticed windows in the southern sanctuary wall opposite which is the entrance door, with built-in external holy water stoup. There is an odd little confessional-box beside the balustered altar-rail. The wooden roof is open, without ceiling. "Inside, the box pews are set on to a stone-paved floor in two ranks, each side of a central aisle. The sanctuary is raised on a simple wooden platform and demarcated by a rudimentary wooden communion rail that is interrupted at the south end by a single confessional. This too is an early piece of furniture, with the penitent placed outside and only the priest enclosed. The rear compartment of the same framework is the sacristy, but there is no special entry door for the priest from the outside. The sanctuary has not been reordered in any way - even the corona candelabra is a contemporary fitting. Where else would you find such a perfect reflection of simple devotion? This is a most remarkable survivor and long may it be cherished" (Oram). All this, in a stone-walled graveyard, with yew trees, almost washed by the lapping water of Strangford Lough.

This little church, like its near-contemporary neighbour, Balligan (16), has received little notice from historians. Mr Kertland of the Ordnance Survey, in 1837, says only "There is a Roman Catholic chapel in the townland of Lisbane. It was erected in 1777 by general subscription. It measures 62 by 24 feet and is capable of accommodating about 400". Samuel Lewis, in the same year, says only "the chapel at Lisbawn is connected with that of Ballygelgat, in the parish of Witter". The Parliamentary Gazetteer just says "the Roman Catholic chapel has an attendance of 700 and upwards, and is served by two officiates, who serve also the chapel of Witter". The usually exemplary Dr O'Laverty has little enough to tell of it; for some reason (perhaps its date was too late?), it does not earn a mention in the Archaeological Survey of County Down; and the listers accord it only a B+, with the description "Simple single-storey church with arched Georgian windows and door. Now used once a year". Perhaps its neglect is due partly to the obstacles placed in the way of access: friends of mine who greatly wished to get married here were refused permission to do so, and were obliged to make do with a ceremony in O'Neill & Byrne's late Victorian church at nearby Ballycranbeg. However, Lisbane featured in the successful film of Sam Hanna Bell's novel, December Bride. It deserves to be better known, and more visited.

Photographs: A C W Merrick.

Situation: Rowreagh Road, Lisbane, Kircubbin; td, Lisbane; District Council, Ards; Grid ref. J 602 588..

References: Listed B+ (24/3/38). OS map, 1833; M M Kertland, OSM, 1837, Down, II, p 2; O'Laverty, 'Down & Connor', I, 1878, p 455; J J Gilmore in JUAHS, II, 1978, pp 8-9; 'Upper Ards Historical Society guide', 1997, p 16; Walker, 'Historic Ulster churches', 2000, p 38; Oram, 'Expressions of faith', 2001, pp 12, 86-87.

Knockbreda (C of I) Parish Church, Newtownbreda

Hugh Dixon says "It is during the early Georgian period that the first consistent use of professional architects is found in Ulster ... the façade of Newtownbreda Parish Church seems serene and uncrowded. The triangular pediment of the doorcase is echoed by that of the pediment of the main bay, and again by the line of the roof. The height and shape of the spire relate to the rest of the façade, and the interior is no plain rectangle but a complex space with a narrow chancel and semi-circular transepts ... Newtownbreda was the work of Richard Cassels, then Ireland's leading architect". For some reason, he dates it to 1747, though most other authorities, including Maurice Craig, suggest 1737; Larmour specifically states, "consecrated in August 1737". J S Curl describes it as "assured ... in its detail and massing ... The tower is ... projected forward and, like St. John's at Moira, there are windows set above the central entrance and the flanking windows. The door is set in a Gibbs surround over which is an entablature with a pulvinated frieze and a triangular pediment that is echoed in the pediment over the crowning cornice of the body of the church".

The Archaeological Survey of County Down says "The church was built c. 1737, at the expense of the Dowager Viscountess Midelton, reputedly from a design by Richard Cassels. It comprised a square-ended chancel, nave with apsidal transepts and W. tower, the ground floor of the tower forming a porch, opening to rooms on N. and S. The present chancel was erected by Sir Thomas Drew in 1883 ... the present apsidal chancel, with organ chamber on N., was sympathetically designed to accord with the character of the original building and is lighted by three windows similar to those in the present nave". Indeed, it looks as though the tracery of the nave window lights was altered by Drew to match his new chancel windows.

Lavens Ewart remarks "The church is believed to have been designed by Castle (or Cassel) a famous architect in the beginning of the last century, and has peculiar architectural features that seem to have been suggested by the plans of the early Basilicas, which were much studied at that time. A chancel was added in the year 1883 of much beauty, in the same style, designed by Thomas Drew RHA, Arch., in which a costly mosaic pavement was placed by Lord Deramore in memory of his brother, Samuel Bateson. Stained-glass windows, representing the twelve apostles, fill the three lights in the apsidal termination of the chancel towards the east". A pity: this early Georgian church might have looked better with only plain glass windows. A vestry was added in 1910 to the design of R I Calwell.

The exterior of the church is, in general, in good shape: it has fairly recently been re-roughcast; the Gibbsian doorcase is nicely painted white, the railings at the (very

18. Haris, in 1744, says "About half a Mile East of *Belvoir*, on an Eminence commanding a Prospect of *Belfast*, the Bay and Town of *Carrickfergus*, and the Country around it, appears the Parish Church of *Breda*, a Building the neatest and most compleat perhaps of this Kind in the Kingdom. It is, exclusive of the Chancel, 50 Feet by 25, and 25 in Heigth. From the middle of the Church on each side springs a Semicircle of 18 Feet Diameter, which, besides enlarging the Room, adds greatly to the Beauty of the Building. The Steeple, with the Spire, built according to the exact Proportions of Architecture, catches the Eyes of all Travellers. This Church was executed under the direction of Mr. *Castell*, at the sole Expence of the Right Honourable the Lady Viscountess Dowager *Middleton*, whose Charities, both publick and private, have been very extensive". Most surprisingly, neither Lieutenant Bordes nor W Heather of the Ordnance Survey mention this church at all, though the latter comments on the architecture of Belvoir Park (now sadly demolished) and says of its setting, "Just beneath you is the serpentine Lagan, winding its slow path that skirts the plantation. You can hear the hoarse boatman's noise urging on the weary horse to catch the tide"; and mentions also Millar's church at Castlereagh (34).

discreet) ramp, painted red. The front windows are divided into an unusually large number of small panes: 18 panes in each window above, 30 in each window below. The spire is topped by a nice ball, cross, and metal flying dove. Unfortunately, this very fine façade is quite spoiled by the insensitivity of whoever attached four very obtrusive electricity lines to the front wall. They should have been taken round to the side or, better still, brought in from the road (no great distance) underground.

The interior is very fine too: well painted with the flat parts of walls and the shallow barrel-vaulted ceiling in a sort of caramel colour, the projections picked out in off-white: the ceiling of the chancel blue. There is a gallery of 1883 with plump Ionic columns. The pews cannot be original, but are harmonious. There are several good

memorials on the walls to members of the Hill, Bateman, Kinahan, and other families. All is neat, seemly, and prosperous-looking. What a pity the same cannot be said of the four splendid listed 18th-century mausolea in the churchyard (see 178).

Photograph: A C W Merrick.
Situation: Church Road, Knockbreda; td, Breda; District Council, Castlereagh; Grid ref. J 351 702.
References: Listed A (25/16/5a). Harris, 'County of Down', 1744, p 72; G F W Bordes, OSM, 1832, and J Heather, nd, Down, II, pp 97-102; Ewart, 'Down & Connor & Dromore', 1886, p 53; ASCD, 1966, p 333; Dixon, 'Introduction', UAHS, 1975, p 35; Curl, 'Classical churches', UAHS, 1980, p 8; Craig, 'Architecture of Ireland', 1982, p 213; Larmour, 'Belfast'.1987, p 105; J F Rankin, in 'Clergy of Down and Dromore', 1996, p 71; Walker, 'Historic Ulster churches', 2000, p 53.

19. ". . . on an Eminence ... a handsome Parish Church finely situated, the Front of which, and part of the Steeple are well executed in hewen Stone. It was built" (in 1723) "at the Expence of the late and present *Sir John Rawdon*" (Harris). "The parish church is situated on the east side of the town. It is a plain, whinstone, rectangular building, corniced with cutstone. It is 83 feet long and 36 feet broad. It has a handsomely ornamented doorway of cut stone. At the north west end is a tower on which is a low, shingled spire. The accommodation is for 400 persons. The general attendance is 250. The interior of the church is plain, the windows are nearly rectangular" (Ordnance Survey memoir, 1837). However, as the Archaeological Survey of County Down remarks, "The side walls each contain three large segmental arched windows with key-block and have an eaves-cornice of cyma-recta profile; the E. window is semicircular arched with key-block". Samuel Lewis writes "the church was erected, at the joint expense of Sir John Rawdon and the Earl of Hillsborough: it is a large and handsome Gothic [?] edifice, with a square tower surmounted by a spire, in excellent repair, and, from its situation on an eminence above the town, forming a beautiful object in this rich and well planted district". Rankin says "The church is little altered; the inner doors came from Moira Castle on its demolition in the nineteenth century and the communion rail is believed to be part of the Castle stairway and bannister. The pews and pulpit were renewed during the nineteenth century and the gallery was built in 1871; the spire was blown down in 1884 and replaced by the present copper coated wooden spire, visible for miles around". The inner doors he mentions are exceedingly ornate, painted in green, white and gilt; it is thought that they may have come from the ballroom of Moira House.

St John's (C of I) Church, Moira

Dixon says of this church, justly, that it is "little more than a barn church with a tower added" (in fact, recessed into it) "at the west end. Its classical features, especially the crushing size of the doorcase pushing up into the window above, are clumsily handled". However, Walker points out that this central window seems only to have been inserted in 1877 "to provide additional internal light after the gallery was installed. Indeed this is verified by a glance at a mid nineteenth-century engraving of the church, which shows the façade without the offending window ... The engraving also shows the original slate-hung spire ... This was replaced by the present copper-clad spire, which is lower than the original. The reduction in the height of the spire, and the choice of covering, serve to emphasise the somewhat graceless quality of the tower". Altogether, it comes as something of a surprise that the listers have placed this church in the 'A' category; perhaps on the grounds that it is an uncommonly early example of amateurish classicising, perhaps because of its portentous cut-stone door-case. Unfortunately, the integrity of its splendid site, at the head of a long tree-lined avenue just where the village used to meet the open countryside, has been much prejudiced by adjacent inappropriate modern buildings - the new Baptist church, and large Baptist Housing Association block - not, in themselves, ill-designed, but very ill-sited indeed. Otherwise, despite much new housing at the side, the long uphill avenue from the main road still survives fairly unspoiled, as does the churchyard with its surprising wealth of obelisks.

The best feature of the interior is the wooden reredos, "of three bays, with intermediate attached columns and terminal pilasters, rising from pedestals, having fluted shafts and Corinthian capitals supporting a full entablature; the frieze is enriched with scrolled foliage, with a vase flanked by cherubs at the centre and scallop shells on the forward breaks, and is surmounted by a dentilled and modillioned cornice. Each bay contains a panel with moulded architrave-surround, the wider central panel inscribed with the Creed and the Lord's Prayer, the flanking panels with the Ten Commandments" (Archaeological Survey) - all very classical and sophisticated.

There are also excellent scumbled box-pews; plain glass Georgian-glazed windows in the side walls, a stained-glass window of St John the Evangelist tucked in above the reredos; a 19th-century gallery is carried on slim and simple cast-iron columns, its front, like the pulpit, painted in bright colours - one could not quite say garishly, yet rather out of keeping with the 18th-century character of the church. On the whole, though, the interior is of greater charm than the exterior; and both are of such respectable antiquity as to command proper regard.

Photographs: A C W Merrick; MBR.

Situation: Up long avenue off Main Street, Moira; td, Clare; District Council, Lisburn; Grid ref. J 154 605.

References: Listed A (19/22/1); in conservation area. Harris, 'County of Down' 1744, p 104; J R Ward and T C McIlroy, OSM, 1837, Down, III, p 117; Lewis, TD, 1837, II, p 377; ASCD, 1966, p 330, pls 113, 117,141; Dixon, 'Introduction', UAHS, 1975, p 35; Curl, 'Classical churches', UAHS, 1980, p 8; J F Rankin, in 'Clergy of Down and Dromore', 1996, p 221; Walker, 'Historic Ulster churches', 2000, pp 49-52.

St Malachi's (C of I) Church and Screen, Hillsborough

20. "The most sophisticated and uniform example of the Georgian style in Ireland" (Hugh Dixon in 1977). Maurice Craig says that in 1760 "the church at Hillsborough Co Down, had initiated, as far as Ireland was concerned, the gothic revival properly so called. Like most notable churches of the century, it owed its existence to a single patron, in this case Wills Hill, Earl of Hillsborough. Almost certainly an English architect was involved, and the likeliest of several candidates is perhaps Sanderson Miller. It is still, of course, gothick with a 'k' and in no way constructional. It is rigidly symmetrical, approached by an axial avenue, with a West tower and spire half-detached from the aisleless nave, and narrow towers at the ends of the transepts. It took, apparently, 15 years to build (1760-1775). Not the least of its charms is that, apart from some savage ribbon pointing carried out under another English

architect in the present century" (now rectified; see below) "it has escaped violation in any way".

John Cornforth, in 1994, wrote: "Lord Hillsborough ... rebuilt the church at Hillsborough on an unusually grand scale for 18th-century Ireland, as if he hoped that it would become the cathedral church" - Downpatrick cathedral lay then in ruins. "It is not known who produced the design, but work is supposed to have been begun in 1760 and finished in 1772. The concept is a sophisticated one, because the previous building, which is incorporated, had a fairly straightforward, cruciform plan. However, all sense of English handwriting in the design is overlaid by the strongly regional character of the detail; and it is known that the young joiners Charles and John Gardiner made many alterations in the drawings and plans, while others were made by the patron and his agent, Samuel

Scott" (*recte* Samuel Smith). "Even so, there is a strong sense of each element in the building making its proper architectural statement, which seems to be a characteristic of Wright's work" - the reference is to Thomas Wright of Durham, to whom Cornforth tentatively attributes Hillsborough Fort, (12). "What Lord Hillsborough did was to build on" (to the previous church of 1662) "a new, single-bay sanctuary, twin towers at the ends of the old transepts and a link to the new western tower. Within, he created a marvellous sense of unfolding spaces and changing levels, beginning with an octagonal vestibule under the western tower, and then moving under the organ gallery into the nave ... At the central crossing, there are steps up to left and right to disguise the fact that the family vault lies under the north transept, while light pours down through the windows of the north and south towers. Happily, the interior retains almost all its original fittings *in situ*."

There is a thorough and scholarly description of the church in the Archaeological Survey of County Down of 1966; there is my own, quite lengthy, description of the state of the church in 1974; there is now Simon Walker's thorough description of the church in 2000. I shall not seek to duplicate any of these. I shall simply try to concentrate attention on the principal features of this excellent church; and on changes which have occurred over the past forty years.

First, it must be said that the outstandingly fine spire can be firmly attributed, like that at Lisburn cathedral, to the stonemasons James and (his son) David McBlain. Like Lisburn, it it is marked out by the elegant annular moulding at the foot of the slim octagonal spire itself. For the main body of the church, the head mason was Hercules Harper, a native of Hillsborough. Robert Parker was also involved.

Next, attention must be drawn to the exceptionally high quality of the interior woodwork, especially the pulpit with sounding-board (see illustration on page 26), the bishop's throne, the chancel stalls, the box-pews, and the double-bow gallery. The joiners were William Gardiner and his two sons, John and Charles. "Charles was a very clever

man, little more than twenty, who drew beautifully, and he and his brother John had the entire direction in building the church and made many alterations in the drawings and plans" (statement of Andrew Jamison, 13 May 1819, quoted by Barry).

The glass is of the highest quality: the top section of the east window contains "a group of overfed cherubs, puffing and flapping amidst cotton-wool clouds, and wearing their wings like mufflers" (Brett, 1974) - a description which deeply, and maybe rightly, offended the (perhaps a bit Trollopian) Canon Barry, then rector, now retired; described in notes in the MBR by Mr H W Clokey as "of little aesthetic value ... pleasing in its setting, and the only glass of its type known to me in Ireland ... no doubt the work of Francis Egington of Birmingham from drawings (or adaptations) by Sir Joshua Reynolds". The tinted diaper-pattern glass in the other windows appears to be original: one of the lower panes in the east window was found, on restoration, to be inscribed 'to the order of the Earl of Hillsborough, April 1772'. The glazier was Andrew Jamison, father of the memorialist referred to above.

There is a Snetzler organ dating from 1773, and an England chamber organ of 1795. There is a very fine peal of bells. There are many interesting and excellent monuments and memorials, including the Leslie memorial, of 1774, by Nollekens, whose bust of the Earl of Hillsborough has been removed for safe-keeping to Hillsborough Castle (51), where it is probably the finest work of art on view. It is clear that the Earl played a very active part in the building and furnishing of his church.

The fabric was enthusiastically 'restored' between 1951 and 1956 under the supervision of Sir Albert Richardson, PRA, whose taste commanded the total confidence of the then rector, Canon Barry. Unfortunately, Sir Albert did nothing to counter a process of prominent ribbon re-pointing in the then fashionable style. Happily, this was reversed as part of a prolonged scheme for the restoration of the stonework under Stephen Leighton, of Leighton Johnston, who embarked in 1991 on a major scheme to repair and repoint. The only other major change to the principal structure has been the insertion in 1994 of a new doorway in the side of the porch to provide disabled access. Though it undoubtedly upsets the original symmetry of the design, it must be remarked that the stairs to the tower are likewise asymmetrically disposed. The work has, however, been undertaken discreetly and with diplomacy; once the new stone has weathered, I think few will notice this modern intrusion. In general, the present state of the church itself, inside and out, is in the year 2000 commendable.

The same cannot quite be said of its environment. The excellent 18th-century entrance screen has been well restored since 1991: the twin pavilions at the sides - both originally school-rooms, today sexton's house and parish room - are linked by railings and splendid gates between four square piers with round shafts at the angles, each surmounted by four ball finials (see also illustration on page 28). This gives access to a double avenue up the hillside to the church and is lined by lime trees - now very mature; it is more than time that thought was given to replacement, or inter-planting. The head of the avenue leads also to the extensive stone-walled graveyard; to the Fort (12); and to the lake beyond: a most important spatial relationship. The insertion, to the left of the avenue, of a very large Fold Housing scheme is just about acceptable, though its design, detailing and colouring add nothing at all to a very balanced 18th-century composition. The threatened insertion, to the right of the avenue, of a fairly obtrusive, and perhaps over-tall, parish hall, does not promise well for the future.

There has been very considerable debate on the authorship of this splendid group. It was Alistair Rowan, I believe, who first advanced the theory that both church and screen were the work of Sanderson Miller (1716-1780), "essentially a gentleman architect whose architectural activities formed part of an active social life" (Colvin); to whom Lord Barrington introduced Wills Hill in 1763. Rowan says "The church is a remarkable example of eighteenth century Gothic and many of the details, such as the crockets at the intersection of the vaults or the machicolation of the towers, are typical of Miller's designs. Miller had already worked in Ireland in 1757, for Bishop Pococke at Kilkenny Cathedral ... Few architects could have built such a large and comparatively competent Gothic structure in the early 1760's, and of those who could, only Miller is known to have made designs for Irish buildings". However, if Miller was only introduced to Hill in June 1763, then either the date of 1760 for the beginning of work must be wrong, or the plans must be by another hand. This seems to me probably to rule out Miller's authorship of the church itself, but I by no means rule out the possibility that he was author of the, later, screen, which seems very much in his style.

Sir Albert Richardsons's proposed attribution for the church was to his namesake (no relation) George Richardson (? - c1813) of London, a former draughtsman in the Adam office. On 28 January 1957, Sir Albert wrote to his friend Canon Barry "My own view is that the designs were supplied by George Richardson, who built a similar church at Stapleford, Leicestershire, for the Earl of Harborough. No other architect of that day had such a command of Gothic, with the exception possibly of Essex who worked directly for Horace Walpole". But Colvin says, "Although he was an accomplished draughtsman and designer of internal decoration in the Adam style, Richardson appears to have designed few complete buildings, and to have made a living chiefly by his publications and by acting as a drawing-master".

My own, always somewhat tentative, candidate was Francis Hiorne (1744-1789) of Warwick, who certainly was concerned in old St Anne's, Belfast, completed in 1776 for Lord Donegall. Colvin says of him, "Hiorne was one of the most accomplished designers of the elegant, decorative, Gothic of the late eighteenth century, of which Tetbury church is an excellent example. As a classical designer he is represented by St. Anne's, Belfast". I still have a weakness for his candidature.

John Cornforth has, in 1994, proposed Thomas Wright (1711-1786) of Durham, on the grounds that Hillsborough Fort as rebuilt for Lord Hillsborough is "in a similar vein to the sketch that he produced for Codger's Fort at Wallington in County Durham ... It has to be accepted that there are no details at Hillsborough that echo those in Wright's drawings, but he could have sent over sketches that were freely interpreted on the spot ... Wright mentions only going through Hillsborough on one of his trips in Ireland in 1746, but he did a good deal of work for Lord Limerick at Tollymore Park". And as to the church itself, as quoted above, "there is a strong sense of each element of the building making its proper architectural statement, which seems to be characteristic of Wright's work".

The reader must make his or her choice: until some lucky researcher turns up conclusive evidence, we can only guess at the architect of Hillsborough parish church; which must in no way be allowed to derogate from our admiration of so elegant and sophisticated a building.

Photographs: A C W Merrick (see also colour illus. 5).

Situation: Off Main Street, Hillsborough; td, Hillsborough; District Council, Lisburn; Grid ref. J 245 587.

References: Listed A (19/5/1,2,3,4). A Rowan, in 'Quarterly bulletin of the IGS', VII, 1964, p 28; ASCD, 1966, pp 327-328; Brett, 'Mid-Down', UAHS, 1974, pp 8-11, 23; H Dixon, 'Historic monuments in Hillsborough', HMSO, 1977, p 1; Barry, 'Hillsborough', 1982, passim; Craig, 'Architecture of Ireland', 1982, p 215; UA, March/April 1991, pp 50-51; J Cornforth, in CL, 28 July, 1994, pp 66-67; Colvin, 'Dictionary', 1995, pp 495-6, 653, 810-811, 1100-1101; J F Rankin, in 'Clergy of Down and Dromore', 1996, p 121; Walker, 'Historic Ulster churches', 2000, pp 63-65; correspondence and other documents in MBR.

St Marys (C of I) Church, Kilmood

disrepair. I had failed to notice, twenty-seven years ago, that the weights of the clock are hung outside, not inside, the tower - a most peculiar arrangement; after many years of disuse, the clock was restored in 1988.

Rankin says "opened for worship in 1822, the foundation stone having been laid in 1820 by David Gordon of Florida Manor, according to an inscription on the tower window. The Gordon family of Florida Manor contributed generously to the building of the church and remained patrons of the living for many years. Their coat of arms is on the front of the tower ... and those above the entrance on the side of the tower are the Londonderry arms ... the top of the spire was blown off in the Great Wind of January 1839. The roof was largely replaced in 1908 and in the following year, the spire was struck by lightning and the top twenty courses of stonework blown off. The height was reduced on re-building. The church ... has three fine chandeliers, the central one reputedly of Dutch origin and the others made locally as replicas" (in 1967). "It also retains the original box-pews complete with acorn shaped hinges. The pulpit, goblet shaped, also merits attention".

The pulpit and box-pews are indeed delightful; the creed and commandments are painted in gilt lettering on black above and beside the altar; the central brass chandelier is quite magnificent; there is a "baby-shaped" black marble font, standing on a fluted stone column, inscribed 'Presented to the Parish of Kilmood by David Gordon Esquire, 1825', in a modest

21. Lewis (1847) says "in 1821 the present church, an elegant structure in the later English style, with a handsome tower and spire rising to the height of 120 feet, was erected near the site of the ancient ruins, at the joint expense of the lord of the manor and the Marquess of Londonderry, aided by a gift of £900 from the Board of First Fruits. The interior is fitted up with Riga oak; the east window, of stained glass, and of large dimensions, appears to have been copied from that of Salisbury cathedral. In the churchyard is a very beautiful mausoleum belonging to the Gordon family". The Parliamentary Gazetteer adds "The church was built in 1821, at the cost of £2,215 7 8¼. contributed by the patrons, by Lord Dufferin, and by the late Board of First Fruits. Sittings, 300; attendance, from 80 to 250". Brett, in 1973, wrote "It is attractively sited on the summit of a drumlin, and is both rather larger and rather more sophisticated than is to be expected in the middle of the countryside. For once, the tower has a rather Early English air, complete with battlements, tall slim un-Irish pinnacles, clock, and armorial bearings. The nave gable makes a pretence at being a pediment, and the eaves are carried on half-hoops carved of ashlar". There is nothing in that with which I now disagree, though one or two changes there have been: for the better, the churchyard has been landscaped, with carved stone cross and path, to expose the rock outcrop upon which the church was built, and a surprising brick coal-hole; for the worse, the once charming sexton's cottage has had its former Georgian-glazed windows blocked up and fancifully painted, is unoccupied, and apart from the roof appears to be falling into

baptistry just inside the entrance. The aisle is stone-flagged; there is a nicely vaulted ceiling in a somewhat Tudor manner; the paintwork is all in the best of order and the best of taste. The gallery, now removed, used to constitute the family pew of the Gordons, firmly marked 'Private'! Altogether, a pleasing example of a modest Irish Protestant country church.

Photograph: A C W Merrick.
Situation: Church Road, Kilmood; td, Kilmood and Ballybunden; District Council, Ards; Grid ref. J 470 628.
References: Listed B1 (24/17/38). Lewis, TD, 1847, II, p 154; PG, II,1846, p 520; Brett, 'East Down', UAHS, 1973, p 46; T C Burrowes, 'St Mary's Parish Church, Kilmood, Killinchy, Co. Down: a brief history and guide', 1989; J F Rankin, in 'Clergy of Down and Dromore', 1996, p 138.

St Mark's (C of I) Church, Newtownards

22. The present church was built to replace the once splendid chapel of the Colville family, erected in the 1690s in Court Street beside the then derelict parish church, which Sir Hugh Montgomery had made from the remains of the former Dominican priory (7) in 1607. The chapel was used as the town's parish church until 1817, when the new church was built. G. Scott of the Ordnance Survey, rather endearingly, writes - around 1833, no date given - "Newtownards church is a neat, ornamental building situated in the Broad Street. It is the prettiest building in the town. (More information could not be procured relative to the church ... in consequence of the absence of Lord Londonderry's agent)." One wonders what his employers thought of that?

Lewis, in 1837, says "The church, a handsome cruciform edifice, was built in 1817, at an expense of £5446, of which £831 were a gift and £3692 a loan from the" (late Board of First Fruits); "the remainder, £923, was a donation from the late Marquess of Londonderry". The Parliamentary Gazetteer says only, "The present parish-church is a handsome structure; but the other places of worship are remarkable more for their number than for their architecture". It is certainly true that St Mark's is one of the handsomest buildings in the handsome town of Newtownards: perhaps because of the financial support of Lord Castlereagh. According to Lavens Ewart, the ultimate cost was £10,000; "It was built by the great Lord Castlereagh, Prime Minister" (*recte* Foreign Secretary) "of England, afterwards Marquis of Londonderry, at a cost of £7000 ... The nave of the church was elongated in the year 1844 ... and additional accommodation provided for the parishioners at a cost of £366 16 5 ... A north aisle was added to the church at a cost of £2500, in the year 1866, so that the church is now capable of accommodating 857 persons". (Richardson, however, remarks that "though the chancel is said locally to date from 1844, the rainwater head at the south-west corner of the chancel is dated 1817").

Rankin writes - "The chancel was added in 1844 and in 1866 the north aisle was created by removing the north transept ... The Londonderry family made many gifts, including the pulpit, designed by Thomas Drew. The baptistry, created in 1965 in the south transept, contains medieval glass from the old church; there is also a stone in the south wall from the ruins of Movilla Abbey. Major modifications were carried out in 1994. The chancel was enlarged ... the pulpit was moved ... a side chapel has been created with a glass screen as partition". The listers just say, "Church in Gothic Perpendicular style with square tower and spire."

Externally, a very good-looking church, set amidst a generous railed-in lawn with noble monkey-puzzler and other trees; the detailing on the numerous pinnacles, crockets, and spire, very lavish, including numerous gargoyles and foliations. Internally, there is a certain loss of unity: the original nave is in a sort of Tudorish style; the additional aisle next door rather different, with a very Victorian character; the windows are very various, some plain, some polychrome, in many differing styles. The jolliest feature of this rather ambitious and expensive church is the pair of square private box-pews, one on either side of the entrance from porch to aisle, and both screened and panelled - one rather dark, one lit by a delicious private window, but both quite private enough to permit the eating of sandwiches or the playing of cards during service - not that I dare assert that such things took place, since one was the rector's pew, the other the churchwardens'!

Excellent as this church unquestionably is, certainly deserving of its place in the 'A' listing category, one may feel that the American scholar Dr Richardson, despite his lucid description, somewhat overstates its merits. "The church was initially planned as a structure of four irregular bays and a slightly shorter one at the west end, to balance the chancel - an unusual feature for the period - at the other end, plus a tower without spire in the middle of the west end. Instead it was built with a spire, and to a cruciform plan. A triple-decker was installed in front of the 'transept' on the south side, which was walled up to form a vestry. This arrangement (long since altered) is not so strange as it seems: Georgian churches with seats on three sides of the box pews, like St Mark's, had a multiple orientation whether or not there was a chancel at the east end, and placing the pulpit in the middle of one side

solved an acoustic problem. In addition this plan put the pulpit opposite the private pew which originally filled the north transept ... St Mark's is a particularly successful example of later Gothic style and might almost be attributed to Francis Johnston himself. The construction is very solid, like all Johnston's work ... the church is also full of robust but graceful refinements, like the Chapel Royal in Dublin ... The window tracery is a better version of the Chapel Royal's, which could hardly be improved from an archaeological point of view. In short, apart from the welcome solecism of transept, which contributes to the plasticity of the building, the exterior is a most exceptional piece of Perpendicular design, probably the best of its date in the British Isles. The plaster and wood interior is sprightly but sparse, more like the entrance hall at Johnston's Charleville Castle than his Chapel Royal ... But even though Johnston came from Armagh in the next county, he is not known to have done anything in Co Down and he does not mention St Mark's in the letter listing his work which he sent J.N.Brewer in 1820. One can only conclude that the church is worthy of Johnston, if not by him".

I must say that, until I read this piece, it had never crossed my mind that this admirable church might have been by Francis Johnston. In the first place, to me the hall-mark of his style is an elegant, austere simplicity; which seems to me to be absent from Newtownards. In the second place, 1817 seems an unduly late date for a church by Johnston: the Chapel Royal was started in 1802, and Dr McParland suggests that, by the time he was designing his church in Tullamore (completed in 1815), "one is inclined to think that, on the whole, St Catherine's is a reflection of Johnston's loss of interest in provincial commissions (apart from country houses) after his move to Dublin". And in the third place, there is, of course, as Richardson admits, the total absence of any documentary evidence supporting an attribution to Johnston.

But it is a very fine church all the same.

Photograph: A C W Merrick. Water-colour drawing: J W Carey, courtesy of Mrs Dorothy Russell.
Situation: Church Street, Newtownards; td, Corporation South; District Council, Ards; Grid ref. J 485 743.
References: Listed A (24/11/1). Unsigned and undated drawings in RCB; Harris, 'County of Down', 1744, pp 57,58; G Scott, OSM, nd, (? 1833), Down, II, p 106; Lewis, TD, 1837, II, p 436; PG, III, 1846, p 31; Ewart, 'Down & Connor & Dromore', 1886, p 54; McParland, 'Francis Johnston', pp 107-108; Richardson, 'Gothic revival architecture in Ireland', 1983, I, pp 196-198, 240; McCavery, 'Newtown', 1994, p 55; J F Rankin, in 'Clergy of Down and Dromore', 1996, p 150; Walker, 'Historic Ulster churches', 2000, pp 96-97.

St Mary's (C of I) Church, Comber

23. A very characteristic church by William Farrell, of 1840, on the site of a much earlier church, perhaps early 17th-century, and possibly incorporating elements of a still earlier Cistercian foundation. According to M M Kertland of the Ordnance Survey, writing in 1837, "The church is a small, very old and oblong building situated near the centre of the town. It is said to have formed a part of some large and ancient ecclesiastical establishment, of which nothing more at present remains. It is capable of accommodating about 300". His colleague Lieutenant Bordes writes, perhaps about the same date, "The church of Comber appears an old building. There is no tower or steeple. It is built like a common house with merely a stone arch erected on its southern gable, in which is a bell". But Rankin says "In the second and third decades of the nineteenth century, the vestry expended considerable sums on repairs and was unable to make up its mind as to whether to go on repairing the church or build a new one. The advice of the Marquis of Londonderry was sought and, by 1829, it was resolved to build a new church on the existing site and existing foundations, raising the floor in order not to disturb graves. The Bishop, Rt Rev. Richard Mant, gave his consent to the plan and appointed William Farrell, the architect to the Ecclesiastical Commissioners, to design the church. Tradition in the parish says that the church was consecrated in 1840".

It is a bit surprising that the decision to rebuild this church, apparently taken in 1829, should have escaped the notice of the Ordnance Survey compilers, of Samuel Lewis in 1837 (but not in 1847), of the Parliamentary Gazetteer in 1846, and of Lavens Ewart in 1886: but such is the case. Perhaps this is partly due to the fact that the new church, having been built on the old foundations, had almost identical dimensions and accommodation to those of the old; also perhaps to the fact that a number of memorial tablets on the walls of the older church were re-erected in the new one. Lewis notes particularly "those to the memory of the Rev. Robert Mortimer; Capt. Chetwynd, Lieut. Unet" (*recte* Unite) "and Ensign Sparks, of the York fencible infantry, who fell in the battle of Saintfield, during the disturbances of 1798 - and of the Rev. Messrs. Birch, father and son"; but (to my sorrow) fails to mention the black marble tablets recording members of the Brett family, starting with Charles Brett of Killough (d. 1758) and ending (at present) with my father, Charles A Brett MC, (d.1988), solicitor, late of the Connaught Rangers, beside whom I hope to be commemorated in due course: for my family is commemorated in Comber, wherever buried. The Archaeological

Survey of County Down remarks, a little sniffily I feel, "The church, rebuilt in the 19th century, is of slight interest, but it contains earlier monuments".

The tower has corner pinnacles, vestigial crenellation, and a clock. The side walls of the body of the church are roughcast, with slim pointed lattice windows; within there are elegant hooped cast-iron trusses, in Farrell's usual style, carrying the roof; and a fine five-light stained glass window in the transept, itself added in 1913, the chancel having been added in 1896. Rankin adds "Comber possesses a very unusual font of polished dark red limestone; its provenance and date of acquisition are unknown, although it is fairly certain that it was transferred from the earlier church, but may, in fact, even pre-date that building".

Photograph: A C W Merrick.
Situation: The Square, Comber; td, Town Parks; District Council, Ards; Grid ref. J 460 692.
References: Listed B (25/15/2). M M Kertland, OSM, 1837 and G F W Bordes, nd (? 1835), Down, II, pp 28, 35; Lewis, TD, 1847, p 377; ASCD, 1966, p 323; 'Gravestone inscriptions', Down, II, 1988, p 180, V, 1970, p 30; J F Rankin, in 'Clergy of Down and Dromore', 1996, p 97.

St John's (C of I) Church, Kilwarlin Upper, Hillsborough

24. A delightful small church, of cutstone, amidst mature trees on a hill-top with striking views out over the length of the Lagan valley. Like its sister chapel-at-ease, St John's, Lower Kilwarlin, designed by Charles Lanyon, free of charge, for the Down and Connor Church Accommodation Society. It bears a certain relationship to the churches Lanyon also designed for the Society at Craigs and Raloo in County Antrim. Canon Barry rightly says "It stands on a splendid hill-top site with a sweep of view that takes in the flat pastures of the Lagan valley, framed between the distant Sperrins and the slopes of Divis. It is a well-proportioned cruciform building carried out in the mellow red of local sandstone, and sheltered from the winds that blow across the height by graceful old trees". "The plan of the building was adopted, with alterations, from that of one erected in the Isle of Man by the late Bishop of Sodor and Man; comprising a Chapel capable of containing 130 persons, and a School-room, separated by a moveable partition, which will accommodate 120 more, so that the whole may be, when required, thrown into one, for 250 persons" (Down and Connor Church Accommodation Society). No trace of this unusual arrangement is now discernible. The church has lancet windows, a bell-cote rather than a tower, and a porch in the re-entrant angle of the nave. The plaque above the porch reads:

> *Erected from the free contributions of the Marquis of Downshire and the inhabitants of Kilwarlin, aided by the Down and Connor Church Accommodation Society, by the Ven. Walter B. Mant MA, Archdeacon of Down, 1840.*

The actual cost of the church was over £600, of which £205 came from the Downshires, £234 from the Society, and the balance from the parishioners of Hillsborough.

Completed in 1840, it was only consecrated in 1842. The church is in good order, apart from the excessively protuberant pointing of the stonework and the deplorable artificial-stone of the later vestry. Major remedial works were completed in 2001.

The interior has a few unusual features. With one exception, all the windows are the original metal lattice windows with hexagonal and diamond-shaped panes of clear glass; but the east window, the gift of Bishop Richard Mant, has tinted glass, and celebrates 'Baptism', 'Fellowship', 'Doctrine', 'Prayers', and 'Breaking of Bread', the central pane having inscribed on it the twelve commandments, but so small as to be quite illegible from the nave. The modern organ pipes are attached to the front of the gallery (the latter carried on slim cast-iron Ionic columns) and sprout up into the air most strangely, but by no means unattractively. Below the organ-loft, a large green-painted safe, with the Marquess of Downshire's D and coronet painted in armorially correct polychromy on the the two doors: a bizarre demonstration of the text, "Render unto Caesar that which is Caesar's", but endearing nonetheless. Altogether, though a bit odd perhaps, a very pleasing and comfortable little church.

Photograph: A C W Merrick.

Situation: St John's Road, Hillsborough; td, Corcreeny; District Council, Lisburn; Grid ref. J 205 576.

References: Listed B (19/5/130). Datestone; Down and Connor Church Accommodation Society, 'Fourth ... report', 1843, p 20; Ewart, 'Down & Connor & Dromore', 1886, p 49; Barry, 'Hillsborough', 1982, pp 81-82; J F Rankin, in 'Clergy of Down and Dromore', 1996, p 143; 'Church of Ireland Gazette, 15/2/2002, p3.

St James's (C of I) Church, Kilwarlin Lower, Hillsborough

25. "An old schoolhouse which had been used for divine worship in the townland of Ballykeel Artifinny was blown down in the storm of January 1839. It was not worth re-building and the rector of Hillsborough, Archdeacon W. B. Mant, asked the Marquis of Downshire for a new site in a more convenient situation. The present site was granted and the church was to be called Halliday's Bridge church. Downshire wished to have James Sands draw up the plans, but Mant insisted on Charles Lanyon, as the Church Accommodation Society had agreed to contribute sub-stantial funds towards the building; Lanyon gave his ser-vices free to the society ... The church was opened for wor-ship in August 1841 and consecrated in the name of St James on 30 December 1842 as a chapel-of-ease to Hillsborough. The chancel was added in 1896" (Rankin). In fact, the General Statement of Account for the Down and Connor Church Accommodation Society shows a total investment of £391; although, for some reason, no detailed description or illustration of this church is included in its Fourth Report.

". . . one of the most complete and beautiful small country churches in the diocese", opines Canon Barry. Originally a symmetrical five-bay church, stuccoed, with two lancet windows to the left, two to the right, of the central tower, which incorporates a tall pointed sandstone-framed doorway under two very tall and slim lancet windows, with a clock above (installed in 1919 and still creditably showing the right time), belfry openings, and pleasing corner pinnacles: so that the church sits up like a four-lugged rabbit, with ears pricked, above the nearby motorway. At present, very well painted in cream, and altogether a most attractive example of Lanyon's generos-ity, though Gordon Wheeler finds it hard to believe that much, other than the tower, survives of Lanyon's work; I am not quite so sure, though I confess that I did not pen-etrate to the interior. The later chancel incorporates, in an elaborate Gothic stone frame, a stained glass window inserted in 1953. In the tower is a tablet inscribed:

Glory to God, Goodwill to Men. This Church, by the name of Saint James', lower Kilwarlin, was built from contributions of the Marquis of Downshire, the Earl of Hillsborough, the Down and Connor Church Accommodation Society, and others by the Venerable Walter B. Mant M.A., Archdeacon of Down MDCCCXL.

At the rear, there is an add-on vestry; and an attractive little school-house (1845), still in use. According to Canon Barry, the addition of the chancel was largely financed by a successful bazaar in Hillsborough Castle and grounds in 1895, at which the principal attractions included exhibitions of "Edison's latest inventions, the Kinetoscope and Kineto-phone"; plus a Living Aunt Sally. How times change!

Photograph: A C W Merrick.

Situation: Lany Road, Kilwarlin, Hillsborough; td, Ballykeel-Artifinny; District Council, Lisburn; Grid ref. J 204 598.

References: Listed (19/5/136}. Datestone; D/671/C/190, in PRONI; Down and Connor Church Accommodation Society, 'Fourth ... report', 1843, p 45; Barry, 'Hillsborough', 1982, pp 77-80; J F Rankin, in 'Clergy of Down and Dromore', 1996, p 142.

Moravian Church, Kilwarlin, Hillsborough

26. "Kilwarlin Moravian chapel is situated in the town-land of Corcreeny, on the side of a by-road. It is a neat, slated and stone building, roughcast and whitewashed. It is 41 feet long and 26 feet broad in the inside. The walls are 2 feet thick. The entrance is at the west end by a passage 3 feet 6 inches wide and 13 feet long, on each side of which is a small vestry over which is a gallery looking into the body of the chapel. The pulpit is very neat. There are no pews but forms for the accommodation of 150 persons, including the gallery. The chapel was rebuilt in 1834 at the expense of the present clergyman. The old chapel was built in 1755 and was in a very ruinous state when he came there, and was seldom used except as a school-house" (Ordnance Survey Memoir).

The exotically-named Rev. Basil Patras Zula, apparently a Greek refugee from the troubles preceding the conclusion of the Greek War of Independence (which ended only in 1832), and married to a Dublin Moravian lady, was appointed minister here in 1834, when he found a congregation of five elderly persons, which he had increased to fifty younger ones by the time of his mysterious death in 1844. "At an early age, with a price on his head and sought by the Turks, Zula forsook his homeland, whither he returned for a brief period in 1822, to fight at Missolonghi. Later, at Smyrna, he was befriended by an Englishman, Sir William Eden, with whom, in 1828, he travelled to Ireland. In Dublin he met and married the daughter of a minister of the Moravian church, and in time became a minister himself" (Jean O'Neill). "Under his leadership new church, manse and schoolhouse were constructed in 1835"... "Such was the affection in which Zula was held that for a number of generations after his death, a great number of local children, both male and female, had the name Zula among their Christian names"

(Walker). A full account of what is known about this extra-ordinary man will be found in J S Curl's and Joseph Cooper's articles, and in Barry's and Walker's books, so will not be repeated here.

The façade is topped by an unconventional bell-cote, with three finials like miniature chimney-pots; and three more, with strange metal coronets on top, at the gable-ends of the church and crowning the outshot return of the manse. The manse with its extension and modern church hall are carried on in a line with the church, as is the case with the Moravian church at Lower Ballinderry in County Antrim of almost exactly the same date: the church has round-headed stained glass windows, the church hall and manse orthodox Georgian-glazed windows, in the latter in round-headed recesses on the ground floor, framing a (probably later) porch. There is a plaque on the façade of the church inscribed, *The Ancient Episcopal Church of The United Brethren commonly called Moravians erected A.D. 1755. Rebuilt October 13th 1834 Restored 1987.* The pre-1987 version of this was set in a classical aedicule within a deep recess, both now regrettably removed. All the walls are of rather dreary grey cement render; the group would look vastly more attractive if the congregation were to revert to the practice of 1837, and keep it all whitewashed once a year, perhaps with window-sashes and doors picked out in black, blue, red, or green.

The interior, as at Ballinderry, is very plain; despite the Ordnance Survey report, the present late-Victorian pulpit is unremarkable; but all is neat, in good repair, and seemly. The grounds are laid out in most unusual humps and hollows, interspersed with yew trees, and kept nicely shorn (it looks a daunting task, even with modern machinery). It turns out that this is the only known example in Ireland of a 'Battle Garden' (see illustration on page 284), a rare enough specimen anywhere, intended to reproduce the terrain of the battleground of Thermopylae fought in 480 BC, so as to cheer up the homesick Mr Zula.

The late Professor Hammond provides a very clear map of the Pass of Thermopylae, and a lucid description: "Leonidas held the narrow passage between the cliffs and the sea, which was some 50 feet wide. Here an ancient wall of dry stone had been repaired by the army to protect their camp. In front of the wall the passage widened and then contracted again to a width of some 6 feet. In the space between the wall and the narrowest point Leonidas intended to fight; here he had a narrow strip of a mile or more in length, over which his men could advance or retire. Behind the wall and at about the same distance the passage narrowed again near the village of Alpeni, which was his base of supply. On his arrival Leonidas had learnt of a mountain path by which his position could be turned; he had therefore detached the Phocian force, which volunteered to hold the path". It was indeed by this path that a body of Xerxes's Persian 'Immortals' by-passed the Phocians, and eventually turned the tide of the land battle against the gallant Greeks, though theirs, both on land and sea, was the ultimate victory.

However, it is quite extraordinarily difficult to reconcile map and description to the layout of the Kilwarlin battle-garden. Several authorities have written about this rarity: the fullest account is that given by Curl in his article 'The Battle Garden at Kilwarlin'; he has recourse to symbolism to reconcile the two. " ... One of the most extraordinary gardens in Ireland ... Six steps lead down to an artificial hollow, and these symbolise the eastward entrance to the Pass of Thermopylae. Opposite these steps, near the entrance, is a low hill representing Mount Oeta. By the church drive is an ornamental lake fed by a stream that symbolizes the Aegean Sea, and from this lake there is an underground stream to signify the hot springs from which Thermopylae derives its name ... The sloping range of artificial mounds represents the foothills of the Callidromos range of mountains through which the Pass runs, and the highest mound on the site is a model of Mount Callidromos itself ... In the centre of the hollow is a pond around which there were once twenty-four flower-beds that represented the letters of the Greek alphabet: only two, representing Alpha and Omega, survive today". (Though all else is very well kept, these too seem at the date of writing to have faded away).

Curl suggests that Zula attributed "a curious protective symbolism" to his Battle Garden; he seems to have believed that he would be pursued even to Ireland, and attacked by Turks. "The paranoiac fear of the Turk caused Zula to construct several escape routes in his new manse, including a gazebo-like room built on columns with a trap-door in the floor through which instant flight would be possible to the churchyard. In the event, the Turks never came for Zula, but Death did, on 4 October 1844, in Dublin, shortly after work on the Battle Garden had been completed". After his death "his widow, Ann, lived on in the manse and using money from his estate built an additional wing to the manse in which she conducted a Boarding School for Select Young Ladies: she died in 1858" (Foy).

There is a graveyard, not dissimilar from those at Ballinderry and Gracehill, at the rear, guarded by cats, as are sundry extensions and outbuildings, all Georgian-glazed. The plan of the manse, which - as at Ballinderry - communicates directly with the vestry and the church - is extraordinarily complex, full of surprising doors and passages. There is also a pretty Georgian-glazed cottage, originally the schoolhouse erected by Lord Downshire under Zula's supervision, latterly a shop, and for a time formerly the caretaker's home, within the curtilege of the church, white-painted stucco to the road, red-brick towards the church; with an enigmatic ecclesiastically-glazed addendum. Finally, the enclave is protected by a delightful gate-screen and railings, the pillars topped by knops with Greek-key pattern surrounds; all nicely painted.

Canon Barry says, dismissively "The present church and adjoining minister's residence ... are of no architectural interest". I must, emphatically, disagree. To my mind, this is one of the most interesting and unusual groups of buildings in the county; of great charm; and could be even more delightful if suitably painted.

Photographs: A C W Merrick.

Situation: Kilwarlin Road, Upper Kilwarlin; td, Corcreeny; District Council, Lisburn; Grid ref. J 209 588.

References: Manse, listed B1, Church, church hall and gate screen, listed B (19/5/133, a,b,c, 134). J R Ward, T C McIlroy, and J C Innes, OSM, 1837, Down, II, p 95; Stanford, 'Ireland and the classical tradition', 1976, pp 119-120; J O'Neill, in CL, 17 December 1981; Barry, 'Hillsborough', 1982, pp 82-84; J S Curl, in 'Garden history', II, 1983, pp 65-69; Hammond, 'History of Greece', 1986, pp 233-234; J H Foy, 'Kilwarlin Moravian church: a visitor's guide', nd, passim; J Cooper, in 'Down survey', 2000, pp 70-77; Walker, 'Historic Ulster churches', 2000, pp 79-80.

Presbyterian Church and School, Dundonald

27. It is fascinating to compare this spiky, prickly, stuccoed Gothic church of 1839 with its exact contemporary, Comber Second Presbyterian Church (36), where the Gothic is still insidiously creeping into the classical frame. The street frontage at Dundonald is in fact the back of the church and is not of great distinction, despite its pointy windows; but as Carr remarks, "only Presbyterians normally get this view" - of its proper front, with twin Gothic-glazed door-ways in the projecting central section, under two-light Gothic window with pointed dripstone, gable, and central pinnacle; tall Gothic-glazed windows on either side.

Even nicer than the church is the little stone-and-brick Congregational National School, built on the Church Green in 1844. In the caption to his illustration, Carr advises "Note the scratches at waist height by the door, made by children sharpening their slate pencils. In the 1840s there was also a small library here". It is in excellent order, and retains its Tudoresque detailing.

Photographs: A C W Merrick.
Situation: On Church Green, Dundonald.; td, Church Quarter; District Council, Castlereagh; Grid ref. J 419 739.
References: Oddly, neither church nor schoolhouse is listed. Carr, 'Most unpretending of places', 1987, pp 128,138.

Presbyterian Church, Conlig, Newtownards

28. The listers say the church is of "about 1854, in a style of Gothic Revival with some classical detail"; Patton says "c. 1848: Spiky church in slightly squared random rubble and ashlar dressings which looks eastward from its hillside location. Gabled front with finialed buttresses and slender colonettes to the door and three lancet windows above; square belfry with finials, and clockface in base; round-headed windows with traceried tops along the body of the church". An inscription on the front informs the world that belfry and clock date only from 1930, which is a bit surprising, since they look like integral parts of the design.

A very tall, rather gaunt and sombre, church, but unexpectedly attractive in its detailing, the silhouette of its curious pinnacled belfry being important to the landscape. The clock had, at any rate when seen, the virtue of showing the correct time. There is an Ordnance Survey bench-mark at the foot of the building. There seems to be no record of the name of the architect, but there must have been one, for, though a little architecturally naïve, this is not a vernacular building. It appears to have been built, "almost entirely at his own expense", by Mr John Sinclair of The Grove, Belfast, in whose memory Sinclair Seamen's Church in Belfast was later built. There is a distressing flat-roofed addendum at the rear, a modern church hall, and a vast expanse of carpark "with a solitary but important beech tree trying to look cheerful in the midst of the tarmac" (Patton).

Photograph: A C W Merrick.

Situation: Main Street, Conlig; td, Conlig; District Council, North Down; Grid ref. J 500 782.

References: Listed B (23/6/4). 'History of congregations' 1982, p 328; Patton, 'Bangor', UAHS, 1999, p135; 'Journal of the Bangor Historical Society', I, 1981, pp 19-20.

Friends' Meeting House, Kiltonga, Newtownards

29. A charming small rubble-stone building, a cube with a hemisphere attached, rescued not so long ago from utter disarray; standing a bit incongruously at the entrance to the Kiltonga Leisure Centre, but still a welcome sight.

McCavery says "Quaker numbers were small in Newtown, only twenty in 1764. Despite the small numbers, however, a meeting house was built in the town in 1780. The congregation seems to have increased, for at a meeting in November 1797 there were four hundred worshippers, although paradoxically enough, given the Quakers' pacifism, this number included some soldiers who were stationed in the town at the time. The district's leading Quaker family was then the Bradshaw family of Bradshaw's Brae who built the" (1796) "meeting house opposite their residence at Milecross House" (89).

Francis Joseph Bigger is more specific. "The Bradshaws became Quakers very early, for William Edmonson" (*recte* Edmundson, 1627-1712) "who 'convinced' James Bradshaw (I) ... was the celebrated Quaker preacher ... '6 of 6th month, 1796. It appearing that some steps have been taken to put forward the building of the meeting-house at Mile-Cross, the committee are desired to collect the subscriptions and pay them into the hands of John Barcroft'. Then, on 13 of 2nd month, 1806 - 'The new meeting-house at Mile-cross having for a considerable time remained in an unfinished state, which has a disreputable appearance, Jonathan Richardson and John Barcroft are appointed to endeavour, with Thomas Bradshaw, to devise the most eligible and speedy means of getting it finished.' I am led to think Mile-Cross meeting ceased about

1830". This seems to be about right, for on 4 June 1834 the Valuation officer records "Quakers Meeting House now occupied as an office by Mr Bradshaw" - this was Robert Bradshaw, lawyer, known as "Mad Bradshaw" (see 89).

The Archaeological Survey of County Down in 1966 says, "Small rectangular building, with apsidal porch, built of harled rubble" (the harling since removed), "with wrought-stone eaves-cornice and slated roof; disused and semi-ruined. The building has an E. window, now blocked, with modern openings above in the gable; the side walls are lighted by pairs of semi-circular headed windows. The porch has an entrance on the N., in dressed stone, with chamfered jambs and flat head with key-block inscribed 1796, and a corresponding flat arched recess on the S.; it is lighted on the W. by a semi-circular-headed window, now built up in the lower part" (but since restored) "... The structure appears to have been commenced c. 1796, but not completed until after 1806". Fortunately, matters have improved since 1966: the building has been nicely restored by the District Council, and is now used for meetings and events.

Photograph: A C W Merrick.
Situation: Off Bradshaw's Brae (Belfast Road, Newtownards) at Kiltonga; td, Milecross; District Council, Ards; Grid ref. J 472 747.
References: Not listed. VAL 1B/322, p 39, in PRONI; F J Bigger, in UJA, 2nd series, VIII, 1902, pp 6, 55; ASCD, 1966, p 346; W Edgar, in 'Further glimpses of the Ards', 1980, pp 53-55; McCavery, 'Newtown', 1994, pp 81-82.

Non-Subscribing Presbyterian Church, Ravara, Ballygowan

30. A very small, plain, boxy, preaching-house, with a hipped roof; four bays wide, with very tall slim Georgian-glazed windows, twelve panes in each sash. The entrance wall is pierced by an upstairs window, lighting the raised pews at the back of the church, above the simple planked door; the wall opposite is blank. Recently nicely painted: the roughcast pink, the plinths, gutters, and reveals of a darker shade of the same tint, glazing-bars correctly white: simple but attractive.

The congregation was founded in the year this little church was built, 1837 according to the Church's aide-mémoire - 1838 according to the notice board outside the church. This seems to be the first of the series of new meeting-houses in North Down - Comber, 1838 (35), Killinchy, 1846 (38), Holywood, 1849 (40) - required after the formidable Henry Montgomery led seventeen congregations out of the main Presbyterian Synod of Ulster to form The Remonstrant Synod. "From 1830 many of these … congregations split into factions of which one set 'kept the property and the other kept the faith'. New Remonstrant meeting houses were needed where the subscribing party kept the church and called for themselves a minister to their liking" (Banham).

Ravara is the simplest in style, and might be described as 'Very-late-Georgian-vernacular'; the others are all more or less classical; but, with the exception of Holywood (and even there, there is uncertainty), and the somewhat tentative attribution of Killinchy and Comber to James Patterson, the name or names of the architect(s) seem to have remained unrecorded: which is a pity.

Oram says "This church, erected in 1837, is a perfect example of the intentionally plain, vernacular, hall-type meeting house, commonly built during the second half of the eighteenth century. The Non-Subscribing Presbyterian congregations have been most diligent in keeping their original buildings in use, rather than seeking replacements in the latest fashionable architectural style. There is a stark, serene simplicity, careful attention to proportion, and relationship of solid to void, that makes this a very appealing little structure".

Photograph: A C W Merrick.
Situation: Saintfield Road, Ballygowan; td, Ravara; District Council, Ards; Grid ref. J 428 634.
References: Listed B1 (24/16/53). Notice board outside church; aide-mémoire, 1999-2001, 'The Non-Subscribing Presbyterian Church of Ireland'; Oram, 'Expressions of faith', 2001, p 83; letter of 22 March 2001 from Rev. D G Banham to the author.

First Presbyterian Church, Donaghadee

31. This is the church recorded by Mr Kertland of the Ordnance Survey in 1837 as being, in comparison with the Shore Street church, "more in the centre of the town and constructed on a more ornamental plan." (The Shore Street church, known as 'Mr Skelly's church', was established by him after he had been "deposed *sine die* for alleged immorality", by a majority of one vote, in 1821 from the First Congregation. He was followed by many seceders, and built the Shore Street church out of his own pocket to accommodate them. He was restored by the General Synod in 1856, a year before his death, and the church building had to be bought back from him for £200).

Of the First Presbyterian church, Kertland continues "It accommodates about 500 and was built in the year 1824 at an expense of 815 pounds, which was defrayed by subscription". It is, to my mind, a slightly clumsy classical building, standing back from the street behind listed railings enclosing a rather stark courtyard of concrete slabs, with only a slight frill of greenery at each side. It is a little oddly painted, though neat and prosperous. But Curl thinks it quite sophisticated: "Compared with the dignified and correct classicism of buildings like the Presbyterian Church in High Street, Donaghadee, with its engaged unfluted Giant Order of Doric columns and robustly modelled pediment, such structures" (as Newry

Methodist, First Dromore Presbyterian and Great Victoria Street Presbyterian, Belfast) "seem curiously naïve in their use of classicism."

Dixon describes it as "A dignified classical building ... The façade is slightly wider than its pedimented portico of four giant attached, unfluted Doric columns. Between the columns on the ground floor two entrances, with modern panelled double doors and semi-circular fanlights, flank a central window also round-headed but filled, quite inappropriately for such a classical composition, with stained glass ... Above, three arc-headed windows retain their Georgian sashes. A plain clock-face is set into the triangular pediment. Except for the heavy cornice, the narrow wings to each side of the portico are quite plain".

The cream-painted columns make an excessive contrast with the mud-brown walls, and create a certain sense of disharmony. A subtler colour-scheme might serve to unify the building's parts better.

Photograph: A C W Merrick.
Situation: 18 High Street, Donaghadee; td, Town Parks; District Council, Ards; Grid ref. J 591 799
References: Listed B (24/7/3). M M Kertland, OSM, 1837, Down, II, p 47; 'History of congregations', 1982, p 383; Dixon, 'Donaghadee and Portpatrick', UAHS, 1977, pp 13, 16; Curl, 'Classical churches', UAHS, 1980, p 19.

St Patricks (RC) Church, Magheralin

32. As Walker remarks, "St Patrick's Church, built in 1843, is a rather rare example of a classical building constructed as an Ulster Catholic church. This was the style of architecture more usually associated with Presbyterianism at this time, and indeed Magheralin would look like many Ulster Presbyterian churches if the cross was removed from the gable. Following emancipation there may have been a number of Catholic churches built in the style, but many of these were subsequently rebuilt in a more flamboyant Gothic idiom. Perhaps its rural location ensured the survival of this particular church."

Of squared blackstone, with red-brick trim round the tall recessed round-headed windows (four in the façade, four in each side wall); nicely detailed sandstone pilasters supporting a pediment with a shield inscribed 'Ad majorem Dei gratiam, A.D.1843' in the tympanum. Walker says that the pedimented porch "was built in the late 1980s replacing the former stuccoed porch which had

two outer pilasters and two Ionic columns ... the new porch is fitting and contributes to the overall classical simplicity of the building". There are particularly good original railings in front of the church. The interior was re-ordered in 1969, retaining few of the original fittings. "The church is basically a two-aisled hall, with an integral sanctuary and a shallow gallery ... The only ornate piece is the communion rail which is composed of Romanesque arches" (Walker again).

Altogether, a small and unusual church of considerable charm.

Photograph: A C W Merrick.
Situation: Beside main road from Magheralin to Lurgan; td, Ballymagin; District Council, Craigavon; Grid ref. J 127 590.
References: Listed B (14/7/15). Oram, 'Craigavon', UAHS, 1971, Pt II, p 9; Walker, 'Historic Ulster churches', 2000, p 85.

First Presbyterian Church, Bangor

33. Set back from the streetline on Main Street behind lawn, tarmac, railings, and central weeping ash, a great asset to Bangor despite the incongruity of the contrast between classical façade and very un-classical tower and spire: seldom a successful combination, except in the hands of a Christopher Wren. The body of the kirk is of 1831-1834; the spire is of 1881; the portico is of 1928, but you would never guess it.

The "new and beautiful building" (Lewis) is horse-shoe or D-shaped, with a very fine semi-circle of box-pews radiating from a point in front of the pulpit, and a deep gallery, similarly shaped, borne on six stout columns - evidently solid timber, like ships' masts, not cast-iron. "There is a large and fine Presbyterian meeting house near the centre of the town. It was finished in 1834 at a cost of 2,400 pounds, which was defrayed by subscription. It will accommodate upwards of 1,000" (Kertland). The church is now said to seat 900 persons, 500 below and 400 upstairs, but some of the corners of the pews would accommodate only dwarfs or children. There is a pitch-pine ceiling. The high, columnar pulpit can, at need, hold around five Ministers; behind it, the organ and organ pipes arrayed in a segmental-headed recess flanked by pilasters. Externally, the church is built of random basalt, with segmental-headed windows (some with stained glass), and a pedimented façade carried on four plain pilasters, now with an oculus in the centre of the tympanum. Moreover, "The north and south elevations of the auditorium are pedimented, with terminal pilasters of wrought sandstone, having moulded bases and capitals with entablature blocks" (Archaeological Survey of County Down).

The "three-stage tower and steeple added in 1881 in unmatching 'scrabo freestone with Scotch red sandstone

dressings' ... The tower, which has Early English detailing, rises from a basalt base above the original vestibule to a sandstone stage ... The slender white spire is octagonal with aedicules at three stages" (Patton); by whose great-grandfather, Rev. Alexander Patton, it was erected; he "energetically set about raising funds, commissioned two designs for the spire, and by the looks of it chose the less appropriate one!" Bassett, no connoisseur, disagreed: writing in 1886, he said, "About 5 years ago this stately old edifice received the addition of a very high and most graceful tower and spire".

The portico, extended forwards and rebuilt in 1928, contains a vestibule and a very fine divided staircase up to the gallery; most oddly, in an arched niche between the two staircases, an acroterion which appears to have come from elsewhere. As Patton remarks, the portico "faithfully reproduces the appearance of the original elevation, with giant-order pilasters supporting the broad band cornice and separating the strange squat semicircular windows with pendant labels at first floor level. There are three doors, the central one of which has a triangular stone pediment".

A fine building; it is only a pity that the modern buildings by which it is flanked are so unworthy of it; apparently, and rather disgracefully, developed by the church around 1975 on the site of the former manse.

Photographs: 1874, before the spire, courtesy of North Down Heritage Centre; A C W Merrick.

Situation: Between 100 and 102 Main Street, Bangor; td, Corporation; District Council, North Down; Grid ref. J 504 816.

References: Listed B+ (23/7/6). M M Kertland, OSM, nd (?1837), Down, II, p 24; Lewis, TD, 1837, I, p 183; Bassett, 'County Down', 1886, p 287; ASCD, 1966, pp 340-341; Wilson, 'Bangor', 1992, p 58; Patton, 'Bangor', UAHS, 1999, pp 131-134.

Presbyterian Church, Castlereagh

34. Set in a large graveyard, with many fine mature trees, just on the ridge of the Castlereagh hills, looking northward over Belfast to Divis Mountain: a very fine neoclassical church of 1834 by John Millar; of almost exactly the same date as his church in Antrim, a few years earlier than his church in Portaferry (37). John Heather of the Ordnance Survey says "The parishioners who held seats in the former old meeting house were obliged to raise 300 pounds. There was 1,100 pounds raised by subscription, making the total amount of the cost 1,400 pounds. They employed some country architect to execute the plan and before 6 months it almost fell to the ground. It is now partly refinished. There are 47 seats in the gallery and 68 in the aisle. It is capable of holding 800 persons, there is 700 of a congregation".

In an ebullient report just before its reopening, on 13 August 1835, the Northern Whig wrote: "This house, it will be seen, is to be opened for public worship, on Sunday next ... It has been erected at a very heavy expense, by the exertions of the congregation and the friends of their respected Pastor, the Rev. Mr. Haslett. A considerable debt, however, still remains upon the house: but we trust, that the liberal individuals of the people of this town and surrounding neighbourhood, will cheerfully co-operate in liquidating it.

"The new house has been erected from a design, and under the supervision, of our talented young townsman, Mr. John Millar, Architect, to whom the lovers of classic architecture owe a debt of gratitude. This house does the utmost credit to Mr. Millar's talents. Viewed in its design, its altitude, or even in its decorations, as a whole, or in part, it pleases the eye and satisfies the taste. It is adorned by a Belfry (the first instance of the kind we know of, on a

Presbyterian house of worship, in Ireland), whose picturesque appearance, and commanding situation, render it very conspicuous. With respect to it, the Architect has boldly ventured out of the beaten track, in not placing the tower or Belfry astride, as has been usual, on a pediment. Here, Mr. Millar has, with great freedom of composition, managed his materials in a masterly manner, in placing the tower on a square basement, rising majestically from *terra firma*, the shadowed recesses of which, and the attached columns that act as buttresses, give to the whole a richness and power which contrast strongly with the flat and ineffective attempts made generally in our public edifices. - The columns, we understand, are adapted from a beautiful example of the Ionic, in the Temple of Apollo Epicurius, in the Peloponnesus". Curl calls it "the splendid Castlereagh Presbyterian Church" and adds "The building is certainly most distinguished, with a severe arrangement of two Ionic columns set *in antis* that recalls Soane at his best, though without some of that great architect's quirky details". Curl went on to remark "Regrettably one of the capitals has recently" (1980) " been ineptly 'restored'". Happily, that has now been put right, and the façade is well painted and in good order. Walker describes it as having "something of the crispness of a freshly-iced wedding cake". The opening of the Castlereagh New Meeting House, "agreeably to public notice", was performed by the Rev. Duncan Macfarlan, of Renfrew; it is satisfactory to note that "The Congregation was not only numerous, but respectable in the highest degree": the collection on the occasion amounted to £137 9 3.

The composition is introduced by railings and very fine fluted gate pillars, with Greek key ornament, topped by urns. The date "1650" is deceptively incised above the door: this is, of course, the date of establishment of the congregation, not that of the building. The slim fluted columns have highly idiosyncratic Ionic capitals: Larmour says "the chief interest" of the church "now lies in the particular choice of Ionic order used on the entrance front. Its columns have the wide flaring bases and distinctive capitals with canted volutes and curved tops which derive from the interior columns of the Temple of Epicurus at Bassae. It is an unexpected choice at a time when more familiar models were usual for the outside of a building, and it may be the earliest external use of the order in the British Isles. Millar would have known the details from the plates in the fourth volume of 'The antiquities of Athens', published in 1830, of which he had a copy". There is no pediment, though a heavy entablature; the "belfry" is more of a slim, tall, circular cupola, on a square base, evidently based on the monument of Lysicrates in Athens. The church is five bays deep, the upper windows round-headed and Georgian-glazed with clear glass; those below, square-headed and (perhaps a little regrettably) now all with colourful but somewhat sombre stained glass.

Inside, there is a horseshoe-shaped gallery supported on seven fluted cast-iron columns with Ionic capitals; good box-pews; a slightly unexpected compartmented ceiling of pitch-pine, and two highly unexpected and (here) rather incongruous chandeliers. The pulpit and organ-pipes fill almost the whole back wall of the church. Inside the front door, there is a good, divided, staircase to the gallery, though the church is normally entered by a side door at a slightly lower level.

Despite numerous protests, a highly incongruous three-storey modern extension has, in 2001, been tacked on to the rear of the church. Its glazing is in the contemporary style; and, though its stucco surface has been painted cream to match the body of the church, the lining-out of the walls has been crudely executed. The best that can be said of it is that its design could be worse; and that it is, from most angles, relatively inconspicuous. Against this, a building of this quality deserves to have its three-dimensional integrity respected. More serious still, the new building seems to have affected the stability of the old: there is now a sinis-

ter crack snaking its way right up the outside wall, close to the junction between old and new, with precautionary tell-tale glasses over it. How serious it will turn out to be for the structure cannot yet be determined, but it emphasises the risks of this kind of architectural philistinism.

Photographs: A C W Merrick.
Situation: 79 Church Road, Castlereagh; td, Castlereagh; District Council, Castlereagh; Grid ref. J 374 708.
References: Listed B (25/13/2; gates and railings, 25/13/3). OS map, 1834; J Heather, OSM, nd, Down, II, p 101; 'Northern Whig', 13/8/1835; J Little, 'Castlereagh Presbyterian Church' 1935, passim; ASCD, 1970, p 341, pl 128; Curl, 'Classical churches', UAHS, 1980, p 14; P Larmour, in 'Perspective', Sept/Oct 1994, pp 55-57; C E B Brett, in UA, Oct 1994, pp 4-6; Walker, 'Historic Ulster Churches', 2000, p 72; church records.

Non-Subscribing Presbyterian Church, Comber

35. A very pleasing late-classical church, with cutstone Ionic columns carrying a pediment; plaque with festoon and date '1838'; pedimented doorcase with console brackets. The side walls of Roman cement, two-storey; the side windows round-headed above, segmental-headed below, all Georgian-glazed. Set (together with congruous manse and church hall) in a delightful hill-top garden, surrounded by trees - though redbrick housing development hems in this surprising enclave ever more closely.

Internally, equally pleasing: a good box-pewed gallery in a double curve, with pretty cast-iron crinoline-bowed front, carried on four exceptionally slim cast iron Corinthian columns, faces an attractive blue-and-white painted recess behind the pulpit, ornamented with scrolls and simplified anthemion motif. Between gallery and recess, two aisles dividing nicely-curved box-pews; above, a simple tongued-and-grooved wooden ceiling; and at the front of the gallery, an array of the flags of the scouts and British Legion. All this, due to the munificence of the Andrews family of Ardara, the town's mill-owners. The name of the architect seems not to be remembered, though it would seem likely that this is another work of James Patterson (see Killinchy Non-Subscribing, 38, and Comber Second Presbyterian, 36, churches). M M Kertland of the Ordnance Survey rather abruptly dismisses this congregation with the note "Within the present year (1837) the upper part of a barn has been fitted up as a place of meeting by that sect of people styling themselves Unitarians. It will accommodate about 200". Was this a temporary place of worship used while the present church was a-building, perhaps?

Photograph: A C W Merrick (see also colour illus. 6).
Situation: Mill Street, Comber; td, Town Parks; District Council, Ards; Grid ref. J 455 692.
References: Listed B (24/15/34). Datestone; M M Kertland, OSM, 1837, Down, II, p 28.

Second Presbyterian Church, Comber

36. A most unusual, if handsome, hybrid between the classical and Gothic styles, dated 1839 in the pediment, in fact opened for worship on 3rd October 1840. Set on a grassy hillock, with yew trees, and standing back from the busy street, it has four fine cutstone pilasters (the stones of two slightly different colours, some pinkish, some buff); a pedimented doorcase on console brackets; the recessed panels between the pilasters being of cream-painted plaster, framing the stone surrounds of tall pointed windows. The cutstone is carried round the corner for one bay on each side, with a blank pointed window recess; then four more tall pointed windows on each side between walls of rubblestone.

Curl says "A similar arrangement" (to that at Killinchy Non-Subscribing Presbyterian Church, 38) "with the orders in stone is found in the façade of the Comber Second Presbyterian Church, ... of 1839, although there are some concessions to Gothic in the fenestration". "The congregation was formed in 1838 by 69 families; the new House of Worship was opened free of debt in 1840" (Church hall appeal booklet); no mean achievement.

It appears that the architect of this church, as also of the Killinchy Non-Subscribing Presbyterian Church, was James Patterson, according to the recollections of his 95-year-old granddaughter, Mrs Maude McConnell. I have, however, been unable to find documentary evidence to confirm this: though such oral evidence is certainly to be treated with respect.

Photograph: A C W Merrick.
Situation: Off Killinchy Street, Comber; td, Town Parks; Parish, Comber; District Council, Ards; Grid ref. J 459 690.
References: Listed B (24/15/21). Curl, 'Classical churches,' UAHS, 1980, pp 12, 18; 'History of congregations', 1982, p 327; Church hall appeal booklet, 1991; information from Rev. R McKee, minister of Killinchy Non-Subscribing Presbyterian Church, and from Rev. D G Banham.

Presbyterian Church, Portaferry

37. Possibly the high point of achievement of the eccentric but accomplished Belfast architect, John Millar (see 34 and 107); as Paul Larmour describes it, "a magnificent Greek Revival temple with a six-columned portico at each end. His precise model here was probably the Temple of Nemesis at Rhamnus whose hexastyle front employing the" (Doric) "order had been published in 1817. For the interior columns at Portaferry, Millar chose the Ionic from Bassae. This idiosyncratic range of orders makes Portaferry one of the most interesting examples of Greek Revival architecture in Ireland, while its 'unity as well as the majesty of mass and outlines' ... makes it one of the most satisfying". And Curl says "Hexastyle Doric porticoes on a high podium distinguish John Millar's nobly conceived Portaferry Presbyterian Church, of 1841, ... a building that would not look out of place in Helsinki or Leningrad. Indeed, this marvellous Greek temple is one of the most distinguished Neoclassical buildings in Ulster, and is in the first rank of Neoclassical designs in the whole

of the British Isles".

The Down Recorder, suitably impressed, reported in 1842: "The style of architecture which Mr Millar has adopted is that which prevailed in Greece during the architectural age of Pericles; its dimensions are sufficiently large to produce an impression of grandeur and sublimity; ... thus stamping his works, where they have been carried out under his own eye, with perfection and harmonious beauty, without stooping to the factitious aid of adventitious embellishments". The congregation's building accounts disclose that he was paid a fee of £69. 3. 0, on an expenditure of around £2,500. In addition, he received £45. 14. 0 for "drawing freestone" - dressed pilasters and triglyphs transported, presumably, in his carriage, from Scrabo quarry (close to his home) of which his father was, or had been, the owner.

The Presbyterian congregation in Portaferry must have been much larger then than it is now. The previous meeting house, according to the Ordnance Survey memoir, was "a large house, has 90 seats in the isle and 14 in the gallery. It was first erected in the year 1694 and was almost rebuilt in 1751 ... the house would accommodate 730"; but it was rendered unsafe by the Great Wind of 1839. Millar's church was far larger: it has a capacious U-shaped gallery, and it appears that a second, upper gallery, was originally envisaged. The ground floor is full of pleasing dark box-pews: though the church is reported to be, as a matter of practicality, inconvenient and uncomfortable. Not that John Millar would have cared. The site slopes steeply, so that the north-west portico gives access to the gallery (there is no internal staircase). The pulpit is reached by a most curious back-stair, with a little porch lit by three small central windows; an arrangement of great inconvenience. But it is unclear how much of this was original. Apparently, according to Anderson and Lyttle, "In 1907 it was deemed necessary for the exterior of the church to be painted, probably because of damp ... At the same time the spaces between the pillars of the upper entrance were enclosed to provide a vestibule for the gallery". Walker suggests that both ends were glazed in 1907; it is now impossible to tell whether the area behind the pulpit was always part of the body of the church, or taken into it later. Williams takes a poor view of all these changes: "alterations due to the refusal of the congregation to treat neo-Classicism as sacrosanct have unwittingly resulted in a shrine to Post-Modernism: tiny windows have been introduced to light the stairs to the pulpit and the porticos have been partially glazed". Myself, I find these alterations, if alterations they all are, so bizarre as to accord quite well with Millar's eccentricity.

Although now in poor order, this is one of the most distinguished buildings in the county: the clarity and elegance of its detailing are quite remarkable. As Gordon Wheeler points out to me, the way in which Millar simplified and stylised triglyphs and guttae into plain unornamented

blocks is noteworthy. True, one of the pairs of Bassae columns indoors is now obscured by irrelevant organ-pipes; true, the whole exterior seems to have been coated with a rather regrettable rendering; but the battered base, the "almost Egyptian" pylons at the corners, the quality of gates and railings, the delicate detailing of the modest fluting not only at the tops, but also at the recessed bases, of the plain Doric columns, are all of great sophistication. This is certainly one of the treasures of Ulster architecture, and in my view ought to be listed 'A'.

Photograph: A C W Merrick. Figure: Ionic column detail, QUB Architecture Library.
Situation: Meeting-House Lane, Portaferry; td, Ballyphilip; District Council, Ards; Grid ref. J 595 508.
References: Listed B+ (24/1/46). G Scott, OSM, nd, Down, p 10; Bell, Brett, and Matthew, 'Portaferry & Strangford', UAHS, 1969, p 12; Curl, 'Classical churches', UAHS, 1970, pp 14, 17; Anderson and Lyttle, 'Portaferry Presbyterian church', 1993, pp 2-4; P Larmour, in 'Perspective', Sept/Oct 1994, p 56; C E B Brett, in UA, Oct 1994, p 5; Williams, 'Architecture in Ireland', 1994, p 111; Walker, 'Historic Ulster churches' 2000, p 85.

Non-Subscribing Presbyterian Church, Killinchy

38. A handsome and well-proportioned classical church of 1846, standing in its own grounds just outside the village in the countryside. Its façade is of cream-painted stucco (not lately though: it is in need of refreshment), vertically divided by six plain pilasters carrying a plain entablature and pediment: the recessed panels linked horizontally by a string-course; two orthodox Georgian-glazed windows in the second and fourth upstairs bays, the first, third and fifth bays with blank recesses; downstairs, a round-headed doorcase with radial fanlight, and the date on the keystone; round-headed blank recesses in the first and fifth

bays; square-headed blank recesses, topped by projecting dripstones, in the second and fourth bays: all very geometrical and symmetrical. Once beyond the stucco façade, the side walls are of random blackstone, with brick headers to the round-headed Georgian-glazed window-openings inset into stuccoed recesses. The interior has a U-shaped gallery on Ionic columns, and good box-pews.

According to the oldest living member of the congregation, the 95-year-old Mrs Maude McConnell, the architect was her grandfather, James Patterson, who also designed the Second Presbyterian Church, Comber (36).

Very fully described in the Archaeological Survey of County Down, which says "The entrance leads to a vestibule with stairs to the gallery on either side; the gallery encloses the church on three sides and is supported on cast-iron Ionic columns; the gallery front is panelled. Behind the pulpit, which occupies the centre of the N. wall, is a recess flanked by pilasters with enriched imposts, with flat elliptical arched head having moulded archivolt and panelled soffit. The walls of the church are crowned by a moulded cornice; the plaster ceiling is flat with elaborate central rose". Unfortunately, unduly obtrusive electric panel heaters attached to the panelling of the gallery-front detract considerably from the visual charm of the interior. There are nice scumbled box-pews, upstairs and down; a curiosity is, that the pulpit has the appearance of sitting on top of the organ, although actually, according to Mr Banham, "It just so happens that the organ, fitted later, fits into the space between the stairways, and the pulpit is so high that the preacher can be seen from around the gallery and thus high enough for him to be seen over the top of the organ". The plain glass in the windows, with its views of rustic greenery on both sides, is very welcome.

Curl says "Such examples" (as at Hilltown) "of classicism reduced to an absolute minimum have their undoubted qualities, but there are also instances where classical Orders are applied in stucco, using only pilasters and the most basic of mouldings. An elegant building in this applied classical manner is the Killinchy Non-Subscribing Presbyterian Church of 1846 that has a front consisting of ultra-simple pilaster-strips, an entablature, and a pediment".

Photograph: A C W Merrick.
Situation: Off Comber Road, Killinchy; td, Ballyministragh; District Council, Ards; Grid ref. J 495 610.
References: Listed B (24/17/39). Datestone; ASCD, 1966, p 345; Brett, 'East Down', UAHS, 1973, p 44; Curl, 'Classical churches', UAHS, 1980, pp 12, 18; information from Rev. R McKee and Rev. DG Banham.

Holy Trinity (C of I) Church, Kircubbin

39. A most uncommon small classical church, in the Main Street, apparently by no less an architect than Sir Charles Lanyon. Paul Larmour writes - though he cites no authority, and I have been unable to find any - "Just as the Church Accommodation Society was wound up, Lanyon built one further small church, not actually under the auspices of the Society but paid for by some of its subscribers, and it shows a truly remarkable departure from the others. At Trinity Church in Kircubbin (1843) in his only essay in the style, Lanyon built one of the finest Greek Revival churches in Ulster. It has a Doric *in antis* façade that is obviously based on the Temple of Diana-Propylaea at Eleusis as represented in 'The Unedited Antiquities of Atticus', right down to the seven sets of triglyphs across the frieze. Although there was occasionally a Neo-classical element of Lanyon's later work he was never again so reliant on an antique model".

"Foundation stone laid, 1843; consecrated, 1843; accommodation, 180 ... Trinity Church was built at the expense of Robert E. Ward, of Bangor Castle. Grecian style of architecture. Completely remodelled in 1876, at a cost of £250" (Ewart). "Before the present church was built, the parish was known as Inishargie and was one of three parishes which made up the union of Saint Andrew using the church at Balligan" (16). "This union was dissolved in 1844 ... Since 1975, Kircubbin has been united to Greyabbey" (Rankin).

In 1831, the Commissioners of Ecclesiastical Inquiry had noted "It is observed that after different fruitless attempts to reside, the incumbent has been compelled, by the repeated illnesses of his wife, to give up permanent residence in the parish"; so the whole large area was entrusted by him to a curate. "This state of affairs was regarded as unsatisfactory both by the Commissioners and by Mr. Robert Ward of Bangor, the local landowner. The former resolved to divide the united parishes so soon as the present incumbent should retire or die; but Mr. Ward resolved to endow the village of Kircubbin with church, parsonage, and parson without waiting. And so, in 1843, Mr Ward built a new classical church in an unexpected Greek-revival style, rare in Ulster, in the main street; a large and commodious new parsonage" (75) "on the hill behind the village; endowed both with a sum of 3$\frac{1}{2}$ per cent stock, which brought in £140 a year; and, after some rather complicated negotiations with the bishop, presented" my great-great-grandfather, the Reverend Wills Hill Brett, then incumbent of Greyabbey, to the living. "This arrangement had its oddities: the new church was never properly constituted a separate parish. Wills Brett received some incredulous letters from his friend the Rev. Hull, formerly a curate in nearby Inishargy, now episcopal minister in a parish in the highlands of Scotland: 'is it so, that henceforth there are to be no fewer than 4 ministers of the Establishment including yourself? ... If they be all spiritual men, you will doubtless receive much mutual refreshment and comfort from Christian intercourse; an advantage I very rarely enjoy" (Brett). The separate parish of Kircubbin was apparently not created until 1850. Wills Brett lived on at Kircubbin, with his wife and children, until his death, aged sixty-four, in 1862.

The interior, like the exterior, is classical. Oddly, the centre, and the left-hand, doorway have been closed up, only the right-hand door being in use, and leading, most unexpectedly, past the back of the pulpit - it seems that, according to the authors of the second historic buildings survey, "the altar was originally on the" (rear) "west wall (where one might expect to find it) but was moved to the east in 1922, an alteration which was said to have been brought about at the behest of a prominent member of the congregation" (? one of the Ward family) "who wished to observe all late comers!" The altar is now housed in a curious semi-circular niche, tucked into the former main doorcase, framed in a pilastered and pedimented aedicule; on whose back wall are neatly inscribed the commandments, and the Lord's prayer. The coffered ceiling is painted blue and white. There are two good marble memorials

on the west wall, both signed by J Robinson of Belfast, one to Colonel Ward, a peninsular war veteran, wounded at Badajoz, who died in 1860; the other to his widow, who died in 1872.

Not only must this be one of the last episcopalian churches built in the classical style, it is also a rarity for an Ulster classical church in being built of cut Scrabo stone, not stucco, though the side walls and back wall are rendered. Each of the two fluted columns in the portico is carved from three great blocks of stone. The second survey listers say "The porch is distyle in antis with full entablature and pediment. In the centre of the pediment is a black faced clock with gold hands and Roman numerals ... The centre door, which ordinarily (on any other building with a façade of this type) would serve as the entrance, has

a stone architrave with full entablature and console brackets ... The site level drops sharply to the rear, giving a full two stories at this elevation". The basement room is now used for Sunday school.

Altogether, a most surprisingly sophisticated little church to find in the main street of a very modest country village.

Photograph: MBR.

Situation: Main Street, Kircubbin; td, Kircubbin; District Council, Ards; Grid ref. J 598 627.

References: Listed B+ (railings B), (24/2/29). D 3303/8/A/12A, D 3303/8/B/6, in PRONI; Ewart, 'Down & Connor & Dromore', 1886, p 53; 'St Andrew's, Inishargy, Balligan', 1966, p 8; Brett, 'Long shadows', 1978, p 75; P Larmour, in 'Irish arts review', 1989/90, p 203; J F Rankin, in 'Clergy of Down and Dromore', 1996, p 145.

First (Non-Subscribing) Presbyterian Church, Holywood

40. Replacing an earlier meeting-house near the shore, a very fine Italian-classical Corinthian façade of 1849, set back from the street-line of High Street behind a rather unworthy tarmac yard. According to the listers, by Thomas Jackson; this is not confirmed by Hugh Dixon's list of his works, and is contradicted by Kelly, writing only a year after the church's completion, who firmly attributes its design to Charles Lanyon, and the supervision to Francis Ritchie of Mountpottinger. Merrick, less convincingly, records that "it is said that Lanyon used it as a model for the County Antrim Courthouse on Belfast's Crumlin Road, which was built the following year". He adds "The church was largely paid for by the widow of John Suffern, a well-known Belfast merchant, and the work superintended by Francis Ritchie, felt manufacturer, of Ballymacarett. For some years afterwards, the view of the front was partially obscured by a row of old houses". It is now somewhat obscured by an obelisk erected in 1891 (after his death aged 80) in memory of the Rev. Charles James McAlester, who had established a Select School in the large hall beneath the church, generally known as "the underground academy".

Of stucco, agreeably painted green with white trim and red doors; topped by a balustrade rather then the expected parapet; the central recessed portico lined with niches and with Corinthian columns; blind arches between Corinthian pilasters to each side. Hipped roof; on a steeply sloping site; side and back walls of economical random stone punctuated by tall, plain, round-headed windows. Thoroughly repaired and repainted, by Gordon McKnight, 1984; and again, 1996; but there is always more to be done.

The interior of the church is interesting, just at the meeting-point between the classical and Italianate styles. A little unhappily, the organ has been moved from the gallery to a very prominent site behind the pulpit; the old pulpit, a splendid piece of carved mahogany, with four Corinthian columns, relegated to the undercroft - but it could without too much difficulty be put back. It seems that the minister used to enter the old pulpit up a ladder and through a trapdoor in its floor; it is said that this jack-in-the-box act kept startling one parishioner so much that he went elsewhere, in consequence of which the arrangements were altered.

The body of the church has excellent box-pews, slightly raised at the rear, and a ceiling of tongued-and-grooved pitch-pine; it is well-decorated and seemly, with three blank arches in the north wall behind the pulpit. There are two charming curly corner staircases leading up to the former organ-loft, now gallery, and one down to the big schoolroom below, with its six cast-iron columns supporting the congregation above. The schoolroom's heating arrangements are unconventional: the two fireplaces (the room was originally partitioned to provide two classrooms) were served by horizontal chimneys venting out through the back wall.

Photograph: A C W Merrick.

Situation: High Street, Holywood; td, Holywood; District Council, North Down; Grid ref, J 397 792.

References: Listed B (23/20/10). Kelly, 'Holywood', 1850, p 40, H Dixon, in PBNHPS, 2nd series, IX,1970/77, pp 27-30; Merrick, 'Buildings of Holywood', 1986, p 66; Congregational history, nd, typescript, passim; file in MBR; information from Rev. D G Banham.

Opposite: 5. St Malachi's Church, Hillsborough (20)

6. Non-Subscribing Presbyterian Church, Comber (35)
7. Presbyterian Church, Hillhall (44)

Presbyterian Church, Waringstown

41. A very strange building indeed, plainly dated in the porch to 1853 - foundation stone 1851, consecration 5 June 1853. The façade incorporates a round-headed central recessed porch, with cut-stone Tuscan Doric columns in antis; apart from these, only the plinth is now of chiselled stone; the rest, perhaps originally of ashlar, is now rendered. There are plenty of round-headed Georgian-glazed windows. At each of the front corners, there rises a kind of Italianate campanile, rather like that of a Victorian railway station. But the side walls are in marked contrast: six bays deep, of blackstone with red-brick dressings to the likewise round-headed windows, on a downward-sloping site. At the rear, not offensive modern church halls and offices.

Internally, a very large barn-church, plain and mildly Italianate, with blue ceiling and ochre walls; box-pews, except where they have been removed at the front; two aisles; interlace pattern on the fronts of the gallery, which is reached by a spiral staircase in the left-hand tower; an elaborate, very wide, multi-columnar wooden pulpit. I personally, in my old fashioned episcopalian way, find it highly disconcerting to come upon an Ulster Presbyterian church filled with the evidences of the happy-clappy tendency: the musical apparatus appropriate to a jazz-band beside the pulpit; in the very front pew, a computer; strangest of all, an enormous screen for audio-visual displays hung above the pulpit. Perhaps this is all very well, but I suspect that it would have astounded Dr Cooke and Dr Hanna.

The listers just say "A two-storey hall with galleries. The front twin towers with recessed entrance bay and interior are detailed in the 'Florentine' style" (?). Oram says "The building is a hall of simple classical proportions constructed of blackstone with brick detailing and slate roof.

In contrast, the interior and entrance façade with twin flanking towers are fully detailed in Florentine Renaissance style" (? again: I never saw anything remotely like this in Florence). This church seems to be universally believed to have been designed by Sir Charles Lanyon. Oral tradition is not lightly to be disregarded; yet to me, this seems not remotely credible, as it is so unlike his polished style of this date. He and his practice had, some years earlier, produced many designs for the Church of Ireland and its Down and Connor Church Accommodation Society; but only a very few for the Presbyterian church; and none of these in this style. I thought I had found a possible answer when I noticed that the History of Congregations in the Presbyterian Church described the church as "designed by Sir John Lanyon in the Florentine style with two ornate towers at each corner of the front". Sir Charles Lanyon's son John was never a knight, and was a much lesser architect: but could it perhaps have been designed by him? Yet no, he was aged only thirteen in 1853; and did not enter partnership with his father and W H Lynn until ten years later, in 1863. I am told that all the church records have been destroyed; and that the newspaper reports of the consecration of the church make no mention of the name of the architect (in itself odd, if he was indeed the, by then highly distinguished, Lanyon senior). Surprisingly, Jeremy Williams seems to have missed this remarkable example of Victorian church architecture. It is included here more for its oddity than for its beauty.

Photograph: A C W Merrick.
Situation: Off Hall Hill, Waringstown; td, Tullyherron; District Council, Craigavon; Grid ref. J 106 553.
References: Listed B+ (14/6/16). Oram, 'Craigavon', UAHS, 1971, Pt II, p 7; 'History of congregations', 1982, p 797; information from Mr Eric McIlroy.

All Saints' (C of I) Church, Eglantine, Hillsborough

42. A very distinguished small country church designed by Sir Thomas Drew, perhaps the very best work of the scholarly Drew. Not at all Irish; in the Early English style; the walls of coursed random blackstone, with ashlar trim; the beautifully carved detailing of Caen sandstone; the roof, very English, of small red tiles. Hard to find, up a long lane at the backside of Hillsborough: by a curious freak, although in County Down, this parish trespasses across the River Lagan and is in the diocese of Connor. Williams, justly, remarks: "Although Thomas Drew designed many churches he was at his happiest when designing them for devout private patrons where he could revert to the hand-made qualities of rural Gothic. Picturesque composition made out of separately articulated elements like a collection of cottages. Open timber porch leading to single-cell nave and apsidal chancel". Thomas Drew (1838 - 1910), was a son of the somewhat Orange rector of Christ Church, Belfast; served his articles with Charles Lanyon, and worked both with Thomas Turner and W H Lynn; in 1862 removed his practice to Dublin, but was nonetheless appointed in 1865 as diocesan architect of Down, Connor and Dromore. "A man of immense energy, Drew seems to have found it impossible not to play an active part in any body or enterprise with which he was associated. Not only did he become president of the RIAI and AAI but also of the RSAI and the RHA, the only person to have held all four positions ... awarded a knighthood in the Queen's birthday honours for 1900, a distinction to which, as the Irish Builder agreed, no other architect in Ireland was so well entitled" (Irish Architectural Archive).

Eglantine House (now a stark burned-out carcase, once a splendid mansion) was leased from Lord Downshire from 1841 to 1917 by a branch of the Mulholland family of the York Street mill, Belfast (see Ballywalter Park, 59). The only son of the family, St Clair Mulholland, died as a child in 1861; his father, also St Clair Mulholland, died in 1872; the distraught family, in particular Mary Mulholland, resolved to build a memorial chapel in their memory. Scott hints that the family had found the services at Hillsborough parish church, "where in those days hymns were not sung, and sermons very long", until 1869 under the formidable Archdeacon Mant, uncongenial. Thomas Drew was engaged as architect. The lower tender was for £1895, but the church in the end cost £3,442 5 10, including all the furnishings. It was consecrated on 13 July 1875 and survives almost entirely unaltered. In due course Eglantine has become a parish in its own right.

Externally, the church is quite modest, though beautifully detailed; there is a splendid porch (re-roofed in 1970, but imperceptibly) "of massive woodwork, resting on a low wall" (Ewart); a tall chimney-stack to the vestry; a nice little gablet belfry, accommodating three bells within its central arch; and prickly guttering, the eaves of the roof carried on pretty trefoil wooden corbels. The stone portal inside the porch is exquisitely carved. Internally, the church is charming, the side aisle carried on plump Caen stone columns supporting pointed arches picked out in brick for contrast. The apse has good windows, a fine alabaster reredos, and even better ornate polychrome tilework. At the junction of nave and chancel, there are dark-green polished marble columns with delightfully crisp floral Caen stone capitals in the Ruskinian manner. The ceiling has a black-and-white hammer-beam pattern. There is a pleasant graveyard behind the church, containing the graves of many war-time servicemen, mostly from the RAF aerodrome at Long Kesh nearby.

High Victorian architecture at its very best.

Photograph: A C W Merrick (see also colour illus. 10).
Situation: Off Eglantine Road, Hillsborough; td, Carnbane; District
    Council, Lisburn; Grid ref. J 243 613.
References: Listed B (19/4/1). IB, XVI, 1874, p 175, XVII, 1875, pp 21

(illustration), 214; Ewart, 'Down and Connor & Dromore', 1886, p 99;
'Short history of All Saints', Eglantine', nd, typescript, passim; Scott,
'Churches of the Diocese of Connor', 1997, pp 89-90; Williams,
'Architecture in Ireland', 1994, p 105; biographical notes in IAA.

St Patrick's (R C) Church, Newtownards

43. "The inventor of the Hansom Cab, J. A. Hansom, designed Newtownards Roman Catholic church": according to the Irish Builder of 1912. Although, as Walker correctly says, there was an intermediate church of 1846 in Ann Street, Dr O'Laverty reports that the church of 1813 (in East Street) "was replaced by the present church which was erected at the sole expense of the Dowager Marchioness of Londonderry. The foundation stone of the building was laid on the 3rd August 1875 by the Most Rev. Dr. Dorrian, Bishop of Down and Connor. The church occupies a commanding position, convenient to the railway station. The style is pure Gothic, and what is known as the late decorative, approaching the perpendicular. The stone used is from the quarries at Scrabo, with facings of freestone. The interior dimensions are one hundred and seven feet by forty-eight, and there is accommodation for six hundred and sixty persons. The building consists of a sanctuary, with a side altar on the Gospel side, and the sacristy on the south side. There are also north and south transepts, nave and aisles. The gallery is at the west end, facing North Street, access to which is gained from the principal entrance by a spiral staircase of Dundonald stone at the south side of the door. At the south-west angle there is a commodious porch, with Gothic door and elaborate traceries, and above it is a niche, in which is placed a statue of St. Patrick, to whom the church is dedicated.

At the intersection of the nave and transepts there is a lantern tower, and immediately beside it a belfry for the sanctus bell. Each side of the building has three windows, and the sanctuary has five; all in the Gothic style ... Messrs Hanson [sic] & Sons, London, were the architects. It was dedicated by the Most Rev. Dr. Dorrian, October 24th, 1877".

Williams says, perhaps with some pardonable over-enthusiasm, "One of the most delightful churches of its time in Ireland, designed by J. A. Hansom and built in 1877. Cruciform with central lantern tower, transepts of one bay each flush with the aisles, and apsidal choir - the ingredients of a cathedral but on a miniature scale. Its formality is subtly disrupted; the facade is made asymmetrical by the staircase to the organ and southern porch, while one Irish round tower is diagonally attached to the central lantern, leaving its fenestration undisturbed - eight rose windows inserted into the spandrels to give a mysterious illumination to the crossing".

Although it stands in ample grounds, close to the centre of the town, with fine trees, on a hill-top, to me, the exterior seems something of a jumble, with its square tower with pyramidal roof at the crossing; circular tower with conical roof attached; tall twin cylindrical chimney-stacks above the sacristy; and confusion of hexafoil, cinquefoil, quatrefoil, and trefoil windows in what appear, from outside, to be port-holes. But the interior is quite another matter. It is spacious, uncluttered, and delightful. The main aisle, and the compartmented roof, are borne on heavy stone clustered columns. The side-aisles are in nicely-timbered pentices. The ceiling of the chancel apse is geometrical and particularly pleasing. Almost all the windows are blessedly free of ornate stained glass, being only patterned compositions of plain or lightly-tinted glass; the one exception the glowing orange-golden glass in the cinquefoil windows of the side-chapel, though Walker says "it is thought that the small circular window in the baptistry may be glazed with fragments of glass from the town's medieval priory". It seems that the Roman Catholics of Newtownards have much reason to be grateful to their benefactress, Lady Londonderry, for a most unusual and charming place of worship; "no doubt influenced by Father McConvey, the Dowager Marchioness who had previously become a convert to the Catholic faith decided to provide at her own expense a completely new church ... often referred to as a cathedral in miniature with its Hiberno-Gothic Architecture and its building material appropriately of Scrabo and Dundonald stone" (Edgar). Although a daughter of the Earl of Roden, she spent most of her life in London, where she corresponded copiously with Cardinals Wiseman, Manning and Newman; she became a Roman Catholic in 1855. The church was re-ordered, quite sensitively, in 1988, with new circular altar, and ambo, though an earlier altar of 1876 still remains in the Blessed Sacrament chapel to the north of the sanctuary.

Joseph Aloysius Hansom, son of a York joiner, "perfected and registered his invention, the 'Patent Safety Cab', and ... devoted himself to the administration of the company to whom he had sold the patent rights". However, he never received the purchase price of £10,000. The 11th edition of the Encyclopaedia Britannica says "The hansom cab as improved by subsequent alterations, nevertheless, took and held the fancy of the public". Henry Russell Hitchcock describes his 1831 competition-winning design for Birmingham Town Hall as "the most striking British example of the temple paradigm", a "characteristic Romantic Classical edifice, raised on a high rusticated podium". Amongst others, he was at one time in partnership with E W Pugin. "In 1834 Hansom founded the *Builder* newspaper, but was compelled to retire from the enterprise owing to insufficient capital. Between 1854 and 1879 he devoted himself to architecture, designing and erecting a great number of important buildings, private and public, including churches, schools and convents for the Roman Catholic church to which he belonged. Buildings from his designs are scattered all over the United Kingdom, and were even erected in Australia and South America" (Encyclopaedia Britannica). He died in 1882.

Photographs: A C W Merrick.

Situation: Upper North Street, Newtownards; td, Corporation North; District Council, Ards; Grid ref. J 490 744.

References: Listed B (24/9/10). O'Laverty, 'Down and Connor', II, 1880, p 148; 'Encyclopaedia Britannica', 11th ed., 1911, XII, p 931; IB, LIV, 1912, p 352; Ware, ' Dictionary of British architects', 1967, p 116; W Edgar, in 'Further glimpses of the Ards', 1980, pp 55-56; Hitchcock 'Architecture', 1987, p 110; 'Solemn dedication of St Patrick's Church, Newtownards', 1988, passim; Williams, 'Architecture in Ireland', 1994, p 111; Walker, 'Historic Ulster churches', 2000, p 128.

Presbyterian Church, Hillhall, Lisburn

44. An interesting contrast with Castlereagh Presbyterian Church (34), and equally good in quite a different way: John Millar and Vincent Craig seem centuries apart; yet only seventy years, the span of Queen Victoria's reign, divide the two architects.

The listers say: "One of the finest architectural compositions in the Arts and Crafts style to be found in the province. The design is complete, incorporating the interior furnishings and fittings in the overall concept". Hugh Dixon evidently thought this church to be by Blackwood and Jury: he writes "The Art Nouveau style is also to be found in more rural settings. Hill Hall Presbyterian church is one of a number in the very personal style created by Blackwood and Jury in the decade before the Great War. Striving for originality, the architects produce a series of unusual shapes and improbable construction details; the style even extends to the design of the gate posts. In a similar if rather more restrained manner Vincent Craig produced designs for Presbyterian churches at Portstewart (1902) and Ballywatt, near Portrush (1910-11)".

Williams and Walker follow Dixon in attributing it to Blackwood and Jury, "at their most experimental, juxtaposing Gothic Revival and Art Nouveau. The belfry has a pyramidal roof interpenetrated by four corner piers that wittily repeat the piers of the entrance gates" - surely it is more likely to be the other way round? -"The main stylistic influence is Charles Harrison Townsend. Stained glass by Ward and Partners". Walker calls it "this rather jaunty church". Paul Larmour correctly asserts that the author of Hillhall was Vincent Craig: this is confirmed by the Belfast Newsletter in 1902, which expressly states "Mr Vincent Craig FRIBA architect, 5 Lombard Street, Belfast, prepared the plans and specification and superintended

the erection of the church"; and adds, somewhat mysteriously, "The design is early English Gothic modified, in character perhaps approaching the English mountain church".

Larmour comments "The influence of Art Nouveau, that most vital new style that swept much of Europe at the time, was slight in Irish church architecture, and was largely confined to Non-Conformist work in Ulster. Its effect can be seen in the quirky forms and decorative details of the Presbyterian churches at Hillhall, Co Down (1901), by Vincent Craig ... and Letterkenny (1907), by Blackwood & Jury, two of the main exponents of a style that was never very widespread elsewhere in Ireland". The foundation stone was laid, according to a plaque in the porch which does not record the name of the architect, in December 1901; the completed church was opened in September 1902. It cost £2,250, of which £1,000 had still to be raised. At the opening service, the Moderator is reported as saying "The house combined the maximum accommodation and comfort with the minimum of expenditure, and yet everything was done without crimping and in admirable taste." Unfortunately most of the records of the congregation were destroyed in a malicious fire in the church hall at the rear in November 1999.

A large, T-shaped church, walls of lime-roughcast with Bath stone trim: a surprising pattern of alternating chequers of the two materials in the tympanum of the gable. Entrance through porch at the foot of the square tower, which is topped by curious corner turrets and a pyramidal slated roof terminating in a weathercock on a pole; clock on two sides superimposed on the louvres of the belfry openings of the tower. "The roofs are covered with blue slates, having horizontal bands of sea-green slates at intervals" (Belfast Newsletter). The principal roof-ridge is shared by a delightfully oriental ventilator lantern and a rather obtrusive (perhaps later?) chimney-stack. Very deliberately angled buttresses to each side of the nave, and to the gable-end of each transept, give an unexpectedly battered (in the technical architectural sense) air to the exterior.

Internally, light and airy; the very wide roof-span clad in panels of sheeted pine; raked pine pews; panelled organ-loft above the low, octagonal and tapering pulpit, the 'east' wall otherwise being blank. At the hour of morning service, the church is flooded with sunlight through the great broad five-light 'west' window above the gallery. This, and the other cusped windows, grouped sometimes in threes, sometimes in fives, contain Art Nouveau glass of great elegance and restraint; the finest windows being

unquestionably those in the gable walls of the two transepts.

Although, externally, a bit grey and dreary on a dull day, this church on closer examination is of astonishing quality: beautifully detailed inside and out; the interior, one of the finest spaces in the county.

Photographs: A C W Merrick (see also colour illus. 7).

Situation: Off Hillhall Road, about 1 mile from Lisburn; td, Lisnatrunk; District Council, Lisburn; Grid ref. J 288 643.

References: Listed B+ (19/9/27). Plaques inside church; 'Belfast Newsletter', September 1902; Dixon, 'Introduction', UAHS, 1975, p 76; Williams, 'Architecture in Ireland', 1994, p 106; P Larmour, in 'Twentieth century architecture, Ireland', 1997, pp 59-60; Walker, 'Historic Ulster churches', 2000, p 150; information from minister and elder.

St Columbcille's (R C) Church, Holywood

45. A strange, but on the whole successful, admixture of 1890s tower and 1990s church: the tower and spire, very tall, slim, and distinguished, by Mortimer Thompson, architect; the circular church, with its conical copper roof and central lantern, by Rooney and McConville, Belfast.

This church was originally the child of that most eminent of local historians, Monsignor O'Laverty, author of the invaluable, five-volume, history of the Diocese of Down and Connor, parish priest of Holywood. "It was when standing at the ruined altar of Iona, whilst delivering a lecture, explanatory of the ancient abbey-church, to a company of tourists, who had gone on an excursion from Portrush, that the parish priest vowed to dedicate, under the invocation of St. Columbkille, the parish church of Holywood; the erection of which he then contemplated. The announcement of this resolve was received with three enthusiastic cheers by the audience, nearly all of whom

were Protestants" (O'Laverty). Alas, the church, designed by Timothy Hevey (who had been an assistant with Pugin & Ashlin) and consecrated by Bishop Dorrian in 1874, was burned to the ground, possibly as an act of arson on the part of Protestant bigots, in the early hours of 25 August 1989. Only the later tower and spire survived, surprisingly quite unscathed. It was resolved not to try to reproduce the "full-blooded French Gothic" church which Hevey had built, but to rebuild in the contemporary style. The result is striking.

The remaining tower and spire, designed and completed by Hevey's younger partner, Mortimer Thompson, in 1891, after Hevey's death in 1878, are now free-standing, of pale brown and pink sandstone, with a string-course on which is incised, on four sides, the legend *Have mercy O Lord on the soul of Patrick Reed / by whose bequest this tower was completed 1890 / The church of Saint*

Columbkille dedicated June 14th 1874 / New church built and tower restored 1993. In fact, the rededication was on 28 May 1995.

The new church was very much the creature of Father Stewart, Parish Priest, who was anxious that the arts should be applied creatively so as to educate and instruct. It has low walls of similar stone to that of the tower; above them, wide curving stained-glass window strips; above that, a conical reddish-brown copper-clad roof rising to a central lantern which strives, not entirely successfully, to harmonise with the corner pinnacles of the adjacent spire. There are two monopitch up-stands, one housing the porch, the other a kind of side-chapel. Internally, the circular altar is placed on a circular plinth in the centre, surrounded by (unusually comfortable) curved and cushioned pews, all topped by the remarkable zig-zag pattern of the wood-panelled ceiling. The glass in the side-chapel is exceptionally colourful, and its iconography unusual:

it features an enormous peacock with swirling tail, and brilliantly-coloured large butterflies. What lesson are these gaudy creatures intended to inculcate? It is not self-evident, but Gordon Wheeler suggests that the peacock symbolises immortality, the butterflies the brevity of mortal life. All the stained glass was designed by Lua Breen, of Donegal; the altar, tabernacle, font, and various pieces of metalwork are by Richard King, of Dublin. The baptistry has a brass dove (presumably the Paraclete) perched on the edge of the font, and a pleasant mosaic backing by H McLain of Holywood.

Photographs: Now, A C W Merrick; as originally built, MBR.
Situation: 52 High Street, Holywood; td, Holywood; District Council, North Down; Grid ref. J 396 789.
References: Listed B+ (23/19/9) (tower and spire only). Datestones; O'Laverty, 'Down and Connor', II, 1880, p 212; Merrick, 'Buildings of Holywood', 1986, p 64; UA, May/June 1995, pp 6-7; file in MBR.

GRAND HOUSES

Music Room parquetry floor by John Ferguson, Mount Stewart, Greyabbey (53). Photograph: Christopher Hill, courtesy of the National Trust

GRAND HOUSES

It would have been convenient to subdivide this introduction into, the splendiferous houses of the aristocracy - the Lords Downshire, Dufferin, Londonderry, and Dunleath; the houses of their younger sons, or dower houses, Glenganagh (55), Bangor Castle (64); the seats of old, but not ennobled, country gentry - Waringstown (46), Rosemount (47), Donaghadee (49), Portaferry (48); the seats of merchant princes - Carrowdore (54), Larchfield (61), Portavo (65), Straw Hill (63); the freak, Quintin Castle (58); and the homes of wealthy Belfast commuters - Craigavad House (62), Craigdarragh (60), Windrush (57), Tudor House (56), Glenmakieran (68), Rathmoyle (66), Ballyalloly (67), Guincho (69). But that, I fear, would be a great over-simplification: for upwards and downwards social mobility greatly distorts the pattern. Merchants turn into gentry, gentry turn into nobility, with surprising alacrity; and, of course, *vice versa*.

The grandest house in the county is unquestionably Hillsborough Castle (51), former seat of the greatest landowners in County Down, the Marquesses of Downshire; then of the Governors of Northern Ireland; today, of the Secretary of State for Northern Ireland . Yet the Hill family is not of exceptional antiquity: Sir Moses Hill first came to Ireland as a military man with the Earl of Essex in 1573; the Viscountcy of Hillsborough was created in 1717, the Marquessate of Downshire in 1789. As with almost all other Irish landed gentry, Mr Gladstone's Land Acts - quite literally - cut the ground from under their feet, and their power and influence in the county quickly disappeared. Hillsborough Castle now belongs to the Government.

The Dufferins of Clandeboye House (52) stem from one James Blackwood of Bangor, a Scotsman born in 1591. The Barony was created in 1800, just after the Act of Union; the Marquessate dates from 1888. The house still belongs to the family.

Alexander Stewart, a successful flax merchant, bought the manors of Comber and Newtownards in 1744, and built the first house at Mount Stewart (53). His son, Robert Stewart, was created Baron Londonderry in 1789; Viscount Castlereagh in 1795; Earl of Londonderry in 1796; and Marquess of Londonderry in 1816. The house now belongs to the National Trust, though Lady Mairi Bury still occupies an upstairs flat in it.

Andrew Mulholland of Springvale, builder of Ballywalter Park (59), was an exceptionally successful Belfast textile manufacturer - first of cotton, then of linen. His son John was created first Baron Dunleath in 1892. The house still belongs to his descendants.

Bernard Ward, of Castle Ward, settled in Ireland in 1570. Robert Ward, MP, was created Baron Bangor in 1770 and Viscount Bangor in 1781. Robert E Ward built Bangor Castle in 1852 with a view to outshining his cousins at Castleward: the house now belongs to, and constitutes the town hall of, North Down District Council.

It is unclear exactly when, or by whom, Glenganagh House, Groomsport, was built; but it served as a dower house for the widow of the first Lord Dufferin from around 1836 until her death in 1865, when the house was sold.

So much for the houses associated with the aristocracy. North County Down is rich also in the substantial houses of the country gentry, and of merchants who, on retirement, set themselves up as gentry: Warings, Savages, Nugents, Montgomerys, Mussendens, Delacherois, Kers. Only a handful of these houses - Waringstown House, the Manor House, Donaghadee, and Rosemount - are still owned and occupied by the descendants of their builders.

All these houses, no doubt, appeared at first as the rather vulgarly ostentatious displays of the *nouveaux riches* of the day. It is only in the course of my own lifetime that the Victorian and Edwardian mansions, and those of the inter-war years, built by the wealthy citizens of Belfast outside the city's boundaries, have come to have their architectural merits recognised. Of these, I have included a selection; but there are very many other examples which I have, equally deliberately, omitted. And I have omitted altogether the rash of enormous, sometimes apparently almost obscenely vulgar, mansions which have gone up in various parts of north County Down over the past three decades: perhaps it will be best to leave it to posterity to decide on their respective architectural merits and demerits.

Waringstown House

46. The front part of this important and interesting 17th-century house, originally of two storeys and attics with dormers, was built by William Waring in 1667; the front wall was raised a storey in brick, and returns and a rear free-standing tower were added in 1673-4. Very obligingly, he left "An estimate of the charge I was at in building my house, &c. 19 April 1673". The grand total, including both parts of the main house, bawn wall, stables, a cow house, and several low walls, came to £586 15 4. The entries include £6 to William Nues and Robert Read for making 6000 shingles; "the charge of shingling was £37 3 3"; 5000 laths cost £1, but "paid Joseph for plastering £7 12 0"; and, expensively, "For nails this year '74 and part '73, £13 15 7".

A report by Dr Philip Robinson in the Monuments and Buildings Record says "This elaborate oak butt-purlin roof of the late 17th century, without ridge purlin and with wind-braces, is one of only four such house roofs identified in Ulster. The others are at Springhill House (c 1680), Ardress House (c 1667) and ... New Row, Coleraine (c 1674). All of these belong to an English vernacular roof-carpentry tradition which appears to have been introduced to Ulster during the Plantations of the 17th century. While such roofs may not be exceptional in England, in Ulster their occurrence and survival is rare and historically significant". "The extension to the South wing ... also contains an oak, principal-rafter roof with butt purlins ... This extension ... contains an early brick hearth and ovens in its gable, and can be identified with a 'bake-house' commissioned to be built at Waringstown House by the Duke of Schomberg when he stayed there en route to the Boyne in 1690". "During the war of 1688, a party of the adherents of James II took possession of this house, which they garrisoned and retained until the arrival of Duke Schomberg,

in the following year, when they were driven out by that general, who slept here for two nights" (Lewis).

The Archaeological Survey of County Down provides an extensive (but, considering the complexity of the building, succinct) description of this very splendid house: "The house was built by William Waring in 1667 and was originally a symmetrical U-shaped building, with rear projecting wings, of two storeys with attics and cellars, reputedly built of boulders in clay mortar; it is now harled, with orange colour-wash ... The main E. front of the house is of" (six) "bays, with V-channelled long-and-short quoins and similar pilaster-strips to the central bay and is flanked by pavilions added in the 18th century ... with similar quoins. The main block has a ... modillioned cornice at attic level ... With two exceptions the windows are all sashed, having external shutters at ground floor; the central" (sandstone) "door is flanked by fluted pilasters, with moulded bases, rising to an entablature, broken forward with guttae at the extremities, which is surmounted by a triangular pediment; the door-surround is perhaps of the 18th century. The side elevations of the main block are in part gabled, and are provided each with a curvilinear and pedimented gablet, constructed of bricks ... which contains a square window with segmental head with plain imposts and keyblock. At the rear the wings are gabled ... with 19th century crow-stepping. In the 18th century," (but see Robinson above) "the S. wing was extended by an addition of two storeys, the gable of which has a brick chimney-stack, with dentilled offset and cornice, which is pierced by a semicircular-headed opening for a bell ... Internally the fittings are entirely 19th century; the flooring, of oak, is probably largely original. All window openings, of sashed type, are 18th century or later, save for two transomed and mullioned lights at first floor, opening to the re-entrant between the

wings, the ogee-moulded timber framing of which is in part original."

Harris reports, " The elegant Seat of this Family is at *Waringstown*; and their House, built on a rising Ground, commands the Prospect of a pleasant well improved Country". In 1834, Lieutenant Bennett of the Ordnance Survey says of Waringstown House that it is "a plain building erected in the year 1666 on the site of an old fort. The floors are of oak and pieces of oak were used instead of tiles for the roof but have this year (1834) been removed".

John O'Donovan called on the Rev. Holt Waring on 29th March, 1834, and got a somewhat mixed reception. "He lives in a castellated" (?) "house, erected in 1666, which presents an appearance of no inconsiderable importance ... At first he paid no attention but the most indifferent to me (the result in all probability of my weather-beaten appearance) ... I perceived immediately that his notions were Aristocratic, and that it was very probable I could get no good of him. So I told him in a few words what I was about; upon which he immediately changed his tone and countenance, and asked me would I take wine, &c ... Mr Waring is very proud of his Cromwellian dynasty (as he calls it) ... He spoke to me at full length about Irish forts; on the site of one of which, he says, his own mansion is erected ..."

Both Oram and Bence-Jones draw attention to the fact that Waringstown House is one of the earliest surviving unfortified country houses to be built in Ireland. Dr Craig writes "When we explain a bout of building fever by the advent of a stable regime we are apt to forget that stable regimes have sometimes been thought unstable at the time, and vice versa. The clearest expression which a building-owner can give to his estimate of danger and security is not to be found in plan-form, but in the treatment of that most critical region where the walls of his house meet the roof ... Richhill has Dutch-inspired curvilinear gables alternating with plain eaves: in other words, no possible provision for defence. Waringstown ... is now

three storeys high, but when first built was of two like Richhill, and still has Dutch gables on its flank-walls, so that the original termination is conjectural, but certainly did not give even such provision for defence as is afforded by a plain parapet. The plan of Waringstown has a deep indentation at the back: deeper and wider even than at Glinsk," (County Galway) "and the stacks are all on the outer walls as they are at Glinsk ... and nearly every house before them except Rathfarnham, Portumna and Raphoe. The timber eaves cornice with dormers above it is the *ne plus ultra* of indefensibility, and it, like the curvilinear gables, is of Dutch derivation, from van Campen by way of Hugh May and Sir Roger Pratt. Both ran their course at the same time, in the town as well as the country, and both in the end yielded to the parapet. A little after 1660 they were very up-to-date".

Lewis remarks, "The ancient name of this place was Clanconnel, which was changed into that by which it is at present known by Wm. Waring, who settled here in 1667 on lands purchased by him from the dragoons of Cromwell's army, who had received a grant of forfeited lands in this quarter. The new proprietor immediately built a large and elegant mansion, which is still the family seat ... Waringstown House, the mansion of the proprietor, is in the immediate vicinity of the town, surrounded by a demesne richly planted with ancient and flourishing forest-trees; the pleasure-grounds, gardens, and shrubberies are extensive, and kept in the best order". Lewis's comment on the grounds is confirmed by J R Ward in his additional Ordnance Survey memoir of the 1830s, where he writes "The ornamental ground is very tasteful. The flower garden is reckoned the best in the county".

". . . a fine demonstration of the merging of different traditions. The impressive symmetrical front, though simple in conception, has both the assurance of the classical tradition and the self-conscious character of designed architecture. By contrast, the side elevations have an agreeable jumble of Dutch and Scottish gables, with windows and chimneys varied in size and style. Here it is the natural growth of vernacular architecture which predominates, for the original thatching" (*sic:* but read shingles) "has been replaced by Welsh slates, the rendered walls of rubble and earth, bound with lime mortar, are perhaps the most typical features of Ulster's native building style" (Dixon). In fact, the lower part of "the front wall is certainly field boulders in clay mortar having some lime mixed with it but very little" (Oram). According to Bence-Jones; "the architect of both the house and the church is said to have been James Robb, chief mason of the King's Works in Ireland" - (Rolf Loeber, however, has shown conclusively that this personage was a figment of the fertile imagination of the late Colin Johnston Robb). "Tall C19 Tudor-Revival chimneys. Surprisingly, for so large a house, the walls are of rammed earth"- but this last statement is incorrect: the lower storeys are (as noted above) of fieldstone and clay, the top storey of brick, both harled over with pink-tinted roughcast.

This has become clear as the result of the very considerable restoration and stabilisation programme, carried out over a number of years, undertaken by the present owner - largely with his own hands, and with the help of a small band of devoted craftsmen; not always by entirely conventional conservation methods, but in general, very successful. A direct descendant of the original builder of the house, and grandson of the well-known broadcaster D G Waring, he inherited it from Margaret Waring, widow of Holt Waring, who had died in the last year of the first World War; she herself died only in 1968. On becoming owner on attaining the age of thirty, he found the house in very poor condition, little having been done to it, except to set a new slated roof above the original timbers (which, though cut, for the most part remain in place), since the 1920s. During his minority, the trustees of Mrs Waring's will felt constrained to sell a large part of the contents. But, with some courage, he has rebuilt crumbling walls; replaced the window-heads and repaired the original sashes; stripped all the walls, set them to rights, and re-harled them; as well as carefully replacing or repairing much interior woodwork which had been subjected to rot and woodworm, and re-assembling many timbers after repair - as in the staircase: though neither the great oak beams holding the house together, the butt-jointed roof-timbers, nor the original oak floor-boards in some of the rooms, required replacement. The results - not yet quite complete; attics and chimney-stacks still await attention - are highly creditable.

The demesne contains a number of subsidiary features of interest. The tower in the back yard; the pineapple-topped gate pillars; the little grotto built of massive flints from Magheralin; and the rare carriage-wash, are all worthy of note; not to mention the Rev. Holt Waring's workshop, including the original treadle lathe he used in carving the Jacobethan ornamentation of the parish church (15) in the 1830s. The village, perhaps regrettably, has grown out of all recognition; too many of its buildings have been spoiled; but the house, set back from the main street, next to the church, amidst ancient trees behind its lawn, remains one of the finest buildings in the county; and indeed, in Ireland.

Photographs: A C W Merrick (see also colour illus. 13). Drawing: Rev. Holt Waring.
Situation: 15 Banbridge Road, Waringstown; td, Magherana; District Council, Craigavon; Grid ref. J 104 549.
References: Listed A (14/6/1). Waring papers, in house; Harris, 'County of Down', 1744, p 105; G A Bennett, OSM, 1834, and J R Ward, nd, Down, III, pp 58,60; O'Donovan, 'Letters ... 1834', 2001, p 21; Lewis, 1837, I, p 466, II, pp 674, 675; ASCD, 1966, pp 437-438; Oram, 'Craigavon', UAHS, 1971, Pt II, p 6; Dixon, 'Introduction', UAHS, 1975, pp vi, vii; Bence-Jones, 'Burke's guide', 1978, p 282; Loeber, 'Biographical dictionary', 1981, p 88; Craig, 'Architecture of Ireland', 1982, pp 142-143; Jupp, 'Heritage gardens inventory', 1992, D/067; Dr P Robinson, undated interim report in MBR; information from owner, and from R Oram.

Rosemount (or Greyabbey House), Greyabbey

47. The name 'Rosemount' is of considerable antiquity: the house, somewhat less so. William Montgomery, in 1683, wrote of "a double roofed house and a baron and fower flankers, with bakeing and brewing houses, stables and other needful office houses; they are built after the forraigne and English manner; with outer and inner courts walled about, and surrounded wh pleasant gardens, orchards, meadows and pasture inclosures under view of ye said house called Rosemount, from wh ye mannor taketh name. The same was finished by ... Sir James Ao Domi 1634". In 1701, William added to his account, "only some small convenient additions of buildings and orchards are made by ye sd William, and improved lately by his sd son James". Harris, in 1744, says "*Rosemount* was the Mansion-house of Sir *James Mountgomery*" (second son of the first Viscount Montgomery of Newtownards) "... He built here a noble House, and stately Out-offices (which were afterwards burned down *Ann*. 1695) and laid out fine Gardens behind it, executed in the Form of a regular Fortification, some Bastions of which are yet to be seen. However, the present worthy Proprietor" (William Montgomery) "... has built a neat and commodious House with handsome Offices, on part of the Site of the former House, and has laid out his Gardens and Out-grounds about it in elegant Taste". It seems that this too burned down and was subsequently replaced. The date of rebuilding is specified by E G S Reilly in 1842, only eighty years after the event, who says categorically, "William Montgomery succeeded his father William at Grey Abbey in 1755. He began to build a new house there in 1762, which is the present one".

James Boswell, on 2 May 1769, visited an "excellent house of Mr Montgomery's own planning, and not yet finished" at Rosemount, which dates it pretty securely. It is shown on Taylor and Skinner's road-book of 1778. The prudent authors of the Archaeological Survey of County Down say "The present house may have been started before 1744 but certainly no definite features earlier than c. 1760-70 are now recognisable". Lieutenant Tucker of the Ordnance Survey, writing around 1835, says "The house consists of 2-storeys", (?) "is commodious, built of the common stone of the county and roughcast, and commands good views across Lough Strangford. The demesne is small, prettily broken and well wooded". The house was valued at £95 6 9 in 1837; in the 1860s, first at £60, then (at an unspecified date) at £80; then, in 1870, at £85; a modest enough figure for such an imposing house; perhaps it was not always kept in very good order.

The main block is of three storeys on basement, six bays wide on the entrance front, rendered in Roman cement, with hipped roof, massive chimney-stacks, and balustrade above modillioned cornice. Externally, everything is quite severely classical, with Georgian-glazed windows in lugged architraves: except for the ground-floor windows in the canted bay at the centre of the garden front, and the charming octangular room within, which are, unexpectedly, Gothick. As Bence-Jones remarks, "This unusual appearance of Gothic in the garden front of an otherwise Classical c18 house would suggest the influence of Castleward, at the opposite corner of Strangford Lough; it seems likely that the Gothic work dates from post 1782, when William Montgomery's son, Rev Hugh Montgomery, married a daughter of 1st Viscount Bangor, whose home was Castleward". The detailing of the exterior and interior of the Gothic windows at Rosemount is considerably more assured than that at Castleward, as is the glazing-pattern; the ceiling rose at Rosemount incorporates both the Montgomery and Ward coats of arms;

and there is a fundamental similarity, which suggests that the same architect might have been responsible for both. But who? No convincing evidence has yet come to light. There have been tentative suggestions that it might have been a pupil of Carr of York; but no proof. I remain of the opinion, which I have long held, that the answer is likely to be found in Bath: resort of many members of the Irish gentry in the late 18th century.

Rosemount is full of puzzles, conundrums, and enigmas for the architectural historian: it has been much altered over the years, there has been much repartitioning, and most of the records were destroyed in a fire at the agent's house. Where was the original front door? Where the original main staircase? Just how many times has it been altered? There are, at the least, five different styles of plasterwork: the elegant Dublin-style mid-18th-century ceiling in the sitting-room; the Gothick work in the octagon room; the heavy triglyphs and guttae of the cornice in the best bedroom; the Greek-key pattern mouldings which some are tempted to ascribe to the Morrisons; and the curious Prince of Wales feathers and floral ornament in the arched alcove of the dining room. There is also, on the top floor, a most enigmatic half ceiling-rose - cut in two by a stud wall - incorporating a pulley, possibly to carry a chandelier: in which case, the bedroom floor must be later, and the front hall ought to be below; but then, that is contradicted by the apparent date of the plasterwork there. The joinery is equally ambiguous. There are shouldered doorcases on the first floor in the oldest parts of the house, very similar to those in Leslie Hill, County Antrim, of 1758; but the woodwork on the ground floor seems later. There is some evidence that the entrance to the demesne, the stables, and presumably to the house, was originally by way of the gate and lodge beside the ruins of the Abbey (5). But then, the gate-lodge seems to be rather later?

The house is also unusual in the addition of segmental-bowed ends. The Archaeological Survey of County Down says that square wings were there in the late 18th century, only the bows being added in the mid 19th century, probably in the late 1840s. That to the right contains the hall and a very grand new staircase, with fine brass balusters like those at the Argory, County Armagh, opening off a most uncommon diagonally-placed entrance porch; at the other end, the answering diagonal feature is a dummy. "The wings were provided with a cornice and balustrade, the main block was similarly embellished and the house was rendered and dressed in Roman cement, with lead and slated roofs" (Archaeological Survey). All this seems to have been to the designs of James Sands, architect, who furnished an estimate of £2,850 for "sundry works" in 1846, and five of whose drawings survive in the house, bearing the same date, and not all executed. "The single-storey block on the garden front to the south-west side of the house dates from 1895. It was built as a smoking room, and to provide space for gentlemen guests to bathe and change from their shooting or hunting clothes before they came into the drawing rooms" (Mussen). There are good stables and subsidiary buildings; in particular, a nice little stone game-larder with its original iron hanging-hooks all barbarously complete.

Photographs: A C W Merrick (see also colour illus. 18).
Situation: Off the Square, Greyabbey; td, Rosemount; District Council, North Down; Grid ref. J 582 679.
References: Listed A (24/ 4/ 17). VAL 1B/33, p 188, VAL 2B/3/4 p 39, VAL 12B/23/16A-F, in PRONI; Montgomery, Description of the ... Ards, 1701, in his 'Montgomery manuscripts', 1830, p 308; Harris, 'County of Down', 1744, p 48; Boswell, journals, 2 May 1769, in 'Boswell in search of a wife', 1957, p 212; Taylor and Skinner, 'Roads', 1778, p10; H Tucker, OSM, nd, (? 1835); 'Down', II, p 69; Reilly, 'Family of Montgomery', 1842, p 63; Bence-Jones, 'Burke's guide', 1978, p 146; ASCD, 1966, pp 171, 263, 405-408; Jupp, 'Heritage gardens inventory', 1992, D/051; J Mussen, in CL, 10 October, 1997, p 46.

Portaferry House

48. Portaferry House is an imposing, but not an especially handsome, building externally, but it has much fine interior detailing, and stands on a magnificent site. Its exact date is unknown, but the central block is thought to have been built by Andrew Savage, a former officer in the Spanish army, who died in 1773 (see Portaferry Market House, 145). He chose the site "because it was near a beautiful spring-well up to which, from the old castle," at the waterside in Portaferry, " he used to walk every morning to drink a cup of its clear pure water". His son, Patrick Savage, "in the winter of 1788-9 ... was dining in company with Mr Robert Stewart of Mount Stewart and Mr Montgomery of Grey Abbey (probably at a meeting of the Down Hunt), when a wager of 500 guineas was laid by Mr Savage that a peerage would be conferred upon Mr Stewart within twelve months. Mr Stewart was raised to the peerage as Baron Londonderry on 20th September, 1789; and Patrick Savage spent the money he won from him in helping to build the west wing (or 'Library Wing') of Portaferry House" (Malcomson).

This lucky win appears to have under-written the employment of Charles Lilley, a Dublin timber merchant, carpenter and architect, much patronised by Lord Downshire; also busy on canal bridges for the Board of Ordnance. Three surviving drawings are signed and dated 1789 and 1790, but how much work was carried out to his plans is unclear. In 1814 Patrick engaged William Farrell to complete the building, following Lilley's designs quite closely. Work began in March 1818, and was completed when on 23 October 1820 Farrell authorised payment of the final account totalling £7,410 4 1, including his fee, calculated at 5% on £7,000. Farrell's earlier estimate of £8,666 19 0 for his alternative Gothick design of 1814, with turrets and buttresses, seems to have been declined.

He was still corresponding with Andrew Nugent (then staying with Mr Hall at Narrow Water) regarding the mantelpieces, and a proposed colonnade at the front of the house, in February 1821: "In the sketch of the colonnade you will observe that the spacing of the columns is not all alike, from the irregularity of the old front it is impossible to make them so, I have brought them as near as possible, the difference will not be very observable, particularly as the approach does not come up direct in front, the effect is more perceptible in the drawing than it will be in execution ... " However, this scheme was never executed.

The family historian, George Savage-Armstrong, just says: "In the year 1790 the House was enlarged by the addition of the Library (or Western) Wing, and was completed, as it now stands early in the Nineteenth Century ... In the pleasure-grounds stands an interesting old sun-dial, bearing the name and date 'Patrick Savage, Esq., 1773' " (apparently this has now migrated to nearby Ballywhite, seat of the Brownlow family).

The Savage family descended from Sir William Savage, "one of the twenty-two knights who accompanied Sir John de Courcy in the invasion of Ulster in AD 1177" (Savage-Armstrong). In 1812, Colonel Andrew Savage "assumed by Royal Warrant ... in accordance with his great-uncle's Will, the name and arms of Nugent"; giving rise to the local gibe "Old Savage, New Gent". Sadly, after the family had lived for over seven hundred years in Portaferry, Roland Nugent's two sons were both killed in the second World War, the elder aged 22 in Tunisia in 1941, the younger aged only 19 in Italy in 1942, both as lieutenants in their father's regiment, the Grenadier Guards. Their father was eventually Speaker of the Northern Ireland Senate at Stormont, and created a baronet in 1961, but died without an heir to the title in 1962. His widow, crippled by arthritis, left the house in 1977 to live in Mrs O'Hara's nursing home at Quintin Castle (58). The estate was purchased in 1986 by the present owner, who has devoted much energy to restoring and modernising it, very successfully; it is now in excellent order. In the process he has sub-divided the house into four connected, but separate, dwellings. However, one of the plaster cornices remains incomplete, to commemorate a difference of opinion with the Department of the Environment over grants: as evidenced by an elegant framed testimonial.

The house appears in Taylor and Skinner's road book of 1778. G Scott, of the Ordnance Survey, merely observes, around 1832, "Portaferry House (the residence of Andrew Nugent Esquire) is an extremely fine house situated near the centre of an extensive and well planted demesne. The ground is prettily ornamented and shows considerable taste": and adds "The only magistrate residing near Portaferry is Mr Nugent, who is respected by the people ... Mr Nugent settles all offences that is in his power at his own residence. This part of the country is extremely quiet part of the country". Samuel Lewis, in 1837, writes of "Portaferry House, the residence of Andrew Nugent Esq., a large and handsome building, finely situated in an extensive and highly ornamented demesne". The Parliamentary Gazetteer is, like other critics, more enthusiastic about the grounds than about the house: "The demesne of Portaferry-house, the seat of A. Nugent, Esq., the proprietor of the town and of an adjacent estate of upwards of 5,000 Conyngham acres, occupies comparatively elevated ground on the immediate shores of the Channel, and in the immediate northern vicinity of the town, but within the parish of Ardguin; it includes 300 acres of woodland, and comprises a series of charming close views; and it commands, on one side, an animated home prospect, southward to the town of Portaferry, and over the lough to the village of Strangford - and a brilliant far-away prospect over the North Channel and the seaboard of Down, to Scotland, the Isle of Man, and the mountains of Mourne". Bence-Jones has not much to add: "A dignified house of 1821, by William Farrell, who apparently worked on a plan produced by Charles Lilley 1790; the 3 storey centre of the house being very possibly a 3 storey block of 1770s ... The house stands in beautiful parkland overlooking the entrance to Strangford Lough".

The late Dudley Waterman provided a thorough, but very dry, architectural description in the Archaeological Survey of County Down; and illustrated many of the finest interior details. Much the best, most lucid, and most sympathetic account of Portaferry House is to be found in Dick Oram's authoritative article in the admirable Journal of the Upper Ards Historical Society.

Portaferry House is unusual in that the central five bays are three-storey over basement, the projecting canted wings two-storey but under the same roof-line - the ceilings of the state rooms, and their windows, being much taller than those of the central block. The central windows in the main façade are triple; all the windows retain their Georgian glazing-bars, but Oram clearly demonstrates (and helpfully illustrates) the different profiles of the glazing-bars used at different dates:

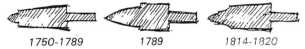

COMPARATIVE WINDOW GLAZING MOULDINGS FOR:-

1750-1789   1789   1814-1820

He adds "What we see today is the result of a number of building operations each carefully designed to give an overall appearance of unity". The roof is hipped; there are now two principal chimney-stacks, which appear to have been at some date cut down, instead of the four envisaged by Lilly; the walls, at one time creeper-covered, are coated in a kind of Roman cement; the porch, with its show of Ionic columns and pilasters, is evidently of about 1823, when four alternative (unsigned) designs were under consideration; there is an extensive single-storey service return. The house is said to have, on the second floor, the first flushing lavatory to be installed in Ireland: inscribed 'The Citadel'. The extensive cellars have splendid vaulted ornamental ceilings, and have been opened up by the removal of the earth banks outside their windows, originally contrived to prevent the servants from spying upon their betters.

Internally, Farrell substantially altered Lilley's layout. "In the centre of the house the old staircase was taken out and what had been the hall, the old stair and the drawing room were combined to form a large Reception Hall with a colonnaded screen; a new floor of 'scotch' stone was laid. The western wing lost its Venetian window and this room

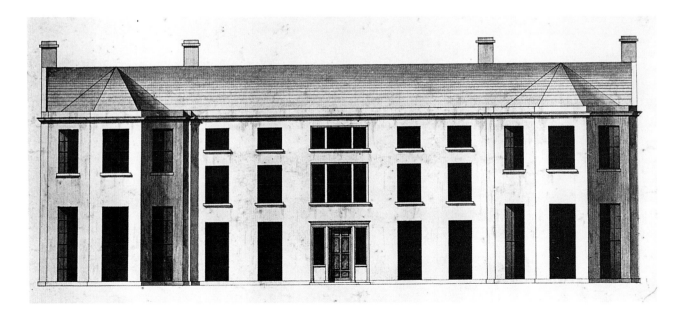

was made The Library ... The return was gutted and the eastern wall demolished and rebuilt a little further eastward increasing the space which was then filled by the new stone built cantilevered Grand Stairway. The stair is very beautiful and extremely elegant ... All the state rooms were replastered and embellished ... All the mahogany doors date from this period" (i.e. 1818 -1820 - Oram).

The interior is much more sophisticated than the exterior would lead one to expect. The anthemion detailing of the entablature above the Ionic colonnade in the hall is of surprising delicacy; as are the various ceiling and cornice details; and the mahogany doors, with roundels, not much inferior to those at Mount Stewart (53). It is odd, though, as Dick Oram remarks, that the opening from the front hall to the grand staircase remains quite plain and unornamented.

I first visited this house in 1956, at the request of Lord Antrim, soon after I had been appointed to the Northern Ireland Committee of the National Trust: Roland Nugent, then Minister of Finance in the government of Northern Ireland, was desirous of minimising his personal liability to death duties, and contemplated presenting the house to the Trust. After some hesitation, I advised that I thought the architectural merit of the house was not quite up to National Trust standards. To that view, I still, hesitantly, adhere; though I should now place a much higher value than I then did on the landscape quality of the demesne.

Photographs: A C W Merrick; MBR. Drawing, C Lilley, copy in MBR.
Situation: Off Kircubbin Road, Portaferry; td, Ballymurphy; District Council, Ards; Grid ref. J 592 517.
References: Listed B+ (24/1/105). D 552/A/3/2, D 552/B/3/4/1-25, D 552/A/6/4, and notes by Anthony Malcomson, all in PRONI; Taylor and Skinner, 'Roads', 1778, p 9; G Scott, OSM, nd, (? 1832), Down, II, p 14; Lewis, TD, 1837, II, p 464; PG, III, 1846, p 80; Savage-Armstrong, 'Savage family', 1906, p 359; ASCD, 1966, pp 379-381, and pls 169-173, 178,179,181; Bell, 'Portaferry & Strangford', UAHS, 1969, p 20; Bence-Jones, 'Burke's guide', 1978, p 232; R Oram, in JUAHS, XIII, 1989, pp 8 - 13; Jupp, 'Heritage gardens inventory', 1992, D/047; file in IAA; information from owner.

Manor House, Donaghadee

49. "The principal house of the town and home of the Delacherois family since the mid-18th century after the marriage in 1725 of Marie Angélique Delacherois with Thomas Montgomery, who later became 5th and last Earl of Mount Alexander" (Dixon). But, Gordon Wheeler asks, can this be quite right? Samuel Delacherois did not inherit from the last Countess of Mount Alexander until 1764; Daniel Delacherois came into possession of this portion of the Montgomery lands only in 1771; is it not more probable that he built the house thereafter? The Delacherois were Protestant refugees from France, of some distinction in their own country, and uncommonly successful as settlers in their new country.

In 1837, "The handsome residence of D. Delacherois, Esq., its proprietor" (Lewis). "House at corner of High Street and Manor Street, of two floors with cellars and attics; a rectangular block with square stair projection at rear fronting the High Street seems 18th century, probably before c. 1780; a large return wing with frontage with large canted bay window projection to Manor Street appears to be an enlargement of the early 19th century ... The elevation to High Street is six windows wide with off-centred door having side-lights and semi-circular arched fanlight; the entrance is fronted by an open timber porch with a pair of fluted Doric-like columns and respondent pilasters supporting a full entablature with triglyphed frieze; this porch is probably c.1800. The stair is of about the same date or somewhat earlier and rises to attic level; it has a wreathed mahogany handrail, turned and moulded

balusters placed two to each tread, and fluted blocks planted on the face of the strings" (Archaeological Survey of County Down).

In itself a somewhat unexciting building, but very important to the streetscape of central Donaghadee: two-storey, roughcast but creeper-covered, set back just a little way from the street-line. As Dixon says, "As a piece of sculpture, the house moulds the street corner with uncluttered assurance, having enough garden to allow privacy, and not too much to suggest withdrawal from the life of the town" (a very shrewd description). The grey nonentity of the façade is redeemed by the white-painted porch and canary-yellow door (though the yellow paint-brush seems to have strayed a little). The loss of its former neighbouring dower-house - Manor Lodge in Manor Street - is to be lamented; despite proposals for restoration, now demolished and subject to current redevelopment. Although the principal (and very fine) stone-walled gardens are on the other side of High Street, there is an enclosed garden and an extensive yard at the rear: "The Manor House has the full range of outbuildings necessary to the proper running of a large Victorian household: coach houses, stables, harness room, loose box, byre, apple-house, wash house - even a mounting block and 'jox box' or doghouse. Chiefly dating from the 19th century, these are grouped irregularly round a pleasant courtyard with trees. The stable range has an important stucco façade along High Street with channelled rustication on the prominent coach arch bay, a rusticated surround to

the former office door, and blank window recesses articulating the wall surface. The wall rises to a parapet which is given extra height and elaboration where the wall breaks forward above the coach arch" (Dixon). All these

are undergoing, or about to undergo, energetic restoration: most encouraging.

Internally, "Beyond the front door an ample hall gives directly onto a returning staircase which disappears to the

heavens or the attics whichever are higher. And from the first half-landing, within view of the hall, another stair errs only slightly from the line of the first flight to give access to the upper rooms of the return. The woodwork of the carefully scaled ground- and first-floor rooms, ranging along the High Street front, appears to date from about 1800 with, in particular, the fan finishes to the window reveals relating to the work elsewhere of Francis Johnston and William Murray. The oldest parts of the building, possibly dating from the late 17th century, are the cellars which are extensive, flagged, much remodelled, but nowhere vaulted. The return south wing was remodelled about 1818, and at that time the ballroom with the canted end was built; this has elaborate (obviously principal reception room) woodwork and a grey marble mantelpiece ... A curved addition to the landing outside the ballroom door - to let crinolines pass each other - results in a charming latter-day bartizan bracketed out over the courtyard" (Dixon again, whose study of this interesting house was very conscientious). The former long drawing-room on the ground floor has now been returned to its original function as dining-room; the upstairs 'ballroom' is now the drawing-room, still with its fine woodwork, plasterwork, and detailing.

The house seems to have been enlarged around 1879, probably to accommodate the then Daniel de Lacherois's eight children: the valuation increased in that year from £44 to £60, at which figure it was to remain for many years. It contains a multitude of family memorabilia, including the water-colour sketch-books of Daniel Louis De la Cherois, a barrister who never practised but portrayed with a sharp eye all around him; and is still in the ownership and occupation of descendants of the Delacherois Crommelin family.

Photographs: A C W Merrick; family collection (The two little girls were to become Mrs Day and the late Mrs Stone).
Situation: High Street, Donaghadee; td, Town Parks; District Council, Ards; Grid ref. J 592 797.
References: Listed B (24/7/9); in conservation area. VAL 12B/23/13/ A, C, E, F, in PRONI; Lewis, TD, 1837, I, p 465; D L Delacherois, 19th-century sketchbooks, in the house; ASCD, 1966, p 396; Dixon, 'Donaghadee and Portpatrick', UAHS, 1977, p 16; Jupp, 'Heritage gardens inventory', 1992, D/102; information from owners.

11-13 The Square, and 35 Main Street, Hillsborough

50. This is one of the grander terraces of town houses in the province: although not quite as grand as some of those in Armagh, such as the houses at Charlemont Place on the Mall, which are of cut stone and rather later. Four big brick houses, all now nicely-painted, and all with original or restored Georgian glazing pattern, fanlights, and railings; their front windows looking out at the comings and goings of the denizens of Hillsborough Castle (51) and of the Court House (146); their back windows agreeably overlooking the grounds and lake of Hillsborough Castle: highly desirable residences. While these are undoubtedly very pleasant dwelling-houses, their interiors are not of any especial distinction.

The Archaeological Survey of County Down quotes a letter from his agent, John Gardner, to Lord Downshire of February 1779 in which he says "we are now clearing the ground for the four houses to be built in the square". The Survey then remarks, "Each house is a semi-basement and three floors high, built of brick in double Flemish bond, with brick eaves-cornice and slated roofs. Two houses are three windows wide, that on the W. is four windows wide and had a vehicle passage at ground floor, with semi-elliptical arched entrance; the entrance has been blocked and the passage converted to living accommodation. The central and E. houses have doors with plain architraves and imposts and semi-circular fanlights with moulded archivolt and key-block; the door of the W. house has been rebuilt; the windows are flat arched and sashed ... The terrace is extended on the E. by a house of equal depth but only two floors high over a semi-basement, which is

probably not much later than those described; it is brick built with moulded stone eaves-cornice and the roof is slated".

These grand houses step in a stately manner down quite a steep slope: the front door of the top house is reached by three granite steps, of the second by six, of the third by nine; that of the fourth house is round the corner, in a stuccoed extension, on Main Street. The top house is called Trevor House; No 12 is Blundell House; No 13 is Trumbull House: names all derived from those of members of Lord Downshire's family, not to say his own names: the seventh Marquess, who inherited in 1918, was resoundingly named Arthur Wills Percy Wellington Blundell Trumbull Sandys. No 35 Main Street is Hill House. The residents of these house have been numerous and distinguished: No 11 was for many years the grace-and-favour residence of Lord Downshire's secretary and his family, and was only sold in the 1970s; No 12 was occupied between 1969 and 1975 by Harvey Bicker, now of

Echo Hall, the Spa, my driver on many of my architectural explorations, then of Robin Eyre-Maunsell; No 13 was for many years home of the painter and poet Patric Stevenson; No 35 Main Street, was, in his latter years, home of the late Sir Ivan Ewart. Canon Barry does not seem to have thought either the buildings or their residents worth a mention in his book on Hillsborough, which first came out in 1962; indeed, when I wrote my own account in 1974, the buildings (if not the residents) were rather down at heel; today, all looks spick and span.

Photographs: A C W Merrick (see also colour illus. 19).
Situation: 11-13 The Square, and 35 Main Street, Hillsborough; td, Hillsborough; District Council, Lisburn; Grid ref. J 243 586.
References: Listed B+ (19//5/39,40,41,29); in conservation area. ASCD, 1966, p 415; Brett, 'Mid Down', UAHS, 1974, p 19; Pierce and Coey, 'Taken for granted', 1984, pp 138-139; information from Harvey Bicker.

Hillsborough Castle

51. Hillsborough Castle is by far the largest and grandest house in north County Down, as befits the seat of, in succession, the Marquesses of Downshire, the Governors of Northern Ireland, and its Secretaries of State. (It is not, and never was, in truth a castle: at most a château.) It also provides accommodation for the monarch, visiting royalty, ministers, and other important visitors; and serves as a sort of Government hospitality centre. Its exterior, however, is much less grand than its interior: unusually for an Irish house, its principal portico is on the garden, not the entrance, front, though the latter has a subsidiary portico of its own. Its close relationship to the village of Hillsborough is also somewhat unusual, and is best appreciated looking out from the front door, where the grand houses of the Square (50) face the Court House (146), between them framing an intimate view of the Georgian houses and shops in the Main Street, all seen across the sweep of front gravel and lawn and through the beautiful 18th-century wrought-iron screen brought here from Richhill Castle, County Armagh, in 1936. (Contrary to the views of purists, I advised some years ago that it be painted white; which it was, and very well it looked, I thought, against the dark-green foliage of the shrubbery beside the house; but others disagreed, and adopted the high ground that railings must *always* be painted black. At present, however, despite the recommendation of the village's Conservation Area booklet - "railings are best restricted to black or white" - they are painted dark blue! But Gordon Wheeler points out that, according to Parissien, late 18th-century external ironwork was painted 'bronze green' or possibly a dark 'invisible green'; sometimes an indigo blue). Bence-Jones suggests that the relationship between mansion and village "is reminiscent of the *Schlossplatz* in a small German capital"; Cornforth says it has the

"sophisticated urbanity of a prince's pocket-handkerchief capital, which is hard to parallel in towns in the British Isles".

The building's architectural history is very fully described in a 1993 publication of the Ulster Architectural Heritage Society of which the principal authors were W A Maguire and Peter Rankin, as well as in John Cornforth's two Country Life articles in 1994. I do not propose to repeat all their findings here, but shall confine myself to a very concise summary, plus some observations of my own on the position in 2000.

"A drawing by R. F. Brettingham was exhibited in the Royal Academy in 1797, the year when the house was 'completed'. Brettingham's contribution however was not to design the house from scratch but to re-vamp, add a library to and make more sophisticated and acceptable to late-eighteenth century metropolitan taste an earlier house by another hand. Though much extended after 1797, the house we see today is still in the understated French-derived style of Brettingham and the Henry Holland circle" (Rankin). Brettingham's work in the house may have commenced as early as 1788. In 1833, it was valued at exactly £100. Further alterations and additions had been carried out by Thomas Duff in the 1820s, and more were to be carried out by William Sands in the 1830s and 1840s: this last was responsible for the enormous Ionic portico at the centre of the long symmetrical seventeen-bay elevation on the south front. The end result is an elongated L-shaped plan, two storey for the principal rooms with their high ceilings, and three-storey for the offices, but under the same roof-line, the whole executed in sandstone ashlar, with numerous stone chimney-stacks; all windows having glazing-bars intact, but some now with the addition of somewhat unhappy protective screens. The

fabric of the house has been little changed since the Downshires decided to economise by reason of the effects of the Land Acts, and let it to Sir Thomas Dixon, who lived there until 1919. In 1910, it was valued at £260. In 1922, the Ministry of Works in London bought the Castle and grounds for the use of the first Governor of Northern Ireland. There was a nasty fire in 1934, and Rankin describes the resultant refurnishing as having "rather the feel of a Maples job-lot from the reproductions department"; my own comment, in 1974, was that "the opportunity was taken of inserting much formal, not to say regal, plasterwork in a style which might fittingly be described as 'Late (British) Empire'". Cornforth says that, after the fire, "the house was rebuilt ... in a weak, modernised Georgian style, with some details cribbed from Holkham but made official-looking - if not more convincing - with crowns and gilding".

In 1987, the then Secretary of State, Tom King, appointed a small committee, chaired by the late John Lewis-Crosby, formerly of the National Trust, to advise "on the structure, decoration, furnishing and maintenance of Hillsborough Castle and the planting and maintenance of its grounds". The Committee appointed John O'Connell, architect, of Dublin, as its consultant. Between 1987 and 1993, they gave the establishment a very thorough overhaul. "We concluded that, while the Castle must be furnished and decorated in a manner befitting its ceremonial purposes, it should in general reflect ... the appearance and atmosphere of an Irish country mansion. It should be friendly, easy to manage and maintain, and its furnishing should bear testimony to the continuity of its history" (Lewis-Crosby). "... it is a friendly house. A little bland perhaps, but not oppressive or severe or gloomy" (Rankin). On the whole, the committee's efforts have been very creditable; but, for my taste, there is a bit too much gilding, and rather too little Irish carved mahogany: in particular, I find the combination of ornate gilded

rococo overmantel mirror, gilded pelmets, gilded cornice decoration, and "half-wreath fillet in gilt cast resin, above dado, in corners and below the gilt cornice", against crimson damask walls, somewhat too rich a plum pudding for my taste. But on the whole, I like it very well: there is a cool spaciousness to the drawing-room and dining-room which is very pleasant, if not especially Irish; and the entrance hall, vestibules, ante-rooms and curving staircase with its cast-iron balusters have been very well handled. The throne room, however, as John Cornforth remarks, remains "the great weakness of the house. It was misconceived in 1934, because it is far too low to be a room of state ... Moreover, the lack of height is emphasised by the crowded design and big scale of the damask hangings".

The grounds and gardens, used regularly for garden parties, are very attractive and well-related to the house, apart from the fact that the lake and most of the demesne are invisible from it. There is a yew walk, planted with Florencecourt yews; a lime avenue; a pinetum; and an absolutely enormous rhododendron bush, said to be the largest in Europe. There is a small, late, circular rotunda or eye-catcher known as 'Lady Alice's Temple'; in 1974 I commented "An oddity, perhaps of about 1880, a domed circular tempietto constructed of ten cast-iron columns of some crudity; it looks better from a distance than close up". And, at the eastern corner of the south front of the house, there is my favourite in 1974 and still: "a charming tiny Greek Doric summer-house of cut stone, very simple in form but with admirably executed detailing - triglyphs, guttae and anthemia. It has a freshness and lightness that are missing in Hillsborough castle itself. Can it have been an integral part of the house, or could it be an earlier exercise in the Grecian style imported from elsewhere? If so, it would be of the greatest interest to trace its history and provenance" (Brett). It is shown on William Sands's drawing of about 1840.

The literary sources are somewhat mixed: the earlier

publications, such as the 19th-century editions of Wilson's Post-chaise Companion, the Ordnance Survey memoirs, and Lewis, are surprisingly reticent, and for that matter the later ones mostly seem to take the place for granted: nonetheless the passing references are too numerous to include any but the more interesting. The Parliamentary Gazetteer is one of them: "Criticism has remarked that the whole Downshire property, or at least that part of it which concentrates at Hillsborough, has been disposed with a view rather to the profitable results of a good estate, than to the fine decorations of a picturesque landscape, and, in particular, that the beauty of the town would have been greater if ... the mansion, with its picturesque home-view, had been removed a little farther from the public road. Yet whatever may be said about the demesne, the town acquires an almost aristocratic air from the proxim-

ity of the mansion, and seems as if caressed between the lawn and the park". Cornforth tellingly quotes from a visitor in 1849: "The Downshires live in regal state. Servants innumerable, silent as the grave, let you want for nothing, plate to no end. The cook shining, eating all day, dinners to twenty, hot luncheons, breakfasts beyond perfection, immense house, corridors and staircases and passages with bedrooms so luxuriously furnished, and all full" (Elizabeth Smith). I will conclude by quoting Rankin's summation: "There are no really big architectural moments in the interior. The principal rooms are comfortable and somewhat domestic, and to modern eyes well adapted as to orientation ... There is no grand conception of rooms enfilade. What we see now is very much in the public works or official embassy type of taste".

Drawing: W Sands, 1840, PRONI. Photographs: MBR.

Situation: The Square, Hillsborough; td, Small Park; District Council, Lisburn; Grid ref. J 241 586.

References: Listed B+ (19/5/76). (An interesting classification; if Government is prepared to spend as much money as it has done on a building in this category, should it not be prepared to spend far more on buildings classified A?). In conservation area. Numerous plans, drawings and papers in D 607, and D 671, VAL 1B/344B, p 26, VAL 12B/20/14D, p 123, all in PRONI; PG, II, 1846, p 298; ASCD, 1966, pp 414-415; Brett, 'Mid-Down', UAHS, 1974, pp 14-16; DoENI 'Hillsborough conservation area', 1976, passim; Bence-Jones, 'Burke's guide', 1978, p 152; Smith, 'Irish journals', 1980, pp 243-244; Barry, 'Hillsborough', 1982, passim; Jupp, 'Heritage gardens inventory', 1992, D/027; 'Hillsborough Castle', UAHS, 1993, passim; Parissien, 'Georgian house', 1995, pp 180-181; Howley, 'Follies and garden buildings', 1993, pp 30,117-118, 144; J Cornforth, in CL, 28 July 1994, pp 64-67, 4 August 1994, pp 48-51.

Clandeboye (formerly Ballyleidy) House, Bangor

52. Much has already been written about Clandeboye, and little remains to be added: but I can hardly leave it out. It is a house of strong character and great charm, rather than one of outstanding architectural merit. The original Ballyleidy, of around 1803, now much added to and altered internally, is attributed to a little-known architect named Robert Woodgate. He is said to have been originally a carpenter, and "entered Sir John Soane's office as an apprentice in June 1778 and received a small yearly salary until the expiration of his articles in November 1791". Soane employed him as job architect, or clerk of works, at Baronscourt, County Tyrone; in a letter of 11 May 1793, the Duke of Abercorn's agent described him as "a lad of much address, seldom embarrassed and full of resource". After the fire destroyed most of Soane's work at Baronscourt in 1796, Woodgate "established himself as an architect in Dublin", and in November 1799 wrote "a grateful letter to Soane, enclosing a plan and elevation of his first house" - probably Clandeboye; the drawings are lost. It may well have been his only work; he seems to have died young; for, though he is credited by the APSD with the design in 1810 of the Londonderry County Infirmary, Hugh Dixon notes that he was described as "the late" in 1805. Two drawings signed by Woodgate survive in the house: one, undated, the detail for a door; the other, dated 18 May 1804, a 'Plan for the finishing of the Hall and Staircase at Ballyleidy' - the signature rather shaky, so perhaps he was already ill.

Woodgate's original design was fairly conventional: an L-shaped two-storey house on the top of a knoll, with a pedimented portico at the centre of the south front, a segmental bow at the centre of the east front, and the services tucked away downhill to complete a square around a small central court. "The east front was of nine bays, the centre three in a shallow bow: the south front of seven, the five inner bays breaking forward with the three in the centre grouped under a slightly projecting pediment. The entrance was under a single-storey four-columned Doric portico below the pediment" (Rankin). The quoins,

string-course, eaves-course and trim are of cut sandstone, the walls plastered in cement render. The central pair of stone chimney-stacks seem to be the sole survivors of the earlier 17th-century house on the site. The single tremendous stack at the rear is later.

Bence-Jones suggests that Sir Richard Morrison had a hand in the house; but I see, and know of, no evidence for this. On the contrary, the basic layout closely resembles Soane's Baronscourt, which likewise "had a centre bowed drawing-room in a similar range of three reception rooms en suite" (Rankin). The ground-floor windows inset in arched recesses, the ceilings and covings of the principal rooms, and above all, the spandrels of the dome room with its central lantern, seem to me likely to be the work of a pupil of Soane.

The house was left in comparative peace for half a century; but, since Frederick, then fifth Baron, later to become first Marquess, came of age in 1847, its structure has been much added to and imbricated, though in essence not much changed. He employed many architects to draw up many ambitious plans - including Benjamin Ferrey, William Burn, and W H Lynn - and hankered after a fairy-tale castle, as Harold Nicolson remarks, "a fusion of François Premier and the Prince Consort"; but, despite a busy diplomatic career as Governor-General of Canada, ambassador to Russia, then the Porte, Viceroy of India, ambassador to Italy, then France, and ultimately Warden of the Cinque Ports; and despite the fabulous collection of mementos he brought back with him, he never succeeded in amassing sufficient money to build afresh.

His alterations to the house seem to have been almost all his own work, in later years with some assistance from W H Lynn. By far his most successful trick was turning the front hall into a delightful library, and creating a completely new entrance at a lower level at the back of the house. Until the addition of the new Doric porte-cochère in 1959, the front door was set in a blank wall, but for a smaller service door beside it. Inside, the outer hall contains a flight of steps flanked by curling-stones and antiquities of all kinds; "a mummy-case, two cannon, a

Burmese bell slung between carved figures, and ... a bear ... were artistically grouped; the wall behind them had been covered with wire netting on which were affixed dirks, daggers, cutlasses, pistols, lances, curling brooms, and a collection of those neat little fly-whisks with which the acolytes dust the high altar at St Peter's at Rome" (Nicolson). (I have often contemplated writing a monograph on the uses of wire netting in British domestic architecture). "The inner hall was larger and more deliberately baronial. It was lit by a vast Tudor window bearing the arms and quarterings of the Blackwoods and the Hamiltons ... On emerging from the inner hall ... one passed under the armorial window and found oneself in a narrow corridor lighted by a glass roof ... It was little more than six feet wide and, having remained a corridor for sufficient time to allow space for the door of the Museum on the right, it ceased to be a corridor and became a flight of steps, leading upwards under its skylight until it terminated in a small but elegant statue of Amen-Hetop II seated upon his throne. One then turned sharply to the right, opened a blue baize door on the left, and found oneself in the great well of the main staircase with the high vault of the gallery echoing beyond" (Nicolson again; and:) " The reasons for this strange structural confusion were partly the conformation of the site and partly Lord Dufferin's optimism regarding his own capacity as an architect ... His passion for glass roofing was in fact uncontrolled. He built a vast series of domestic offices - including gun-rooms, still-rooms, boot-rooms, servants' halls, housekeepers' rooms, stewards'-rooms, lamp-rooms, brushing-rooms, laundries, drying-rooms, storerooms and linen-rooms - which were concealed from the view of the approaching stranger by a high blank wall and which were illuminated, in the full spirit of the industrial revival, by windows in the roof". "Late in the century, presumably at the end of the 1880s and in the 1890s, Lord Dufferin transformed further back quarters on either side of his inner and outer halls into a large billiards room lined with book shelves, a table tennis room, a strong room, a museum room, a commodious gentlemen's cloakroom - plus a series of domestic offices. All were top-lit" (Rankin).

And, in the outer yard, he adapted former farm buildings to include a banqueting hall - of somewhat uncertain purpose (Harold Nicolson says "we were never quite certain what the banqueting hall was all about. It was a long high room with an arched roof, a platform at one end, a deal floor which squeaked at the slightest touch, and a long range of skylights. In those days it contained some models of sailing ships, the skull of a caribou and some stuffed beavers") - and a very remarkable chapel (Peter Rankin says, of 1862, but Mrs Armstrong, the curator, says, of 1898; the former was perhaps the date it was first conceived, 1 January 1898, certainly the date when it was ultimately consecrated), which was restored, and improved, in its centenary year, 1998. The exterior of the chapel is of random stone, with remarkably accomplished frilly carved Irish Gothic porch and windows; although the building is attributed to Lord Dufferin himself, he must surely have had help from W H Lynn with, at least, the detailing. The Dowager Lady Dufferin, in her contribution to Carey's history of Bangor parish of 1963, says that Lord Dufferin himself, "after 24 years of service abroad" ... "planned and supervised the alterations necessary to an old building, which had hitherto been used as a barn, into a chapel ... the door was copied from the door of an ancient Irish cathedral, while the windows and all the ornamentation were taken from correct architectural

drawings". The interior is airy, commodious, but (Nicolson again) "much to my mother's disquiet - had forgotten all about the Reformation and remembered much too much about Rome. Upon the damp plaster walls hung huge oil paintings in the style of Luini, heavily framed in gold ... And let into the wall to the left of the altar was a tablet of (there could be no doubt about it) heathen origin ... nor do I, to this day, know how my uncle justified the presence, in a place of Christian worship, of the cartouche and title of Tirhakah, King of Ethiopia".

This nice touch well exemplifies the endearing mixture of the sumptuous, the cosmopolitan and the dotty which characterises Clandeboye and its contents: it is magnificently Irish in its rich variety. Its present châteleine, and her late husband, have contributed notably to the collection, which includes works by (amongst many others) Duncan Grant and David Hockney, as well as by Lady Dufferin herself. They have also added a flight of steps on the south terrace using stone from the platform of the disused railway station at Strabane; Thomas Jackson's beehouse of 1828 from Altona; bee gardens, bear gardens, rhododendron gardens, and arboreta to add to the clumps, plantings, screens and lakes created by the first Marquess. As the present Lady Dufferin has written, Clandeboye "is a house of dreams and enchantment that fill my thoughts and, as I grow older, the pleasure of being part of it grows greater".

There are twelve excellent colour photographs of Clandeboye in Hugh Montgomery-Massingberd's Great Houses of Ireland.

Photographs: A C W Merrick.
Situation: Off Belfast Road, Bangor; td, Ballyleidy; District Council, North Down; Grid ref. J 475 794
References: Listed B+ (23/10/2); chapel B+ (23/10/5). VAL 12B/23/7A,7D,7G,8A,8B, in PRONI; APSD, VIII, 1892; Nicolson, 'Helen's Tower', 1937, passim; Dowager Lady Dufferin, in Carey, 'Abbey and parish of Bangor', 1963, pp 49-52; M Bence-Jones, in CL, October 1 and 8, 1970; 'Introduction to the Abercorn letters', 1972, p 181; Dixon, 'Soane and the Belfast Academical Institution', 1976, p 4; Bence-Jones, 'Burke's guide', 1978, p 83; 'Clandeboye', UAHS, 1985, passim; Jupp, 'Heritage gardens inventory' 1992, D/012; Montgomery-Massingberd and Sykes, 'Great houses of Ireland', 1999, pp 160-171; drawings and documents in Dufferin and Ava archive, Clandeboye, and in PRONI.

Mount Stewart, Greyabbey

53. In 1744, Alexander Stewart, a successful flax merchant who had married a rich wife, bought from Robert Colville the manors of Comber and Newtownards, including the property now known as Mount Stewart. Alexander lived at first in Newtownards, but soon built himself a house, which he called 'Mount Pleasant', on the present site on the shores of Strangford Lough. Daniel Beaufort, who visited it in 1808, described it as long and low and "all painted blue". After inheriting in 1781, Alexander's son, Robert, later first Marquess of Londonderry, added the Temple of the Winds (173) to the demesne and had James Wyatt draw up plans for remodelling Mount Pleasant: these were never carried out but, instead, a temporary timber wing was added to the west of the house. The expense of political advancement conflicted with the expense of building: "Stewart's father was required to spend £60,000 to win his son the seat" (in Parliament) "expenditure that involved selling off old family portraits and the curtailment of building plans for Mount Stewart; so that he 'lived the remainder of his valuable life in an old barn, with a few rooms added' " (Richey). In 1805, Robert Stewart, by then Earl of Londonderry, employed the fashionable London architect George Dance (1741 - 1825) to build him a new west wing for the now renamed 'Mount Stewart'. Sir Howard Colvin says "It is as a pioneer of neoclassicism that the younger Dance has his place in English architectural history ... In Newgate Prison he designed a monumental building of the first rank ... Sir John Soane was Dance's principal pupil ... Architecture was by no means Dance's only interest. He played well on the violin, flute and 'cello, and in later life spent much of his time making skilful but rather stereotyped pencil portraits of his contemporaries." According to Gervase Jackson-Stops,

"Dance is thought to have been the lover of Lord Londonderry's sister-in-law, Lady Elizabeth Pratt, with whom he came to Ireland in 1791 whilst her father, Lord Camden, was Lord Lieutenant. It is likely that he visited Mount Stewart at this date, and first discussed the possibility of alterations then". (It seems that the usually very reliable Jackson-Stops did not get this quite right; the visit took place in 1795, it was her brother, not her father, who was Lord Lieutenant - information from Mrs Jill Lever). Certainly, according to Colvin, "In about 1790 he made designs for the 1st Lord Camden for the layout of the Camden estate in Kentish Town, but after the building of Camden High Street this degenerated into haphazard development".

Recent research by Jill Lever, who is cataloguing Dance's drawings and correspondence in Sir John Soane's Museum, throws much new light on the history of Mount Stewart, and I am extremely grateful to her for letting me use her copies and notes. It seems that "about 1803 Lord Londonderry decided to enlarge the house and turned first to John Ferguson", the very skilled carpenter-turned-architect who had worked at the Temple of the Winds. (His talented near-contemporary in Belfast, Roger Mulholland, was also carpenter-turned-architect). However, Lord Londonderry's eldest son, Lord Castlereagh, found Ferguson's ideas altogether too rustic, and persuaded his father to seek advice from Dance. In an undated letter to Dance, the son writes: "we have succeeded in our first point namely knocking at Ferguson's next detestable plan and also in putting the business which I consider is most material in your hands". Dance responded at length in 1804 to Lord Londonderry, setting out his ideas: "the great point seems to me to be to form your entrance on the

East side because by that means you retain complete use and beauty of the Whole of the three rooms" ... "with respect to the Chimney under the window in the Music Room it is by no means an uncommon thing in this country but in France it has been very generally used for a Century past ... The reason for adopting it in the Music Room is obvious as the room cannot afford any other convenient and symmetrical situation". He then advises as to the proportions of the rooms and windows; and "I strongly recommend to make very large folding Doors so as occasionally to lay the three rooms into one", with detailed instructions. And: "It is better to avoid all Quoin stones or any dressings or Mouldings round the Windows, they by no means add any beauty to the work and always increase expense. The whole Masonry should be of one description ... I have proposed in my sketch to erect a Coach porch or Portico at the entrance wch is both ornamental & extremely convenient at night and bad weather to drive under" and just such a coach is nicely included in his drawing in Sir John Soane's Museum.

Lord Londonderry then sent Dance a survey elevation, presumably prepared by Ferguson, with some comments: "Before I had received your letter I had determined these two Points" (the height of the windows and storeys) "the blame or bad taste as to the Proportion of the Windows I must take upon myself for altho' the Builder wished to have made the Windows somewhat higher I would not hear of it ... I also decided on making the Bedchambers higher than you propose ... I make the walls very thick and substantial ... I mean this to be a permanent Dwelling which may be added to" ... "I wish to finish & compleat every Part of the New work in a Substantial, & neat plain manner; for which Reason, I shall certainly have the Porch of Free stone" ... "I have now Twelve Masons at work & the Building is going on so fast the sooner you can let me hear from you" (sc. "the better"). This is followed

by a sensible, if ill-spelled, letter from Ferguson to Lord Londonderry in London, this time dated 29 February 1804, enclosing a "Ruff Draft" of the entrance front: "I do think that the Columns Must have baces as it will in sum misure be a protection to the shaft from the Rubb of a Carride wheel ... I wish also that" (Mr Dance) "would have the goodness to give a Ruff Draught and Explanation of the foulding Doors as we Irish are so apt to blunder" - this last is either unexpected modesty on the part of so exceptionally talented a craftsman, or heavy sarcasm from a man now acting only as site architect. Jill Lever concludes that Dance must have sent drawings and instructions from London which were executed by Ferguson, for there is no record of Dance having returned to Ireland before 1815. On 14 March 1804, Dance had been paid £54 3 4 for his services, but just what services is not known.

In about 1832, Lieutenant Tucker of the Ordnance Survey remarked of Mount Stewart: "The house is plain and small for a nobleman's residence, consisting of 2-storeys, with a range of sleeping apartments on the ground floor which have been added to the house". The "sleeping apartments" were in fact part of the original early 18th-century house lying behind Dance's wing. The Ordnance Survey map of 1834 shows the old house covering a substantial area. In 1837, Samuel Lewis writes "Mount-Stewart, the splendid residence of the Marquess of Londonderry, is a spacious mansion, situated in an extensive demesne richly wooded and pleasingly diversified with water". The Parliamentary Gazetteer remarks in 1846: "The mansion combines some old masonry with comparatively modern architecture, and exhibits a style more Grecian than Roman, yet not strictly classical; and its apartments are numerous and splendid".

About 1835, the distinguished Dublin architect William Vitruvius Morrison was invited by the third Marquess to

prepare plans to knock down the old house, and greatly to enlarge Mount Stewart. As Jackson-Stops says, "As one of the younger exponents of the Greek Revival Morrison would certainly have respected the work of one of the acknowledged pioneers of Neo-Classicism, but his tactful treatment of Dance's work at Mount Stewart is nonetheless interesting ... Morrison repeated both the north and south elevations of Dance's building at the far east end of his new block. As a central feature on the north front he introduced a giant Ionic portico, wide enough to serve as a porte-cochère and with the columns raised on high pedestals ... As the smaller, one-storey porte-cochère, built by Dance on the north side of his west wing, was now redundant, Morrison replaced it with a tripartite bracketed window frame, echoing the 'Wyatt' window on the first floor above. A new loggia, supported by coupled Ionic columns was at the same time built in the centre of the long south front, further emphasised by a pediment over the three first floor windows ... The windows on the west front are narrower and set closer than those on the long fronts, and the masonry is more uniform in bond. But in both stages of the building the same dark grey local stone was used, with lighter dressings for the windows, string courses and pediments; in addition Morrison added a heavy balustrade all the way round the parapet (partly concealing the shallow-pitched roofs) so as to give a coherence to the design as a whole". In fact, the earlier stonework, with much galleting, is clearly distinguishable from the later work, though both are quite harmonious. Work seems not actually to have started before 1845, by which time Morrison was long dead. Between 1845 and 1849 expenditure of £19,175 was incurred, the work being supervised by a Newtownards builder named Charles Campbell, who left behind him a rather dubious reputation. His slightly later differences with Lady Londonderry at Garron Tower, County Antrim, are well documented. There seems no doubt, however, that Campbell was working to the plans supplied by Morrison.

Whilst all this may be accounted a considerable success, the result is rather confused: Mount Stewart's merits lie rather in its contents, its associations, its remarkable gardens, and the even more remarkable intricate relationship between garden exterior and floral interior, than in its architecture. Nonetheless, there is much of interest both in Dance's rooms and in Morrison's. Of the former, Jackson-Stops considers the staircase-hall the finest from a purely architectural point of view. "The staircase itself rises in a single central flight to a half landing, where it divides into two flights on the return walls reaching a gallery on the first floor ... The very broad shallow arch supporting this gallery and the similar one above helping to support the skylight dome are typical of Dance (as of the young Soane), and the gently curved indentations of the dome itself, giving it a shape rather like an umbrella, are reminiscent of his Council Chamber at the Guildhall in London built nearly thirty years earlier. The resulting interplay of curves, and the lightness of the whole effect, is far from the pomposity of much contemporary Neo-Classical architecture, and this delicacy is enhanced by the cast-iron balustrade ... and John Ferguson's handrail of mahogany inlaid with ebony". Above the half-landing hangs Stubbs's 'Hambletonian Rubbing Down', exhibited at the Royal Academy in 1800, the finest of all the treasures in the house.

The Music Room has a splendid parquetry floor, by John Ferguson (see illustration on page 75), matching that in the Temple of the Winds, and reflecting also the pattern of the ceiling: "Both floors are of oak and mahogany, with a central patera surrounded by a guilloche pattern and honeysuckle motifs, and radiating bog-fir boards of a beautiful mellow colour" (Jackson-Stops). It is the most elegant room in the house, with a triple window as adumbrated by Dance, lovely Adamesque shutters, horizontally sliding sashes, anthemion ornaments, beautifully inlaid double doors on three sides, and (perhaps later?) inlaid chair-rail and skirting-board; approximately as shown on Dance's drawings, though the ornaments and the door and window openings are somewhat different.

Dance's original 'study' (subsequently for a time the dining-room, then library, and now 'the Castlereagh Room') has intriguing book-presses and book-backed shutters, probably not original, but excellent of their kind. The library, later Lady Londonderry's sitting-room, also has interesting floor, shutters, and window reveals, carved by John Ferguson, "designed in a very individual manner with reeded panels decorated with rosettes, set in circles, ovals and ellipses. Ferguson's floor is again inlaid with oak, bog-fir, yew, holly and other woods - a rare feature in an Irish (or English) house of this date ... The delicate plasterwork of the cornice, and the rosette in the centre of the ceiling, are obviously by the same hand as the more elaborate ceiling in the Music Room next door" (Jackson-Stops).

Of the Morrisonian elements in the house, a number were (regrettably) altered in the 1920s, but the central hall is "one of William Vitruvius Morrison's most ambitious Classical interiors, in surprising contrast with the long, low proportions of the exterior, and with Dance's compact and homely rooms at the western end. Probably conceived during the period of partnership with his father, Sir Richard Morrison, it is reminiscent of the domed rotunda at Ballyfin in Co. Leix, their joint masterpiece of the 1820s ... From the entrance hall, the central door leads into a vast octagon with double pairs of Ionic columns painted to resemble dark green marble, and lit, through the well of the gallery, by a large dome. Beyond the columns either side are lateral extensions, also lit from above ... Like the famous gallery at Londonderry House in Park Lane, the room was probably intended for sculpture" (Jackson-Stops). The Irish Architectural Archive volume on the Morrisons says "Inside the house, the rectangular entrance hall leads, as at Ballyfin, into a vast two-storey top-lit hall, which has some affinities with Joseph Bonomi's recently completed gallery at Wynyard. This octagonal space, with a gallery running round it at first-floor level, is separated by double screens of Ionic columns from single-storey top-lit lobbies on both sides ... the upper level was completely remodelled after the First World War, when the balustrade and stained glass were replaced. On the far side of the hall, double doors lead into what was originally a two-storey top-lit saloon with a gallery supported on four columns; this room, which is behind the loggia on the south west front, was likewise altered after the First World War, when it was divided horizontally into a smoking room with a bedroom above".

The drawing room has been much altered over the years; it originally had two fireplaces, not one - the present mantelpiece came from the ground floor of the Temple of the Winds when the room was remodelled in the 1920s - but the screen of Ionic columns at each end lend it much dignity. The chapel is a surprising space, with curving front and back walls, capable of seating a congregation of 80 souls - it was largely remodelled in the 1860s, when the (slightly garish?) polychrome ceiling was inserted; it

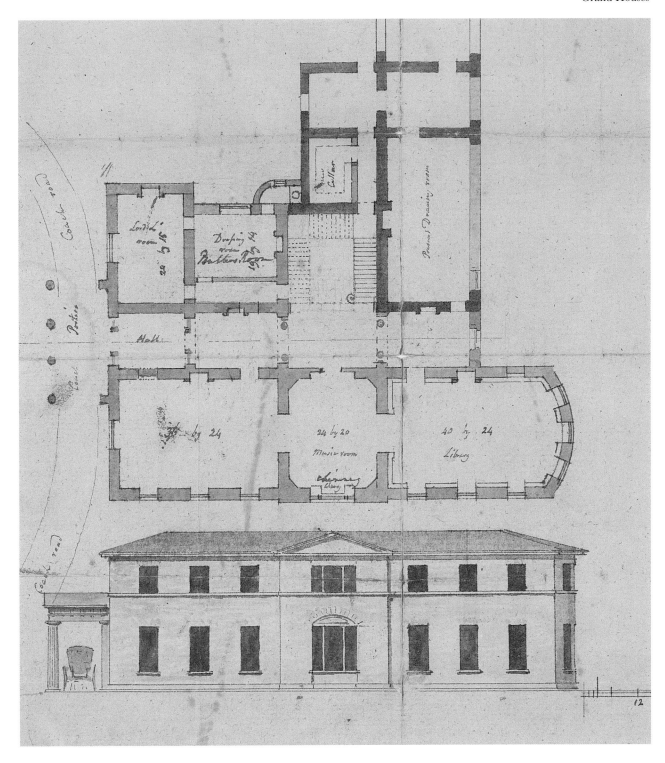

contains a very colourful set of heraldic banners and a number of suitable paintings, some copies, some not; the walls are blue, the carpet dark red, as is the velvet reredos above the altar. Rich and interesting, but by no means a typical Church of Ireland place of worship - the reason for this being, presumably, an indulgent redecoration after Elizabeth, 4th Marchioness, converted to Roman Catholicism in 1855 - the same lady who, as dowager, paid for Newtownards Roman Catholic Church (43).

Taken all in all, Mount Stewart, if not quite an architectural masterpiece, is a fascinating house: especially considered in relation to its gardens, and the contributions of Edith Lady Londonderry to the overall impression. I am certain the National Trust was right to take it on, and owes gratitude to Lady Mairi Bury for offering it, with an endowment, in 1977.

Photographs: A C W Merrick (see also colour illus. 15). Drawing: G Dance, 1804, courtesy of the Trustees of Sir John Soane's Museum (see also colour illus. 12).

Situation: Off the Newtownards - Portaferry Road on the north-east shore of Strangford Lough; td, Mount Stewart; District Council, Ards; Grid ref. J 552 697.

References: Listed A (24/4/52). D3/9/1a-d, and D3/9/1-5, in Sir John Soane's Museum; D 654/112/7, in PRONI; Lt Tucker, OSM, nd, (? 1832), Down, II, p 69; OS map, 1834; Lewis, TD, 1837, I, p 674; J Morrison, 'Life of the late William Vitruvius Morrison, of Dublin, architect', in 'Quarterly papers on architecture', I, 1844, passim; PG, II, 1846, p 808; C Hussey, in CL, 5 Oct 1935, pp 357-362; 'ASCD', 1966, pp 374-376; G Jackson-Stops, in CL, 6,13 March, 1980 pp 646-9, 754-758; 'Architecture of R and W V Morrison', IAA, 1989, pp 132-134; Jupp, 'Heritage gardens inventory', 1992, D/037; Colvin, 'Dictionary', 1995, pp 288-292; Brett, 'Buildings of County Antrim', 1996, p 107; G Jackson-Stops, NT guidebook, 1997, passim; Montgomery-Massingberd and Sykes, 'Great houses of Ireland', 1999, pp 198-207; R Richey, unpublished Ph D thesis, QUB, 2000, p 296.

Carrowdore Castle, Millisle

54. An inscribed stone over the entrance proclaims *Nicholas de la Cherois Crommelin /Built this Castle AD 1818.* Mr Kertland of the Ordnance Survey, writing in 1837, says: "Carrowdore Castle, the residence of Nicholas Delacherois Crommelin Esquire, is situated in the townland of Ballyrawer. It is a fine and capacious building of imposing proportions and bold and effective design, but has an unfinished appearance arising from its being built partly from brick and partly from stone and having no external plastering. As a piece of architecture, it has had to contend with the difficulties arising from the combination of the military characteristics of a fortification with the large windows of a modern dwelling house; but on the whole it is a very fine building and very ornamental to the surrounding country. The quantity of planting about it is small and by no means proportioned to itself ... The present building has been erected within the last 20 years".

Bence-Jones describes it as "A Georgian Gothic castle built 1818 by Nicholas de la Cherois-Crommelin. 3 storey; 4 bay front with 4 slender polygonal turrets; Gothic portico. Round tower at one end. Very graceful Gothic plaster work fretting on hall ceiling". The listers just say "3-storey castle house in a Gothic style with deep-set basement and with towered gatehouse to stable yard and gazebo in boundary wall". There is a surprisingly complete account of this house in the Archaeological Survey of County Down: "House built 1818, of three storeys with cellars, facing N.; it is of rectangular plan with central stair projection at rear

and large attached circular tower of four floors on the S.W. It is constructed of rubble and brick with sandstone dressings and has slated roofs. At the angles of the main block are turrets, of square plan to first floor level and semi-octagonal above, with additional turrets to the front elevation which is three bays wide. The central bay is two windows wide, the side bays a single window; the windows are flat-arched and dressed in brick. The central entrance is framed by a pointed opening with moulded surround and is fronted by a porch and approached by steps ... The porch is of wrought sandstone, consisting of three arched bays and single return bays, with intermediate and angle buttresses which have tapering pinnacles rising above a cornice and battlemented parapet". . . "Internally there is a central hall and stair-hall flanked on each side by a pair of rooms ... The decoration of the main rooms is derived from both classic and Gothic sources. The cornices and ceiling borders are generally detailed in the classical manner" ... "The stable-yard S. of the house has a gatehouse contemporary with the main building".

Suzie Pack-Beresford, historian of Carrowdore, says "Nicholas ... married in 1810. After the death of his father in 1816, they moved to Carrowdore and by early 1818 had commenced the building of the castle. Previously there had been a farmhouse on the site which Nicholas' father had used only occasionally, apparently adding to it from time to time 'simply to make it habitable as a bathing-lodge or place for receiving his rents during his occasional visits' ...

By the spring of 1820, the castle was apparently sufficiently advanced to permit them to occupy a few rooms, but sadly a few days after they moved in Mrs de la Cherois-Crommelin died soon after giving birth to a son."

In his notes of June 1977, Hugh Dixon says "For the site of his new house Mr Crommelin chose a piece of rising land, then, no doubt, bare of trees like much of the parish still remains, now surrounded by mature plantings giving the house at once shelter and framed views of the countryside and the sea beyond. The choice of the castle style is predictable, though the precise idiom - a combination of symmetrical castle front but with a great tower dominating a rear corner of the house - reflects the arrival of John Nash's picturesque compositions at Killymoon, Cookstown, and (perhaps with more relevance in view of the Crommelins' Co Antrim connections) at Kilwaughter above Larne, and Shane's Castle by Randalstown. The architect is unknown but a strong contender must be J B Keane whose northern houses include Necarne at Irvinestown which, like Carrowdore, combines castle-Gothic outside with classical interiors. The romanticism of the style is extended with great conviction into the outbuildings by the use of garden 'bawn' walls, a 'flanker' summer house, and a stable yard with a great pointed archway beneath a tall tower, bearing with pardonable deceit the date '1690'".

J B Keane? Perhaps; but I wonder. It bears no resemblance whatever to his work at Lisanoure, County Antrim, of 1829; and not really very much to his work at Necarne, County Tyrone, of 1833; both a decade later. On the other hand, whilst certainly there is no direct evidence, I came to think, on the basis of photographs, that there was a definite resemblance to the Morrisons' Ballyheigue Castle, County Kerry, of about 1809: to a slightly lesser extent, to their Castle Richard, County Waterford, built before 1819; and to their Castle Freke, County Cork, started about 1815. I also took the plaster dove in the hall ceiling as corroboration, since the bird appears again in the ceiling of the octagon bedroom of Glenarm Castle, certainly by William Morrison, completed in 1824 - another County Antrim connection. So I would, fairly tentatively, have voted for an attribution of Carrowdore Castle to either Richard, or William Vitruvius, Morrison; or the two in concert. But I am over-ruled by my friend Dr McParland, to whose expertise I am never ashamed to defer. Having examined the photographs, he writes "I have to say I'm not fully satisfied by either the Keane or Morrison attribution. It's very (too?) early for Keane, and I don't think that the Morrisons would have left the C 18 style sash windows: the three parallels you draw - with Ballyheigue, Castle Freke & Castle Richard - have traceried, or casement, or mullioned windows. The gothic tracery on the stucco ceiling of the hall (surrounding the bird) is too 'thin' for Morrison: even Borriss, which is thin enough in the gothic stucco line, is meatier than this. And even our bird doesn't help since I don't think it is a Morrisonian dove. If it is, it's acting badly out of character, clutching that thunderbolt!" And, when I obtained access to the interior, I found that he had been quite right: the 'dove' turned out to be an eagle the size of a turkey! So the authorship of Carrowdore, like that of Quintin Castle (58), remains up in the air.

The exterior has very considerable charm and character, although, as Mr Kertland noted in 1837, the mixture of mellow brickwork and rubblestone is disconcerting: only the pointed-arch porch is of cutstone. The most attractive feature is the tower giving access to the stable yard, which is itself neatly kept, whitewashed, and home to the present owner's racehorses. The house, however, has for the most part stood empty since 1988, except for a couple of rooms adjoining the curious modern sun-parlour added at the rear, which are used temporarily by the adjacent Strangford Integrated School.

Nicholas de Lacherois Crommelin senior (1783-1863), who built the castle, incurred enormous debts in trying, vainly, to develop the family's property at Newtown Crommelin, County Antrim: so much so, that "Towards the end of 1847 it was found that all these purchases and speculations had so much embarrassed his affairs that it was considered advisable not only to sell a considerable portion of his property, but also to leave Carrowdore Castle as a residence. Mr Crommelin himself then retired to live at Cushendun where he possessed a small romantic abode only accessible through an entrance cave". In 1847, "his father's removal to the Caves occasioned his son's return to Carrowdore Castle" (M Crommelin): the first son to do so being Samuel, inventor of 'Carrowdore Cigarettes', with (at first) his brother Nicholas de Lacherois Crommelin junior who unwisely quarrelled with his brother-in-law John Mulholland (later first Lord Dunleath) of the York Street Flax Spinning Company and also went to live at Cushendun. Nicholas junior, too, made unwise investments, and was actually declared bankrupt in 1868; notwithstanding which, he went to live in some style at Blackheath, near London. By 1875, the castle was occupied by Samuel and his family, and valued at £55, then £60, at which figure it remained well into the 20th century. The youngest brother, Frederick Armand, last of the

Crommelins to live at Carrowdore, seems to have inherited it in 1886, and to have died himself aged only 32 in 1902, when a sale of the contents was held. The place was leased by the Hon. Somerset Ward, formerly of Isle O'Valla House, Strangford; who was succeeded by a Major Workman. Subsequently, the castle was acquired in 1931 by a Mr McNeill; it then passed to Mr George Kinnaird, "who carried out extensive renovations". I used as an adolescent to visit there - below stairs, as a friend was courting the cook. It was then acquired by Dunsmuir and Pearl Mitchell, formerly of Rathmoyle (66); and in 1978 by the present owner. It is said that, like the Mitchells before them, the present owner and his late wife were much troubled by the ghost of a female Crommelin, presumably Elizabeth (daughter of Lord Ventry) who, as recounted, had died in childbirth in 1820; so in 1988 they built a large and palatial modern house in the ample demesne, into which they removed. The old house is beginning to deteriorate, and its longer-term future must be at some risk.

Photographs: A C W Merrick.
Situation: On outskirts of Carrowdore village; td, Ballyrawer; District Council, Ards; Grid ref. J 589 731.
References: Listed B+ (24/5/1). Inscription on building; VAL 1B/32, p 84, VAL 12B/23/10A - E, in PRONI; M M Kertland, OSM, 1837, Down, II, p 49; Lewis, TD, 1837, I, p 465; Bence-Jones, 'Burke's guide', 1978, p 59; ASCD, 1966, pp 355-356; H Dixon, notes in MBR, 15 June 1977; 'Architecture of R and W V Morrison', IAA, 1989, pp 20, 58, 69; M Crommelin, typescript formerly in possession of the late Mrs Stone, of Donaghadee, chapters X, XIII; Jupp, 'Heritage gardens inventory', 1992, D/083; Pack-Beresford, 'Christ Church, Carrowdore', 1994, p 42; Brett, 'Five big houses', 1997, pp 41-45; letter of 16 April 2000 from E McParland to author; information from owner.

Glenganagh, Groomsport

55. In appearance, a large L-shaped two-storey roughcast Regency mansion, standing back behind a very high sea-wall and lawn, amid woodlands, looking out over Ballyholme Bay to the mouth of Belfast Lough. It is on the borderline between the grander kind of middling house, and the more middling kind of grand house: but because of its wooded demesne ("the shady copses of Glengannagh" - Praeger), its extensive out-buildings and farms, its relationship to the rocky headland of Bally-macormick Point, and the fact that it has belonged to the same family for well over a century, I classify it as a Grand House.

The front facing the sea contains three large triple windows, Georgian glazed, and is plain but handsome. The entrance front is very different, with Tudoresque stone doorcase and windows, dripstones, and lozenge-shaped chimney-stacks disposed in twos, three, and a foursome. There are two excellent cast-iron conservatories, one at each end of this façade, linked by a sort of glass-roofed iron colonnade, all painted green and topped by pretty

cresting; in surprisingly good order on a site so exposed to the sea air. Major internal alterations were carried out between 1911 and 1916: the inner and outer hall and dining-room were panelled in the Edwardian manner, a canted stone bay window in Jacobean style was added to the dining-room, and a large new panelled and top-lit square stairwell and staircase inserted at the centre of the house, with a gallery round the upper level serving the bedrooms. These alterations were carried out under the supervision of James Hanna, architect, who had put up the gate lodge a few years before. It is unclear whether the massive cut-stone archway dividing the inner from the outer hall was also his work, or earlier. He seems to have made no material changes to the exterior.

There was probably an earlier house on this site which was incorporated into its successor, since the walls of the large drawing-room are thicker than the others. It appears as 'Glengannah' on an Admiralty chart in the house, compiled evidently in 1831, and on the Ordnance Survey map of 1833, as also in the Valuation book of 1835, but it is

probably at least fifteen years earlier, perhaps more. It did not form part of the Dufferin estate earlier, but it provided a dower house for Anne Dorothea (daughter of John Foster, Lord Oriel), whose husband, Sir James Blackwood, had succeeded to his mother's barony of Dufferin and Clandeboye in 1808. He died in 1836, and around then she moved into Glengannah, where she lived on until her death at the age of 93 in 1865. She appears to have been a formidable lady, a notable gardener (Lord Dufferin's rent books show that he expended the large sum of £31. 7. 9 on her garden in 1865-6), and a lady of the highest moral principles; who was irreverently known as 'Anna of Glengannah', and who heartily disapproved of the frivolous Helen Sheridan (of Helen's Tower), wife of the 4th Baron: who evidently reciprocated the dislike. In 1835, the Valuation book records "Lady Dufferin's house and offices, valued at £25. 6. 0, in category 1A, measuring 56 feet 6 inches by 26 feet by 18 feet high". Improvements must have been made over the next few years, for the valuation crept up from £25, to £30, to £38. It is unclear whether the house was originally built as a seaside bathing-lodge, or as a dower house, and by whom: since it was not on Hamilton land, it may have been bought ready-built for Anna, there having been already a Dufferin dower-house (now demolished), at Conlig.

Knox says, "Glenghanna, near Groomsport, was the residence of the late Baroness Dufferin, but it is at present occupied by Mr. Andrew Cowan, formerly of Ballylintogh House, near Hillsborough". In 1871, six years after her death, her name was struck out from the Valuation book and that of Andrew Cowan, a Belfast linen merchant, substituted. In 1880, his name in turn was struck out, and the owner was shown as Samuel Kingan: great changes must

have been made, for the value leaped up to £60. 5. 0 ; and in 1883, to £65. 5. 0, at which figure it remained until 1916, when it leaped up again to £110. Samuel Kingan JP, in whose family - my first cousins - it remains, had been a partner in J & T Sinclair, bacon merchants, of Tomb Street, Belfast. The firm was a very prosperous one, with a sister concern in Chicago, and Samuel Kingan "expended vast sums in ornamenting the place" and adding the "vineries, fernery and conservatories heated on the most approved principles" (Lyttle). On Samuel's death in 1911, the place passed to his sons (my uncles) Willie and Tom; but family history relates that the major alterations carried out at this time were instigated by their energetic sister Elsie, later Mrs Done.

For family reasons, I spent many holidays here during the war. And here, in 1944, my aunt used to line up the family on the drawing-room hearth-rug on Sunday evenings: my cousins and I were expected to stand to attention while, after the nine o'clock news, the national anthems of all the Allies - by then, a very long list - were played over the wireless. And here, on the lawn, I remember vividly the taste of my first post-war banana.

Photograph: A C W Merrick.
Situation: 39 Bangor Road, Groomsport; td, Ballymacormick; District Council, North Down; Grid ref. J 528 829.
References: Listed B (23/1/1). VAL 1B/ 31, p 84, VAL 2B/3/1C, p 28, VAL 12B/23/7A, D, G, and VAL 12B/23/8B, in PRONI; OS map, 1833; Knox, 'County Down', 1875, p 545; Lyttle, 'Bangor season', 1885, p 39; Praeger, 'BCDR. Official Guide to County Down', 1898, p 91; Jupp, 'Heritage gardens inventory', 1992, D/126; Dean, 'Gate lodges', UAHS, 1994, p 77; Patton, 'Bangor', UAHS, 1999, p 18; notes by Denis Mayne in MBR; information from Lola Armstrong, curator, Clandeboye, from Ian Wilson, and from owners.

Tudor House and Tudor Hall, Holywood

56. "'Tudor Houses', a prominent feature in the picturesque entrance to Holywood from the North East ... They consist of two separate buildings, each containing two mansions which have been built in the Tudor style of architecture from which they derive their name. The cost of their erection was upward of £6,000. The proprietor of these is the enterprising merchant of Belfast, Henry Murney of High Street" (Kelly, 1850). (Murney is also described as "the snuff and tobacco king"). On the staircase landing of Tudor House, there is a stained glass window inscribed 'Tudor House. HM. 1848'. He and his family have expansive memorials inside the old Priory Church (6).

Merrick says that these houses were built in 1849 - "Located on an escarpment overlooking very spacious and wooded grounds that swept right down to the road, they enjoyed a superb vista of the Lough. It is a matter of considerable regret that so much of the woodland and the little gate-lodge with the castellated entrance gates to the demesne were lost when the private housing estate was built in 1970. Tudor House is a fine example of the fully-fledged neo-Elizabethan style of architecture and the roof-line which is alive with chimneys and gables looks most impressive as it rears above the surrounding trees". The listers are markedly less enthusiastic: they award Nos 17/19

Bangor Road (I think, Nos 4 and 6, Tudor Park, but it is hard to be sure: the numbering seems to have changed, perhaps more than once) a grudging B1, with the brusque comment "2-storey block of 2 houses with Tudor influence in style - mid-19th century"; and a similar description and classification to Nos 21/23 Bangor Road (I think Nos 3 and 5, Tudor Park, next door) - though in my view the latter are much inferior.

Although I have learned from bitter experience to beware of attributions unsupported by documentary evidence, I felt at first sure that Tudor House, and Tudor Hall, with their inimitable chimney-stack details, gables, and cylindrical pinnacles on every gable and gablet, were by the irrepressible John Millar; they resemble so closely his documented villas at Old Quay Road, Marino (107), and are so unlike the work of anyone else. Having now seen the interiors, I am not so sure: the Tudoresque halls and staircases could be his, but the very florid ceiling roses and cornices throughout the ground floor rooms do not at all look like Millar's work.

This is a splendid great thumping pair of tall, mock-Elizabethan, stucco semi-detached houses, two-storey-and-attic, the dormers with ornate bargeboards, quoins, dripstones, and all the Tudorbethan trimmings, No 6 well painted in pale brown; its other half, rather more seedy at present, but still fine despite the rather obtrusive conservatory added in the 1930s. Externally, Tudor House, facing north and west, getting the morning sun, would appear to be the grander of the two; but maps disclose that the two houses are divided, not along the centre-line of the block, but in such a way that Tudor House is the narrower of the two - Tudor Hall, facing north and east, so getting the evening sun, is considerably the larger and grander of the pair. Each house is extraordinarily high, long, and thin, consisting of little more than one room and a corridor on each side of the spine wall. Of the two, Tudor House has been much less altered over the years than Tudor Hall: its marble mantelpieces and above all its remarkable staircase, with fancy ironwork banisters in a style foreshadowing Art Nouveau, are all intact. Although said to have been originally semi-detached, there used to be a connecting arch and doorway between the two houses, on the first floor, so that at some date, this must have been used as a single enormous dwelling; but the opening, it seems, was blocked up after a severe fire in 1907 in which two members of the Murney family perished.

The other pair (Nos 3 and 5, Tudor Park) are three-storey, with very tall pointed gables, of multi-coloured patchy stucco: with plain rectangular chimney-stacks, quite lacking in the bravado and panache of Millar's work.

I think that these are certainly by some lesser mortal; unless, perhaps, Mr Murney's money ran out before Millar could complete the second block. Both buildings were the subject of extensive, expensive, and co-ordinated repairs between 1989 and 1992.

Tudor House was valued at £52, occupied until 1925 by Annette Gardiner, and from 1926 until the 1950s by William Dunn, grandfather and father of the present owner; the latter, in my young days, the last Chairman of Holywood Borough Council. It is said that the house was requisitioned to provide billets for troops during the second World War, and various initials carved into the woodwork appear to bear witness to this. Its other half was valued at £54, and occupied by Thomas Orr; later bought by John Irvine, then by the present owner. The two, lesser, neighbouring houses were valued at £45 each. It is a pity that the grounds were invaded in 1970 by so many red-brick villas and bungalows, though their design (by Robert McKinstry) is quite inoffensive.

Photographs: A C W Merrick.
Situation: 4, 6 Tudor Park, Bangor Road, Holywood; td, Holywood; District Council, North Down; Grid ref. J 402 793.
References: Listed B1 (23/20/18a and b). VAL 12B/17/10F, G, in PRONI; Kelly, 'Holywood', 1850, p 61; Merrick, 'Buildings of Holywood', 1986, p 57; files in MBR; information from owners.

Windrush House (formerly Ardville), Marino, Cultra, Holywood

57. A very grand house indeed, looking out from the top of a slope across its lawn, and through its fine trees, to Belfast Lough, with its great bow, topped by a curly parapet, framed in Ionic columns and pilasters. Exceptionally well-painted stucco; quoins; five-bay; semi-Regency glazing pattern; good chimney-stacks and pots. Everything is in excellent order, inside and out, though there have been various discreet additions and extensions. Not earlier than 1834: Tony Merrick points out that a careful comparison of the 1834 and 1858 Ordnance Survey maps indicates that Ardville was a replacement for an earlier group of buildings looking very much like a farm. A planning submission of 1984 in Monuments and Buildings Record, in preparation for an appeal which was not pursued, says "Between 1834 and 1856 the principal apartments of Ardville were remodelled and a new classical façade was added to what had previously been the north-west side of the house. The design is classical in its symmetry and detailing. Two features make it of particular interest. Externally the large segmental bow form of the central bay with engaged columns is unusual. The only other building in Ulster with this feature is Castle Coole. Internally the stairway and hall are conceived on a very grand scale and are beautifully detailed. Windrush is well-proportioned and clearly the design of an architect. From the styling and date it could be the work of either Charles Lanyon or Thomas Jackson". But it would not altogether have surprised me to learn that this, like Marino Villas (107), just across the road, was in fact the work of John Millar; before he had abandoned the classical style for his crockety neo-Elizabethan manner, he had displayed a considerable predilection for the curvaceous volutes of the Ionic capital, in the portico of Castlereagh Presbyterian Church (34) of 1834, and the interior of his Portaferry Presbyterian

Church (37), of 1841, though, as Gordon Wheeler points out, the segmental-headed windows are not in his style.

However, the evidence from the deeds and documents, and from local knowledge, seems to suggest a date for the remodelling of around 1860. In 1830, a lease for ever of three acres to the Rev. Henry Wallace (of Holywood, Presbyterian minister) had imposed upon him the obligation to build one or more houses within three years at a cost of at least £300. In 1852, presumably having complied with the covenant, he sold the principal part to James Lennon ("a prosperous ship's chandler and manufacturer of rope and canvas at premises in Corporation Square Belfast: he was also a ship-owner"- Merrick) for £350. In 1871, the place was bought by James Barbour for £2637; he was "a wealthy engineer and iron-founder of the firm of Combe, Barbour & Combe who ran the Falls Foundry in North Howard Street" (Merrick again). To him is attributed by tradition the construction of the bowed façade, which he required to house his seven sons (and one daughter); but this oral tradition is not confirmed by the entry in the 1862 Valuation book - see below.

The interior of Windrush is as grand as the exterior: an ornate porch, at the side, gives access to a tremendous two-storey top-lit front hall, with a screen of Tuscan columns, and very solid staircase with pierced wooden banister panels. Off this are three very large and splendid rooms, north-facing but all with magnificent views over the sea - sitting-room, drawing-room with its great bow, and dining-room - with fine coving and ceiling plasterwork. Members of the Barbour family lived on here until 1907, when the house was sold to William McMullan. In 1936, it was bought by Mr Garrod, the headmaster of the Royal Belfast Academical Institution; in 1942, divided into flats and let parts furnished, parts unfurnished; and in

1943, bought from Mr Garrod by Ralph Gordon Cully, merchant, of Belfast, who soon thereafter proceeded to carve the house into three separate dwellings. In 1966, Windrush was bought by a Mr Frank Lamont, of the linen family, who emigrated to Australia in 1979 since when it has changed hands twice.

The 1984 planning submission continues: "The original house Ardville has been sub-divided into three units, Windrush, Ardreagh, and a reduced Ardville. The original house faced south-west towards Old Quay Road and the entrance is still on that façade. The remodelling turned the house to face north-west looking across landscaped gardens. Later the dwelling was sub-divided with the main front apartments forming Windrush House and the rest of the main house becoming a much reduced and more modest Ardville. These dwellings are shown on the map as 33 and 31 Old Quay Road respectively. Later the servants' quarters, a two-storey structure to the rear of the original house, were hived off to form a third dwelling now known as Ardreagh (40 Farmhill Road)". The present Ardville is a lower two-storey house, of stucco painted black and white, with Regency glazing-pattern in the upstairs windows; probably the house originally built by the Rev. Henry Wallace about 1833; but considerably altered over the years: it seems to have changed hands very frequently.

Ardreagh is a very much smaller house carved out of the rear quarters of the main house, for which it provided laundry and servants' bedrooms. It is at right angles to

Farmhill Road and has a large garden. The original relationship of the three houses is now difficult to disentangle.

The house now known as Windrush was first, apparently, occupied in 1849 by Theodore Bozi, a linen merchant who was also consul for Spain and Portugal (Merrick). By 1862, it was valued at the formidable figure of £110. A pencilled plan in the margin of the Valuation book, and the notes "large sheet-glass windows all through - projecting front with pillars and pilasters. A very elegant house"; and: "A very fine house in excellent repair"; would seem to dispose of the suggestion that rebuilding post-dates 1870. My own conjecture is that the exterior of Windrush is earlier, but that the interior was extensively revamped around 1870, judging from the style of mantelpieces, cornices, ceiling roses, the pierced banister panels, and other internal details. It is a matter of some regret that the original house has been carved into three, for it must originally have been one of the finest mansions on either side of Belfast Lough. But it is still a little-known and most impressive establishment.

Photographs: A C W Merrick.
Situation: 31 and 33 Old Quay Road, and 40 Farmhill Road, Cultra; td, Ballycultra; District Council, North Down; Grid ref. J 408 800.
References: Listed - Windrush and Ardville B1, Ardreagh B (all 23/18/40). VAL 1B/318; VAL 2B/3/182, p 29; VAL 12B/17/10A, p 3, B, VAL 12B/17/10C, p 9, in PRONI; OS maps 1834, 1858; notes, and draft planning submission, in MBR; A C W Merrick, in 'Holywood Advertiser', March 1987; information and title deeds from owners; information from Mrs Moyne Ramsay and from A C W Merrick.

Quintin (or Quinton) Castle, Kearney

58. One of the most attractive, and exciting, romantic buildings in the north of Ireland. Jeremy Williams's description is: "Dramatically sited cliff-top castle protected from the spray of the sea by long, castellated curtain-walls leading to flanking towers. The core of the castle is 17th- century ... No architect is recorded ... There is certainly a Byronic air of menace and exoticism. Formality is surrendered to the freedom of an organic composition where the major tower with its machicolations and Irish battlements are replicated on an increasingly reduced scale. The ranges in between are underplayed but are designed with wide windows set in regular fenestration to enjoy the view. Earlier this century Quintin was an appropriate setting for séances and pentagons chalked upon the floor-boards. Now" (1994) "it has settled down to a more mundane existence as a residence for the elderly". Williams's suggestion that the rebuilding was the work of an Ancketill "long-forgotten playwright and novelist" acting as his own architect is plainly unsustainable: the castle was clearly completed in its present form long before the Ancketills moved in, in about 1875; and this, very sophisticated, composition, with its harmonious counterpoint of square and octagonal towers, symmetrical and asymmetrical elements, must surely have been the work of a skilled architect.

Barbara Jones says "Quintin is a splendid castle house with a heavy square tower in the centre and four smaller

ones at the corners, all with stepped castellations, and walls to match, set on jagged rocks above the sea. The gates are like stage-settings too, with stout wood portcullises painted white between a a tall square tower and a shorter one. Then the drama ends, and to the south, parallel to the sea, run three quiet terraces, hanging gardens on castellated walls, and at the end of them is the little octagonal tower".

It is built of split-stone rubble, random laid, horizontally, except that the western and southern façades have been coated in rendering, with cutstone trim. There are doubled windows in each wing. It is surrounded by (once) well-trimmed lawns in a series of terraces and enclosures, incorporating a well with an antique hand-pump. The central tower rises, romantic and forbidding, above the whole complex. I understand, though I have not seen it, that the upper room in the tower contains a painted zodiac ceiling. Subsidiary towers - some square, some octagonal, but all with Irish crenellations - punctuate the lower two-storey ranges. The asymmetrical gatehouse, with one octagonal tower and a lesser square one, is of exceptional charm. Of it, Dean says, "There is no lodge here, but a charming folly gateway worthy of notice. Like a stage set in slaked rubble stone are a tall octagonal crenellated tower decorated with arrowloops and pointed pedestrian door giving access to a spiral stair leading nowhere in particular. At the other side of the entrance the same but

smaller, and spanning the opening an unusual rectangular arch over sturdy timber 'portcullis' gates. An early tower house beyond of the Smith family in the early to mid-19th century was enclosed and extended in the castellated Romantic style by the Rev Nicholas Calvert who had come by the property through marriage to the Ross heiress. There is a tradition that the architect William Vitruvius Morrison was employed here and if that is so these works may precede 1838."

I wish I could believe in the Morrison attribution; but there seems to be no documentary evidence whatever, and it does not much resemble any of his known works: nor was he greatly given to Irish machicolations, the hall-mark of this building. However, I remain firmly of the opinion that this group was not the work of an amateur. Perhaps research will, in the end, turn up its author.

This is a fascinating mixture of old and new. The castle appears on Lord Burghley's map of Ulster of about 1580. Lewis dates it precisely to 1184, and says that it was built by the Norman, John de Courcy, but the core of the present central tower seems to be a typical simple tower-house of the 16th century. William Montgomery, writing in 1683, speaks of "Quintin bay Castle wh commands ye bay, that is capable to receive a bark of forty tunns burthen. Sr James Montgomery of Rosemount" (47) "purchased the same, and lands adjoining therunto, from Dualtagh Smith, a depender on ye Savages of Portneferry, in whose manor it is: and ye sd Sr James roofed and floored ye castle, and made freestone window cases, &c, therin: and built ye baron, and flankers, and kitchen walls contiguous; all wh, Wm Montgomery, Esq., and his son James (joyning in ye sale) sold unto Mr George Ross, who lives at Carney, part of the premises". (This was Mr Ross of Mount Ross: see 85). Sir James had carried out a very similar

restoration of the nearby tower-house of the Savages at Portaferry in 1635.

By the 1830s, when G Scott was adding his notes to the Ordnance Survey memoir, James Montgomery's flankers had gone, and "The castle is now roofless and much out of repair, owing to persons taking stones from it for their own houses. The base storey, which is arched over, is made use of as a store place for fragments of boats". However, as Savage-Armstrong records, matters were soon to improve: "The Castle and lands of Quintin Bay subsequently passed to the Rev. Nicolson Calvert, on his marriage with Elizabeth Blacker, daughter of the heiress of the Ross family; the present group of buildings, of which the old Keep, much altered in appearance, still forms the principal feature, was erected by him towards the middle of the Nineteenth Century. The Castle, after being for a time in the possession of the Anketill family, is now the property of Miss Ker, a granddaughter of Mr. and Mrs. Calvert, and a descendant of George Ross above mentioned. The Castle appears on most of the old maps of the district, and is almost invariably designated 'Smith's Castle'. QUINTIN CASTLE, as renovated and enlarged, is a picturesque structure with machicolated Towers and walls, some of the latter being built on the natural rocks which form the barriers of the pretty little Bay". Knox just says "it was one of the old square keeps, but it was re-built and modernised, by the late Mr Calvert, into whose possession it had come".

The local historian, Thomas Byers, in an excellent article in the Upper Ards Historical Society's journal, says that the castle was first built in 1184; and that Sir James Montgomery of Rosemount and his son William "made great addition to the original pile. They built the walled Courtyard and added a number of smaller Towers, a large

house adjacent to the Central Tower and also a Great Kitchen to seaward of the Castle structure. They re-roofed the castle and put in new floors. This was the first reconstruction of the castle and was probably carried out before 1659". He adds "The Montgomerys sold the castle to George Ross who lived at Kearney. Ross never lived in the Castle and therefore it was allowed to become a nearly ruined structure." In 1826, a Miss Blacker, heiress of the Ross fortune, married the Rev. Nicholson Calvert, rector of Childerley in Cambridgeshire; "and Mr Calvert conceived the idea of restoring the old ruins, which he did about 1850 at very considerable expense. The central keep was raised considerably and a walk made within the battlements; he built the drawing room opening onto the inner gardens, and the dining room which is situated on the lowest floor of the great tower. The grounds he enclosed with a massive stone wall and the main entrance took the form of a barbican with portcullis. The stone used was quarried whinstone while the library and the drawing room have solid granite floors ... Mr Calvert died soon after the restoration was completed leaving two daughters, one of whom became the wife of J. C. R. Ker, M.P. for Downpatrick ... Two of Mr Ker's sisters married Anketells, of Anketells Grove, Co. Monaghan, and when the widowed Mrs Calvert sold her interest in the estate in 1870, Mr W. R. Anketell bought it and on his death in 1889 his son Mr A. W. Anketell resided in the castle for some years".

The Valuation books, some of which are unfortunately missing, do not mention Quintin at all in 1835, as presumably there was nobody in residence; but clearly show "Elizabeth Calvert, in fee", as owner in 1861; the valuation set at £50, soon after raised to £60; with sundry notes: "let furnished and with garden at £20 per month for 3 months"; "I understand that the castle furnished and the farm would be let for £150 - which I think cheap, and

there would be three years of it"; and, most tellingly, "From the peculiar style and bad situation of this castle it is very difficult to form a fair estimate of its value - Were it well situated it would be worth much more than £50". Indeed, before the introduction of the motor car, it must have been very remote. Mrs Calvert's name appears to have been struck out, and that of Mr W R Ancketill substituted, only in 1875; the name of Amyott W Ancketill appears in 1892, when the Calvert estate seems to have been "in the Court of Chancery"; in 1896, the occupier is shown as Rose Jane Ker, with the observation, "castle now let for £200 and repairs. Castle wants papering and painting only", so it must have been in fair order.

I do not know whether Jeremy Williams is right in saying that Ancketill (of Ancketill's Grove, Monaghan) was a "long-forgotten playwright and novelist". What I do know is, that in 1874 W R Ancketill published two regrettably 'begorrah-style' novels, Mick Callighan, MP: a Story of Home Rule, and The De Burghos: a Romance. The latter opens with an engraving of 'De Burgho Castle', plainly a delineation, from the seaward, of Quintin; and the opening paragraph of the book goes: "On the margin of a beautiful bay on the western" (sic) "coast of Ireland stands a castellated building, the central portion of which dates from the invasion of Strongbow, the remainder having been added in the course of successive centuries. Viewed from the sea the structure presents an imposing appearance, and conveys to the mind of the spectator ideas of the feudal power and grandeur that, no doubt, formerly attached to the ancient stronghold". Coincidence? Perhaps.

After the Ancketills apparently came a shipping man, a Mr Allen, who was the first person in the district to own a chauffeur-driven motor car. "When the Estate was sold in 1897 to the tenants, Mrs Ker re-entered, as purchaser, under the Land Commission, of the castle with about sixty acres of land. Miss Ker, her daughter, died in 1921, making her niece, Miss Kinghall, her heiress" (Byers). Magdalen Ker is shown as owner in 1918; Olga Louise King-Hall in 1924; and here Madeleine King-Hall wrote her best-seller, The Young Lady of Fashion, published under the name 'Cleone Knox' in 1925; and, by marriage, became Mrs Patrick Perceval Maxwell of Finnebrogue, Downpatrick, County Down. So late as 1949, she published a sinister and Gothick novel entitled Tea at Crumbo Castle, from which it may be suspected that her memories of Quintin Castle were not entirely happy ones. Her heroine, having bicycled past "the absurd little castellated lodge" ... "could not help thinking that in its bogus, pretentious way (for with its false battlements and meaningless towers it bore the unmistakable marks of the Victorian Gothic revival) it made a striking effect". Of the dining-room, she thought no better: " ... not a cheerful room. The architect had evidently had some thoughts of a medieval refectory when he designed it, and the results did not accord happily with the darkened flock wallpaper, the monumental mahogany furniture, the carpet of a dark yet violent pattern, and the heavy red-plush curtains trimmed with fringes, tassels and cords. The general impression was unpleasantly sombre". Against this background, the novel proceeds by way of laudanum, suicide, murder, séances, and the appearance of the ghost of a twenty-one year-old red-head, to its foreseeable conclusion.

In the days of the King-Halls, the gardens at Quintin were especially notable. But about 1926 the estate was sold to one General Maxwell, who soon sold to a Colonel E D Kennedy, who soon sold to Mrs Burges of Parkanaur, County Tyrone, who lived here until the 1950s, and kept a pet owl (called 'Owlie') in the tower. When the local stock of mice ran short, it is said that Mrs Burges asked all her friends to post her dead mice for Owlie: which they did, until the village postman, understandably, went on strike.

The property has not only changed hands with uncommon frequency; it has also had some fairly Bohemian occupants. It was owned for a number of years by a Mr 'Skeets' Martin - I have not been able to discover the origin of the epithet - a horsey Belfast estate agent with a glamorous wife; to her chagrin, he left it to the Presbyterian Church, which put it on the market. Then in 1977 it was (in part) restored as an old people's home by Mr and Mrs James O'Hara; I had occasion quite often to visit Lady Nugent (late of Portaferry House, 48) there. Subsequently, it passed into the ownership of a company which contemplated ambitious plans for re-opening those parts of the complex not used as an old people's home, for medieval-style banquets; but nothing came of this scheme. The castle now stands much as before: sometimes occupied, often empty, yet overall apparently in fairly good order. It is in 2002 reported to have changed hands once more.

I have always thought, and still think, that this is the most romantic and delightful bogus castle known to me in the whole of Ireland. The Irish Times speaks of the "breath-taking views from the ramparts"; Bence-Jones describes it as "A romantic early C19 castle, part of which dates from C17, surrounded by battlemented walls and outworks and rising spectacularly from among the rocks on the sea coast". I wholly concur: it is one of my favourite buildings in north County Down.

At the foot of the cliffs on the seaward side of the castle there is a very private and secluded cove, where seals come to enjoy sex: an inexhaustible, and unmentionable, source of entertainment for the highly respectable old ladies and gentlemen who lived in Mrs O'Hara's nursing home; and, no doubt, for other owners too.

Photographs: A C W Merrick; P. Rossmore, courtesy of IAA. Engraving: from 'Savage family in Ulster'.
Situation: Off eastern road from Cloghy to Portaferry; td, Ballymarter; District Council, Ards; Grid ref. J 632 505.
References: Listed B1 (24/1/ 78, 79, 80). Burghley map, c. 1580, MPF 90, in PRO; VAL 2B/3/10, p 16, VAL 12B/23/27A-D, in PRONI; Montgomery, Description of the ... Ards, 1701, in his 'Montgomery manuscripts', 1830, p 304; G Scott, OSM, nd, Down, II, p 126; Lewis, TD, 1837, II, p 724; Knox, 'County Down', 1875, p 469; Savage-Armstrong, 'Savage family in Ulster', 1906, p 358; ASCD, 1966, pp 245-246; Jones, 'Follies and grottoes', 1974, p 429; Bence-Jones, 'Burke's guide', 1978, p 236; 'Irish Times', 28 /5/1979; T Byers, in JUAHS, VI, 1982, pp 7-9; Jupp, 'Heritage gardens inventory', 1992, D/049; Dean, 'Gate lodges', UAHS, 1994, pp 90-91; Williams, 'Architecture in Ireland', 1994, p 111.

Ballywalter Park (formerly Springvale)

59. Arguably the grandest of all the private Grand Houses, the stateliest of the private Stately Homes, of north County Down, - (I exclude Hillsborough Castle, 51, as being *hors concours*) - Ballywalter Park, in its present form, was built soon after 1847 to designs by Charles Lanyon for Andrew Mulholland, proprietor of the York Street Flax Spinning Mill, Belfast, on the site of an earlier house, Springvale, which had for many years been a seat of the Matthews family. Harris, in 1744, had remarked of one George Matthews that he had been a notable collector in the early 18th century: "This Gentleman (who has travelled in the Eastern Countries) has made a Collection of several Curiosities, and among others has many antient Coins ... as also Gems, Seals, and *Egyptian* Pebbles. Add to these some antient *Egyptian* Hieroglyphicks ... with several figures of Mummies ... petrified Mushrooms, Stones having clear and starry Impressions, and the Skeletons of Fishes thrown out of a Quarry in great quantities on the side of Mount *Lebanon*."

As Alistair Rowan points out, "It is surprising ... to discover that it is not all an early Victorian building but a radical remodelling of a late-Georgian house called Springvale, built between 1805 and 1812 for Major George Matthews whose family had held the estate from early in the 18th century. Before Andrew Mulholland altered Springvale the house that stood on the site occupied exactly the same area as the main block of Ballywalter today. Its principal façade faced south, with a slight recession in its centre, and it was two storeys high, with the ground floor raised on a semi-basement. Though Springvale has vanished to be absorbed into Ballywalter Park a number of stone doorcases with simple keystones survive in the present basement, while some of the original stonework of the house was revealed recently" (1980s)

"when the stucco on the garden front was removed for maintenance work. The walls were built of large blocks of squared rubble stone decorated with galleting ... From details such as these we may imagine that Major Matthews' house was a low, relaxed sort of place, carefully built yet rustic rather than metropolitan in its appearance". The long stone stable-block at the rear, with its central arch and tower, and Regency glazing pattern, appears to be the only other survivor of the original complex, apart from some of the doors of the old house which appear to have been parsimoniously re-used in the bedrooms on the top floor.

Rowan's supposition is confirmed by M M Kertland of the Ordnance Survey who, in 1837, writes "Springvale House, the residence of Major Mathews, is a building of considerable size. It is erected in the style of modern country residences and has a quantity of planting about it, principally fir of different kinds". On 6 April 1846, Mulholland bought both house and estate for £23,000. It is interesting that the Valuation books treated it as the same house at all times; the name 'Springvale House' was only struck out, and the name 'Ballywalter Park' substituted, in 1893. It was valued at £180 13 2 in 1836; after the change of ownership from Matthews to Mulholland, at £200; and this valuation increased by modest steps to £265 in 1879, "new billiard room, kitchens, etc." (of about 1863 and also by Lanyon), at which figure it remained for many years.

Bence-Jones says: "Ireland's finest C19 Italianate palazzo; in the words of Dr Rowan, 'a building with a metropolitan air and all the architectural trappings of a London club'". Indeed, it is very evident that the style of the building derives from the Italian Renaissance palaces of Florence and Rome, transmuted through the medium of

the London club-houses of Sir Charles Barry. Though it is notable that Ballywalter is encased in painted stucco not stone - like Barry's Travellers' Club of 1829-32, but unlike Decimus Burton's Athenaeum of 1828-30, or Barry's Reform Club of 1837-41, both faced in ashlar. But, as Pevsner remarks, "the Travellers' - an epoch-making design - is modest in size and altogether modest in treatment; which is its great attraction", in contrast to its neighbour, of which the secretary of the Anti-Corn Law League "is supposed to have said when introduced by Bright ... to the Italianate opulence of the Reform Club, 'John, John, how can we keep honest if we live in such palaces as this?'". Externally, Ballywalter may have more in common with the "modesty" of the Travellers; but internally, it seems to me to have more in common with the "opulence" of the Reform. (Of neither club am I a member; in each club I have been a guest.)

In essence, the front consists of a solid three-storey-on-basement central block, quoined, five bays wide, topped by a broad dentilled cornice, hipped roof, and tall chimney-stacks; Georgian-glazed windows in generous architraves, three-light windows on the ground and first floors flanking the broad central Doric portico. On both sides there are advancing single-storey wings, quoined and incorporating Corinthian aedicules framing tall three-light windows to library and office respectively. The single-storey wings at each end of the garden-facing façade have generous bows, with pedimented windows: one, internally full-height, housing the drawing-room (or ballroom); the other housing breakfast-room below, with false windows above to an agreeably oddly-shaped bedroom. To the left of the garden façade extend offices, billiard-room, smoking room, and (at right angles) the extraordinarily fine conservatory of 1863, with its sandstone Corinthian columns, iron, and glass: presumably not unconnected with Lanyon's former principal assistant, Thomas Turner, a son of the well-known Dublin iron-founder who built the palm houses at Kew, Glasnevin, and the Belfast Botanic Gardens.

Internally, though the dimensions and proportions are always ample, the design shows a commendable balance between the ornate on the one hand, and the plain, almost austere, on the other. The outer hall is darkly panelled, incorporating the Dunleath (not Mulholland) coat of arms, a modern insertion, however; though the panelling may well date from 1892, the year in which Andrew Mulholland's son John became Baron Dunleath. The sitting-room and study are comparatively plain. The ornate bookcases and panelling in the library - which Alistair Rowan rather unkindly describes as "ornate tabernacle shelving in a debased Pompeian style" - incorporate John Mulholland's initials, and look very much High Victorian in style, are also perhaps of around 1892; or perhaps a bit earlier, since there is no reference to the new title. The very large dining-room is not over-decorated, though it could not be called plain. The great drawing-room is divided into two unequal parts by a screen of Corinthian columns - a feature Lanyon was to use again in the splendid drawing-room of his Ulster Club in Belfast, alas, now demolished. The polychrome grey, white and gold plasterwork of the ceiling is of the utmost magnificence, but without the over-ornamentation which rendered so many fine Victorian rooms fussy or even vulgar.

The glory of the house is its great central top-lit staircase hall, or saloon. I cannot improve on Alistair Rowan's summation: "The saloon from the point of view of the family and its visitors is the focal point of the house. All the other reception rooms open off it. In terms of formal analysis too this great space, vigorously articulated by classical columns, by monumental balconies and by arcades on the first floor, is the logical resolution of the architecture on the entrance front. The facades of Ballywalter lead us to expect some bold stroke, some architectonic resonance within: Lanyon's great central saloon supplies it". It

is appropriately furnished with niches, marble statuary, geometrical balustrades related to those on the exterior porte-cochère, and organ-cases.

The house has endured threats of demolition, a serious fire, outbreaks of dry rot, and sundry other vicissitudes: it has had to endure also extensive re-wiring and, more recently, the modernisation of its plumbing arrangements in order to bring the bedrooms on the top floor back into use. However, it has been treated with affection and discretion, in somewhat differing styles, by its successive owners and occupiers - now a collateral branch of the original family. At the date of writing, the house has just come through a fifty-seven week programme of refurbishment and renewal: that which needed cleaning has been cleaned, that which needed repainting has been painted; everything is delightfully fresh, sparkling, and new.

Surrounded by a large demesne, acres of fruit and vegetables, acres of woodland, magnificent gardens and extensive farmland, it is one of the most attractive, as well as one of the most imposing, houses in the county.

Photographs: A C W Merrick (see also colour illus. 16, 17).
Situation: Outside Ballywalter village; td, Springvale; District Council, Ards; Grid ref. J 625 680.
References: Listed A (24/4/28). VAL 1B/39, p90, VAL 2B/3/A, VAL 12B/23/6A-C, in PRONI; Harris, 'County of Down', 1744, p 68; M M Kertland, OSM, 1837, Down, II, p 16; A Rowan, in CL, 2, 9, March 1967, pp 456-460, 517-520; Pevsner, 'London', I, 1973, p 612; Bence-Jones, 'Burke's guide', 1978, p 29; A Rowan, in 'Ballywalter Park', UAHS, 1985, passim; Jupp, 'Heritage gardens inventory', 1992, D/004; Montgomery-Massingberd and Sykes, 'Great houses of Ireland', 1999, pp 260-267; P Smith, in TLS, 6, Oct., 2000, p 3; information from present and previous owners.

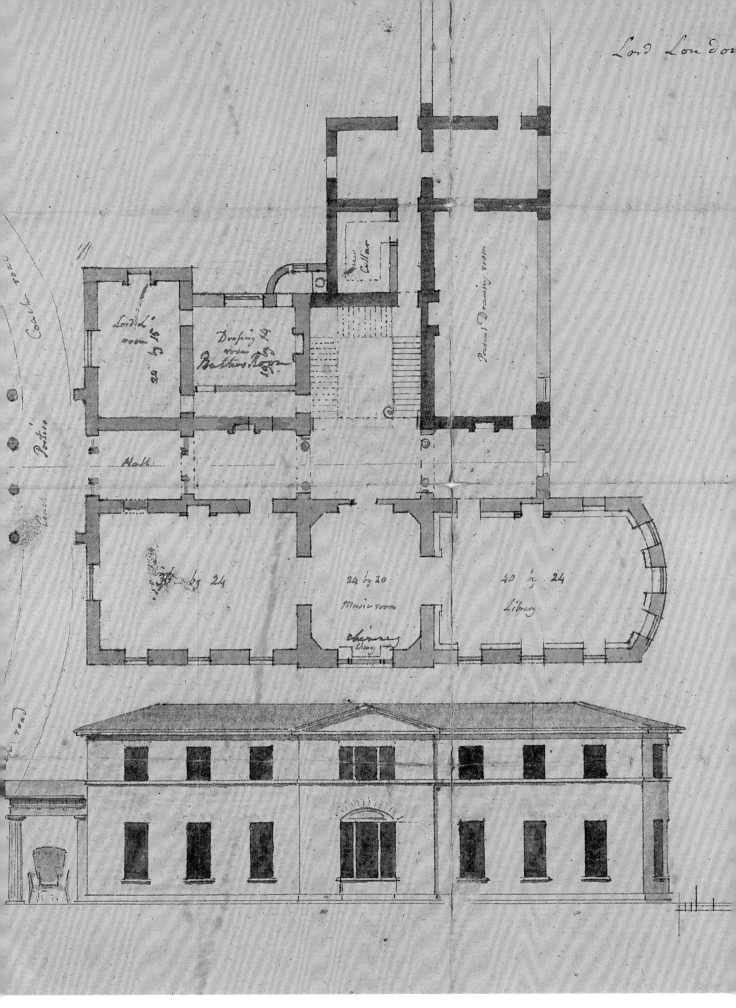

12.   George Dance, plan, and elevation, 1804, for north front of Mount Stewart, Greyabbey (53),
courtesy of the Trustees of Sir John Soane's Museum, London

13. Waringstown House (46)
14. Larchfield, Annahilt (61)

Opposite: 15. Mount Stewart, Greyabbey (53)
16. Garden front, Ballywalter Park (59)

17. Drawing-room ceiling, Ballywalter Park (59)
18. Rosemount, Greyabbey (47)

19.   11-13, The Square, and 35 Main Street, Hillsborough (50)
20.   Guincho, Helen's Bay (69)

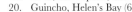

Opposite: 21. New Forge, Magheralin (95)
          22. Ard View House, Killinchy (96)

          23. The Lough House, Greyabbey (86)
          24. Marino House, Cultra, Holywood (97)

25. Grace Hall, Magheralin (101)
26. 65 Main Street, Moira (92)

Craigdarragh House (now St Columbanus Nursing Home), Helen's Bay

60. A very fine, grand, house, in Charles Lanyon's most ornate style: externally, if not internally, almost as grand as Ballywalter Park (59), built at much the same time (the exact date of neither house is known). The listers say 1850, and cite "records of former owner's family." If their informant was the late Mrs Garner, a descendant of the Workmans, this is likely to be accurate, for she was a conscientious local historian. Dean says "A big stone and stucco house designed by Charles Lanyon in his Italianate palazzo style c 1850 for Francis Gordon. It seems that the client ran short of funds for he never occupied the place, it being tenanted for many years. Nor could he afford a gate lodge because what stands today was built by Thomas Workman upon his purchasing the property". Craigdarragh appears in the Valuation book for 1863, occupied first by George Hamilton, then by Lord Dufferin, and valued at £120. Lord Dufferin was followed in 1864 by Joseph Jaffé; in 1874 by John Patterson; then "Earl Dufferin" appears again. In 1879, house and demesne were advertised "to be let unfurnished" at £325 per annum, applications to the Dufferin Estate Office, Clandeboye.

The two-storey-on-basement house stands at the top of a grassy slope running down to a little sandy bay. The main entrance is on the inland side; there is a garden entrance with columns *in antis* on the eastern side; the back, despite the fact that it contains the drawing room and dining room (both looking out over the lough) is very much plainer and less ornate. The front is, in essence, of five bays, with a tremendous Doric porch; all the glazing-bars are complete on the two principal façades; there are aedicules around the windows; quoins; a hipped roof, with the original chimney-stacks and pots, borne on terrific ornate cornice and frieze. The pierced balustrade of the porch is almost identical with that at Ballywalter Park; above it, a wide window flanked by two narrow ones divided by vertical strips ornamented with overlapping paterae. This last is, so far as I know, a decorative feature rare in Ireland, though to be seen in the Hofburg in Vienna: I know of only two other examples in Ulster, the Northern Bank in Derry and the former rectory at Ballinderry, both attributed to Thomas Turner, who was Lanyon's senior assistant throughout the 1840s, until he set up on his own in 1852: so it seems reasonable to suppose that he had at least some hand in the design of Craigdarragh.

The square front hall is very fine, with six elaborate doorcases, and a series of round-headed niches, in the three walls facing the visitor once he is within the front door. Unfortunately, the ceilings of the drawing room and morning room have been covered in plastic panelling; but the magnificent dining room remains intact, some of the extravagant ceiling ornament picked out in gilt. On the conversion of the house to a nursing home, a number of utilitarian alterations were made, and, on the west side, a completely new wing rather unhappily added. But on the whole, it is surprisingly unspoiled, thereby doing much credit to its new owners.

I do not know who Francis Gordon was. Thomas Workman was "a naturalist of note and president of the Belfast Natural History and Philosophical Society from 1898 to 1900" (Killen). Son of linen merchants, he served his apprenticeship with Harland & Wolff, and then prospered as one of the founders of Workman, Clark, shipbuilders, Belfast. He bought the freehold of Craigdarragh from the Dufferin estate in 1883, when the valuation increased from £120 to £150. His son, Major Robert Workman of the Royal Irish Rifles, 1878 - 1949, a great traveller and a zealous yachtsman, was still living there when I was a boy. He had been wounded at Ypres in 1917; was for many years chairman of Down County Council, Commodore of the Royal North of Ireland Yacht Club, and was President of the Linen Hall Library from 1928 until 1949. He was a kindly old boy, good to his neighbours: he used to take us out once a year in his large sailing-yacht, anchored in the cove below the house; he permitted my family to walk down through his delightful glen to the shore to swim in the chilly waters of Belfast Lough, or to collect hen-grit for the Twelve Apostles who provided us with unrationed eggs in the early years of the second World War (the broody one was called Judas Iscariot; they were Rhode Island Reds). During the war, the house was not (like so many) commandeered by the army; but a large hutted encampment was constructed in the demesne, used to house some of the first American troops to arrive in Europe. My parents thought it proper to show some of the doughboys hospitality, and I well remember an excruciating meal of misunderstandings: they were accustomed to a diet of fried chicken, ice-cream, and coca cola; in those days of stern rationing, we could only offer boiled cod, apple pie, and, with luck, Kia-Ora lemonade. When the Americans left, the camp was used to house German prisoners-of-war, whom we watched moping behind the barbed wire.

After Major Workman's death, the house was sold to the Sisters of Mercy, and converted into a nursing home specialising in the care of the elderly: a function that it performs very well, and blessedly free from the *bondieuserie* sometimes found in Roman Catholic institutions of this kind. It is only a pity that it has been found necessary to close off the still-extensive parkland from the path along the shore, and that there is no longer any means of access from glen to shore, or vice versa. It is surprising that this, really very architecturally important, building has gone so little noticed: unremarked by R M Young, by Mark Bence-Jones, (so far as I know) by Paul Larmour, and by Jeremy Williams.

Photograph: A C W Merrick.
Situation: Down a long avenue at 57 Craigdarragh Road, Helen's Bay; td, Ballyrobert; District Council, North Down; Grid ref. J 444 823
References: Listed B (23/16/17). OS map, 1859; VAL 12B/17/10A, p 20, VAL 12B/17/10B, p 114, VAL 12B/17/10 C, p 42, in PRONI; Workman family papers in D 2778, in PRONI; A J Rowan, in 'Ballywalter Park', 1985, UAHS, p 20; Killen, 'Linen Hall Library', 1990, pp 203-204; J A K Dean, 'Gate lodges', UAHS, 1996, p 71; R Blackwood, genealogical notes in Linen Hall Library.

Larchfield, Annahilt

61. The listers just say "A small late classical country house with fine interiors and plasterwork set in a designed 'natural' landscape"; and "c 1750. Built for the Mussenden family; re-modelled and added to c 1858". The history of the house is not quite as simple as that, though it is true that it has belonged to only three families in 250 years; and the house is now by no means a small one.

Daniel Mussenden, a prominent Belfast merchant, decided to retire to the country in 1755; and to build himself a new house. In April 1756, building must have been well under way, for he ordered two marble and four stone chimney-pieces from Marsden & Benson in Dublin, and one more a month later; and in the same month Mr Benson, then taking the waters at Bath, sent him "two

Marleborough vases with doves, which are the Mussendens' crest" for him "to put on the two piers in the front court of his house in the country". He seems to have moved in by 1757. Extensive planting and landscaping was carried out in the park. He made his will in 1763, leaving Larchfield to his son William.

In 1772, a mob of 300 Hearts of Steel assembled to burn the house down, but were with some difficulty dissuaded. Rosemary Richey, perhaps correctly but perhaps a little unkindly, observes that "William Mussenden ... was perhaps the most domineering landlord, possibly because he was an arriviste, his father having made money in trade. In general, those who acquired estate and title through commercial activity were inclined to be hard on their tenants, possibly feeling that this was the way to emphasise their position in the landed élite. Of all the County Down gentry it was Mussenden who suffered most at the hands of the Steelboys". In the spring of 1783 the Earl-Bishop of Derry, then aged 53, came to stay for several weeks with his 19-year old cousin, Frideswide Bruce of Killyleagh, who had married Daniel Mussenden junior in 1781; and addressed correspondence from Larchfield to his architect, Michael Shanahan, at Downhill, County Londonderry. Mrs Mussenden died, two years later, aged 22, and the Bishop named his Temple at Downhill in her memory. It is not entirely clear whether their relationship was scandalous or innocent: Lord Charlemont, "always hostile to the Bishop", made "general charges of immorality against him"; but the balance of probability seems to be that the relationship was perfectly innocent, though perhaps a little indiscreet. The second William Mussenden, born in 1836, was the last of his family to live at Larchfield.

The then rector of Annahilt parish, the Rev. John Dubourdieu, wrote in 1816: "About 60 years ago, the present Mr. Mussenden's grandfather made extensive plantations and built a mansion house at Larchfield, which received its name from the tree he was fond of: his grandson has been a most extensive planter: and by exciting the same spirit among his tenants, the estate has assumed a very cultivated appearance". Atkinson claims to have visited Larchfield in 1817, and remarked that the seat of "Mr. Mussenden, who resides upon his own estate, is represented to be a most respectable feature of improvement, the proprietor having planted much, and encouraged a similar spirit in his tenantry"; or, as Gordon Wheeler suggests, was he, as so often, just cribbing from Dubourdieu? In 1834, the house, measuring 63' 6" by 24' 6" by 27', was valued at £53 17 0; in 1862, at £60; but in 1863, still shown as the property of Capt. William Mussenden, the house, offices and gate-lodges soared in value to £100: in consequence of extensive enlargement and rebuilding.

Soon afterwards, probably in 1868 or 1869, Mussenden, who was childless, sold the estate to Ogilvie B Graham, first of a family (like the Mulhollands) of hereditary directors of the York Street Flax Spinning Company, who extended the house still further. The valuation gradually rose, between 1876 and 1885, from £100 to £145, explained by successive notes: "new offices"; "part of house raised a storey, 1883"; "two new gate lodges". At that figure it remained until well into the twentieth century. I well remember the last Colonel O B Graham, a man of an imperious manner, from whose family it was bought in 1968 by the present owners.

The Georgian house has been almost entirely swallowed up by the 19th-century one. Dixon says "The woodwork in the one surviving early Georgian room, with lugged heads to the door and window cases, and modest scale, suggest a date in the second quarter of the 18th century. This house faced west and comprises the middle section of the present house, running from the present portico on the south to the present north wall". (In fact, there are two surviving Georgian rooms with lugged doorcases.) "About a hundred years after the original building was erected, it was radically remodelled in the late Georgian fashion then current. The orientation was changed, the new entrance placed on the south end of the old building and a new range of rooms built in front of the old house. The new façade was pulled together ... to present a two-storey appearance. The two middle bays advance slightly from the wings and gain further importance from the presence of the severe but neatly-scaled single-storey Ionic portico and its surmounting balustrade. The large tripartite windows of the ground floor of the wings are recessed in arches, in a manner typical of late Georgian designs elsewhere in Ulster".

This is in many ways a puzzling house, much altered over the years, but a very handsome one both externally and internally: the rooms are tall, well-proportioned, and well-detailed. Hugh Dixon advised the present owner that he thought the 19th-century work was probably to designs by Charles Lanyon, and stylistically this would be plausible, if the Victorian alterations could be dated to the 1840s or 50s: but the Valuation books appear to indicate the contrary. The library is the most charming room in the house, with a segmental bow opposite the triple windows, and a screen of a pair of Ionic columns: the cornice above the screen incorporates the Mussenden doves. The drawing-room ceiling, however, has the Graham coat of arms in each corner. There used to be a doorway between inner and outer hall, but Colonel Graham threw both into a single large space with a picture-frame moulding around the opening; the present owners removed the frame and substituted new Doric columns framing the opening between the two: a great improvement. The staircase (evidently moved by the Grahams) rises from the back of the inner hall, is lit by a great round-headed window at the landing, and both it and the upstairs gallery are topped by an elaborate coved ceiling and flanked by arched alcoves in the side walls. There are extensive three-storey out-offices at the rear, including, unexpectedly, the remains of a Turkish bath.

The house is in effect L-shaped, and stands serenely amidst rolling parkland and mature trees and gardens. It is partly of stone, partly of brick, all faced in an agreeably mellow Roman cement softened by creepers, with stone quoins. The two windows above the porch, part of the original house, have been heightened with dummy sashes above the level of the ceiling inside, so as to range with the windows in the higher-ceiled rooms at either side. The hipped roof to the front range is topped by two tall stone chimney-stacks. A surprisingly grand house, and in very good order.

Photograph; A C W Merrick (see also colour illus. 14).

Situation: 375 Upper Ballynahinch Road, Annahilt; td, Aghnaleck; District Council, Lisburn; Grid ref. J 310 585.

References: Listed B (19/6/3). VAL 1B/338B, p 43, VAL 2B/3/35, p 83, VAL 12B/20/1A-E, and D/354/753, 895, 1035, 1047, 1056, all in PRONI; Taylor and Skinner, 'Roads', 1778, p 277; J Dubourdieu, in Mason, 'Statistical account', II, 1816, p 11; Atkinson, 'Ireland exhibited', I, 1823, p 233; Lewis, TD, 1837, I, p 26; Childe-Pemberton, 'Earl Bishop', 1924, I, pp 293-5, II, pp 334-336; Rankin, 'Irish Building ventures', UAHS, 1972, p 29; Jupp, 'Heritage gardens inventory', 1992, D/086; R Richey, unpublished PhD thesis, QUB, 2000, p 3; H Dixon, notes, and T Reeves-Smyth, notes, in MBR; information from owners.

Craigavad House

62. Craigavad House, now club-house of the Royal Belfast Golf Club, was designed in 1852 for John Mulholland, son of Andrew Mulholland, of Ballywalter Park (59), by Thomas Turner, whose drawings turned up at Ballywalter in the late 1960s. It is a fine cutstone two-storey mansion, five bays wide and four bays deep, with hipped roof and stone chimney-stacks, standing on a splendid site at the top of a wooded and grassy slope descending to the shore of Belfast Lough. All the windows have segmental heads; the glazing-pattern is unusual, Georgian upstairs and Regency below. On the landward side, there is a broad portico of Doric columns *in antis*; on the seaward side, there is a great two-storey semi-circular projecting bay with fine views over the Lough. As Dixon and Rowan say, "Its exterior is severe though nicely detailed". Recently well restored at enormous expense, but it is a pity that the Ulster predilection for picture windows has been allowed to upset the symmetry of the fenestration. The sundry club-house extensions are somewhat less obtrusive than usual.

The interior is remarkable for the sumptuous circular central hallway or rotunda, surrounded by an upper gallery with very fine cast-iron Roman-pattern balustrade, and top-lit by a wide circular dome of lightly-stained glass. The walls are divided into a series of round-headed niches, alternative lunettes being ornamented with very fine plaster figures from the classical myths - Arion riding his dolphin, and so on - picked out in white against a dark-grey background: one of the most effective rooms in the county, very grand though not very large. The same cannot be said of the very fine ball-room, now dining-room, which is both grand and large. The rooms are agreeably proportioned, and the plasterwork is crisp but fairly restrained: this is a house that has more in common with late

Georgian simplicity than with high Victorian opulence.

Thomas Turner was a son of Richard Turner, the well-known Dublin iron-founder who designed the palm-houses in the Botanic Gardens at Belfast, at Kew, and at Glasnevin in Dublin. He came to Belfast in the early 1840s as principal assistant to Charles Lanyon, the County Surveyor for Antrim, and from then until 1852, when he set up in practice on his own, he must have been responsible for much of the work of this busy practice - see in particular Craigdarragh House (60). A lifelong bachelor, he was described by Robert Young as "a good-looking, amiable man, easy and well-bred, and a favourite at once in any company he entered". In abilities he appears to have rivalled Charles Lanyon; regrettably, his achievements were far fewer, and this is arguably the best of them.

John Mulholland, only son of Andrew Mulholland, was as capable a businessman as his father; rather more of a public man; and inherited Ballywalter Park on his father's death in 1866, soon after which he seems to have removed there, renting Craigavad House first to one George Washington Charters; then in 1880 to Sir Edward Porter Cowan, who must have carried out extensive works, for the valuation rose from £210 in 1880, to £240 in 1882, to £300 in 1883, when Mulholland sold the freehold to Robert Kennedy. In 1892 he was created first Baron Dunleath of Ballywalter, "on the recommendation of the outgoing Conservative Prime Minister, Lord Salisbury" (Ballywalter Park, UAHS), in recognition of his public service, his parliamentary career, and his role as a commercial adviser to the government.

The house seems to have changed hands with uncommon frequency: a note in the club-house records that, after John Mulholland, it was occupied in succession by Sir Edward Coey, Sir Edward Porter Cowan, Mr A Kirker,

and Mr J C White, from whose heir, Lady Edith White, the property was bought by the Golf Club in 1925, the valuation by then having fallen back to £270. Rather surprisingly, this imposing house attracts no mention either in Bassett's County Down Directory, or in R M Young's Belfast and the Province of Ulster.

Photographs: A C W Merrick (see also colour illus. 11).
Situation: Off Station Road, Craigavad, at the end of a long avenue; td, Craigavad; District Council, North Down; Grid ref. J 430 815.
References: Listed B+ (23/16/1). VAL 12B/17/ 7A, p 35, VAL 12B/17/10C, p 48, in PRONI; H Dixon and A Rowan, in CL, 24 May 1973, p 1495; 'Ballywalter Park', UAHS, 1985, passim; Jupp, 'Heritage gardens inventory', 1992, D/117.

Straw Hill, Donaghcloney

63. A very fine example of large-scale mid-Victorian domestic architecture in the Jacobean style at its best; deceptively, much more spacious than its exterior would suggest, due to a clever if irregular layout. Built for William Nicholson, a prosperous linen merchant, of imported Scottish sandstone - smooth-faced in the front part of the house, rough-faced at the rear. There is a wealth of gables and gablets, all with very ornate fretted bargeboards, and topped by a variety of tall, decorative, chimney-pots, much like those employed by Playfair at Brownlow House, Lurgan, not far away.

There seems to be no documentary evidence as to authorship, and conflicting evidence as to date. Jupp says 1846; the un-named author of a typescript history of the Nicholson family says firmly 1851, which seems to me the likelier of the two. William Playfair would by no means be an implausible guess for its architect: but Dean notes that "there is much about the architecture of the house reminiscent of the work of William Spence of Glasgow, also to be seen in the gate lodge". The attribution is quite a persuasive one: David Walker tells me that Coulter Mains, in Scotland, "is an extremely good Jacobean house which suggests that he spent some time with John Bryce's brother

David and his then employer William Burn, as it is indistinguishable from the latter's work"; and the influence of Burn and Bryce is indeed perceptible at Straw Hill. Gomme and Walker, in their classic Architecture of Glasgow, describe Spence as "(?1806-1883). Rather a shadowy figure in Glasgow. He was assistant to John Bryce, but was working on his own by 1837. He designed a number of theatres, all now destroyed; and his remaining buildings are chronologically widely spread; but all show an adventurous and resourceful mind". Dean says that he designed Gilford Castle, County Down, about 1855 for Benjamin Dickson, and Elmfield, nearby, about 1856 for his brother James Dickson (although the authors of Linen Houses of Banbridge suggest c.1864 for the latter). Both (like William Nicholson) were beneficiaries of the linen boom of that period. Gordon Wheeler tells me that Spence also designed Edenderry House, now part of Banbridge Academy, about 1865.

Internally, the house contains some surprisingly good plasterwork in the ceilings of the principal rooms, the entrance hall, and stair-well; and some fine, if rather heavy-handed, joinery. There are extensive out-buildings, with stabling for polo ponies, and the gardens and

grounds are of some magnificence. During 1851, the year when I think the house was a-building, William Nicholson planted well over 10,000 trees in the demesne, including an avenue of deodars from seeds sent home by his in-laws, the Birnies of Downpatrick, two of whom were colonels in the Indian Army: one is said to have married a maharajah's daughter, the other a niece of Lady Dalhousie.

The house was built on the site of a much more modest farm-house, named Straw Hill, bought in 1827, with 11 acres, from one Robert Boyce; Nicholson rather grandly named his new residence 'The Hall' or 'Donaghcloney Hall'; it has now reverted to the earlier name. In the Valuation book for 1861, the house is shown as belonging to Robert G Nicholson, his name struck out and "Reps". inserted; valued at first at £37, then £70, "including gate lodges". Thereafter, it seems to have had a chequered history: in 1866, the owner is shown as William Cosby, who took in lodgers; "the whole of this house is not occupied by the present owner". By 1876, it had passed to Abraham Coombe; by 1899, the valuation had dropped from £70,

to £63, to £51, then to £42: "John Hale, lessee from Abraham Coombe ... A fine large house, but much too large for farm". However, by 1901 onwards it was valued at £80, and evidently either Abraham Coombe, or Emilie G Coombe, lived in it. After the second World War, the house was bought by a wealthy horse-breeding Arab, a Mr Ali Reza Soudevar; then, in 1983, it passed to Mr David Prentice; and was acquired by the present owner in 1989.

Photographs: A C W Merrick.

Situation: 2 Hall Road, Donaghcloney (but principal entrance in village Main Street); td, Banoge; District Council, Craigavon; Grid ref. J 128 538.

References: Listed B1 (14/6/5). VAL 2B/3/46, p65, VAL 12B/21/4A-F, in PRONI; Atkinson, 'Ulster parish', 1898, p 80; Gomme and Walker, 'Architecture of Glasgow', 1987, p 300; Jupp, 'Heritage gardens inventory', 1992, D/141; Dean, 'Gate lodges', UAHS, 1994, p 97; 'Linen houses of Banbridge', 1995, pp 30,54,60; information from owner, Nicholson papers in his possession, and correspondence with David Walker.

Bangor Castle

64. An imposing Tudorbethan mansion, on a wooded hilltop looking out over the town to the mouth of Belfast Lough. Credited by Colvin and most other authorities to William Burn; but there is evidence also for the involvement both of William Walker of Monaghan, and of Anthony Salvin, to whom the listers, I think wrongly, attribute it. (Mark Girouard, no doubt unconsciously, manages to attribute it both to Burn and to Salvin: with some justification, for it appears in the list of buildings given in each man's obituary, in each case at a cost of £9,000). One theory is that the original conception was that of Walker, the main house was by Burn, the somewhat different stable-block by Salvin. Another theory, supported by David Walker, is that Burn may have started the building and Salvin finished it.

It seems that on the death of Colonel Edward Southwell Ward in 1837, his son, Robert E Ward, determined to replace the late Georgian Gothick "very elegant house" which he had inherited, and first commissioned plans from Walker, but did not execute them. Patton says that "in 1847 he approached William Burn, who had built Dartrey, Co Monaghan, for Lord Dartrey in 1845 and was to prepare designs for Elizabethanising Ballyleidy House (ie Clandeboye House) in 1848" (see 52). Williams says "A characteristic gesture of a younger brother in the Romantic era to fabricate an ancestral home that appears to predate by several hundred years the family seat" - Castle Ward!

Certainly the main house is very much in Burn's manner. A Scotsman (1789-1870), he was trained in Robert Smirke's London office. "By 1840 he had already designed or altered over ninety country houses, besides thirty churches and twenty-five public buildings ... a man of vigorous and independent character, frank and plain spoken, but very patient in meeting the wishes of his wealthy and sometimes idiosyncratic clients". He turned out "innumerable houses in Elizabethan, Jacobean or

Scottish vernacular dress as the occasion required ... their dry, repetitive detailing rarely succeeds in recapturing the charm of their prototypes: what commended them to Burn's clients was the convenience of their planning - above all, the care taken to safeguard the owner's privacy from both servants and guests ... Burn's output is more remarkable for its quantity than for its quality ... Nevertheless Burn is a remarkable figure in British architectural history, epitomizing in a single career the whole course of nineteenth-century architecture from Greek Revival to Scottish Baronial" (Colvin). And David Walker sums up Burn's importance: "He played a central role in the transition of the country house from the rigid formality of the eighteenth century to the comfortable asymmetry of the nineteenth. Above all, he was adept at reconciling the conflicting requirements of his clients - for grandeur, privacy, outlook, guests' accommodation, logistic convenience and segregation of servicing. Indeed, his thinking on how buildings should function was on a more sophisticated level than that of any previous British architect".

In essence, a large rectangular house of Ayrshire sandstone, two-storey and attics on a sizeable basement, with a three-storey tower topped by a corner clock-turret beside the porch: windows in bays (some canted, some square, some bowed) divided by mullions into two, three, or four tall sections; scalloped quoins; tall gables without crow-steps embracing triple windows; with curly stone fretwork topping the bay windows (though some of it seems to have fallen off). The castle is at the time of writing in the early stages of an extensive programme of stonework restoration: it is greatly to be hoped that the tall stone chimney-stacks, an important, indeed essential, element in the composition, whose post-war removal is rightly reprobated by Marcus Patton, will now be restored. There are various heraldic plaques, carvings and monograms, as well as numerous pinnacles and finials, which go some way to alleviate the lack of chimney-stacks. The stable courtyard

(now containing restaurant and the North Down Heritage Centre) is of a paler stone, and in a more Gothic style, with slit windows and an octagonal turret.

The entire Castle and grounds were acquired by Bangor Council on the death of Lady Clanmorris, R E Ward's daughter and heiress, in 1941. In 1952 the building became Town Hall for Bangor Borough Council; now for North Down District Council. The Council Chamber fits very well into the Great Hall or Music Room, which used to contain a large organ (sold off), and still contains a splendid wall-window of stained glass, part heraldic, part family portraiture; panelling; and a fine hammer-beam roof. Off the hall opens the grand staircase (for the use of family only) with strapwork banisters not dissimilar to the curly stonework capping the window-bays outside. On either side of the hall is a screen-passage leading to the three principal rooms of the house - dining-room, drawing-room and library. All of these have ornate compartmented ceilings: the richest is that in the dining-room, where there are also a tremendous wooden chimneypiece

and overmantel, the latter framing an unexpected view of Segovia. The library has a concealed door to allow the owner to slip out unseen, as at Castle Ward. There are two subsidiary staircases, both elegantly cantilevered, for the use of the servants. Each of the principal bedrooms on the first floor had a tin bath painted to match the walls; there was no running water in any of them.

The house is, on the whole, very well cared for by the Council, both inside and out: apart from the matter of the chimney-stacks.

Photographs: North Down Heritage Centre; R J Welch, UM, W05/15/42,45.
Situation: In Castle Park, off Abbey Street, Bangor; td, Corporation; District Council, North Down; Grid ref. J 504 812.
References: Listed A (23/7/1). Wilson, 'Post-chaise companion', 1803, pp 12-13; D M Walker, in 'Seven Victorian architects', 1976, p 31; Bence-Jones, 'Burke's guide', 1978, p 30; Girouard, 'Victorian country house', 1979, pp 439, 441; K R Gillen, notes for conducted tour, 1980; Jupp, 'Heritage gardens inventory', 1992. D/005; Williams, 'Architecture in Ireland', 1994, p 101; Colvin, 'Dictionary', 1995, p 182 ff; Patton, 'Bangor', UAHS, 1999, p 34 ff.

Portavo (or Portavoe) House, Donaghadee

65. By the mid 17th century Robert Ross, a friend of and officer to the Hamilton / Clandeboye family of Bangor, was in possession of a house at Portavo (Carr). William Montgomery's Description of the Barony of the Ards, written in 1683 and up-dated by him in 1701, says "Then about two miles from Donagadee, is James [Ross] Esqr. his great house of Portavo, and large office houses - all of stone, brick, and lime, slated; gardens walled in, and fenced orchards and pastures - all his own erection, since K. Ch. ye 2nds the happy restoration, all whh and his estate in lands, he conveyed by feofment to his coson Geo. Ross, called Gaaston, himself wanting heirs of his own body. In view of Portavo are ye Copeland Isles, part of his estate, being convenient places for a deer-park, warrons, and other chaces, now well inhabited". This seems to have been the house built about 1670, and shown, probably extended and modified, in a late 18th-century water-colour tentatively attributed to William Hincks. (Gordon Wheeler points out that, if the water-colour *is* by Hincks, it must have been painted before 1780/81, when, according to Strickland, he left for London. No evidence is cited for a subsequent return to Ireland). In 1732, John Sloane executed a 'Survey of the extensive property at Portavoe, and elsewhere in County Down, of the Honble Capn Iames Ross'. Harris, in 1744, refers to Portavo as the seat of James Ross, Esq.; but by 1777 Taylor and Skinner show it as the seat of - Kerr, Esq. The parkland and the serpentine lake for this house were laid out by the eminent landscape gardener John Sutherland. It accommodated a fine collection of paintings, statues and furniture acquired by David Ker during a stay in Italy from 1792 to 1794 (Carr). Between 1817 and 1820 David Ker built a new Regency house in front of the old house. Unhappily, this, which seems to have been of some importance, was burned down in 1844, though extensive under-buildings remain.

As Dixon says, "Little is known of the house at Portavoe before the fire. It was apparently a Palladian building of some distinction; the two rough sketches seem to agree on there having been a high vaulted basement of which the remains still exist". Dean says "James Ross is recorded as living here in 1740 but some time later it passed to the Ker

family who built a grandiose square Palladian mansion consumed in 1844 by a calamitous fire." Bence-Jones says, a little dismissively and not altogether accurately, "A house extensively altered in the early years of c19 by David Ker, who bought Montalto from Earl of Moira. Burnt 1844, rebuilt 1880". However, Gordon Wheeler, who has looked closely into the matter, believes that a little more may be deduced of the appearance of the Regency house from a study of the sketches and from other clues on the ground. He writes: "David Ker's own 'plan' of 17 December 1822 is perhaps what he would have liked to have had in his wildest dreams - a multi-porticoed and multi-pedimented affair raised on an arcaded podium and complete with dome; owing much to Palladio's Villa Rotonda. (A drawing of the same period by an unknown architect for an unexecuted gate-lodge, in the form of an elaborate neo-classical screen, possibly demonstrates further how Ker's mind was working). What eventually went up would appear to have been a good deal simpler, though still impressive. The Ordnance Survey map of 1833 shows a square block with a projection breaking forward across the main front which commands a view of the lake below across a broad sweep of driveway. The sketch of the house on fire on 13 January 1844, though possibly drawn from memory at a considerably later date, would indicate that this projection was pedimented and with pilasters at its corners; and that the whole two-storey house was indeed built on such a podium or raised basement as David Ker had envisaged, possibly due to the rocky nature of the ground beneath. Furthermore, Mr Kertland, writing his Ordnance Survey memoir in 1837, speaks of 'a very handsome house principally built of brick' - not stone.

"(An interesting comparison can be drawn with David Ker's procedure at the two-storey Montalto in Ballynahinch, which he had bought from the Earl of Moira in 1802 to be his principal residence. Here, in 1837, according to J H Williams of the Ordnance Survey, he created an extra storey by cutting back the ground around and under the house, 'thus forming an understorey which is supported by numerous arches and pillars').

"The notice of the fire, which appeared in the Downpatrick Recorder, speaks of the 'entire destruction' of 'this ancient edifice', although, as noted below, a fragment of the earlier house lying behind it has survived." The Ker family, who lived here until 1980, indulged themselves in many schemes for rebuilding or alteration over the years, by Lanyon & Lynn, W & R D Taggart, Arthur Jury, and Robert McKinstry; none of them, however, was executed.

The present house, built across the north-eastern gable-end of the 17th-century house and to the rear of the site of its early 19th-century successor, dates from 1884/1885, but looks twenty years earlier; it is an old-fashioned design by an unknown architect (if any). Nevertheless, it is a pleasant three-storey three-bay T-shaped rendered house, with most attractive stone-built out-buildings. The shank of the T contains a long first-floor drawing room and study with Georgian-glazed windows on either side which appear to have survived from the first house. The rather florid plasterwork in the well-proportioned principal rooms is in the style of the 1860s; so is the front doorcase, with thick-ribbed fanlight, at the head of a flight of nine steps; the windows in the front part of the house are Victorian-glazed, with a little peak or pediment accommodating a single attic window; and there are brick chimney-stacks.

If the house itself is rather undistinguished, its surroundings are delightful. It is built on solid rock, the soundest of foundations: there is a walled garden, and stables, and an ice-house with a long tunnel: best of all are the surviving extensive under-buildings of the former Regency house, a maze of stone tunnels and arches, some with brick dressings, some blocked-up, some not, grassed over above, with a number of stairways and entrances: I cannot imagine a more enchanting place to play hide-and-seek.

Acquired from the Ker family by the present owners in 1980, and not much altered, apart from the relocation of the kitchen from the basement, and a new staircase. A house with a very comfortable atmosphere, as I remember from visits in the days of Dick Ker, a considerable local magnate. I remember also a memorable occasion, when I was an articled clerk in the family firm, and my father invited me to sit in on a consultation with Dick's father, David Ker. He was a tall, bald, old man, dressed in gingery tweed plus-fours and a long shooting-coat; I noticed at once that his tummy seemed to be undulating in the most unaccountable manner; all was explained when, after twenty minutes, he removed from his poachers' pockets two hound puppies, and placed them on my father's desk!

Photographs: A C W Merrick; owner's collection. Water-colour: ?W Hincks, copy in MBR.
Situation: Groomsport Road, Donaghadee; td, Portavoe; District Council, Ards; Grid ref. J 562 822.
References: Not listed. T1451/1, 1732, in PRONI; William Montgomery, Description of the ... Ards, 1701, in his 'Montgomery manuscripts', 1830, p 312; Harris, 'County of Down', 1744, p 64; Taylor and Skinner, 'Roads', 1778, p 6; OS map, 1833; M M Kertland, OSM, nd (? 1837), Down, II, p 22; J H Williams, OSM, 1837, Down, IV, p 107; 'Downpatrick Recorder', 20/1/1844, p 3; Strickland, 'Dictionary', 1913, I, pp 485-487; Dixon, 'Ulster architecture', UAHS, 1972, p 14; Brett, 'Mid-Down', UAHS, 1974, p 35; Bence-Jones, 'Burke's guide', 1978. p 233; Jupp, 'Heritage gardens inventory', 1992, D/084; Dean, 'Gate lodges', UAHS, 1994, p 89; heritage garden file in MBR; information from owners and from Peter Carr.

Rathmoyle (formerly Eldon Green), Helen's Bay

66. The listers, surprisingly, classify this suburban house, by Vincent Craig, of 1901, "A", justifying this judgement by the description: "This is a very complete and unspoiled example of a 'turn of the century' house on a large scale. It stands in well-kept gardens and is one of the most attractive examples of domestic architecture of its period in Northern Ireland, designed by a leading local architect". "A large gabled and towered symmetrical house of two and three storeys, designed by the architect Vincent Craig" (an elder brother of Lord Craigavon) " for himself ... It is built of roughcast walls, red tiled roofs, some half timbering to gables, and is characterised by the variety and number of its window types, projecting bays of various shapes, and unusual details such as the wavy head to the front entrance porch surmounted by carved heraldic beasts. The interiors contain a variety of original fireplaces, a fine oak stairway in the entrance hall, and a number of attractive and colourful decorative leaded windows in Art Nouveau style". The whole house is as much Arts and Crafts as Art Nouveau in style. The ground floor is of cutstone, as is the trim on the upper floors; the red roof tiles are unusually small, the chimney-stacks very solid; the stone porch is topped by a pair of carved lions holding up shields, that on the right inscribed with date 1901. Dean says "A big house on an elevated site overlooking Belfast Lough for the architect who also designed the gate lodge."

Vincent Craig moved to England in 1911 and sold the house to Herbert Brown, a Belfast linen merchant; it was valued at £143 15 0 in 1925, almost as much as the nearby Craigdarragh House (60). Brown in turn sold it in 1927 to the Mitchell family: in 1940 I used to visit Sub-Lieutenant Dunsmuir Mitchell, RNVR, who, when on leave, would enthral me as a boy with tales of life in the

Royal Navy. I cannot recall much of the architectural setting then, apart from an impression of dark and rather gloomy panelling. The house was rented until 1947 to Captain Sam Duffin, and then passed to new owners who have ever since used it (and still use it) to accommodate overseas visitors, for hospitality, and for training and conferences, for all of which purposes it is admirably suited; though they have managed to retain its domestic character, with many fine pieces of Edwardian furniture.

Apart from the front hall and generous reception rooms, there is, at the rear of the house and linked to it by a curving conservatory, the so-called 'Great Hall', originally a billiards room or games room, with a very fine tiled Art Nouveau mantelpiece, and mural paintings in the segmental spandrels at each end of the room. The dining-room has an extraordinary oak ingle-nook. The 'Watch Tower' at the centre of the house contains a triple window looking out over Belfast Lough, and must once have provided splendid views of the passing war-time shipping and indeed of the flying-boats landing on, and taking off from, the water, a magnificent sight as I well remember. There are eleven suites of bedrooms. The house was refurbished, and in parts redecorated, in 1993 under the supervision of Michael Priest of London, who did an excellent job. A quite exceptionally handsome and well-furnished house, amidst beautifully-kept gardens: a real treasure even for this well-heeled Gold Coast.

Photograph: Owner's collection.
Situation: Craigdarragh Road, Helen's Bay; td, Ballyrobert; District Council, North Down; Grid ref. J 449 818.
References: Listed A (23/16/30). VAL 12B/17/7A, p 26, in PRONI; Dean, 'Gate lodges', UAHS, 1994, p 74; notes by Paul Larmour, 1994, in MBR; J E M Crosbie, 'Rathmoyle', booklet, nd.

Ballyalloly House, Comber

67. Nearly on the site of an earlier Georgian house - said to have been built in 1792; foursquare, three-bay, three-storey - knocked down to make way for the present seven-bay two-storey house, designed by Blackwood & Jury in 1924 for "Captain the Rt Hon. Herbert Dixon DL MP", later Lord Glentoran. A very successful and interesting exercise in the neo-Georgian style built (by the Dixon's family firm of builders) to the highest standards and of the best of materials: the mahogany doors are of remarkable quality. The house seems not to have been completed until 1930 or even later. It stands amidst fine trees on a hillside, looking south over a splendidly laid out garden of lawns, terraces, flower-beds, and lake, principally the work of Mrs Billy Stephens, whose husband bought the house after the death of Lady Glentoran. It was acquired by the present owner in 1988; both house and grounds are now in excellent shape.

The layout is an unusual one: a short avenue amidst

mature trees leads to a hedged and gravelled forecourt onto which the central front door opens. The façade has angled advancing blocks on either side, giving a sense of enclosure; white-painted roughcast walls, Georgian-glazed windows, some paired, some single, in a symmetrical pattern; hipped roof and good chimney-stacks; very traditional doorcase with segmental fanlight and side-lights. If the principal front is, in effect, concave, the garden front is, in effect, convex, with the wings sloping back at either side of the centre, and a complicated pattern of projections and bays to take advantage of the view over the gardens.

A comfortable and pleasant house, and apparently a considerable achievement on the part of the youthful Arthur Jury, who did not enter partnership with his father until 1931, though he had started his pupillage in 1920. It is just possible that it is not by him; but it is in such marked contrast to the earlier buildings of William Blackwood and

Percy Jury, with their unfailing quirky detailing either in Art Nouveau or Arts and Crafts style, so faithfully recorded by Paul Larmour, that it seems reasonable to attribute it to the younger man. He liked country-house work, and had a talent for it: the new house built at Shane's Castle after the second World War was also his work, and I was perhaps remiss in omitting it from my Buildings of County Antrim; or perhaps my interest in Edwardian and later buildings has grown.

Photographs: A C W Merrick.
Situation: Off Ballyalloly Road, Comber; td, Ballyalloly; District Council, Ards; Grid ref. J 430 682.
References: Not listed. Jupp, 'Heritage gardens inventory', 1992,, D/002; P R Millar, Blackwood and Jury, unpublished dissertation, QUB, 1993, passim; architect's drawings in possession of owner; information from owner.

Glenmakieran (formerly Mirronhurst), Cultra, Holywood

68. An extremely grand Edwardian merchant's house, in the so-called free-style, by a, to me, unknown, architect, built for Ernest Herdman: the foundation stone was laid in 1909. Herdman was son of the founder of Herdman & Co of Sion Mills, County Tyrone, John Herdman, who had been shot dead by his own nephew after a family difference whilst walking on the Antrim Road, Belfast, in 1862. He was a very prosperous man: managing director of Henry Matier & Co, May Street (he had married Lucy

Lambert, whose mother had been a Matier), and a Belfast Harbour Commissioner.

The house is a staggeringly large three storeys, part white roughcast, part hung with red wall-tiles. It has steep sweeping red-tiled roofs; tall clustered chimney-stacks; eyebrow-dormers; square-paned lattice windows, no doubt inspired by Edwin Lutyens's house of 1901 at Deanery Gardens, Sonning; great canted bays looking out over Belfast Lough; front-door-case with rectangular oriel

above it set into an internal corner; in grounds of no less than 15 acres, with mature trees, lawns, stable blocks, and a later gate lodge (Dean says of 1928); and its own water supply from two reservoirs higher up the Whinny Hill. Occupied for over 20 years by a prominent Belfast eye surgeon, Eric Cowan; sold in 1993 to an absentee owner by whom it was considerably neglected; resold in 2000 to an un-named purchaser: it is to be hoped he will look after it, whoever he may be.

Next door, there stands an almost equally large house in equally extensive grounds, 'The Hill,' built for Herdman's fellow Harbour Commissioner Fred Heyn, head of the shipping firm, G Heyn & Sons, by the Belfast architect Henry Seaver, at almost exactly the same date, 1908. (Is it a coincidence that the two gentlemen's portraits and entries appear on the same page of R M Young's book?) It is listed B+, and the listers say "A large two-storey Edwardian 'Free-style' house ... built of red brick and white-painted roughcast, with red-tiled hipped roofs and half-timbering", with many Arts and Crafts features. Paul Larmour writes that this is "the best example of his work in the 'Old English' style ... a magnificent half-timbered

house ... virtually hidden from public view". Although I have recollections of attending children's parties in this house, before the second World War, I have not lately been able to see it: its present owner refused me access. But it seems worth wondering whether the two rich colleagues, who built expensive houses next door to each other in extensive grounds at almost exactly the same time, might not have chosen the same architect? There is no evidence for this that I can find, so perhaps they employed rival architects: in which case, Vincent Craig would not be an implausible candidate for Mirronhurst: compare his work at Rathmoyle of 1901 (66).

Photographs; A C W Merrick.
Situation: South of Bangor Road, Cultra: Glenmakieran, 141 Bangor Road; The Hill, 143 Bangor Road, td, Ballymenagh; District Council, North Down; Grid ref. J 417 801.
References: Glenmakieran, not listed; The Hill, listed B+ (23/18/52). Young, 'Belfast and province of Ulster', 1909, p 393; 'Edwardian architecture', I, 1975, p 89; P Larmour in 'Perspective', III, Jan/Feb 1995, p 59; Glenmakieran, information from Miss Aleen Herdman, and Mr Denis Templeton; The Hill, D 1898/1/54, in PRONI; IB XLIX, 1907, p 729, and information from Miss Aleen Herdman.

Guincho, Helen's Bay

69. To the best of my knowledge, the first house in the Hispanic style in Northern Ireland: fore-runner of a thousand hacienda style bungalows; but this one is Portuguese, not Spanish. Built by Alan Craig and his wife Ida to celebrate their honeymoon at Praia do Guincho, near Cascais, north of Lisbon, the White Park Bay of Portugal, and

completed around 1933 - by then, I was the little boy (aged seven) next door. I well remember the scorn my "Aunt Ida" (as I was invited to call her - pronounced ee-dah) poured on anyone who was fool enough to call it "Gwincho": "You wouldn't call it Gwinness, would you?" she used to ask, crushingly - a crack which acquired added savour when, after the sudden death of Alan Craig, she married *en secondes noces* Melville McClure, owner (with Brian, later Sir Brian, Morton) of Morton's Red Heart Bottled Stout, sold to connoisseurs at a penny a bottle above the going rate for bottled Guinness; and also owner of Melville's Funeral Furnishers: a man of substance.

Originally, a long, low, white-painted house, with red Mediterranean-style pantiles; a roof curving down to the wide, over-sailing, eaves, and twisting pinnacles like goats' horns at the corners; two tall chimney-stacks, with extravagant tiled brims; a blue-and-white *azulejo* tile inset into the front wall, above and to one side of the treble-recessed arched granite doorcase. All this at the heart of a large and splendid garden, first laid out by Ida Craig, though generally credited to Mrs Vera Mackie, who certainly introduced the numerous species plantings, but was perhaps not really responsible for the original layout of this notable garden, which is described by Malins and Bowe as an "Irish compartmented garden". Mrs Mackie's former head gardener, William Harrison, says "In 1948 Mr and Mrs Frazer Mackie bought Guincho, whose sixteen acres contained mostly herbaceous and bedding plants (not at all to Mrs Mackie's taste). Mrs Mackie never lost her head; she made a plantsman's garden, with the emphasis on rarity".

The glen and stream, in which I used to sail toy boats, remain as delightful as ever. The round pond, which then seemed too large for the sailing of boats, seems unaccountably to have shrunk. But the Guincho gardens remain extremely rewarding; private property, but opened for charity, and for the National Trust Gardens Scheme, from time to time.

The Mackies eventually sold in 1979 to a somewhat unsympathetic owner, a Mr Armstrong, who made some unfortunate changes in the house, which then passed to a Nigerian, Dr Moshida, who painted it brown. After lying vacant for some considerable time, the house was bought by its present owner in 1987: he was obliged to spend almost a year on restoring it to good order, and on putting the gardens (now once again very notable) back into shape. His alterations, some for the better, some not, included the removal of the *azulejo* panel, of the corner curlicues, and of the original striking chimney-stacks, for which puny and inappropriate Irish cottage chimneys have been substituted, all somewhat regrettable changes; but also the re-arrangement of the window-openings, and especially the deepening of the upstairs windows at each end of each façade, with the addition of very appropriate wrought-iron balconies: unquestionably an improvement, although it is a pity that the replacement window-frames are plastic. The house is now re-coated with roughcast, painted cream, with white trim, and externally very handsome; not quite symmetrical, but then it never was. It would still look quite at home in the hills above Estoril, where it had its conception. Internally, only a few of its original features survive: but there are still doors (including the fine front door) and one floor of solid American oak. A well-planned, light and airy house; and a most uncommon example of untypical 1930s architecture. Alas, architect, not known; did the Craigs bring back the plans from Portugal? Did they employ a local supervising architect? Or did they just do without - Alan Craig, of Greenhill & Craig Ltd, being a very competent and successful builder and developer in his own right? Neither the present owner, nor I, know the answer to these questions. Nevertheless, this building, though un-noticed and unlisted, remains an important milestone in Ulster's architectural history.

Photograph: A C W Merrick (see also colour illus. 20).
Situation: 69 Craigdarragh Road, Helen's Bay; td, Ballyrobert; District Council, North Down; Grid ref. J 445 816.
References: Not listed; but in the supplementary section of the DoENI register of historic parks, gardens and demesnes; Malins and Bowe, 'Irish gardens and demesnes', 1980, pp 160-161; W Harrison, in 'In an Irish garden', 1986; Jupp, 'Heritage gardens inventory', 1992, D/026; Belinda Jupp, notes in MBR.

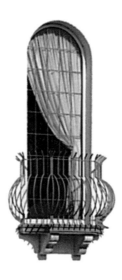

CHAPTER FOUR

CLERGY HOUSES

The northern part of County Down is far from rich in clergy houses of architectural interest, whether rectories, manses, or parochial houses. And of the handful considered worthy of inclusion in this book, not a single one is still used for the purpose for which it was built. However, a few have been well refurbished to make extremely attractive dwelling-houses.

It seems that Bishop Alexander built himself a handsome Regency palace, called Ashfield, at some time between 1804 and 1823, in the townland of Knocknagoney, outside Holywood; in a classical style not dissimilar from that of his other palatial house at Portglenone, County Antrim. M M Kertland of the Ordnance Survey says just "The palace is handsome though not large and the plantations

around it are not extensive"[1]. Unlike Portglenone, which remained in his family, this house was after his death the home of Bishops Mant and Knox; but by the 1880s was in poor order, and was sold to the War Office, which demolished it, and built on its site the Palace Barracks. A print of the house illustrating an article of 1923 by F J Bigger on 'Holywood 100 years ago', shows an imposing hipped-roof building, its wings linked by a balcony carried on six columns: a considerable loss to the town[2]. It was succeeded by Culloden (79), for a number of later years the palace of the Church of Ireland Bishops of Down, Connor and Dromore; whose private chapel is now part of the bar of the very sizeable and luxurious Culloden Hotel, in which the older house has been almost completely engulfed.

Daniel Louis Delacherois, of the Manor House, Donaghadee (49), an inveterate amateur water-colourist, sketched his rector, the Rev. John Hill, preaching and conducting service in his double-decker pulpit at Donaghadee; c. 1835. This double-decker pulpit was replaced in 1888, though probably already removed in the 1878-1881 remodelling of the church.[3] The artist was called to the bar in London, but never practised; instead he travelled and sketched whatever took his fancy. His sketchbooks are still in the Manor House. Although neither Donaghadee parish church nor rectory are included in this volume, it seems permissable to show these unusual illustrations of the clergy of the day.

The Rev. John Hill was incumbent from 1830 until 1877.[4] Although these pictures are to be found in a sketch-book containing other paintings

dated 1868, they appear to be a good deal earlier; as Gordon Wheeler remarks, "the gentleman is wearing collar and neckcloth of the 1830s. The clerical collar, without bands, would have been worn by 1868. Both sketches are of the same man: he wears his preaching gown when in the pulpit; and his surplice when at the reading-desk conducting service. The proper use of the surplice was a great bone of contention in the 1830s and 1840s".[5]

1. M M Kertland, OSM, nd (? 1835), Down, II, p 82. 2. F J Bigger, in BNL, 28/ 2/1923. 3. Dixon, 'Donaghadee and Portpatrick', UAHS, 1977, p 10. 4. 'Clergy of Down and Dromore', 1996, pp 105-106. 5. Mayo, 'History of ecclesiastical dress', 1984, p 94.

Old Rectory, Annahilt

70. The Rev. John Dubourdieu wrote in 1816: "The glebe-house was built in 1790 and 1791 by the present incumbent, at an expense of nearly £1200. He built under the old act of Parliament, by which he was obliged to find the money himself, and as he has exceeded the two years' income of the parish, he cannot recover from his successor more than three-fourths of what he laid out in the mere buildings. In addition to this he has made a good garden, and has improved the glebe lands by draining, ditching and planting, at a considerable additional expense; but he is in some degree remunerated by seeing a dreary wild converted into a substantial and comfortable residence for himself and for his successors".

Dubourdieu was, of course, the author of the Statistical Surveys of County Down (1802), and of County Antrim (1812). He was rector of Annahilt from 1789 until 1817, and had four sons and four daughters, so needed a substantial residence. Dean Swanzy says "Local tradition represents him as saying that a goose was an unsatisfactory table bird, too much for one, too little for two". When he was an old man, in 1834, the young John O'Donovan called upon him and got an "ungracious" reception. "I have called this morning upon the Revd John Dubourdieu, Rector of Drumballyroney and Drumgoolan, and you will be surprised when I say that I have been quite disappointed in him. He is now a very old grey-headed, peevish man, and a haughty, aristocratic, half-civilized, self sufficient little bit of an Irish Frenchman ... I was never so

disgusted with any little *Cur, whelp* or *pup* in all my life. His petty aristocratic assumptions and ungentlemanly remarks had a very disagreeable effect upon my sensitive nerve". Intellectual snobbery on the one part, or youthful inferiority complex on the other? Who knows? It seems that Dubourdieu also built the glebe-house at Drumgooland. He died in 1839 aged 85.

The rectory was sold by the Church of Ireland after the second World War, and after some years fell into dereliction. It was subsequently extensively (and expensively) restored, re-roofed, and, in parts, rebuilt, with an indoor heated swimming pool and cocktail bar, amenities undreamed of by Mr Dubourdieu. The central block is two-storey and attic on basement, four bays wide, with massive chimney-stacks; there are single-storey wings containing respectively front and back door. The area affording light to the basement has attractive railings. The house is encased in nicely painted white roughcast, and all the glazing bars have been reinstalled: it now looks very handsome on its hillside amidst mature trees.

Photograph: A C W Merrick.
Situation: Glebe Road, Annahilt, Hillsborough. Grid ref. J 301 574.
References: Listed B (19/6/1). J Dubourdieu, in Mason, 'Parochial survey', II, 1816, p 11; O'Donovan, 'Letters ... 1834', 2001, pp 37-38, 40; Swanzy, 'Succession lists of ... Dromore', 1933, pp 142-144; undated press cutting in MBR.

Old Rectory, Portaferry

71. Samuel Lewis, in 1837, says, under Ballyphilip, "The glebe-house was built in 1818, at an expense of £1090, of which £825 was loan from the late Board of First Fruits, and £265 was added by the present incumbent, and is chargeable on his successors"; and, under Portaferry, "The glebe-house of Ballyphilip, the residence of the Chancellor of Down, stands on the site of the ancient parish church, which is said to have been once an abbey. The first Marquess of Londonderry received his early education in this house". In his second edition of 1847 Lewis corrects this to "The late Marquess of Londonderry" (ie, Lord Castlereagh, the Second Marquess) "received the rudiments of his education in the glebe-house, under Dr. Sturrock, then chancellor of Down, and incumbent of this parish". Knox adds the disconcerting detail that, "In a garden adjoining, there was a crypt, mentioned in Archdall's Monasticon, which, in a boyish frolic, was blown up by Robert, second Marquis of Londonderry, and his schoolfellow, who were, at the time, under the tuition of the rector, the Rev. Dr. Sterrock [*sic*]".

G Scott, in his Ordnance Survey memoir of about 1837, says: "Glebe House, the residence of the Reverend W. St John Smyth, in the townland and parish of Ballyphilip ... is highly characteristic of a Glebe House, almost surrounded by a plantation". Lavens Ewart, writing in 1886, says "The original church of Ballyphilip stood within the glebe, and the glebe-house is built upon a portion of the ancient graveyard ... In confirmation of this, it may be stated that, when the glebe-house was being enlarged some years ago, human remains were met with during the process of laying the foundation for the walls. On this occasion an eminent living ecclesiastic, who at the time was in the neighbourhood, made the witty suggestion that that portion of the house should be designated 'the scullery'". Ugh!

The rectory is described in the UAHS List of 1969 as follows: "a very pleasant white two-storey Georgian house: unfortunately the good doorcase and fanlight are obscured by a Victorian porch; and there are distressing yellow-brick chimneys. The three-storey addition at the rear is congruous": no doubt this embraces 'the scullery'. In 1982 the then incumbent, and occupant of the building, the Rev. J P O Barry, took issue with this Georgian dating of the rectory, maintaining that it was in fact much earlier: he illustrates the "beautiful 17th Century fanlight"; and asserts "There can be little doubt that the Rectory was built at least a century before 1818, by Archibald MacNeale, M.A., who was the incumbent of Portaferry 1684 - 1707"; and supports this view by reference to the opinions expressed by his father's friend, the eminent Mr Dykes Bower. There is no doubt that Mr Dykes Bower was a great authority on English church architecture: but it may be doubted whether he was an authority on Irish domestic architecture. Certainly, the doorcase and fanlight would have been old-fashioned in England after 1800; but he perhaps did not allow for the fact that, in provincial Ireland, such details were still to be found in new houses built in the 1820s, the 1830s, and even occasionally the 1840s. As Mr Scott of the Ordnance Survey says, Portaferry "is highly characteristic of a Glebe House", of the kind erected under the auspices of the Board of First Fruits. Despite Dr Barry's arguments, and with all due respect, I remain confident that Lewis got the date of the present building right.

It should perhaps be added that all the Georgian-glazed windows in the front wall are triple windows; and that the roughcast walls have vermiculated quoins. The rectory was sold off by the church in 1998. At the date of writing, though the garden is tidy, the house appears to be empty and, perhaps, at some risk.

Photograph; A C W Merrick.
Situation: Cloghy Road, Portaferry; td, Ballyphilip; District Council, Ards; Grid ref. J 600 514.
References: Listed B1 (24/1/52). Lewis, TD, 1837, I, p 161; II, p 464; Lewis, TD, 1847, I, p 154; G Scott, OSM, nd (?1837),'Down', II, p 14; Knox, 'County of Down', 1875, p 468; Ewart, 'Down & Connor & Dromore', 1886, p 38; Bell, 'Portaferry & Strangford', UAHS, 1969, p 12; J P O Barry, in JUAHS, VI, 1982, pp 11-14.

Wellington Lodge, Culcavey, Hillsborough

72. It seems legitimate to infer from its name that this house was built, rebuilt, or re-named, not too long after the battle of Waterloo: though I have been unable to track down documentary evidence about its origins, or to identify it in the Valuation book of 1834. The listers say "About 1780. A two-storey Georgian house with slated roof and coloured rendered walls. The central door has an elliptical arched fanlight". They also say that it is in Carnreagh townland; but it appears in the Griffith valuation in Culcavey. Pierce and Coey describe it as "A three-bay two-storey house, formerly a mid-17th century coaching inn but altered to its present appearance about 1790". So far as I can discover, the evidence for this is purely local oral tradition; not that that does not deserve to be taken seriously.

What is certain is the entry in the Griffith valuation of 1861: "Wellington Lodge. Rev. Edward Kent from Marquis of Downshire, lessor. Mr. Kent purchased this place about two years ago, and paid £400 for the outgoing tenant's interest. He has also expent about £300 on the improvement of the house". Mr Kent was rector of Annahilt until 1847, when he became Treasurer and Rural Dean of Dromore. This seems to have been his private house, not a glebe-house, He lived here off and on, between 1859 and his death in London in 1863. Perhaps Kent's widow lived on here; but from 1873 until 1876 it was the private house, in his retirement, of Rev. Edward Smyth, who had been rector at Rathfriland until 1873, and who died in Wellington Lodge in 1876. After 1863, Culcavey had formed part of the parish of Christ Church, Lisburn (as opposed to Lisburn Cathedral); following the creation of the new parish of Eglantine, Wellington Lodge became its rectory in 1876 and was occupied by Rev. Stephen Campbell, evidently a rather awkward customer, who "complains of the value of the house. A large portion of

the rere is at present" (1879) "being rebuilt and roofed".

Valued first, in 1861, at £12 10 0, then at £15 10 0, then at £24 10 0; in category 1A; measurements, 50 yards by 22 yards by 18 feet. Mr Campbell's successor, Rev. F W Hogan, vicar of Eglantine parish from 1882 to 1915, apparently spent nearly £500 on the house in 1880, with the result that its valuation rose to £27 5 0. He was still there in 1913, when apparently the freehold had been bought in by the Church under the Land Purchase Acts. The photograph shows Canon A D Mitchell and his wife shortly before his retirement in 1961. The house has been substantially altered and restored since it was sold by the Church in 1967, when a new rectory was built beside Eglantine Church. It was occupied for many years by Mr Jeremy Bryson, who sold in 1998 to the present owners.

It is a pleasing house, in the style of a rectory even if not built as such, two-storey, three-bay, of cream-painted stucco with quoins; a pretty doorcase with reeded pilasters, good fanlight, and side-lights; gabled roof with a chimney-stack at each end: standing in agreeable grounds amidst fine mature trees. The ground floor windows on either side of the door are wide triple ones, those above them narrower triple ones; the central window, above the front door, is an orthodox single Georgian window. All now have restored Georgian glazing-bars, the sashes and astragals white-painted.

Photograph: Courtesy of Rev. C W Bell, rector of Eglantine.
Situation: 67 Lisburn Road, Hillsborough; td, Culcavey; District Council, Lisburn; Grid ref. J 255 606.
References: Listed B (19/4/3). VAL 2B/3/43, p 54; VAL 12B/20/16A - E, in PRONI; Pierce and Coey, 'Taken for granted', 1984, p 137; 'Clergy of Connor', 1992, pp 247, 394; 'Clergy of Down and Dromore', 1996, passim; Scott, 'Churches of the Diocese of Connor', 1997, pp 89-90.

Dromara House

73. In 1974 I wrote: "1821; possibly by James McBlain, but more probably by Charles Lilley; but very evidently from Lord Downshire's stable of local architects. An attractive L-shaped house, three-bay, two-storey and basement, with

hipped roof, the ground-floor windows inset in round-headed recessed arches; three-light doorcase and fanlight; stucco, the ground floor of the entrance front rusticated. The stone outbuildings at the rear include one used as a manor court house, and the basement incorporates a 'black hole' to which the squarson incumbent could consign offenders".

J Hill Williams of the Ordnance Survey remarked in 1837 that "The Glebe House of Dromara is a good 2-storey house nearly a quarter of a mile to the westward of the town, at the meeting of the Banbridge and Dromore roads. It is the residence of the Rev. Hannington Elija Boyd, rector; was built in 1820 at a cost of 1,125 pounds, 100 of which were a gift and the remaining 1,125 a loan from the Board of First Fruits". Lewis just says that the glebe house was erected in 1821. The listers say, "A typical Church of Ireland rectory of the period that has suffered very little change through time".

Now a private house; and at the time of writing, undergoing extensive refurbishment.

Photographs: A C W Merrick.
Situation: 50 Banbridge Road, Dromara; td, Dromara; District Council, Lisburn; Grid ref, J 283 498.
References: Listed B1(19/7/9). J H Williams, OSM, 1837, Down, III, p 69; Lewis, TD, 1837, I, p 503; ASCD, 1966, p 361; Brett, 'Mid Down', UAHS, 1974, p 32.

St Elizabeth's Court, Dundonald

74. "... in 1819 the Rev. Dillon laid the foundation stone of a splendid new rectory. However, in spite of a generous grant, the building work left Dillon out of pocket, and the entry" in the Vestry minutes "covering it has a slightly martyred air: 'cost £830 - received only £800 from the Board of First Fruits: erecting offices and all other improvements amounting to nearly £400 sterling, at the sole expense of the Incumbent'" (Carr). However, as rectories go it was a large and comfortable one: in which Mr Dillon lived on until his death, in the house, in his 82nd year, in 1851. Lt Bordes of the Ordnance Survey merely includes "the Glebe House" amongst the gentlemen's seats of the Parish. Lewis writes in 1847 "The glebe-house, a handsome residence, was built in 1819 by a gift of £300 and a loan of £500 from the late Board of First Fruits; the glebe comprises 15 acres".

Now converted into housing association flats for old people, with subsidiary buildings all around in the former ample garden, the whole under the title of St Elizabeth's Court. (The parish church is dedicated to St Elizabeth -

not the mother of St John the Baptist, but, for some obscure reason, to the 13th-century St Elizabeth of Hungary). The central block is three-bay, two-storey, with hipped roof and broad chimney-stacks; two bays deep; glazing-bars complete; sill-course; central doorcase with wooden Doric columns and simple geometrical fanlight; walls now covered in a slightly unpleasing cement stucco. At each side there is a pseudo-pedimented subsidiary block with a tall round-headed window. Fairly sympathetically converted, but somehow it has acquired a more institutional air than it really ought to have.

Photograph; A C W Merrick.
Situation: 28 Ballyregan Road, Dundonald; td, Ballyregan; District Council, Castlereagh; Grid ref. J 419 741.
References: Listed B (25/5/1). Vestry minutes; OS map, 1834; G F W Bordes, OSM, 1834, Down, II, p 65; Lewis, TD, 1847, I, p 559; Leslie, 'Clergy of Diocese of Down', 1936, p 118; Carr, 'Most unpretending of places', 1987, p108; 'Clergy of Down and Dromore', 1996, p 110.

Old Rectory, Kircubbin

75. How fortunate was my great-great-grandfather, Wills Hill Brett, to be provided in 1843 by his patron, Robert Ward of Bangor, with such a handsome rectory! Kircubbin Church (39) is certainly by Charles Lanyon; it seems very probable that the rectory is likewise from his hand, or at any rate, from his office. Gordon Wheeler has pointed out to me the similarity between the pierced balustrade above the porch to those used by Lanyon (or possibly his assistant Thomas Turner) both at Ballywalter Park (59) and Craigdarragh House (60); likewise the suspended garlands both on the gate piers of Kircubbin Church and on the rectory porch; and details in common with their glebe-house at Upper Ballinderry, County Antrim, attributed to Thomas Turner.

Wills Brett was born at Charleville (123) in the 'year of liberty', 1798. Family tradition has it that his nursemaid hid him under a hedge in the Castlereagh hills for fear the rebels should come that way after the Battle of Ballynahinch. Educated at Trinity College, Dublin, son of a prosperous Belfast merchant, he was appointed incumbent of the parish of Greyabbey in 1822, and remained there for twenty-one years. It was "by no means an enviable appointment. There was no parsonage, no glebe-house, no glebe; there were no tithes; the total income of the parish was a mere £55 per annum". In 1831, aged 33, he married Mattie Garrett, daughter of a Belfast solicitor, keen on natural history, and something of a blue-stocking. "She was a woman of literary and musical tastes. She was interested in botany, and contributed to Sir Joseph Hooker's *British Flora*. Family tradition has it that she spent most of her life, when not bearing children, lying on a sofa studying Greek and Hebrew texts ... thirteen children were born, at regular intervals, of whom ten survived, and three died in infancy" (Brett).

It must have been a great relief all round when Robert Ward presented him to the living of Kircubbin, which the latter had endowed with church, parsonage, and income of £140 a year, in 1843. The tithes war of the 1830s was followed by the famine of the 1840s: but the fortunate Wills Brett remained comparatively snug until his untimely death in 1862, leaving his eldest son (my great-grandfather Charles Henry Brett), then a young solicitor aged 23, responsible for the upkeep of his widowed mother, his elder sister, and eight younger brothers and sisters. Wills died leaving an estate of between £4000 and £5000, of which only £20 was left to his eldest son. His assets including a cow valued at £12 15 0; a heifer valued at £6 17 6; and a piano valued at £3 5 0. House, offices, and land were valued in 1863 at £22 - that is, their rateable value representing the rental they might be expected to generate. Wills Brett was succeeded in the following year by Rev. Edward Lyle, who moved into grander premises at Tubber na Carrig soon afterwards, letting the parsonage to one Anne Shaw. In 1900, Rev. Charles Johnston moved into the rectory; in 1920, he was succeeded by Rev. Falkiner Wilkinson. The valuation remained unchanged throughout. The house was sold by the Representative Church Body to the present owner when the parish was united with Greyabbey in 1975.

The house is a large, comfortable, roomy, foursquare, parsonage in the late-Georgian manner, with commodious coach-house, stabling and out-buildings. Two-storey on extensive basement, three bays wide and deep, with a little peaked pediment above the hipped roof (the date '1843' inset in the course of re-roofing in 1997), and a rather grand porch, ornamented with garlands, almost certainly original; the windows all Georgian-glazed; quoins and string-course, rendered walls, now clothed in

Virginia creepers and climbing roses. Four large rendered chimney-stacks; good entrance gate-posts with pineapple finials. The rooms are very tall and spacious, but not very numerous: it is a puzzle to see how two parents, ten children, nursey, and servants, could all be fitted in: but they were. The house has been very little altered, and retains almost all of its original character, in a generously leafy garden: except that most of the original mantelpieces have gone; the kitchen has been brought upstairs from the basement; and the cobbled stable-yard has been tarma-cadamed over.

Photograph: A C W Merrick.
Situation: 52 Parsonage Road, Kircubbin; td, Kircubbin; District Council, Ards; Grid ref. J 602 628.
References: Listed B1 (24/2/22). D 3303/8/A/12A, VAL 2B/3/13, p 41, VAL 12B/23/19A - F, all in PRONI; Brett, 'Long shadows', 1978, pp 75, 110; J F Rankin, in 'Clergy of Down and Dromore', 1996, p 145; information from owners.

Albertville (formerly Rose Lodge), Groomsport

76. Patton says "c. 1840 and later", but the quality of the spidery fanlight and sidelights would to me have indicated a rather earlier date, perhaps around 1825. Unfortunately, this is masked from the road by a later porch. A two-storey three-bay rendered house with quoins, glazing bars complete, but its appearance somewhat marred by over-obtrusive slatted shutters. According to Patton, "it appears to have started life as a Perceval Maxwell house - *Rose Lodge* ... the Presbyterian Rev Isaac Mack lived here c. 1870 and extended or partly rebuilt it, but by 1855 it was used as a Rectory, and had become known as *Albertville*" - the name incised in the cap of one of the gate pillars.

Photograph; A C W Merrick.
Situation: 11 Bangor Road, Groomsport; td, Groomsport; District Council, North Down; Grid ref. J 534 838.
References: Listed B2 (23/1/9). Patton, 'Bangor', UAHS, 1999, p 17.

Mullaghadrin House, Dromara

77. A charming Victorian ex-manse of around 1850, on a steep hillside amidst fine mature trees, very well kept, now a private house. The listers say: "The form is symmetrical with the central bay advanced to form a porch. There is a ground floor and attic. This particular format was favoured by the Presbyterian church for about a generation but few examples survive with so little alteration". A report of 1991 in the Monuments and Buildings Record from Denis Piggot says "An interesting one-and-a-half-storey house, smooth-painted render and quoins and mouldings to semi-circular windows; in good condition, it has not been spoiled, is set in very attractive surroundings, on an elevated site, with plenty of trees around it".

At present the stucco is painted pale yellow, with white quoins and trim. All its windows are round-headed, some paired in double architraves, some not, though something awful seems to have happened to the front attic window; otherwise a very pleasant house.

Photograph; A C W Merrick.
Situation: 90 Hillsborough Road, Dromara; td, Mullaghdrin; District Council, Lisburn; Grid ref. J 286 506.
References: Listed B2 (19/7/8). D Piggot, notes in MBR.

Ballyblack Lodge, Loughries, Newtownards

78. A pleasant three-bay, two-storey former manse, very much in the Georgian glebe-house tradition: cream-painted roughcast; yellow brick chimney-stacks; nice doorcase, with sidelights and Gothicky fanlight; good garden and trees. Altogether, a most attractive establishment.

Built about 1860 by the Rev. Marcus Mitchell, who also at the same date caused to be built Ballyblack Presbyterian Church, just along the road. He was succeeded by Mr Graham; then Mr Roulston; then Mr Williamson. By this time, the congregation was in somewhat low water: the minister, who had eked out his existence by cattle-dealing, went off to Scotland. In 1955, the elders decided to sell the house, and build a new and smaller manse just across the road. The old manse was bought by my widowed aunt, formerly of Glenganagh, Groomsport (55), then of the Roddens, Ballywalter; she added a new return, modernised the house, and kept her horse there; and, in due course, went to live in a more modest house at Loughries, and passed Ballyblack on to her daughter and her family, in whose ownership it remains.

Photograph; A C W Merrick.
Situation: Ballyblack Road, Loughries, Newtownards; td, Loughriscouse; District Council, Ards; Grid ref. J 529 728.
References: Listed B1 (24/8/9). Copy correspondence in MBR; information from owners.

Culloden, Cultra, Holywood

79. Culloden was first built, not as a clergy house but as a private residence, for William Auchinleck Robinson, a Scot, between 1876 and 1879, probably to designs by Young & Mackenzie. Their specifications, of July 1875, for building a lodge at 'Back Avenue, Cultra', are recorded by Dean; there are also specifications for a stable block, coach house, coachman's house, and other offices which survive in the Public Record Office. Whilst there is nothing in this grubby roll of paper to indicate that they were the architects of the house itself, it seems extremely likely. As Dean says, Robinson "came with his wife to Ireland in the 1850s to make his fortune as a stockbroker, settling on Belfast's Antrim Road. The extent of his success can be seen in this big mansion and outbuildings in appropriate

Scots Baronial style ... Most of the stone came from Scotland by boat, landed at Portaferry and brought by horse and cart to the Craigavad site. It took 2 years to build during which time the client resided in a small cottage in the gardens. For a while, after Robinson's death in 1884, the residence of the Bishops of Down, Dromore and Connor to whom it was conveyed by his wife Elizabeth Jane Robinson (*née* Culloden)". (Any connection with the infamous battle of Culloden is indignantly repudiated; apparently the lady pronounced her maiden name 'Cullowden').

It is a very imposing, but rather uncomfortably-proportioned, sandstone building in a kind of compromise between the Gothic and Scottish Baronial styles: its original appearance well shown in the Hogg photograph here reproduced. When newly built, it was valued at the high figure of £250. Williams comments: "Entry tower at one end. Adjoining garden front with asymmetrically treated bay windows, lively decorative stone carving ... The finest interior is the staircase hall, especially suitable when the house was a residence for Church of Ireland bishops (1898-1919), lit through an impressive Gothic window. Stained glass by Heaton, Butler and Bayne". He illustrates it with a contemporary engraving for which, as usual, alas, he offers no individual provenance: I have not succeeded in finding it. The suitability of the style of this house for ecclesiastical use is debatable: the interior detailing is so rich as to be sumptuous, if not vulgar; and its furnishing as a luxury hotel has not made it any more chaste or austere.

Culloden was used as the palace of the Church of Ireland bishops of Down, Connor and Dromore certainly from 1899, perhaps earlier, until about 1923, so may here qualify as a clergy house. In 1898, the then bishop, Dr Thomas Welland (son of the distinguished Irish ecclesiastical architect Joseph Welland) moved in; in 1886 the church had sold to the War Office the previous palace in Holywood, on the site of which the Palace Barracks now stand, and Dr Welland's predecessor, Dr William Reeves, had rented Conway House, Dunmurry, County Antrim, from the Barbour family until his death in 1892; after which Dr Welland had lived at Ardtullagh, near Redburn, in Holywood. Welland died in Culloden in 1907, and was succeeded by Dr Crozier, who had himself been rector of Holywood from 1880 to 1897. Dr D'Arcy was the next bishop; then Dr Grierson, during whose episcopate the house was sold, about 1923, to Sir John Campbell, a Belfast gynaecologist, whose widow and family lived on there until 1959, when it was bought from his son by a Mr

Reid; then, in 1962, it was bought for £18,500 by Mr Rutledge White (of White's Milk Bar, in Fountain Street, Belfast), who turned it into an hotel. It was subsequently acquired in 1967 by William Hastings as a hotel; in which capacity it has greatly prospered under the management of his company; and tremendous additions have been made, largely overshadowing the original house. So early as 1975, a note in the Monuments and Buildings Record observes that the extensions "already in existence are greater than the fabric of the original building".

The chapel, in the Early English style, was added in 1910 by Bishop Crozier to designs by W J Fennell, and dedicated on 7 August 1910 as the Bishop Jeremy Taylor Memorial Chapel, since the pulpit which he had used at Magheralin apparently provided the timber for the altar. It was designed for 24 persons, not just as a family chapel, but also "for devotional services and the celebration of Holy Communion when candidates for Ordination are staying there". It is now incorporated into the large and spacious bar, and provides a suitably morally improving drinking-parlour for the establishment. The front dining-room remains unchanged and is used for dinner-parties; most of the rest of the original house is now barely recognisable.

Photograph: A R Hogg, UM, H05/57/12. Engraving: from Williams, 'Architecture in Ireland'.
Situation: 142 Bangor Road, Cultra; td, Ballycultra; District Council, North Down; Grid ref. J 419 804.
References: Listed (23/18/17). VAL 12B/17/10C, pp 6, 59, D 2194/101/4, both in PRONI; 'Church of Ireland Gazette', August, 1910; Dean, 'Gate lodges', UAHS, 1994, p 72; Williams, 'Architecture in Ireland', 1994, p 103; J F Rankin in 'Clergy of Down and Dromore', 1996, p 216; notes by C Grant, and H Dixon, in possession of A C W Merrick; leaflet, 'Culloden Hotel', nd, passim; notes in MBR; information from A C W Merrick and G Wheeler.

Stairwell in Drumnabreeze House, Magheralin (99). Photograph: A C W Merrick

CHAPTER FIVE

MIDDLING-SIZED HOUSES

Though few traditional middling-sized houses survive in the densely-populated areas of north Down, Bangor, and Donaghadee, a surprising number still stand unspoiled and well cared-for in the western part of the county. These vary considerably in size and importance: most were originally either farm-houses, or the houses of mill-owners; some of each have risen to the pretensions of the gentry; one or two, such as Belvedere (98), and Drumnabreeze (99) seem to have been the homes of successful merchants or East India nabobs. A large proportion of them must originally have been little more than single-storey cottages. Some were three-bay, some five-bay, some more. Some had one storey added, a few two storeys. Many had extensive barns, weaving-sheds, water-mills, steam-mills, chimneys, and other out-buildings added over the years: others remained rustic and little altered. The majority were built of fieldstones, many subsequently roughcast or stuccoed, with no doubt in most cases thatched roofs at first, though later slated, whether with local or Bangor blue slates, but a few, regrettably, now tiled - a practice not in itself objectionable, but quite foreign to local tradition. Almost all except the grandest shared a similar pattern of sheeted doors, solid chimney-stacks, Georgian-glazed sash windows, and ornamental door-cases (rectangular, segmental, or semi-circular) often with delicate fanlights and sidelights.

The cantankerous Dr John Dubourdieu - as to whom, see Annahilt Rectory (70), - summed up the general housing position - large, middling, and small - in the county very justly, in his Statistical Survey of 1802. "Besides the several spacious habitations of the principal proprietors of this county, there are numerous and elegant modern built mansions belonging to the gentlemen; and others also, of an earlier date, modernized with taste and judgment. Those, though pleasing and enchanting objects of consideration, as so many proofs of the attachment of their owners to the soil, from whence they derive their resources, do not so properly come within the idea of an agricultural report, as the farm houses and offices ... Which, as may be supposed from the general size of the farms, are neither large nor convenient; they consist for the most part of a low cottage, the dwelling house, which contains a kitchen, and two or three rooms on the ground floor opening into each other, without any apartments over head; and seldom containing any other fire place than that of the kitchen; those in the other rooms having been shut up on the alteration of the hearth-money tax ... Where farms are large the houses are in proportion good, and amongst this class you see proportional attention to comfort and cleanliness in every department, within doors and without; many farmers of this class have houses with a second storey, slated roofs, and all the offices necessary to carrying on their business to advantage ... Amongst the resident gentlemen much attention is paid to their farm yards, &tc. and there are some very capital ones ... A well-sized barn, one proportioned to the farm, is absolutely necessary ... The cottages of the labourers, who have no land, are but poor, yet even they are superior to what they were ... Great attention has been paid by many of the gentlemen, to have comfortable, and often elegant cottages built for their labourers".[1]

There still survive, not too much altered, at least three, perhaps four, examples of the English yeoman's planter style, the first four houses in this chapter (80, 81, 82, and 83), but alas, these are now all too rare. It is good that three out of the four have recently been carefully and sensitively restored; one has been on the market, and must be regarded as at some risk, if only of deterioration to its setting.

There is a little group of blackstone buildings in the area between Moira, Lurgan, and Aghagallon, which stand out as a bit different from the rest. Local oral tradition has it that these were all built by Scottish stonemasons who, having been brought over to build the churches of Lurgan and Portadown, married local girls and set up in business in this area. I do not know whether to believe this or not. It does not seem very likely, since most of the blackstone churches seem to be later in date than the houses in question; but it is never wise to dismiss too quickly an oral tradition such as this.

There are a few bathing-lodges for the gentry, mostly on the south shore of Belfast Lough; but one or two also around the shores of Strangford Lough. Quite a substantial number of vernacular middling-sized town or village houses are of merit, but, for reasons set out in my general introduction, I have included only a handful. Very few middling-sized houses of the twentieth century appear to me to be of real architectural merit.

Nevertheless, all things considered, I found on my travels a good many more unspoiled houses of the middling size than I had foreseen: and the section which follows is, I am a bit surprised to say, considerably longer than I had anticipated.

Reference: 1. Dubourdieu, 'Statistical survey', 1802, pp 32-36.

The Grange, Waringstown

80. Although a stone inscribed '1698' is built into the corner of the garden wall, the building seems to have been considerably earlier: indeed, it may have been the original home built for William Waring when he first came to the village, before the construction of Waringstown House (46). Despite the fact that the thatched roof had been removed, and a slated roof substituted, in the 1920s, enough stumps of timber trusses remained to permit examination by way of dendrochronology. Of the four samples taken, two appeared to be from trees felled in 1658; and two from trees felled in 1692. This "raises the possibility that originally the Grange was a single-storey cruck building like the others in the village. The occurrence of the roof truss of 1692 presumably signifies the raising of the house to two storeys at that time. This could be a house upgraded for one of the weavers brought to Waringstown from the Low Countries ... These dates also explain why the more important buildings, Waringstown House and the parish church of 1667 and 1684, were well away from the centre of the village. The village was already there when they were built! ... The dates established for these three seventeenth-century Ulster

buildings lend strong support to the correctness of the Belfast chronology. Each date fitted well with either the specific or the general historical framework. Of particular importance in this respect were the samples with complete sapwood, as these specified exact felling years" (Baillie). The Archaeological Survey of County Down thought this house to be 18th-century: so nobody is infallible.

Originally two houses under one roof, part of a terrace of thatched cruck houses, situated well above, and set back from, the line of the main street of what used to be a most attractive village. Presumed to have been at first a yeoman planter's house, then perhaps the house of a weaver, it was occupied as a farmhouse by the Irwin family for many years, but by 1969 had fallen into disrepair and lay empty: proposals to redevelop the site encountered a public outcry, and in consequence it was acquired for £1,850 by the Craigavon Development Commission, which in 1972 sold it on to the late John Lewis-Crosby, who personally undertook its restoration. In 1980 its was successfully converted into a restaurant, but in 2000 was back on the market. At the time of writing there are proposals to build four red-brick houses in the orchard on the hillside behind the house; if this is permitted, it is likely to prove highly detrimental to its appearance.

This is a seven-bay two-storey building of random blackstone, with two doorways and Georgian glazing-bars, the gables and rear roughcast and painted white, all very handsome. The gables had to be taken down and rebuilt during the restoration of 1972; early in the 20th century the thatch had been removed, the long walls raised, and the roof then slated, as it remains; there are later outbuildings at the rear.

Photographs: A C W Merrick; R J Welch, UM, W05/91/5.
Situation: Main Street, Waringstown; td, Tullyherron; District Council, Craigavon; Grid ref. J 104 552.
References: Listed B (14/6/18). Datestone; OS map, 1833; ASCD, 1966, p 439; Oram, Craigavon, UAHS, 1971, Pt II, p 7; Baillie, 'Tree-ring dating', 1982, p 133; correspondence in MBR.

Berwick Hall, Moira

81. A very fine six-bay two-storey whitewashed and thatched farmhouse, with Georgian glazing-bars, a rare example, and an epitome of its kind. Dixon says "Almost exclusive to the areas where English plantation was predominant are the two-storey thatched houses, generally referred to as yeoman's or planter's houses. Unlike the single-storey 'long houses' which are never more than a single room wide, the planter's house could often be on a fairly large scale, as at Berwick Hall, near Moira, with its high-pitched roof and tall chimneys. Size alone, however, connects such buildings with the tradition of designed architecture. The materials, stone, thatch, rendering and whitewash, and the unorganised irregularity of the facade all place the house firmly within the vernacular tradition".

The Archaeological Survey of County Down describes it as "rectangular, 60 ft. by 24 ft., and has both long and gable walls 2 ft. 2 in. thick of random rubble harled over ... The first floor windows are squat and lie directly under a small projecting eaves-cornice. There are small windows at first floor in both gables". It draws attention to, and illustrates, the original front door with its 'mouth-organ' fanlight; very unfortunately, both were removed some twenty years ago in order to increase the head-room at the front entrance to the house, though still referred to by Dr Gailey in 1984 as "the earliest surviving door ... a fairly thin panelled door; the panels have raised fields the upper two of which are shouldered with curved tops". (It seems that this door and doorcase survive in the Ulster Folk Museum. It would be possible to reproduce both door and fanlight by reference to the very clear photograph at plate 141 of the Survey, and this would be well worth while). Apart from the generally agreeable appearance of the house, its most interesting feature is the timberwork of the roof structure. Berwick Hall has traditionally been dated to 'c 1700', but this can now be refined since, in the course of recent restoration work and rethatching, a core was taken from the roof timbers and sent off for dating by dendrochronology; and was found to be from a tree probably

felled in 1682. Of course, that does not necessarily mean that it was built in the same year, for the timber would have needed to be seasoned; although probably none too much time was allowed between felling and use in the late 17th-century.

The house was named after the Berwick family, who were said to have been its builders, and who were certainly its tenants from the Batesons of Moira for many years. One of them was the Rev. Edward Berwick (1750-1820), a literary clergyman of considerable attainments, who was vicar of Tullylish before moving to livings in the south of Ireland and becoming domestic chaplain to the Earl of Moira. He edited The Rawdon Papers, published classical and theological works, and was a friend of Sir Walter Scott. In the time of the next Edward Berwick, in 1834, the farmhouse was valued at £16 5 5; in 1862, home of Mark Berwick, valued at £15, with the comment "Neat concern. House old". In 1883, the Berwicks gave way to the Wilson family: John A Wilson inherited from Sarah Wilson in 1926, when the farmhouse was still valued at £15. The house is still in the ownership of, and well cared for by, members of the latter family; there have been some modern additions at the rear, but there are still attractive farm out-buildings, perhaps surprisingly not considered worthy of including in the listing.

Photographs: A C W Merrick (see also colour illus. 29); MBR.
Situation: 1 Hillsborough Road, Moira; td, Aughnadrumman; District Council, Lisburn; Grid ref. J 159 606.
References: Listed A (19/22/3). VAL 1B/347, VAL 2B/3/47A, p 31, VAL 12B/21/7A-E, in PRONI; OS map, 1833; Sergeant, in DNB, II, 1885, p 414; Swanzy, 'Succession lists of ... Dromore', 1933; ASCD, 1966, p 354, pls 137, 141; Oram, 'Craigavon', UAHS, 1971, Pt II, p 10; Dixon, 'Introduction', 1975, p 31; Gailey, 'Rural houses', 1984, p 130.

98 Dromore Road, Waringstown

82. A beautifully-restored 17th- or 18th-century vernacular roadside farmhouse: the older part, four-bay, two-storey, recently very well rethatched with flax; openings irregularly spaced; harled and whitewashed: the newer part, slightly lower - formerly potato-house - slated; Georgian glazing-pattern complete in both, and in end gables. Admirably painted with bright red surrounds to the windows: I do not know who chose the colours, but they could not look better. An absolutely outstanding example of first-class restoration, by a private citizen, of what had in 1999 been a bedraggled wreck, in the midst of a pig-farm. The only thing that detracts just a little from an otherwise exemplary achievement, is the fact that the chimney-stacks are not painted white to match the walls.

Pierce and Coey say it is of "about 1680". Oram says "Dating from c. 1700, a yeoman planter's house in exceptionally unspoiled condition. Fieldstone, mud, harled and limewashed with a thatch roof" and assigns it to category

A. The listers accept the date of 1700 - though Gailey, more dubiously, says "perhaps 18th-century"; for my part, I think, perhaps, it is a bit later than 1700; and the maps suggest that the extension was added after 1858. The farm has belonged to the Gregson family for over 150 years: and still does. In 1862, Thomas Gregson held it as tenant at will, with 32 acres of land, from George Douglass, at a rent of £38 15 0 per annum; valued first at the low figure of £3 15 0, soon after increased (perhaps upon the addition of the potato house?) to £4 5 0; at which modest figure it remained, for Thomas Gregson's life, for that of his widow Sarah from 1885 until 1903, and thereafter for Thomas junior's life, at least until 1929.

The Buildings at Risk description of 1999 reported "This thatched farmhouse at Edenballycoghill, just north east of Waringstown is sadly deteriorating. The importance of this building should be recognised ... The house has deteriorated very rapidly recently, with the loss of a chimney stack, and is currently very vulnerable". Happily, in 2001, it has been rescued by its owner: one of the gable walls had to be rebuilt, the potato store has been considerably altered, as have some of the internal arrangements, but the missing chimney-stack has been replaced; on balance, a triumph of successful restoration.

Photographs: A C W Merrick; Marcus Patton.
Situation: 98 Dromore Road, Waringstown; td, Edenballycoghill; District Council, Craigavon; Grid ref. J 116 565.
References: Listed B (14/7/2). VAL 2B/3/46C, p 20, VAL 12B/21/6A-F, in PRONI; OS maps; Oram, 'Craigavon', UAHS, 1971, Pt II, p 8; Gailey, 'Rural houses', 1984, pl 187; Pierce and Coey, 'Taken for granted', 1984, p 87; BAR, VI, UAHS, 1999, p 57.

160 and 162 Ballygowan Road, Hillsborough

83. A two-storey slated and whitewashed cottage, presently, and perhaps originally, divided into two dwellings. Georgian glazing-bars complete, the window-heads recessed; three white-painted chimney-stacks; two square-headed door-ways. There is a lower extension to the left of the façade. The listers suggest, early 19th-century; but I wonder? Perhaps very much earlier: this seems to be the very last survivor of the farmer's-and-weaver's-cottages on the Downshire's Kilwarlin estate. Perhaps 18th-century; perhaps even 17th-century; the roof-timbers would no doubt tell much: but the present tenant is elderly, and I was unable to secure access; and the file in the Monuments and Buildings Record has unaccountably gone missing. Gordon Wheeler has pointed out the resemblance to the not so very distant house at 98 Dromore Road, Waringstown (82).

Well restored, as a single entity, in 1998, the woodwork very authentically and pleasingly painted a traditional brown to contrast with the white walls. It seems to have been occupied by the Gilliland family, as tenants of the Downshire estate, for many years; thereafter, also for many years, by the Cantley family, said to be of Huguenot descent. In 1913 James Gilliland bought out two small houses, which seem to have been these ones, under the Land Acts; they were valued at only £1 10 0 and 15/-, respectively. In 1915 George Cantley bought ten acres of land nearby; and in 1929 he seems to have bought another 16 acres, valued at £16 5 0, together with buildings then valued at a mere £2 15 0. It looks as though these are the listed buildings in question: though it is far from easy to interpret the records with confidence.

Photograph: A C W Merrick (see also colour illus. 31).
Situation: 160 and 162 Ballygowan Road, Hillsborough; td, Ballygowan; District Council, Lisburn; Grid ref. J 193 571.
References: Listed (19/22/63). VAL 12B/21D p 53, E p 45, in PRONI.

Ballyvester House, Donaghadee

84. Dixon says, "Early 18th century; an exceptionally fine five-bay, two-storey farmhouse with whitewashed stone walls. The central doorway has a rusticated surround-frame and a radiating fanlight. On the front elevation three dummy windows are painted to match the other six-pane sashes, a skilfully executed and convincing trick, which maintains the symmetry of the building"; illustrates it; and accords it an 'A'. The listers say "About 1660. 2-storey early house with later Georgian detail believed to have been altered about 1715 and about 1890 - owner's information".

The title deeds show that the property was granted in 1624 by Viscount Montgomery to William Edmonstone; in 1630, the latter sold to William Catherwood, in whose family it remained for many years. In 1828, it passed to Robert Bailie, who had married a Catherwood; but his mother-in-law stayed on as tenant-for-life until 1882. In 1836, valued at no less than £15 2 8 in category 1A; occupied by Mrs Margaret Catherwood: in 1861, valued at £11 with the note "a large house but neglected looking". In 1890, sold to James Craig, father both of Lord Craigavon and of Vincent Craig, architect. At some time thereafter, the house was divided into two. Part passed to Fullertons, then to McCalls; part passed to John Craig, then to Armstrong, then to Stevenson, then to Mawhinney, then to Rt Rev John Hind, retired bishop of Fukien, then to J B Condell: the two halves were re-united only when the present owners bought the place in 1961.

Set inland a little, amidst rolling countryside, in a good garden with good trees and good outbuildings, it looks charming from the winding country road near which it stands. It is a rather puzzling and confused house of many levels, and many stairs: part apparently built for giants, part for dwarves. The front doorcase, with Gibbsian blocks and fluting, is of exceptionally high quality. So are many of the details of the windows, all Georgian-glazed, with shutters and fluted fans at the corners; but clearly of several different dates, some with brick surrounds, some with inset reveals, others not; all nicely painted in black and white. There are several good plaster ceiling roses, and an uncommonly nice staircase and bannister-rail. A quite exceptionally pleasing, and little-spoiled, house.

Photographs: A C W Merrick.
Situation: 84 Ballyvester Road, Donaghadee; td, Ballyvester; District Council, Ards; Grid ref. J 578 778.
References: Listed B1 (24/7/44). VAL 1B/32, p 105, VAL 2B/3/3A, p 26, in PRONI; Dixon, 'Donaghadee and Portpatrick', UAHS, 1977, pp 32-33; Pierce and Coey, 'Taken for granted', 1984, p 143; information from owners; owners' title deeds.

Mount Ross, Portaferry

85. A pleasant, solid, roomy, Georgian farmhouse, on a hill; the date 1749 chiselled into one of the purlins of the roof (the byre alongside, now disused, has a similar date for 1769). Two-storey and attic on basement; five-bay; Georgian-glazed; a fairly recent porch masking the simple rectangular doorcase and fanlight; a lunette in a sort of peaked pediment lights the top of the stairs and the attic landing; white walls, with grey-painted quoins. According to Savage-Armstrong, " The House of Mount Ross, now in the possession of farmers, stands in a rather imposing and lofty situation some distance from Ballygalget - a solidly-built, small, white house, with two wings." It seems in fact never to have had wings, only farm outbuildings at either side. The best feature of the house is its staircase, broad and shallow, and the pair of reeded wooden archways in the hall, one arch containing the bottom of the staircase, the other the passage down to the back quarters.

The house is said to have been built, at a cost of about £1,500, by one James Ross, a Belfast merchant, and a descendant of the George Ross who had bought Quintin Castle (58) and Kearney from the Montgomerys of Rosemount about 1680. It seems then to have passed to a younger son of the Rock Savage branch of the Savage family, for Savage-Armstrong refers to "James Savage of Mount Ross, born 15th October 1740 ... died at Mount Ross on 18th May 1803, aged sixty-three, and was buried in the Mount Ross family-grave at Ardkeen", leaving one

son and three daughters. The house was subsequently occupied by a Mr Hamilton.

On 25th October 1769, Francis Little, a wheelwright in Portaferry, married Mary McMullen of Mount Ross, a farmer's daughter. Their son Francis Little, born in 1802, was the first of that family to live at Mount Ross. In 1863, when he is shown as occupier, the house was valued at only £7, with the notes "Being repaired, all very old" and "new offices in progress. House and remainder of offices very old". The valuation gradually climbed to £9, then £12, then £14, no doubt reflecting a programme of improvements. Francis died there in 1869, aged sixty-six. He had seven daughters and, at last, a son, Francis, born in 1846, who married a Miss Woods of Blackabbey. This lady, perhaps injudiciously, insisted that the spelling of the name be changed to Lyttle. Their descendants live there to this day, and run a very successful fruit farm. The family tradition is that the inheritance of Mount Ross always goes to the younger, not the elder, son.

Photograph: A C W Merrick.
Situation: 20 Ballygavigan Road, Portaferry; td, Ballygavigan; District Council, Ards; Grid ref. J 629 527.
References: Listed B (24/1/98). VAL 2B/3/10, p4, VAL 12B/23/27A-D, in PRONI; W Montgomery, Description of the ... Ards, 1683, in his 'Montgomery manuscripts', 1830, p 304; Savage-Armstrong, 'Savage family in Ulster', 1906, p292; typescript notes compiled by Ms Amy Anderson; information from owner.

The Lough House, Greyabbey

86. An attractive L-shaped frontage to the village square: two-storey, five-bays and a projecting porch (with nice segmental fanlight and side-lights) in the main façade. It is believed to have been an inn, very possibly a coaching establishment, a tradition corroborated by the numerous bedrooms and the numerous stalls in the stables. The oldest part, the range to the right in line with the court-house next door, is thought to date from 1735; the lintel carved with this date, however, is modern, though based on the date found in the roof-beams of the house next door. The five bays at right angles appear to date from around 1780. The house is largely creeper- or ivy-covered - indeed, in late summer, the front windows are almost completely masked in foliage. With the former court-house next door (now used as a parish hall), and the adjacent two-storey corner block, this makes an uncommonly attractive group, all Georgian glazing bars complete, and all very well kept and painted.

However, there is a lot more than a pretty frontage to the Lough House. A third range of rooms stands at right angles to the rear of the house, evidently of about 1790 to 1800: with lower ceilings in the rooms downstairs, higher ceilings in some of the upstairs, so that it includes a magnificent upstairs drawing-room with very tall Georgian-glazed windows looking out over the shore to Strangford Lough and the Mourne Mountains, and with pretty plasterwork - possibly later, but charming nonetheless. Moreover, there are quite unsuspected, and splendid, gardens on the three sides of the house not fronting on the square. Altogether, a considerable surprise, and a very pleasant one.

The house became home to the agents who managed the Rosemount estate for the Montgomerys in the mid-nineteenth century. It seems to have been valued at £20, and occupied for many years between 1862 and 1908, by James Atkinson; then by James Phair whose wife is still remembered in the village as a teacher of music. On the death of Mrs Worsley, widow of the last agent, in 1952, the house was sold to one Wally Stewart, a wealthy Tyrone businessman, who spent much money on alterations and improvements, mostly, if not quite all, for the better. It was bought from him by the present owners in 1964; and they have looked after it with loving care. It is now in the best of order.

Photographs: A C W Merrick (see also colour illus. 23).

Situation: 1 The Square, Greyabbey; td, Grey Abbey; District Council, Ards; Grid ref. J 578 679.

References: Listed B1 (24/4/1). VAL 2B/3/4, p 63, VAL 12B/23/16A to F, in PRONI; OS maps; title deeds in possession of owner; information from owner, and from W H C Montgomery.

Mill House and Windmill Stump, Greyabbey

87. The Mill House seems originally to have been built by the Newtownards Montgomerys in connection, not with the windmill just behind it, but with a mid-17th-century water-mill just beside it: the flat field behind the house is still known as 'the dam field', and a stream and various flumes and water-courses still run through it and under the road through culverts to the sea. William Montgomery says, "This ... gave occasion to Sir Hugh's Lady" (in 1607) "to build water mills in all the parishes, to the great advantage of her house, which was numerous of servants, of whom she stood in need, in working about her gardens, carriages, etc ... The millers also prevented the necessity of bringing meal from Scotland, and grinding with quairn stones (as the Irish did to make their graddon)".

Parts of this attractive house may well date from so early a date, though it has been considerably altered and enlarged over the years. Today, it comprises a long two-storey range of rendered but creeper-covered Georgian-glazed buildings, with slated roof and four brick chimney-stacks, set back somewhat from the road but close to the sea in a charming walled garden, and with fine views from its windows out over Strangford Lough. The main house is six bays wide, with a modern but very congruous creep-er-clad square porch; the four-bay section to the right, now a separate dwelling, originally provided sail-loft and storage space for the boating activities of the Mont-gomerys of Rosemount (47). For very many years the water-miller's house - but never that of the windmiller - it was by 1838 the steward's house, the dwelling rated B, measuring 52 feet by 20 feet by 14 feet, valued, "including mill and kelp shore", at £16 3 9; the water corn-mill however separately valued at £17 0 7. From 1881 to 1883 it was used as a Royal Irish Constabulary station, where a cell for malefactors (still there, though enclosed) was inserted into the old kitchen return. Then it became the Rosemount shepherd's house, where Sandy Regan, shepherd, lived for many years; then, on the marriage of the

heir to the estate, it was brought into use as a kind of dower-house, and considerably enlarged and modernised in the 1960s: though without diminishing its character.

A deed of January 1779 recites that, at a slightly earlier date, the late William Montgomery "built on part of the said fee farm lands and premises a windmill for grinding corn and by his last will and testament devised to his eldest son William now of Rosemount aforesaid Esquire and his heirs the said windmill together with ... land contiguous thereto". A windmill is recorded on the site by Taylor and Skinner in 1777. In 1838, the mill was worked by William Bailie; "diameter 18 feet by 34 feet high by 24 feet; two pair of stones; machinery valued at £15". From 1862 until 1897, it was worked by Andrew Linton, valued at either £4 or £5: in the latter year, he was succeeded by William Linton, but in 1901, the corn mill was struck out of the Valuation book altogether, and presumably then closed down. It is now a roofless stump, quite cylindrical, its stone walls without batter, but complete right up to the original eaves. It is set on the summit of a most attractive drum-lin site, with a superla-tive view out over Strangford Lough to the Mourne Moun-tains. In the 1940s, when the field sur-rounding the windmill was let in conacre to Jack Bailie, I worked the reaper which cut the hay in that field; and after the war, about 1946, when I was aged 18, I asked my father to buy the

field for me, from his friend, Major Hugh Montgomery: so that I might plant it with trees, and convert the windmill to a weekend house, in later years. He was very sympathetic, but (perhaps wisely) declined the proposition, as he had, at that time, other more pressing calls on his generosity. I have always rather regretted it: what a lovely oakwood I might have owned now!

Photographs: A C W Merrick.
Situation: Shore Road, Greyabbey; td, Mill House, Bootown, windmill, Ballybryan; District Council, Ards; Grid ref. J 585 664, J 587 663.
References: Mill House, listed B1 (24/4/21); windmill stump, not listed. T 1030/31, 1779, VAL 1B/33, p 190, VAL 2B/3/4, p 40, VAL 12B/23/16A-F, all in PRONI; Taylor and Skinner, 'Roads', 1778, p 10; Montgomery, 'Montgomery manuscripts', 1830, p52; Green, 'Industrial archaeology', 1963, p 54; information from Mrs Anne Montgomery and Mrs Sheila Regan.

Unicarval House, Comber

88. Externally, an uncommonly appealing eight-bay two-storey Georgian-glazed house, with grey window-surrounds, of yellow-washed roughcast clad in trellises covered in wistaria, clematis and climbers, set in a delightful demesne with many mature trees; said to date from about 1740, although to me it looks some twenty years later. Gabled roof, with chimney-stacks at each end. Considerably altered inside, and at the rear, where the extensive outbuildings seem to incorporate at least parts of the two flax mills which supported the house. At a guess, the original single-storey house comprised the five right-hand bays, with central segmental-headed doorcase with fan and side-lights; the three more bays to the left, and the upper storey, seem to have been added after the property passed from the Cumming to the Allen family.

The place was granted by Lord Clanbrassil to John Cumming, for ever, in 1673, and remained in the family for some 150 years. Unfortunately, in 1797, a party of United Irishmen "arrived at Unicarval seeking weapons. Cumming refused them, barred the house, and shot at the crowd. If he had intended to scare them, the plan back-

fired, for they immediately broke open the windows and door, rushed into the house, and murdered him" (Carr). He seems to have left a widow, three sons and two daughters - the children all minors - and from then on the family's circumstances ran downhill: they were obliged to borrow substantial sums on the security of the property, and in 1841 the mortgagees foreclosed, the Cummings being constrained to sell the place for £6100 to one Alexander Montgomery. He, in turn sold it on, and it was acquired in 1849 by George Allen, in whose family it was to remain for many years. Carr says, "The Allens kept Unicarval until about 1930, building two fine stone yards and greatly adding to the farm. The Allens were Comber people and with their arrival the southern tip of the parish effectively became a part of Comber". George Allen died in 1886; his widow lived on until 1914. In 1919, their son John Allen returned to his childhood home from Oxfordshire.

The first valuation, on 17 October 1833, categorises the house only 2C+, measurements 60 feet by 21 feet by only 13' 6" high, and valuing it, with return and offices, at a

total of £21 18 0 in all, despite its being "well circum-stanced". The names of Robert and John Cumin were soon after struck out, and that of George Allen substitut-ed. Evidently he made considerable improvements; by the time of the Griffith valuation of 1862, the house was val-ued at £33, flax mill and store were valued at £30: "Flax mill has 12 metal stocks, is worked by Water Power at pre-sent, but the owner is remodelling the concern so as to work by Steam Power and Water Power - one set of rollers & Water Wheel of first class make etc". The mill was at some distance from the house; the photograph of 1907 shows both water wheel and chimney.

Four years later, however, "Mr Allen states that his mill works but 4 months and is employed but one half the power and machinery, and seeks a reduction": which he did not get. The first mill apparently finally ceased working in 1907, when it is reported as used for storage, its value reduced to £2; and in 1918, the second mill was likewise reduced to

£4 10 0. In 1931, the place was sold by John Allen to a member of the Glentoran family; who in turn sold it, as an investment, to the Abercorns; during which period it was rented out to Henry and Patricia McLaughlin of McLaughlin & Harvey, he a very prosperous builder, she a moderately flamboyant Unionist MP at Westminster. The house was acquired by the present owners about 1987 from a Mr Ken Wheeler. It appears that, until 1919, it was usually - but not invariably - spelled Unicarville.

Photographs: A C W Merrick; the Allen family, c.1880, the mill, 1907, both courtesy of A W Anderson.
Situation: 35 Ballyregan Road, Dundonald; td, Unicarval; District Council, Ards; Grid ref. J 449 711.
References: Listed B2 (24/11/37). D 2064/1-29, VAL 1B/317, p 44, VAL 2B/3/17, VAL 12B/23/5A-F, all in PRONI; OS map, 1834; Carr, 'Most unpretending of places', 1987, pp 91, 92, 104, 237; information from A W Anderson.

Milecross Lodge, Newtownards

89. A simple, austere, but most attractive Quaker bleacher's house of the mid-18th century, with extensive outbuildings, grounds, and beech walk, all in apple-pie order: from 1627 until 1885, seat of the Bradshaw family (of 'Bradshaw's Brae'), until their unhappy downfall. The estate, until its sale in bankruptcy, comprised over 400 acres - on both sides of the Belfast Road - including the Kiltonga dam, bleach-green and bleaching mill. Rodney Green says "The bleachworks" (now departed) "only date from about 1874, but they are on the site of one of the oldest bleachgreens in the county ... The Linen Trustees sent James Bradshaw to Holland in 1720 to join Richard Hall who was already there to study Dutch methods. In 1729 the Trustees recorded the invention of a sleaing table for diapers by Richard Bradshaw. Bradshaw's name was traditionally associated with the introduction of damask and diaper weaving into north Down ... In 1797 Robert Bradshaw described himself as a 'manufacturer and bleacher of fine linens and diapers upwards of forty years at Newtownards' though 'not in the trade now' ".

Knox (followed by McCaverty) says "In 1728 Mr James Bradshaw visited Hamburgh, where he acquired an intimate knowledge of the diaper manufacture, having paid most earnest attention to the mode of fitting up looms, the selection of yarns, and the style of weaving. After gaining ample practical experience, he returned home in about two years, and getting looms constructed on principles much superior to those then in use, he introduced a new system which greatly improved the diaper trade in his native country. He was born in the beginning of the eighteenth century, and died towards its close, at an advanced age, at his house at Milecross, where his son, the Rev. Joseph Bradshaw, who has effected great improvements on his property, still" (1875) "resides". No mention here of

"Mad" Bradshaw; nor of the decay of the firm; yet in the Valuation of 1834, the place is described as "bleaching establishment long out of repair: £10 17 9." There seem to be numerous discrepancies in the published accounts of this property and family, which I am unable to resolve.

Unhappily, it seems clear that the Bradshaw family came to a sticky end, and the extensive property was divided into two: the bleachworks seems to have been sold separately; the house, after sundry vicissitudes, passed to Mr John Tate, JP, of Downpatrick; then to one James Carter Rollings; then to the family of the present owner about 1906. The bleachgreen, dam, and mill were bought by Mr W Sibbald Johnston, JP, who, in 1874, built the new and, for many years, successful bleachworks, amply described by Bassett: "Mr. Johnston's buildings, of stone and wood, cover about four acres, and in these 90 people are employed in bleaching and finishing yarns ... The stream running through the bleach works, used for power and other purposes, rises in what is called the Cairn Hill, one of the Scrabo range. It is impounded at Kiltonga, where it forms a handsome pond, and during the season of ice, is taken advantage of by the Kiltonga Curling Club, of which Mr. Johnston is president". Now the resort of wildfowl, not curlers: rather a come-down, perhaps?

The house is two-storey, with hipped roof and stone chimney-stacks; L-shaped, with five bays in each front; roughcast over bluestone, but the walls almost entirely masked by well-trimmed creepers. There is a simple stone Gibbsian doorcase in the centre of what is now the entrance front, a rather more ambitious and complex one with triple keystone in the centre of the original front (now side) looking out across the valley to Scrabo hill. There is a three-light window in the ground floor at each end of this garden front. All the windows are Victorian-glazed, the sashes and glazing-bars painted bright scarlet and said "always" to have been so: the result is strikingly effective, if somewhat unconventional. The interior is very plain and simple, as befits a Quaker merchant's home: no ornamental plasterwork or fancy fireplaces here. The ground-floor rooms, however, are light and well-proportioned, and there is an attractive curving staircase.

The house is reached up a long winding avenue from Bradshaw's Brae; it is quite invisible from the road, and is surrounded by well-kept lawns, gardens, and very fine trees - especially the charming close-planted beech walk at the side, sometimes known as "the soldiers' walk". This is said to have been planted by soldiers of the Yeomanry billeted in the house in 1798: one version having it that the number of trees equals the number of soldiers quartered here; another, that it equals the number of their regiment killed at the battle of Ballynahinch. Behind the house are almost two acres of walled yards, offices, stabling, and gardens. There are two burying-grounds within the original demesne, one Quaker ("the Lambs' Fold"), the other (Killysuggan) Roman Catholic. It was apparently part of the original arrangement for the latter that an empty coffin should always be available to provide a hiding-place for goods smuggled in by the Bradshaws through Portaferry. A later member of the family tried to impose a levy of ten pence a burial, but "Three local Catholics took the Rev. Joseph Bradshaw to the High Court in Dublin, which re-instated their right to a free burial" (McCavery).

In the first valuation - on 4th June 1834, to be exact - the house and its extensive offices were classified 1B, and valued at £27; but with a note "These offices are of little use to Mr Bradshaw". By the time of the Griffith valuation of 1862-4, the valuation had dropped to £23, "a large old-fashioned house, upper storey very low", occupied by Jonathan Bradshaw under the Rev. Joseph Bradshaw. In 1867 Jonathan's name was struck out, and the Rev. Joseph evidently carried out considerable "additions and improvements", for the valuation rose to £40. However, in 1885 the Rev. Joseph was declared a bankrupt, and the house, with 401 acres 2 roods and 10 perches was put up for auction: according to the advertisement "On Lot 2 stands a Mansion House, called Milecross Lodge, which is well built and commodious. It is situate on an eminence, and surrounded by ornamental plantations and timber, and there are good gardens and suitable offices attached". Bigger says that "The furnishings of Mile-Cross house were old, rare, and valuable, bringing very high prices at the auction. It is said they came from England, and all by sea, up Strangford Lough".

The earlier Bradshaws were respectable Quaker merchants, and people of substance (see 29): Thomas Bradshaw (1746 - 1810) married Sarah, "daughter of Samuel Hoare of London, banker"; they had eight children, of whom the eldest son, Robert, the lawyer, was known as "Mad Bradshaw".

The present owner recounts a tale that Robert engaged

in litigation with Lord Castlereagh over the water rights at Kiltonga; that he drove his carriage, drawn by four white stallions, to the courthouse at Downpatrick where he won his case; and that, so overjoyed was he at this success, he galloped them all the way home from Downpatrick, with the unfortunate result that all four of them were found dead in their stalls next morning. But Bigger has a different tale: "One of the Mad Bradshaw peculiarities was the use of bullocks in his carriage - a large van with a stove inside, in which he used to traverse the country. It was said that a by-law was made in Belfast to prevent horses travelling on the then rude footpaths, and that Bradshaw exercised his legal acumen and got over the difficulty by substituting oxen. He and his van were well-known figures in Belfast about 1840. My father often described them to me. He had also remarkable ideas in regard to agriculture, and practised many new devices, chemical and otherwise, with varied success. This was doubtless the commencement of the incumbrance of the Mile-Cross property; but it is also stated that the Bradshaws were the victims of fraud".

In a postscript, Bigger remarks that Robert Bradshaw married his housekeeper, by whom he had seven children. "Other curious accounts of Robert Bradshaw have come to hand. The Belfast Corporation made a bye-law that all carts were to bear the owner's name. Bradshaw placed his underneath; he was summoned for non-compliance with the law, and allowed the case to go before the magistrates, when he confounded justice by revealing his name. When driving bullocks in his wagon he often had a servant mounted on another as escort, all with tails docked, Bradshaw's idea being that a great deal of strength was wasted by tails. He had two such vehicles, one with a stove that smoked vehemently; he had also an outside car with 'patent' harness that had all the gamins of the town running after it. There was a rookery at Mile-Cross - the crows being much encouraged by the owner, who fed them systematically on carrion: they were known everywhere as 'Brodshaws's craws'".

Eventually, the place was inherited by the Rev. Joseph Bradshaw. "Finding the family estate heavily encumbered, he sold all, including the rare old furniture, in discharge of the family debts, and devoted himself to his sacred calling" - first, evidently for a short period, as a curate in the Isle of Wight; "then, in 1885, rector of Mursley, in Buckinghamshire, where he died a few years later".

Photograph: A C W Merrick.

Situation: 77 Belfast Road, Bradshaw's Brae, Newtownards; td, Milecross; District Council, Ards; Grid ref. J 472 751.

References: Listed B1 (24/11/21). D 654/ LE /31, T 2486/12A - J, T 2571, VAL 1B/ 322, p 39, VAL 2B/3/22A, p 72, VAL 12B/ 23/ 24A-F, all in PRONI; Taylor and Skinner, 'Roads', 1778, p 6; Knox, 'County Down', 1875, p 558; Bassett, 'County Down', 1886, p 343; F J Bigger, in UJA, 2nd series, VIII, 1902, pp 4, 54; Green, 'Industrial archaeology', 1963, p 29; McCavery, 'Newtown', 1994, pp 82, 92, 101; information from the owner, and from his niece, Miss Betsy Trevor.

Chrome Hill (formerly Lambeg House), Lambeg

90. An interesting T-shaped house of great character, secluded in a wooded hill-top above a bend and weir on the County Down side of the river Lagan. There are noble trees in the garden, including a yew walk, and a pair of saplings said to have been twined together by John Wesley. It was for many years the mill-house associated with the Wolfenden family's ventures into the manufacture of linen, paper, calico and muslin; their blanket factory was on the other side of the river (see Wolfenden's Bridge, 165). The present exterior appearance, a five-bay two-storey white-painted roughcast house with lower extension to the right and taller extension to the left, is mostly of the early 1830s, when Richard Niven bought the Lambeg works, and established extensive printworks where he produced patterned calico by using bichromates to fix the colours, with such success that he changed the name of the house, formerly known as Lambeg House, to Chrome Hill. Samuel Lewis, in 1837, writes "Chrome Hill, ... a spacious modern mansion, was erected by R. Nevin, Esq., late of Manchester, who established here some extensive works for printing muslin, in which he first applied with success his invention of the 'Ba Chrome', now universally used, and also introduced the oxyde of chrome into the

ornamental department of the china manufacture, from which circumstance he named his estate". (But was there in fact ever a china manufacture here?)

Parts of the house are substantially older than the 1830s, as witness many of the details and the numerous changes of level. Knox, in 1875 says "Chrome Hill is occupied by Mr Richard Niven, son of a Scotch gentleman, of much enterprise and ingenuity, who established in this vicinity, extensive works for printing coloured muslins, in which he first applied with success, his invention of the 'Bichromates', and he also introduced the oxide of chrome, into the ornamental departments of the China manufacture".

According to the researches of the present owner, from whose account (by permission) I quote extensively, "the original small farm dwelling, out of which the present house has grown, was probably built some time during the second half of the 17th century ... If he was not the builder" Abraham Wolfenden "is the earliest known occupant" who, in 1690, sheltered King William while a wagon was being repaired. "Chrome Hill developed from a two unit, two storeyed or lofted house of hearth/lobby formation, with the stairs at the rear of the chimney stack between it and the back wall".

"Sometime around the 1760s ... the original house was heightened, remodelled and extended, by adding a three storey wing on the west side, three rooms long. The difference in floor levels between the old and new blocks, and the way that they are set at right angles to each other, suggests that this wing may have already existed as a cloth store, positioned close to the house for security ... At this time, the front door was moved westward by three bays ... a fine staircase was built to a spacious landing" and "a large sitting room made out of the original loft above the hearth room". The house has many features of this period: lugged doorcases with panelled doors; the carved sandstone pedimented entrance; Georgian-glazed windows with shutters intact and window seats, and the lovely big Venetian window in the north wall of the upstairs drawing-room; the newel posts and balusters of the staircase; fireplaces; the original cornices; and the rococo plasterwork, with scrolls and the Wolfenden arms, in the hall ceiling. Much of this detailing is a little rustic and unpolished; but none the less charming for that. The owner suggests that this ambitious rebuilding was probably carried out by the second Richard Wolfenden, perhaps on his marriage. Musson writes "Chrome Hill is an exceptional house in

its own way ... a representative of a Georgian tradition, resonant with the self-confidence of an industry-owning class of the mid 18th century. It has a pleasing dignity and modesty".

When Richard Niven bought the place in 1830, he made various changes: he inset his own crest in the pediment above the front door, and he added the wide two-storey elliptical bow on the west of the house, at the same time remodelling the dining room inside the bow with arched recesses for sideboard and cupboards. He seems to have been a conscientious housekeeper: the Valuation book of 1862 values the place at £32, with the comment "An old house in good order and well kept". Some Edwardian alterations, reasonably modest, were made in the early years of the 20th century: the entrance hall was enlarged, and a large stained glass Art Nouveau window was inserted; there were also, unsurprisingly, changes to the plumbing arrangements, and the provision of a top-floor "Smoke Room".

Niven died in 1866, but his widow lived on in the house until 1899. It was then bought by John Milligen, coal merchant and speculator, who made some changes, but rented it out to a Major Jenkins, then to Benjamin Hobson of Ravarnet Mill; then he sold the place to a Mr F G Barrett, who used it to stage an exceptionally grand wedding for his daughter to a McCausland seed merchant of Blaris. Next, in 1924, it was sold to the Downer family: Mrs Downer lived on there until 1967, when it was acquired by the present owners, who, naturally enough, made some further alterations: the shape of the dormer above the west bow was improved; and a demi-lune window was inserted in the gable, in place of a chimney-breast, involving the removal of the chimney-stack and the closing-up of the original pair of attic windows in the gable end. All of these changes, and a few others, have been completed with sensitivity. As its owner has written: "Above all, there has been the joy of space and light and plenty of room. Yet the scale is intimate and there is a mystery about the way the rooms lead into each other ... The place looks its best in

spring or autumn sunlight, when the trees are not heavy with leaves, and a slanting light pours through the old windows, across the panelled shutters and onto the boarded floors". Just so.

Photographs: A C W Merrick. Drawing: W W Legge, Lisburn Museum. Plan: R McKinstry.

Situation: Ballyskeagh Road, Lambeg; td, Ballyskeagh; District Council, Lisburn; Grid ref. J 285 669.

References: Listed B (19/9/1). W W Legge, sketchbook, 1816, photocopies in Lisburn Museum; VAL 1B/333 p 13, VAL 2B/3/30, p 46, in PRONI; OS map, 1834; Lewis, TD, 1837, II, p 243; UJA, 1st series, I, 1853, p 135; Knox, 'County Down', 1875, p 512; Marshall, 'Parish of Lambeg', 1933, p 39; Gailey, 'Rural houses', 1984, p 188; Pierce and Coey, 'Taken for granted', 1984, pp140-141; R McKinstry, in 'Lisburn Historical Society journal', VI, 1986-7, p 20; J Musson, in CL, 13/9/2001, pp 168-173.

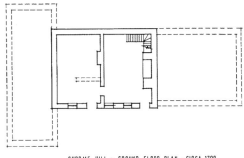

CHROME HILL · GROUND FLOOR PLAN · CIRCA 1700
scale 1/16"

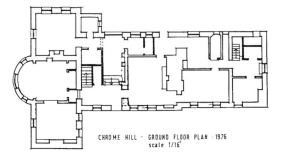

CHROME HILL · GROUND FLOOR PLAN · 1976
scale 1/16"

104 and 106 Main Street, Moira

91. A very fine pair of two-storey-and-attic-on-basement houses, at the eastern end of Moira Main Street, believed to date from 1760, and to have constituted the land steward's house and office for the Moira estate. Described at length, and illustrated, in the Archaeological Survey of County Down. "The elevation to the street has red sandstone quoins and is faced with basalt rubble, with sandstone levelling courses and areas of sandstone over the entrances; the mortar joints are galleted. The windows are flat-arched and dressed in brick; the walls rise to a fluted sandstone frieze and moulded eaves-cornice, the gabled roof is slated with shaped skew-corbels. The E. tenement is four windows wide; the door ... has flanking Roman Doric columns supporting entablature blocks, with frieze enriched with flutings and scallop-shell, and triangular open bed-mould pediment framing a semi-circular fanlight. The W. tenement is three windows wide; the door ... has side pilasters with moulded capitals and semicircular fanlight with moulded and enriched archivolt and moulded key-block. The basement openings of the E. tenement alone remain exposed, although now blocked; they have red sandstone lintels and elliptical brick relieving arches. The house is fronted by a terrace with wrought iron balustrade."

No 106 was restored in 1989 by the Hearth consultancy for the present owners who had shortly before acquired it from a Mr Allen; No 104 had been somewhat earlier restored as a family home by Dr Damoglou, a Greek-Irish physicist, but was acquired as an extension for the next door shop in 1995. From outside, the two houses appear to be of the same date, but once inside one wonders: 104 has a good curly-banistered late-Georgian staircase; 106, a much wider and grander staircase with barley-sugar black-oak balusters, looking a good deal earlier. No 106 , formerly called 'Dewey House', has now been renamed 'Beaufort House', but not because of any local connection. Both are now in excellent order, though the extensive gardens at the rear have been built over.

Photograph: A C W Merrick.
Situation: 104 and 106 Main Street, Moira; td, Carnalbanagh East; District Council, Lisburn; Grid ref. J 151 607.
References: Listed B1 (19/22/4A and B); in conservation area. ASCD, 1966, p 419, pls 158, 210; information from owners, and from Marcus Patton of Hearth.

65 Main Street, Moira

92. The last Georgian house in the excellent Main Street of Moira to remain completely unspoiled, without the slightest fascia, nameplate, or shop-sign; and one of the last to remain a private dwelling. By the look of it, built about 1770, though it could well be earlier; Harris in 1744 says that this "thriving Village, consisting of one broad Street", was even then "inhabited by many Dealers, who carry on the Linen Manufacture to good Advantage". By the 1830s it seems to have deteriorated: Kertland notes, a bit sourly, "Size of the houses very irregular, some thatched and some slated, some very low and some high; streets and houses very dirty. The town is built of basalt or limestone, no brick houses". (No best-kept village competitions then!)

The Archaeological Survey of County Down picks out this house, and illustrates it too: "it is of three floors with harled and colour-washed walls" (at present a warm and cheerful Venetian red, with cream-painted woodwork and stone-coloured trim); "the roof is slated. The street elevation at ground floor has a semi-elliptical arched cart opening on the E.; the door has flanking attached fluted columns with moulded capitals, an entablature broken out over the columns and a semi-circular fanlight with spider-web glazing, framed by a moulded archivolt with moulded key-block; the door has on either side a three-light window, the central light being twice the width of the flanking lights, framed in wood with fluted pilasters and entablature with fluted frieze. The upper floors are each lighted by four windows, diminishing in height at each storey; there are three-light windows centered above the ground-floor windows and single lights above the entrance and cart opening; the windows are sashed throughout".

Bought by the present owner in the 1950s, from a Mr John Irvine (or Irwin) who had lived there for over eighty years. In 1884 the value of house, offices and garden was set at £13 15 0; for some reason it fell soon after to £7 15 0, and remained at that figure for many years.

Photograph: A C W Merrick (see also colour illus. 26).
Situation: 65 Main Street, Moira; td, Carnalbanagh East; District Council, Lisburn; Grid ref. J 150 605.
References: Listed B (19/22/39); in conservation area. VAL 12B/21A - E; Harris, 'County of Down', 1744, p 103; MM Kertland, OSM, nd, Down, III, p 122; ASCD, 1966, p 419, pl 210; information from owner.

Prospect House, Donaghadee

93. Very important in relation to the group embracing the Manor House; formerly near-derelict but now once again an asset to the town. In 1977, Dixon wrote: "pre 1779; a fine five-bay, two-storey house raised on low basement, and with unusually high first floor and attics. The central front door, reached by a flight of four stone steps, has a rusticated stone surround frame and a pretty semi-circular fanlight. To the right an extra, wide bay has been added with a coach arch below and a tripartite window above; curiously, this does not conform either to the height of the other first floor windows or to the placing of the coach door below, yet this irregularity, though disturbing to the sensitive, has an attraction of its own. The house plays an important part as an introduction to the main street and at the junction of the Millisle and Killaughey Roads".

I concur. Very well restored and repainted: the rough-cast walls a sort of grey-brown, the trim white; all glazing-bars complete; interesting double T-quoins at the junction of the original house and the addendum. Apparently, despite the difference of levels, the drawing-room comprises an extension over the coach-arch from the main house. Sold to the present owner in 1983 by Mr Kenmuir who largely restored it.

Photograph: A C W Merrick.
Situation: 4 Millisle Road, Donaghadee; td, Town Parks; District Council, Ards; Grid ref. J 592 797.
References: Listed B1 (24/7/25); in conservation area. OS map, 1834; Dixon, 'Donaghadee and Portpatrick', UAHS, 1977, pp 19, 30; documents in MBR.

Millmount, Dundonald

94. The listers say: "Two-storey, double-fronted Georgian house with basement and piano nobile approached by a flight of steps. The same formality is echoed at the rear". Peter Carr is more informative: "Millmount looks like a Merrion Square townhouse which has been transplanted in the country. Oddly enough, though built around 1810, the house does not appear in any of the contemporary lists of gentleman's seats. This may have been because its owner, William Galway, was a farmer. His hobby was smithwork (he is said to have invented Ireland's first horse-drawn potato-digger) ... The Galways ... moved here from Malone around 1818 ... The farm then consisted of the house and outbuildings, a corn and flax mill, eight workers cottages, and 104 acres of top quality land. If William was not considered a gentleman, his son and grandson were, and the estate faithfully reflects the family's rise in status. In 1833 Millmount seems to have had few pretensions. By 1900, however, it could boast magnificent mature gardens (amongst which strutted peacocks, until they broke the byre windows), a croquet lawn, tennis court, a leafy tree-lined avenue and a small ornamental lake. Raspberries, damsons, pears and gooseberries grew plentifully ... This natural abundance contrasts sharply with life indoors. William and his wife Margaret raised their family with a puritanical severity ... The rising generation was very much in the same mould." "Millmount under John Meneely Galway" (William's grandson) "was a model farm. The hedges were dressed, outhouses whitewashed, and ditches dredged every year or every other year. The yard was kept spotless and the stacks were roped and trimmed so neatly that one well-intentioned English visitor remarked that it would 'put a home counties village to shame' ... The Galways

left in 1922, after John became crippled with arthritis ... none of his sons wanted the farm, and it was sold".

Thereafter, the place ran downhill for many years: it was extensively vandalised; but has now been extensively, expensively, and very courageously restored by Gifford & Cairns, Belfast, for the estimable Mr Gerry Meehan, who was determined to defy and repel all intruders. At the date of writing, it is on the market, with three acres and planning permission for four houses in the grounds - for an asking price of £500,000.

Externally, rather a gaunt house, devoid of ornament apart from the arched doorcase and surmounting moulding, and the ceremonial approach to the front door up no less than eleven cement-rendered steps: how much better if they could have been stone, and railed. All the Georgian glazing-bars have been restored; the walls are of cement render, lined out, and still a bit raw, but could look much better, either painted, or creeper-covered, or both. The house is unusual in making no attempt to screen the basement; there are attic windows in the gables. Internally, no expense has been spared. Externally, it is on an attractive site, with good views, and with many fine trees, but the gardens have sadly gone to seed, and it will take much labour to return them to good order. I wish good luck to whoever may be found to take this on.

Photograph, A C W Merrick.

Situation: 9 Millmount Road, off Comber Road, Dundonald; td, Ballylisbredan; District Council, Castlereagh; Grid ref. J 432 727.

References: Listed B2 (25/6/1). OS map, 1834; Carr, ' Most unpretending of places', 1987, p 140-142, 165, and passim; sale particulars, August 2000; information from Marcus Patton.

New Forge, Magheralin

95. Taylor and Skinner's map of 1777 shows a house here as "Newforge, - Close Esq": though whether this is the present house, or the older one still standing at the rear, is unclear. My bet is, that it is the present one. Both houses, like everything else in Magheralin, belonged to the Waddell family. Lewis mentions it as the seat of Cosslett Waddell, Esq., and adds that "A suphureous chalybeate spring on the lands of Newforge is said to equal in efficacy the waters of Aix-la-Chapelle". The Valuation book, revised in 1838, shows the occupier as Frederick Hole, under Coslett Waddell, house, works and offices valued at £35; but it is not easy to disentangle this from the Waddells' other property on the southern side of the River Lagan at Drumcro (106). So late as 1886, Bassett describes Coslett Waddell as owner of "Mills, Corn and Whiting", and "Henry Mathers, Newford" (*sic*) as "Linen Manufacturer"; and shows Coslett Waddell as resident at Ballymakeonan, north of Magheralin, and Robert Waddell J P as resident at Drumcro House.

Green reports "New Forge House ... is an attractive eighteenth-century building. Behind the house are the ruins of a covered-in yard used for hemstitching and hand-loom weaving ... On the main road is a derelict corn mill formerly operated by the Waddell family. There probably was a bleach-green on this site from an early date ... There is a newspaper notice in 1781 of the theft of six pieces of cambric from Coslett Waddell's bleachgreen at Newforge, Magheralin ... Coslett Waddell also owned a flax mill and a corn mill built in 1834". The Ordnance Survey memoir suggests that the flax mill had been built in 1787, but in the late 1830s "had not been in use for some time". Oram says of the house, "c. 1790. Apparently superseding an earlier two storey house which remains as outhouses at the rear. The present house has three floors with cellars. Harled

and white-washed on rubble, the roof is slated. The door-case is elaborate and crudely pedimented. Behind the house is the site of a bleachworks converted to a Whiting Mill ... Close by is a derelict Corn Mill, c. 1787". The listers say "A three storey with basement simple symmetrical Georgian house with Adamesque doorcase. Behind are the remnants of an earlier house."

For many years, the Pickering family of Magheralin lived here. In 1846, James Pickering died aged 47, leaving a widow Selina and five young children (another had died in 1836): she lived on until her death here in 1892, an apparently formidable lady. In 1861, her daughter Elisabeth Ann married Henry Mathers, who took over the mill, and who seems to have moved into the big house with his mother-in-law: he and his descendants successfully managed the Maralin Hem-stitching Factory, which exported largely to America, until the Wall Street crash, when it was forced to close; and they have lived on at New Forge ever since.

The older house at the rear, which is believed by family tradition to have been struck by a thunderbolt in the 1750s, is in the process of being rebuilt so that the younger generation can move into the big house. The latter has fine big well-proportioned rooms, and many original features, including a good staircase; the basement is reached by an external door in a hollow in the side lawn. The walls are built of very large stones, roughcast and now covered in creepers. The pedimented doorcase, its flanking fluted columns with delicately hinted-at capitals, appears to be of finely-carved sandstone, but all is painted battleship grey. The chimney-stacks are smooth-rendered. The house has a very tall hipped roof; in which were found newspapers of the late 1790s and later years. It is surrounded by old plantings and fine trees. Altogether a most impressive piece of work, if somewhat old-fashioned for its apparent date.

Photograph: A C W Merrick (see also colour illus. 21).
Situation: 58 Newforge Road, Magheralin; td, Ballynadrone; District Council, Craigavon; Grid ref. J 130 584.
References: Listed B (14/7/4). Pickering gravestones in garden; VAL 2B/3/46B, p 48, in PRONI; Taylor and Skinner, 'Roads', 1778, p 16;

BNL, 26/6/1781; OSM, nd (?1837), Down III, pp 110-111; Lewis, TD, 1837, II, p 334; Bassett, 'County Down', 1886, pp 275-276; Green, 'Industrial archaeology', 1963, p 25; ASCD, 1966, pp 316, 377-378; Oram, 'Craigavon', UAHS, 1971, Pt II, p 9; Pierce and Coey, 'Taken for granted', 1984, pp 123-124; information from owner.

Ard View House, Killinchy

96. Standing in good grounds, with old trees, a handsome early Georgian five-bay two-storey-on-basement-with-attic farmhouse of cream-washed stucco, originally of 1722, but embellished in about 1780 with a fine glued-on central façade; and flanking pavilions at each side. The new front embraces a shallow pediment, with a little mouth-organ window to light the attic; Georgian-glazed windows in arched recesses; and a pedimented doorcase with semi-circular fanlight. There are good original chimney-stacks, each with seven chimney-pots, at the gable-ends. Behind the house and its return of 1929 there is an excellent large farm- and stable-yard; in the centre of the yard a free-standing square building, its original use unknown, with a pyramidal roof, and a little stone urn at the apex. A smaller, but somewhat similar, building in the garden - one might think, inconveniently far from the house - houses a three-seater privy of some sophistication: just now, though separately listed, in rather poor order, and lacking its urn.

The interior of the house has had to be extensively renewed because of problems with rot, but still boasts its original mahogany doors, with oddly chamfered tops. The house belonged for many years to the Potter family, by whom it may well have been built; in 1929 it was bought by the Groves-Raines family; in 1974 it passed to a Mr Steele; from whom the present owner bought in 1985.

Photograph: A C W Merrick (see also colour illus. 22).
Situation: 31 Ardview Road, Killinchy; td, Killinchy; District Council, Ards; Grid ref. J 507 595.
References: House, listed B+ (24/17/7); dry closet, listed B2 (24/17/8). OS map, 1834; information from owner.

Marino House, Cultra, Holywood

97. "Marino House, originally Marino Farm, dates from the mid-eighteenth century" (Merrick). Now hemmed in by modern houses, it is nonetheless most attractively sited, looking out over a small park and Belfast Lough towards Whiteabbey. Two-storey, of nicely-painted stucco with white trim, the main house three bays wide, with the addition at either end of single-storey wings with tripartite windows and end bows. The porch is evidently not original, (but is nevertheless shown on the 1834 Ordnance Survey map). The exterior of the house is plain and modest, apart from somewhat unsophisticated but nicely painted urns on the wing parapets.

The interior comes as a very pleasant surprise: the quality of the plasterwork, chimney-pieces, shutters, niches, and internal detailing is unexpectedly high, and the disposition of spaces and proportions uncommonly happy. There are, unusually, two returns at the rear which, with the old stable-block, embrace an enclosed courtyard. The progression from front door, through hall and staircase, to the arched upper landing is effective. The two principal reception rooms, with their fine detailing and bow-ends, are charming, and do not look as if they are much later than 1790, perhaps somewhat earlier; though the jump in value between 1838 and 1862 does go to suggest a much later date. There used to be a remarkable circular walled garden, but this, along with a fine clump of beech trees, disappeared in the mid-1960s, when most of the then remaining 14 acres of grounds were sold for development.

In 1834, known as Marino Cottage; in 1838, the house of Mr McCammond, valued at £18 16 0. An 1854 directory shows Joseph Magill as the occupier, probably tenant, of "Marino House"; the next occupier was Andrew, then in 1862, Thomas, McCammon: in the Griffith valuation of that year, "House offices and land - pasture meadow along the shore - land £30, house £54 - stone finish and oil painted - not modern - offices small and inferior". Before 1872, the house seems to have been let to a Mr McAuley; in that year, it passed to Charles H Ward. By 1885, the valuation had dropped to £44, when the house was let to James Connolly at an annual rent of £75. Marino House has since then passed through a number of hands, but until recently was owned and occupied by Mrs Marcelle Moody. Widow of a barrister, she was a discriminating collector of antiques, and the carved wooden doorcase attached to the coach-house, in appearance but probably not in fact 17th-century, must surely have been one of her adornments to the place. Since she left it, the house has undergone very extensive restoration, and is now in excellent order.

It is hard to decide whether or not this was originally just a three-bay farmhouse; or one of the bathing-lodges built along this shore for holiday-makers from Belfast; or, from the beginning, a gentleman's seat. In view of the quality of the detailing, I personally lean to the third alternative. On the other hand, Lewis, in 1837, says of Holywood "The village, which is delightfully situated on the eastern shore of Carrickfergus bay, and on the road from Belfast to Bangor, previously to 1800 contained only about 30 dwellings, chiefly poor cabins; but from its proximity to Belfast, and its fine sandy beach, it has since been greatly extended, and is now become a favourite place of resort for sea-bathing". But in his new edition of 1847, he counted this amongst fifteen gentlemen's seats at Holywood.

A substantial part of the former farmland seems to have been sold off, around 1825, to Thomas Ward, later to be Secretary of the Belfast and County Down Railway Company, for a house of his own, and villas for letting to summer visitors, all to designs by John Millar, architect, and all but one still standing almost unaltered (see 107).

Photograph: A C W Merrick (see also colour illus. 24).

Situation: Old Quay Road, Cultra; td, Ballycultra; District Council, North Down; Grid ref. J 406 799.

References: Listed B (23/18/41). VAL 1B/318, VAL 2B/3/182, p 29, VAL 12B/17/10A, p3, VAL 12B/17/10/B, VAL 12B/17/10C, p 10, in PRONI; OS map, 1834; Lewis, TD, 1837, II, p 6; Merrick, 'Buildings of Holywood', 1986, p 19; supplementary information from A C W Merrick.

Belvedere House, Drumbo

98. A large, bland, stuccoed, merchant's house, two-storey-and-attic on basement, four bays of windows and a central doorway with Tuscan porch at the head of stone steps; nicely painted cream and off-white; hipped roof with four tall symmetrical chimney-stacks; quoins; otherwise unadorned. Three bays deep. At the rear, a fine two-storey bow, externally canted, internally segmental, with three windows. Internally, the house has a spacious square central hall, with original staircase off to one side. All the principal rooms are large, airy, and well-proportioned, though lacking elegant detailing or plasterwork: this is a nabob's house, not that of a nobleman. The delicate detailing of the slim (original) glazing-bars, intact shutters, and staircase, tend to confirm a date of around 1790: and, for once, there is corroborative evidence. Under the wall-paper in the bookshelf-recess of the sitting-room, a copy of the Belfast News-Letter for Tuesday March 6, 1792, which had been used as lining-paper, was recently discovered by the present owners.

It seems that James Watson Hull, who either bought or built Belvedere, "was born in 1758, the eldest of thirteen children of Anthony Hull, a Lisburn tanner; he spent his early years in Bombay with the East India Company where he amassed a large fortune, returning to Ireland in 1786, where he purchased Belvidere, near Ballyaughlis" (Rankin): he must then have been aged only 28. He is described as "of Belvidere" in a deed of March, 1787. Like his near-contemporary Francis Turnley of Richmond Lodge, Holywood, he was known as "the Nabob". He was at once recruited as a churchwarden for the parish of Drumbo, and appointed treasurer for the building of the new parish church; no doubt on the principle enunciated by my paternal grandfather that the wealthiest member of any body should always be chosen as its treasurer, as being subject to the least temptation towards embezzlement. In 1791, Hull was reduced to sending a begging letter to Lord Downshire to make up a hefty shortfall in the finances of the new church; Lord Downshire declined this honour, and in the end the Nabob had to make it up himself,

contributing in all £170 12 6 to the cost. Possibly in disgust at this, he went to live in York in 1793, and ultimately died in London in 1831.

In the meanwhile, one Andrew Durham appears to have purchased the Belvedere estate. He was a churchwarden in 1796, again in 1805, and again in 1815; and was still there in the 1830s, when Mr Scott of the Ordnance Survey wrote "Belvedere House. A fine house around which there is a good deal of planting. Is the residence of Andrew Durham JP". The Valuation book shows Mrs Elizabeth Durham as the occupier in 1834; presumably the trees encompassing the house had not yet been planted, or at any rate had not yet grown up, for there is a note "Belvedere House, rather exposed": the value was then £33 16 0.

By 1849, Robert Calwell "of Belvidere" had become a churchwarden; Elizabeth Callwell was the occupier of the "nicely situate" house in 1861; for some rather puzzling reason, between that date and 1865, the valuation had leaped up from £25 to £70 - perhaps the house had been put back in repair; perhaps the out-offices had been built? By 1869, Mrs Callwell was followed by Francis Dwyer. He appears to have died in 1907; his widow Bessie Dwyer lived on at Belvedere until 1916; when it was acquired by one David Thompson, who seems to have owned the place at least until 1929. The property then came into the ownership of the Morrison family of the Ulster Spinning Company, one of whose number married Brigadier Ronald Broadhurst, a somewhat exotic Englishman, an Arabist, "a member of the Beersheba Camelry, an Equerry to King Abdullah of Jordan", ex-chief of staff to Glubb Pasha and the Arab Legion, who on retirement to Ulster became a zealous supporter of the late Brian Faulkner, and was Deputy Speaker of the Northern Ireland Assembly between 1973 and 1974. After his death, his son lived on in the house for a short while, but then it fell into decay and dereliction only to be acquired in the early 1990s by the present owner, who has very thoroughly re-roofed and restored it, while making some quite acceptable additions at one side.

The lack of information about this house, and its very

considerable demesne, woodlands, and farmland, is rather surprising. There are the remains of extensive farm out-buildings; and a business-room for the factor or land-steward was neatly tucked into the ground floor room at the right-hand front corner of the house itself. It rates no mention either in the Post-Chaise Companion, or in Taylor and Skinner's roadbook, and only a passing mention in Lewis's Topographical Dictionary. However, the Parliamentary Gazetteer of 1846 remarks of the parish of Drumbo: "The land is all arable and fertile. The river Lagan traces the western boundary. Amongst the mansions and villas are Belvidere, New Grove, Edenderry, and Fairview" - can this last be the house in the parish of Knockbreda now known as Newtown Lodge (126)? "Much of the surface possesses the undulating character and the luscious and charming aspect which so generally distinguish the lower part of the vale of the Lagan". No longer so: the valley now has much light industry, not of an attractive character, and much intrusive modern development; but, girdled in thick woodland, Belvedere conserves its integrity.

Photograph: A C W Merrick.
Situation: 228 Ballylesson Road, Drumbo; td, Drumbo; District Council, Lisburn; Grid ref. J 315 660.
References: Listed B (19/23/19). T 514/11, VAL 1B/327, p 80; VAL 2B/3/25B, p 32; VAL 12B/20/11A - E, all in PRONI; vestry records cited by Rankin; G Scott, OSM, nd (?1837), Down, II, p 56; Lewis, TD, 1837, I, p 494; PG, II, 1846, p 81; Rankin, 'Heritage of Drumbo', 1981, passim; BNL 6/1/1987, p 8; information from owner.

Drumnabreeze House, Magheralin

99. A three-bay, three-storey-on-basement (and attics, but to the rear only) late Georgian house, roughcast with creepers. The roof is hipped, behind parapets, with two tall chimney-stacks placed centrally, each topped by six chimney-pots. At the front, there are tripartite windows in each of the three storeys, the upper ones Georgian-glazed, those on the ground floor with later sashes. The central bay advances, with a (rather later) projecting porch: the latter incorporating a very fine doorcase with granite Doric columns and fanlight, acquired by the last owner from a merchant's house on the canal quays at Newry being demolished in the 1950s, and here re-erected by him.

The detailing inside is somewhat uneven: good fluting and reeding here and there, but little plasterwork; generously proportioned, and very light, rooms. The glory of the house (though it takes up a disproportionate share of the internal space) is its curly staircase, one of the finest I have ever seen, with its generous double whorl (or sheaf) at the foot of the balusters, and arched openings or recesses all the way up. The banister-rail is of mahogany, with the grain running crossways not longways; a feature sometimes attributed to the shortage of timber during the Napoleonic

Wars. This, and the absence of the house from Taylor and Skinner's map of 1777, leads me to guess that it may date from between 1795 and 1805. It is set, probably on the site of an old rath, amidst beautiful woods, gardens, and 88 acres of land, with fine trees; also contemporary coach-houses and stable-yard, all somewhat the worse for wear, as is the house itself, but by no means beyond restoration.

Drumnabreeze first appears in Atkinson's 'Directory to the seats of Downshire', an appendix to his Ireland Exhibited of 1823, as "Dromnabreeze, Lurgan, Matthew Studdart, Esq." Then in the Valuation book, finalised in 1838, appears the entry - "Drumnabreeze, W Matthew Stodhard, house and offices, category 1a, 55 feet x 27' 6" x 29', £55 16 5; note - the Walls of a new flax mill are built by Mr Stodhard." In 1850, it was bought by Augustus Edward Brush, one of the sons of a wealthy Dubliner, holding from Coslett Waddell; valued at a mere £35. By 1867 the valuation had risen again to £50; by 1888, it had dropped again to £45; in 1901, while the value remained unchanged, there was a note "no new buildings as reported, existing buildings very old". Augustus Brush lived on here until his

death in 1923, when his grand-daughters Lucy Mary Mildred Brush, and Olive Frances Elizabeth Brush, both holding under lease from Matthew Stodhard, continued to occupy the place; each died at the age of 99. In 1946, Augustus Brush's grandson Colonel Peter Brush, on retiring from the army, came to live here which he did until his death: the house remains in his family at the date of writing.

Photographs: A C W Merrick.
Situation: 64 Drumnabreeze Road, Magheralin; td, Drumnabreeze; District Council, Craigavon; Grid ref. J 143 569.
References: Listed B1 (14/7/18). VAL 1B/346, p 43, VAL 2B/3/46B, VAL 12B/21/1/A - F, in PRONI; Atkinson, 'Ireland exhibited', 1823, I, p 321.

Lisnabreeny House, Knockbreda, Castlereagh

100. Lyn Gallagher says : "Lisnabreeny was given to the National Trust by Nesca Robb, of the well known Robb family who had a large department store at Castle Junction", Belfast: the gift was offered in 1937, and accepted in 1938. "One hundred and sixty-four acres of National Trust property lie on the very skirts of south-east Belfast. These lands exactly fit the aim of Octavia Hill, one of the national founders of the Trust in 1895, who wanted to safeguard 'open-air sitting rooms' for urban populations. Fields edged with beech and hawthorn hedges fringe housing developments at the top of the Cregagh Road, and give extensive views over central Belfast ... An attractive glen path, which begins at the busy dual carriageway, takes the walker alongside a stream, through a mix of native trees growing on steep banks, into rural Co. Down and the grounds of Lisnabreeny House ... further on, the walk leads to a well preserved hill fort ... this fort at Lisnabreeny would probably have had a simple clay dwelling within. It is approximately forty yards wide, with a rampart twelve feet high in some places, surrounded by a ditch about ten feet wide".

Of the house, she writes "... a graceful, unpretentious building of the early nineteenth century, with an entrance flanked by Ionic columns, an elegant Diocletian window in an arched recess above the door, and a five-bay front sitting on a low podium". It was for many years the Robb family home; used by the Youth Hostel Association, as its first Irish hostel, in 1938; requisitioned by the army, and occupied by American troops during the war. One field was used as a temporary cemetery for US servicemen, established in 1943; the remains were taken back to America in 1948. Afterwards, let to farm tenants, but eventually abandoned and subjected to severe vandalism. "One of the Trust's most long-standing but problematical properties ... the building was the main problem" (its shell had become the haunt of glue-sniffers and drug addicts,

who lit fires to keep warm on cold nights). "Throughout the 1970s negotiations had been carried on in the hope of finding a suitable use for it. Interested organisations included the Glencraig Curative School, the Ministry of Home Affairs, the British Horse Society, and Castlereagh Borough Council, but to no avail" (Dixon). A sore problem for the National Trust, and a property which for some years did it little credit. Eventually rescued in 1986 to 1991 by Lagan College, the first of the new integrated schools, when it was restored to provide the school's Music Centre: though, it must be said, with a rather heavy and institutional hand. There is a rather uncomfortable addition at the rear. However, its external appearance from the front has been satisfactorily restored, even if it is not quite so visible or accessible as might be thought desirable for a National Trust property. The Georgian-glazed windows, each sash with nine panes, have been properly restored; the (unlined) stucco walls are painted pale yellow, the woodwork white, the front door red: but its elegance is quite marred by an enormous notice shouting FIRE EXIT - KEEP CLEAR. Still, it is nice to see a fine building, once despaired of, put to a good new use.

Atkinson says that, in 1817, "Lis-nabreen" was the seat of H S Harvey, Esq. The Robbs acquired house and farm later (see also 109). I well remember Dr Nesca Robb. When I first joined the Northern Ireland Committee of the National Trust in 1953, at the age of 25, when the membership in Northern Ireland stood at 400 (it is now, in 2001, nearly 35,000), the Committee was rather an elderly one. We met in the modern office of King George's Fund for Sailors, of which Lord Antrim was also local chairman, in Castle Street, Belfast. Dr Robb - an eminent historian, authority on King William III, poet, and essayist - had by then become a little frayed and dozy; she was however a regular attender at meetings, throughout which she alternately lit up cigarettes, and slept. The trouble was, that the two activities overlapped: so that it was the duty of the most junior member of staff present - usually David Good - discreetly to remove and stub out the butts before she set fire to the office. For all that, she was a nice old lady, and a good friend to the National Trust, to which she left a fair part of her estate when she died, in England, in 1976.

Photograph: A C W Merrick.
Situation: Manse Road, Castlereagh; td, Lisnabreeny; District Council, Castlereagh; Grid ref. J 367 702.
References: Listed B (25/2/1). Atkinson, 'Ireland exhibited', 1823, I, p 325; OS map, 1834; H Dixon, notes in NT archive, 1974; Gallagher and Rogers, 'Castle, coast and cottage", 1992, pp 76, 177.

Grace Hall, Magheralin

101. A voluptuously bosomy double-pile house, three-storey above cellars, of brick cased in unpainted stucco, with two generous bows, tripartite windows of Georgian-glazed appearance (from a distance) in each bay. The late 19th-century porch linking the two bows unfortunately masks the very fine doorcase with fanlight, fluted pilasters, and plaster olive leaves on the internal arch. There are good fans in the coved interiors of the shutter-cased windows.

A house here appears on Taylor and Skinner's map of 1777, but this probably refers to the smaller and earlier house of 1711 at the rear. Following his visit in 1817, Atkinson says "Grace-Hall, the seat and part of the estate of Thomas Douglass, Esq. comprehends a very fine modern edifice, and 150 acres of a demesne lightly and ornamentally planted". Lewis notes in 1837 that it is the seat of C Douglass, Esq. Very fully described in the Archaeological Survey of County Down: "House and walled farmyard ... The original house, much altered internally and now largely disused, lies on the S.E. side of the enclosure and bears a stone with date and initials, 1711 REP" (or perhaps ERP?). " ... The original house is rectangular in plan, 59 ft. by 27½ ft. externally, comprising two storeys, the upper floor partially within the roof space; it is built of stone rubble, with modern cement-rendering, and has a modern slated roof ... The later house faces S.E. with a wide view extending to the mountains of S. Down. It is square in plan, of three storeys above cellars; the entrance,

with an added semi-octagonal porch, is flanked by wide semicircular bows which are carried the full height of the building. The bows have a single square-headed tripartite window at each floor, the central bay has a similar window, framed by pilasters with moulded capitals, to each upper floor ... The entrance comprises a door and narrow flanking lights, framed by fluted pilasters with moulded caps and surmounted by an elliptical fanlight with spider-web glazing; internally the door is flanked by fluted pilasters with moulded and fluted capitals from which rises an archivolt, moulded in plaster and bearing a straight wreath of leaves and flowers."

By 1990, when it was bought by the present owner, already considerably altered, and in poor order; he has re-roofed it, but has found it necessary to strip most of the plasterwork and replace much of the woodwork. Although the original Georgian-glazed sash windows had rotted, he has retained them, so that it would still be possible to reproduce the originals. He still hopes to restore the house to its original state. At present, it stands empty, used only for storage. A note of 1994 in the Monuments and Buildings Record says "the interior has been stripped out of this house and so I would rate it as B2 quality" unless and until restored.

In 1866, the Valuation book shows the house as the property of Charles Douglass, in fee, valued at the very considerable sum of £70, with 182 acres. In 1881, it passed to John Blacker Douglass, a Douglass having married one of the Blackers of Elm Park, County Armagh: the 1912 edition of Burke's Landed Gentry shows it as the seat of "Maxwell Vandeleur Blacker-Douglass of Grace Hall". However, this grand-sounding gentleman does not seem actually to have lived there, since before then the occupancy had passed to William Wardlaw; the house being now valued at only £50. In 1898, it passed to David Johnston, who bought it out in fee under the Land Acts in 1909: yet by 1903, the valuation of this very fine house had slipped to a mere £25, at which figure it was to remain

until 1929. It subsequently became the home of Jackson Blakely; from whose son the present owner acquired it.

Photograph: A C W Merrick (see also colour illus. 25).
Situation: 59 Cottage Road, Dollingstown, Magheralin; td, Tullyanaghan; District Council, Craigavon; Grid ref. J 105 594.
References: Listed B (14/7/20). VAL 12B/21/6A - F, in PRONI; Taylor and Skinner, 'Roads', 1778, p 264; Atkinson, 'Ireland exhibited', 1823, p 175; Lewis, TD, 1837, II, p 334; Burke, 'Landed gentry', 1912, p 190; 'The Ark', May 1912, p 10; ASCD, 1966, p367-368, pl 157; Oram, 'Craigavon', UAHS, 1971, Pt II, p 8; information from owner, and cuttings in his possession.

New Grove, Drumbo

102. Tucked away at the end of a long avenue, in a wooded agricultural setting, a somewhat unusual house: single-storey on part-basement in front, the remains of a cramped old two-storey settler's farmhouse behind, in the midst of more recent farm outbuildings. "Newgrove, McNeill Esq" appears on the map in Taylor and Skinner's roadbook of 1778: but whether this refers both to the older and newer parts of the house is unclear. On the one hand, the back part on its own would hardly seem to have amounted quite to a gentleman's seat; on the other hand, the front part does not look quite so early. But perhaps it really is. Roger McNeill seems to have been a Volunteer Officer in 1780.

A long, low, well-painted house of white roughcast, with bright blue trim: a broad doorcase with surrounding quoins, semi-circular radial fanlight, the modern door and sidelights inappropriate but not irremediable; two tall Georgian-glazed windows to the left, three to the right of the doorcase; graded slates and domical chimney-stacks; and, most delightfully, the left-hand gable wall is not straight, but forms a segmental bow, with a central Georgian-glazed window.

Mr Scott of the Ordnance Survey says, under "Gentlemen's Seats" - "New Grove, the residence of Councillor Thomas Hutchenson, a small but desirable residence". (What sort of "Councillor" can he have been? Presumably a barrister?) Tradition has it that this was the house of the agent for the Purdysburn estate; very likely, since Mr Narcissus Batt, the pioneering banker, was in 1834 the owner of the whole of Ballycarn townland and half that of Ballylesson; though his agent is given as Mr Malcolm, Hillhall. Lewis gives New Grove as the seat of J Russel, Esq. The Parliamentary Gazetteer just says that New Grove is "amongst the mansions and villas" of the parish. The vestry lists quoted by Mr Fred Rankin show Crommelin Irwin of Newgrove as a vestryman of Drumbo in 1870, Surtees Irwin of New Grove as a churchwarden

in 1871, and W Moore of Newgrove in 1915. The house and farm were acquired by the father of the present owner around 1940, from a family named Dick.

Photograph: A C W Merrick.
Situation: 191 Ballylesson Road, Drumbo; td, Ballycarn; District Council, Lisburn; Grid ref. J 318 668.
References: Listed (no rating?) (19/23/30). Taylor and Skinner, 'Roads', 1778, p 5; OS map, 1834; G Scott, OSM, nd (?1837) and GFW Bordes, nd, (?1834), Down II, pp 56, 59; Lewis, TD, 1837, I, p 511; PG, II, 1846, p 81; Rankin, 'Heritage of Drumbo', 1981, passim; information from owner.

Holly Park, Killinchy

103. A cruciform two-storey five-bay Georgian house, said by neighbours to be of the 1720s but it looks a good deal later; stuccoed and painted cream; Georgian glazing-bars complete; chamfered two-storey porch looks later, except for the chiselled cutstone doorcase on its right-hand side, with nice radial fanlight, no side-lights, at the head of four stone steps : could it have been moved and re-used? Pleasant courtyard at the rear; good grounds; walled garden. Like Ard View (96) near by, this house boasts a separately listed dry closet - this time however, only a two-seater. According to the listers, the basement contains cells built for the temporary accommodation of prisoners, in the custody of the magistrate, on their way to Downpatrick.

On the Monuments and Buildings Record file, Dick Oram notes "The building is a straightforward late Georgian country house of modest proportions and pretensions. Front door and kitchen have cutstone dressings. Well maintained with original fittings". Before the present owner acquired it, it belonged to a Mr Payne; before that, to his daughter Mrs Hayes.

Photographs: A C W Merrick (and see following page).
Situation: 37 Holly Park Road, Killinchy; td, Ballymacreelly; District Council, Ards; Grid ref. J 493 589.
References: House, listed B1 (24/17/13); dry closet, listed B (24/17/13). OS map, 1833; R Oram, notes in MBR.

173

5 - 8 The Crescent, Holywood

104. A Regency or late Georgian three-storey terrace, certainly earlier than 1831 when these four houses appear on a lease map from John Hunter to Hugh Stuart. Built "by Hugh Stuart, probably in the previous decade", according to Tony Merrick, who says that the three-bay end house, No 8, "began life as an isolated farmhouse, most probably in the late 18th century". At right angles (for there is no semi-circular, or Muslim, curve), a later terrace of four polychrome brick houses built in 1864. Both groups are enclosed in a pretty, secluded, triangular garden with fine trees, close to the heart of Holywood. The houses in the earlier of the two terraces are stuccoed, with console-bracketed doorcases and ground floor canted bay windows; Georgian glazing-pattern upstairs, Regency glazing-bars in the bay windows below. Nos 5 - 7 are of two bays only.

Fine big houses, the largest No 8, valued for many years at £20; in this house, after his marriage in 1863, my great-grandfather Charles Brett settled his widowed mother and his five sisters, Elizabeth Corne, Annabella Matilda, Anne Catherine, Mary, and Martha Alicia. The last (and youngest) got married, and went to New Zealand, in 1881; her mother died here in 1886. The other sisters lived on here for half a century: the last of them lived in this house until her death in 1935. "I remember being taken to see my great-great-aunt Mary when I was about six. She was a little old lady in a lace cap sitting up in bed. I have a much more vivid recollection of the enormous fluffy grey cat, which towered above me as it stood on the bed. It was

called Phyllis Doreen, I am told, and was a tom-cat" (Brett). To my mortification, this was a house to which I was very curtly denied access.

Photographs: A C W Merrick.
Situation: The Crescent, Holywood; td, Ballykeel; District Council, North Down; Grid ref. J 400 792.
References: Listed B (23/20/34). 1831 lease map of John Hunter's property at Ballykeel, copy in possession of A C W Merrick; VAL 12B/17/10G, p 128, VAL 12B/17/12B, p 81, in PRONI; OS map, 1834; Brett, 'Long shadows', 1978, p 77; Merrick, 'Buildings of Holywood', 1986, p 54.

Woodford House, Dromara

105. The listers say "Early 19th century. An elegant country villa built for the mill owner in restrained classical style. It was the seat of James Black who owned the adjacent Bleach Works. This house is a good example of late Georgian symmetrical classical design". Lewis says, in 1837, "Woodford, formerly the residence of Jas. Black, Esq., has extensive bleach-works, and was once the seat of a flourishing branch of the linen manufacture". The Ordnance Survey officers, however, make no mention of this house or mill, then evidently in decline.

Rodney Green is much more informative. He says "Dromara Flax Co. Ltd., Woodford ... A modern flax rettery on the site of the highest bleachgreen on the River Lagan. There is" (1963) "a disused beetling mill with a turbine still in position. The house has an early nineteenth-century façade with a noteworthy doorway, but the rear is clearly of eighteenth-century date. Woodford belonged to the Black family and there are references to them as being in the linen trade as early as 1758. The bleachgreen is marked on Williamson's 1810 map of Co. Down. In 1816 Henderson Black of Woodford carried out bleaching experiments for the Linen Trustees. The Valuation surveyors record" (in the 1830s) "that 'this concern is nearly in a state of dilapidation'. There were then two boiling houses, a beetling mill, and a wash house and drying loft. The two wheels of 14 ft. in diameter had not been in use for more than a month in the year for nine years past".

Denis Piggot's notes of 1991 in the Monuments and Buildings Record remark, "The front doorway is magnificent, with its beautiful fanlight and sidelights, and a fine six-panel door, complete with original lock. Inside, very fine hall with attractive staircase". The five-bay two-storey house is cement-rendered, with quoins; glazing bars complete and painted white; reeded pilasters in the doorcase; fine upstanding chimney-stacks at the gable-ends. There are extensive, and pretty ruinous, industrial remains, on a large scale, in the valley; but the mill-owner's house survives intact.

Photograph: A C W Merrick.
Situation: 21 Woodford Avenue, Dromara; td, Dromara; District Council, Lisburn; Grid ref. J 281 503.
References: Listed B1 (19/7/10). VAL 1B/341, in PRONI; Lewis, TD, 1837, I, p 503; Green, 'Industrial archaeology', 1963, p 23; D Piggot, notes in MBR.

Drumcro House, Magheralin

106. A generously creeper-clad five-bay two-storey-and-attic rendered rubble-stone house, with cellars, an unusual half-hipped roof and two central chimney-stacks; Georgian glazing-bars complete; doorcase with narrow sidelights, fluted pilasters and excellent semi-circular radial fanlight, painted white and green. The Archaeological Survey of County Down says "House c. 1820-30 (on the 1833 o.s. map but there named 'New Forge House') ... It is L-shaped in plan, the main block facing W., with a rear return containing kitchens which is probably a later addition" (*sic:* but the owner and I both think it probably earlier, not later); "... At first floor the central window is of three lights, the central light being wider than the others. The main block contains a small hall and stair-hall with a large apartment on each side; a door to the rear, opening from the stair-hall, has a semicircular arched fanlight with spider-web glazing and the window above, lighting the half-landing of the stair, is semicircular arched".

The Valuation book of 1838 shows Mr Corbett (*sic*) Waddell as occupier of house and offices, in category A, valued at £55 19 3, plus "mills" valued at £16 15 9; on the same page is Mr Robert Waddell, whose house, offices, and old bleach mill not used were valued together at £52 5 3. It is not clear from this which is Drumcro and which New Forge (95) on the northern side of the River Lagan. The next valuation, however, of 1861, shows Drumcro House, held by Robert Waddell from the Earl of Clanwilliam, valued first at £36, then £42; New Forge house, works and offices held by Frederick Hole from Coslett Waddell, £35; and another house, £7, corn mill kiln and

offices, £28, and beetling flax mill, £28, all occupied by Coslett Waddell: with the note "NB This Bleaching mill has not been used for some time past - but arrangements are in progress for working it". The present owner's grandfather bought the place from the last of the Waddells in 1918; at present the big house, though in good order, is used only for storage, and the owner lives in the lesser house, known since 1967 as Cedar Lodge, in the ample yard at the rear. There are considerable outbuildings and attractive trees; the riverside site is delightful.

Photographs: A C W Merrick.
Situation: 2 Orange Lane, Magheralin; td, Drumo and Drumcro; District Council, Craigavon; Grid ref. J 130 581.
References: Listed B1 (14/7/12). VAL 1B/346, p 42, VAL 2B/3/46B, p 47, VAL 12B/21/1/A - F, in PRONI; ASCD, 1966, p 361; Oram, 'Craigavon', UAHS, 1971, Pt II, pp 5, 9; information from owner.

Marino Villas, Cultra, Holywood

107. A remarkable enclave of Regency Tudor bathing villas built around 1830 for Thomas Ward by the ebullient and eccentric Belfast architect, John Millar, originally comprising seven houses: six of which survive unspoiled, now known as Nos 6 and 7, Marino Villas; and Nos 1 (Linden Lodge), 3 (The Cloisters), 5 (Marino Villa), and 7 (Brook House), Marino Park. All are shown on the Ordnance Survey map of 1834, three years before Queen Victoria's accession. Lt Bordes of the Ordnance Survey says, in 1834, "Several new houses have been built on the shore to the north east of the village" (that is, Holywood) "for the bathing season, when they are generally filled from Belfast. They are built of stone and in the Gothic style". Of stone apparently they are not, but of brick, all today stuccoed and painted. (The listers assert that these houses were "part of Marriage Endowment by Kennedy family", but cite no authority, and I have been unable to discover any corroboration).

Three years later, Samuel Lewis writes "There are several good lodging-houses in the village and its environs; and from the increasing number of visiters [*sic*], several houses in detached situations, and chiefly in the Elizabethan style of architecture, are now in progress on the Cultra estate, by Thomas Ward, Esq., after designs by Millar. These houses are sheltered with thriving plantations, and beautifully situated on a gentle eminence commanding a richly diversified and extensive prospect of Carrickfergus bay, the Black mountain, Cave hill, the Carnmoney mountains, and the town and castle of Carrickfergus, the view terminating with the basaltic columns of Black Head". Unhappily, most of the "thriving plantations" are gone. In 1980, the residents petitioned, unsuccessfully, to have this declared a conservation area; but the trees were cut down, and the grounds of Marino House (97) (including its unusual circular walled garden, possibly on the site of a much earlier enclosure) built over

with twenty-odd villas and bungalows. In consequence, in 1986, all the houses were renumbered, but the listers do not seem to have amended their records, which makes the study of the area exceptionally confusing. At a later date, an unfortunate infill house between Marino Villa and Brooke House secured planning permission, despite opposition from Historic Buildings branch of the Department of the Environment. For many years, all these houses had been rented out for £20 per annum, the occupants had no incentive to repair, and most of them fell into considerable disrepair. In the post-war years, they were all bought by a Mr Mullan, who proposed to knock them down and redevelop the site; it was he, apparently, who unfortunately irrevocably ruined No 5, Marino Villas, by inappropriate alterations.

It seems that Thomas Ward, who was (according to a pencilled note in the Griffith valuation) by 1862 Secretary to the Belfast & County Down Railway Company, himself lived in what is now Linden Lodge, No 1 Marino Park. No doubt he was in a position to influence the convenient siting of the Marino Halt, only a few steps from his front door; the railway line from Belfast to Holywood was opened in 1845, but the extension from Holywood to Bangor was only completed in 1865. His house, presumably the first of the group to be built, was valued at £31 12 0 in 1838; £27 in 1862, when it was "let to Thomas Valentine for the Bathing Season, unfurnished, at £12 per month"; it was "unoccupied" in 1863.

On the opposite corner of Old Quay Road and what is now known as Marino Park is a cleverly interlocking group of three semi-detached houses, each valued at £19 in 1862: one then occupied by William Wilson, one by H G Burrell (later by Thomas Walkington), one by Mrs Mary Anne Davis. The middle house used to be known as Green Gables; that name was in 1984 transferred, oddly, to the house next door; but since none of the three has, in fact, green gables, it does not seem much to matter. In 1976, the middle house (today No 6 Marino Villas) was described in most unusual detail in the Monuments and Buildings Record files: "Middle house in two-storey block of three pre-1834 houses. Roof slated and gabled. Diagonal-set chimneys with crenellated head. Walls rendered, lined and painted. South-west front has octagonal tower as central bay with pavilion roof and pinnacle, and gabled parapet. Entrance doorway has four-centred arch head and sheeted and headed door. Diamond-framed casement dormer windows, casement windows on ground floor, horizontal astragals and label mouldings". The house next door to the north has, as remarked above, been disastrously mutilated; that next door to the south has recently been repaired, with much new plasterwork, but awaits repainting at the time of writing.

On the opposite side of Marino Park and next door to Linden Lodge, a semi-detached pair - The Cloisters and Marino Villa - in my view, the finest of this group; linked by a cloister-like arcade through which access is gained by separate Tudor doorways to each house and to the central enclosed yard. Each valued at £34 9 0 in 1838; at £39 in 1863; one then occupied by Robert Patterson, the other by Captain George Frazer, "late of the Coast Survey". It is said that this delightful pair may have been based by Millar on a design in J C Loudon's Cottage, Farm and Villa Architecture. The left hand house has an interior cloister, of angled arches, as well as an external one.

The last of the group, Brook House - now No 7 Marino Park - was valued at £16. 14. 0 in 1838 (perhaps then not completed?), £32 in 1862, when it was occupied by Captain Richard Hoskin. It is somewhat plainer than the others, but shares their remarkable crenellated diagonally-placed chimney-stack patterns and detailing, including Tudor label-mouldings. Most of the houses have been somewhat altered over the years, not always for the better, but they retain numerous idiosyncratic and delightful details: doors and doorcases; fluted mouldings; mantelpieces with odd diamond-pattern ornament; angled arches, windows, and arcades; narrow diamond-paned lancet windows; sliding shutters, and even sashes sliding sideways into the walls; and cast iron ridge-tiles.

It would be marvellous if the owners of these six houses,

perhaps even in collaboration with the owners of Marino House (97), Windrush (57), Ardville and Ardreagh, could come together in some sort of residents' association to co-ordinate repainting - preferably, as often as possible, in sparkling white - and replanting, in order to maximise the merits, and minimise damage caused by intrusions into its original environment, of this quite exceptional group of pre-Victorian buildings.

The architect John Millar (1811 - 1876) trained under Thomas Hopper, worked with him on the drawings for Gosford Castle, County Armagh, worked also on the completion of Nash's Kilwaughter Castle, County Antrim, but specialised in neo-classical churches - in Belfast, Antrim town, Castlereagh (34), and Portaferry (37). He also built the Scotch church at Crumlin, County Antrim in an Elizabethan-Gothic style, and (possibly) Tudor Hall, Holywood (56). After a promising start, he seems to have gone bankrupt in the 1840s, and emigrated first to Australia, then to New Zealand, where he mainly undertook engineering work, earned a gold medal for heroism in a shipwreck, and was memorably described as an "odd fish whose element is hot water". According to one Dunedin historian "Millar ... proved to be a highly capricious person ... the touch of the fantastic which he contrived to introduce into most of the schemes he undertook, undermined confidence and invited derision". However, a report in the local press was more complimentary, "Mr Millar, however eccentric, at any rate possesses ability, which is more than can be said for the Town Board" with whom he was in dispute because of his "heretical opinions on tidal scour". His memory should be treasured by the residents of Marino.

Photographs: A C W Merrick.
Situation: Old Quay Road, and Marino Park, Cultra; td, Ballycultra; District Council, North Down; Grid ref. J 407 799.
References: Listed: Linden Lodge and Green Gables B, others all B1 (23/18/36, 37, 38, 39). VAL 1B/318, VAL 2B/3/182, p 30, VAL 12B/17/10A p 3, D 2285/2, all in PRONI; OS map, 1834; GFW Bordes, OSM, 1834, Down, II, p 74; Lewis, TD, 1837, II, p 6; 'Otago Daily Telegraph', 14/1/1864, p 4; M A Ronnie, unpublished MA thesis, University of Otago, 1965; McDonald, 'City of Dunedin', 1965, passim; P Larmour, in 'Perspective', Sept/Oct 1994, pp 55 - 57; C E B Brett, in UA, Sept/Oct 1994, pp 4 - 6; information from owners.

The Glen Farm, Greyabbey

108. A pretty mid-Georgian farmhouse, tucked away amongst fine trees on a hillside amidst 60 acres of pasture, at the end of a very long lane which passes through a farmyard. Originally, this appears to have been a seven-bay single-storey stone house; so it appears on a map of two townlands of the Montgomery demesne of 1789. By degrees, extensive stone out-buildings were added, and at some point the house was 'new riz and slated', probably quite early in the nineteenth century: it appears much as now on the 1834 Ordnance Survey map. It was bought out by the then tenant farmer, William John Carson, in 1933; he left the place to his son Hugh, with a right of residence to his daughter, who survived her brother. After her death, it was bought by a neighbouring farmer who grazed the land, and left the house empty and boarded up. The present owner and her late husband bought the property for the grazing and stabling, but came to realise the charms of the house, and set about restoring it, and laying out the gardens, in 1995. This they have done with great success and sensitivity.

The main part of the house is five-bay, two-storey, the walls encased in lined-out smooth render, with creepers and climbers; slated roof, and yellow brick chimney-stacks at the gables; with a single-storey bay at either end, each with its tripartite window. All the windows have Georgian glazing-bars, careful replacements of the original ones. The doorcase with its rectangular fanlight is original, but the porch is made of disparate elements found in a scrap-yard, and knitted together most persuasively. The interior is plain, as befits a farm-house, though there is one large room, now dining-room, with windows both at front and back. The house looks south-west over rolling farmland with glimpses of Strangford Lough.

Photograph: A C W Merrick.
Situation: 3 Carrowdore Road, Greyabbey; td, Ballymurphy; District Council, Ards; Grid ref. J 583 691.
References: Not listed. T 1031/1, and Montgomery estate rent rolls, in PRONI; OS map, 1834; information from owner.

Islet Hill Farm, Groomsport

109. Patton just says, rather dismissively, "c. 1840: Two-storey three-bay stucco house with outbuildings on the site of a former rath". Still worse. the listers just say "Mid 19th Century. Neo-Georgian farm house". But its occupier, who clearly loves it, has written a charming account of its history, principally for the benefit of those who come to stay at the B & B he and his wife have established there.

This is a modest farm-house, the main block flanked by single-storey wings; all the ground-floor windows set in arched recesses, though unfortunately most of the original Georgian glazing bars have at some date been removed. The walls are of grey roughcast, with a slightly off-centre round-headed chiselled-stone doorcase with small cobweb fanlight. Much of the internal detailing is original, including window-shutters and very slim banisters. Very well cared for. Few such traditional late-Georgian (certainly not "Neo-Georgian") farmhouses survive so little altered in this part of North Down: the owner describes his door-way and fanlight as "quite unique in this area". The house overlooks the rocky but whinny headland of Bally-macormick Point, generously given, with thirty-five acres of land, by the late Jack Kingan to the National Trust in 1952. All this was originally part of the Hamilton, then Dufferin, estate of Clandeboye. The farm of fifty seven Cunningham acres and one rood was let to the Agnew family in 1731. A lease of 16 October 1787 contained a covenant that, by 1791, there should be built a "sufficient dwelling house of stones and mortar" 60 feet in length and 8 feet high and thatched. In 1832 Patrick and James Agnew put the farm up for auction; it was bought by James Clarke, who soon afterwards built a "neat two-storey slat-ed building" - the present farmhouse. In 1882 it was up for auction again, and bought by John Robb, the proprietor of Robb's store in Castle Place, Belfast (see also 100). By then, the landlords were no longer the Dufferins, but the Kingans of Glenganagh (55).

In 1939, a battery of four 3.7 inch anti-aircraft guns, in pits which are still discernible, with supporting Nissen huts for the gun crews (male and female) was built for the defence of Belfast Lough between the farmhouse and the shore. I well remember the embarrassment when, out for a family walk one sunny Sunday afternoon with my aunt and cousins, we almost fell over a comely member of the ATS and a squaddie locked in a posture of considerable indelicacy on the grass beside the guns; and the determi-nation with which we all looked fixedly out to seaward. The occasion must have been at least as embarrassing for them as for us.

Photograph: A C W Merrick.
Situation: 21 Bangor Road, Groomsport; td, Ballymacormick; District Council, North Down; Grid ref. J 530 837.
References: Listed B1 (23/1/7). Clandeboye leases, in PRONI; Gallagher and Rogers, 'Castle, coast and cottage', 1992, p 11; Patton, 'Bangor', UAHS, 1999, p 18; 'Fifty-seven acres and a rood' (unpublished his-torical notes by owner), copy in MBR.

Cherrymount, Lurgan

110. Although this house is just over the boundary between Counties Down and Armagh, I missed it when compiling Buildings of County Armagh, and therefore take the liberty of including it here. On the outskirts of Lurgan, set back from the main road to Aghagallon, a large and imposing five-bay two-storey house, said to have been built - like Kilmore House (121) - by the Langtry family. It must be earlier than 1834, for it is shown on the Ordnance Survey map of that year; but its present appearance is somewhat later: it has been stuccoed all over with heavy quoins, architraves to the lower windows, ornate label mouldings over the upstairs ones, and a good deal of stained glass. However, the Georgian glazing-pattern is intact - there are lunette attic windows in the gables - as is the doorcase with radial fanlight and side-lights, all painted dark red; whilst the walls are off-white, with cream trim.

An undated and unsigned report in the Monuments and Buildings Record, apparently by Hugh Dixon, says: "The house is L-shaped with its main entrance front facing SW into an orchard-garden. Its generously-scaled 5-bay front has two main rooms on each storey divided by a grand central stairhall on the ground floor and a corresponding landing above ... There is a long return aligned with, and apparently built at the same time as the main block's N. gable ... The walls are built of large, very roughly shaped stones packed with smaller ones and joint-harled; the window lintels are straight arches of local brick ... The staircase is the house's most sophisticated and dramatic

feature. It rises in a long ramp from each level and the stairs continue round each outer curve; the handrail echoes the curve at the first-floor landing and seeps on again up to the attics. The treatment of the first ramp with four balusters per tread and Adamesque enrichments to the outer frets has not been recorded elsewhere in the county and is probably extremely rare. There are also Regency enrichments to the wide doorcase, and to the doors and panelled reveals of the hall doorways to the dining and drawing rooms. This is the house which appears on the earliest O.S. map of 1834. Later changes neither enhance nor harm the building's essential character ... A Dovecot to the SW. of the house is also late-Georgian".

In the Griffith valuation of 1862, shown as the property of George Cordner, valued first at £18 10 0, then at £23 10 0. In 1872, George Cordner added a linen store at the rear, which brought the valuation up to £37 10 0. Between 1890 and 1894, the place passed to James Bowden, now valued at £60, "A fine house in good repair, only a small part used for business purposes". Occupied for many years by a Dr Smith; and by members of the Ellis family, from whom it was bought by the husband of the present owner in 1981.

Photograph: A C W Merrick.
Situation: 45 Cornakinnegar Road, Lurgan; td, Cornakinnegar; District Council, Craigavon; Grid ref. H 095 605.
References: Listed B (14/8/5). VAL 2B/2/20A, p 32, VAL 12B/14/5A-B, in PRONI; OS map, 1834; notes in MBR.

Legacurry House, Annahilt

111. A very pleasant mill-house just above the rushing Ravernet river: part of a group, clustered around Legacurry bridge, comprising mill-owner's house; cottage; derelict water-mill buildings; and the remains of a small and early inn, with accommodation for yeomanry at the rear. The principal building is, in effect, L-shaped: the four-bay two-storey part of the house, facing the Crossan Road, is plainly the earlier part, probably mid-18th century; the newer and taller part at right angles, three-bay, two-storey, with its hipped roof, architraves to the upper Georgian-glazed windows and label mouldings below, was added perhaps around 1840. Its walls are of white-painted roughcast, with smooth quoins, parapet, and string-course, ornamented with wistaria. The porch looks later, but incorporates a doorcase with an excellent broad fanlight. A pair of solid chimney-stacks crown the roofline.

The place seems to have belonged to the Morrow family, under lease from Lord Downshire, for the best part of a century. The entries in the Valuation books, though uncommonly confusing, are as usual much more informative about the mill buildings than about the house. On 18th February 1834, the house was shown in only category C+, measuring 50 feet by 21 feet by 14 feet 6 inches, so presumably still single-storey: not separately valued, but lumped in with offices, outbuildings, corn kiln, corn mill, and dust house, at a total of £57 2 0. The flax mill, classified B, measuring 47 feet by 17 feet 6 inches was separately valued at £13 13 6. The diameter of the wheel (or each of two wheels? - unclear) is shown as 11 feet; with the notes: "James Morrow holds but 10 acres Irish with the Mills and Houses and too many offices or houses ... Note. This mill has not a constant supply of water, about 8 months, but one pair of stones, but little business done".

Matters do not seem to have improved much by the time of the Griffith valuation of 1861: it is hard to see when, or how, the mill prospered sufficiently to support the building of so fine a new house. "Robert Morrow, from the Marquess of Downshire, house, offices, corn mill, kiln and land" - total value, £38, of which £16 appears to have been attributable to the house. "Corn Mill valued and built at £11. Three pair stones in this mill, only two used at one time and third occasionally for grinding flour - which I have not taken into account as it seems not to be used more than once per week during the season which is about eight months". No mention this time of the flax mill.

In 1868, "house offices corn mill kiln and land" were valued together, in the ownership of Robert Morrow under Lord Downshire, the buildings being valued at £38; at which figure they remained until 1901, when Robert Morrow's name was struck out, in favour first of Francis Walkington, then of Samuel Brown. By 1897 the corn mill and kiln, though still valued at £18, were described as "at rest"; the house and offices valued at £17. It seems that Samuel Brown bought out the lease under the Land Acts, for by 1915 he was shown as the owner in fee, the house being still valued at £17, the "corn mill and kiln at rest" at £18, and the farmland at £50. So the figures remained until 1929. It appears that the property passed then to the Simpson family; then to Baird; and to the present owner in 1982.

Photograph: A C W Merrick.
Situation: 1 Crossan Road, Annahilt; td, Legacurry; District Council, Lisburn; Grid ref. J 298 601.
References: Not listed (why not?).VAL 1B/327, p 74, VAL 2B/3/25C, p 12, VAL 12B /20/8A - E, in PRONI; information from owner.

Ringneill House, Comber

112. A classic example of a very modest late-Georgian one-and-a-half storey house, perhaps of about 1790, later enlarged (possibly in the 1840s?) to provide a very comfortable moderately-sized gentleman's residence. It is on a marvellous site, on a low rocky knoll where a little river flows out into the western shores of Strangford Lough, looking across at Horse Island and the woods of Mount Stewart, with extensive stone-walled stabling, out-buildings and mature trees; but, characteristically, the old part of the house turns its back on the sea views, so that only the back door looks out over the lough. Most unusually, it retains - as a divider within the hall - the original wide doorcase, incorporating, however, within its rectangular glazing bars red- and blue-tinted glass which, if not a replacement, would argue for a rather later date than 1790: possibly around 1820. The old part of the house, with its cramped L-shaped staircase, is little altered from its original state, apart from replastering and new window-frames.

At some date in the mid-19th century, considerable forward-projecting extensions were added to the front of the older house: there is a long, broad, hallway, with bedrooms opening off it on either side, terminating at the front in generously-proportioned drawing-room and dining-room, each with attics above. Externally, this addition is contained in two broad gabled bays with a somewhat lower and narrower gablet between them, each topped by a turned wooden pinnacle. Breaking forward on either side of the front door are lower single-storey gabled wings with similar finials. There is a hood-moulding over the front doorcase; all is of white-painted lined stucco; not quite original, but seemly replacements after a fire in the 1970s.

The house is said to have been first built for a younger son of the Gordon family of Florida Manor and Delamont who lived there until the mid-19th century; subsequently to have been occupied by the Barry family, ancestors of Canon John Barry, lately of Hillsborough. On December 3, 1834, the valuers placed the house, then occupied by Robert Barry, in category A , and valued it at £14 14 1: with the somewhat surprising note, "has but 29 acres. The House Built as a speculation of getting lodgers". By the time of the Griffith valuation of 1863, the house (now valued at £9) and 39 acres in the (then) townland of Ringneill, and (then) parish of Tullynakill, were still held by Robert Barry under lease from James Dalzell. The valuation rose to £11 10 0 in 1878, in which year Robert was succeeded by Mary Barry. She remained there until 1900, when the occupier was Samuel Galbraith; succeeded in 1905 by his son John, who bought out the freehold from the Dalzells under the Land Acts. The house remained in the occupation of John Galbraith at least until 1929. About 1970 it was bought by a Mr Goldstone; from whom the present owners acquired it in 1996.

In pretty good shape, and well-loved, but it could do with a determined effort to restore it so far as possible to its mid 19th-century condition: there are too many different kinds of rendering, and too many not-quite-right glazing-bars in the windows. However that may be, a house of very considerable charm and character.

Photographs: Anthony C W Marrick.
Situation: 16 Ringneill Road, Comber; td, formerly Ringneill, now Ballydrain; District Council, Ards; Grid ref. J 503 661.
References: Not listed. VAL 1B/323, p 8, VAL 2B/3/23, p 27, VAL 12B/23/28A-E, in PRONI; correspondence in possession of owner.

Beech Park, Lurgan

113. A very handsome two-storey, the listers say three-bay but in fact five-bay, blackstone house, with galleting and brick dressings; Georgian-glazed, with a fine segmental-headed doorcase with fanlight and sidelights; bull's-eye attic windows in the gables. Set in a splendid garden and demesne, with magnificent trees, just on the outskirts of Lurgan.

This was the house of Henry Mercer, descendant of a Lisburn Huguenot family called Mercier. In 1836 the house here - it may have been a previous and smaller one - was placed in category B-, valued at only £9 11 1; by 1861, the valuation had risen to £28, the classification to B+. According to the recollections of H P Watson, written in 1956 when he was only 78 (he lived to be 89), "This house I am living in was built I think circa 1830 at a time when apparently a lot of building was done. Built by a Mr Boyd from County Tyrone, a brother of Mrs Mercer of Farm Lodge adjoining ... My grandfather came here in 1848 and would have bought the place but Mr Mercer refused to sell ... My father came here on his marriage". In 1861 the house was occupied by Hugh Watson under Henry Mercer: and so remained until 1911, when the property passed to Henry P Watson and Mary G Watson jointly, and the freehold was bought out under the Land Acts. The present owner acquired it from the Watson family in 1965, and has lavished loving care upon it and its gardens.

At some time in the late 19th century an extension was added between the main house and the stable-yard at the rear, it is said to the designs of Henry Hobart, architect, of Dromore: its canted bay looking out over the garden was designed to provide a new kitchen, but the present owner very sensibly turned it into a pleasant sitting-room.

Photograph: Anthony C W Merrick; Victorian postcard.
Situation: Set back somewhat from Dromore Road, Lurgan; td, Ballymacateer; District Council, Craigavon; Grid ref. J 102 578.
References: Listed B+ (14/7/19).VAL 1B/346, p 38, VAL 2B/3/46B, p 67, VAL 12B/21/6A -F, in PRONI; Oram, 'Craigavon', UAHS, 1971, Pt II, p 12; copy notes by H P Watson in possession of owner; information from owner.

Kilmore House, Cornakinnegar Road, Lurgan

114. The townland of Kilmore is one of the largest in Ireland: large enough, indeed, to contain two 'Kilmore Houses' (see 121); of which the present building on this site may well be somewhat the earlier; but the site of the other claims greater antiquity.

A very handsome five-bay two-storey blackstone house, with grey-painted stucco quoins and long-and-short window-surrounds; Georgian glazing-bars in the very tall windows; chimney-stacks at the gables; and a fine portico with paired Ionic columns at either side of the central doorcase, with its radial fanlight and elaborately patterned sidelights. Judging from some of the interior details, such as the fluted wooden doorcases, staircase and cross-grained banister-rail, it might be as early as 1810; though the excellent plasterwork in the ceiling roses and cornices looks rather later. It may well be from the same hand as Leansmount (115), in the same townland. There is a particularly nice little 19th-century conservatory at the side.

The house is believed to have been built by members of the Hoop family; it then passed to a linen family, the Macouns. The Valuation books show John "McKeon" as owner in 1836; John Macoun in 1867; William McCoun in 1906; valued by then at £34 - the way the family spelled

its name seems to have changed over the years. It appears to have been John Macoun who added the back half of the house, the porch, and the extensive outbuildings, together with the machicolated bell-tower (dated either 1861 or 1881), topped by a nice cast-iron wind-vane. Unfortunately the ornamental archway into the yard had to be taken down to allow modern cattle lorries to get in. Various plans for improvements, prepared for "John McCoun by James Entwhistle, architect, Sydenham", seem not to have been executed. In 1937 the place was advertised for sale by the last of the McCouns, and was bought by Hercules Jordan, grandfather of the present owner. The farmland and buildings are extensive, the garden contains good beech trees, and all was very spick and span at the time of writing.

Photograph: A C W Merrick (see also colour illus. 27).

Situation: 107 Cornakinnegar Road, Aghagallon; td, Kilmore; District Council, Craigavon; Grid ref. J 092 619.

References: Listed B (14/8/1). VAL 1B/349, p 19, VAL 12B/21/5A-D, in PRONI; Oram, 'Craigavon', UAHS, 1971, Pt II, p 11; information from owners, and documents in their possession.

Leansmount, Lurgan

115. A pleasing classic five-bay two-storey-and-attic black-stone farmhouse, with long-and-short stucco window surrounds, fanlight and sidelights, Georgian glazing-bars complete. It is situated near the tip of the finger of County Down that runs right up to Lough Neagh, driving a wedge between Counties Antrim and Armagh: something of a geographical curiosity. The present house crosses the T of a much older one, now a return, said to date from the 1680s; and alleged to have been built by an Earl of Clanwilliam to provide a dowry, with its hundred acres, for his daughter, who married a soldier called Captain Magill and was considered by her father to have married beneath her. There are two problems, however, about this agreeable tale: the title was not created until 1776; and Burke's Peerage contains no record of any Clanwilliam (or Meade) daughter marrying a Magill.

The Magills sold to a Captain Ellis, who built the present house in front of the old one, some time in the first half of the 19th century: as Oram says, "Probably 1830s", judging from outward appearances, but perhaps a good deal earlier, for there are a very delicate plasterwork ceiling decoration in the hall, and reeded doorcases; and the mahogany banister-rail has the grain running crossways not lengthways, often a sign that it was constructed during the timber shortages of the Napoleonic blockade: so that a date around 1810 seems plausible. In the 1835 Valuation book the house appears in category A, measuring 51 feet 6 inches by 24 feet by 25 feet, valued at the considerable sum of £34 11 1, with a "Note. There are more offices here than required for the farm".

The Ellises went bankrupt as a result of too many expensive building ventures, and the place was then sold to the Belfast family of Turtle: in 1886 the Valuation book shows Thomas Turtle holding under lease from the Earl of Clanwilliam, the valuation having fallen to £27. Thomas was succeeded by Robert Turtle in 1902; his daughters Mary and Christina Turtle were still here in 1923; the father of the present owner bought the place from the last of the Turtles in 1954.

Photograph: A C W Merrick.
Situation: 37 Leansmount Road, Aghagallon; td, Kilmore; District Council, Craigavon; Grid ref. J 083 623.
References: Listed B (14/8/3). VAL 1B/349, p 35, VAL 12B/21/5A-D, in PRONI; Oram, 'Craigavon', UAHS, 1971, Pt II, p 10; information from owner.

Magherahinch House, Moira

116. A substantial five-bay two-storey double-pile farmhouse, with the date 1838 and the coronet of the Downshires above the front door. The windows are Georgian-glazed, and there is a good wide segmental-headed fanlight, though it looks as if the original sidelights have been replaced. The house is, somewhat unusually, of black-painted random-laid stone, with quoins, and brick surrounds to the openings, picked out in cream paint. The striking and very successful paint-scheme is rather let down by the rendered but unpainted chimney-stacks at the gable ends. According to the listers, three-bay, but this does not seem to be right. They suggest that part of the house, one room deep with stair return, is probably considerably older, but much remodelled in 1838. The extensive range of farm buildings and yard, with datestone of 1847, is also listed. Oram describes the property as "Two-storey five bay basalt house of distinction ... The formal front seems to have been added to an older building; the staircase, for example, might easily be early 18th century. At the rear is a court framed by a full range of excellent farm outbuildings roughly contemporary with the formal house front. The whole range is" (1969) "beautifully maintained". It still is.

In the Valuation book of 1834 this farmhouse was shown as tenanted by Reps Joshua Green, and his brother, valued at £16 12 3. In 1862, the valuation had risen to £22, with the note - "An old house remodelled". But in 1868, the name of James Greene was struck out, and that of Adam Ager substituted; and by 1888 his valuation had been reduced again to £20 10 0. Early in the 20th century, James Turner became tenant, and exercised his rights under the Land Purchase Acts about 1909. In 1929, the Turners were struck out, and the new owner was shown as Joseph H Creswell.

At the end of a long laneway opening off Moira's main street, surrounded by good trees, on a marvellous hillside site looking out over the Lagan valley below; but new housing, and industrial buildings, are creeping closer and closer.

Photograph: A C W Merrick.
Situation: 33 Main Street, Moira; td, Magherahinch; District Council, Lisburn; Grid ref. J 151 601.
References: Listed B1 (19/2/54). Datestones; VAL 1B/347, VAL 2B/3/47A, p 46, VAL 12B/21/7 A-E, in PRONI; OS map, 1833; Oram, 'Craigavon', UAHS, 1971, Pt II, p 12.

Annaghanoon House, Waringstown

117. Approached by a very long lane, an attractive five-bay, two-storey, Georgian farmhouse; the walls are of very large stones, encased in yellow-painted stucco, channelled on the ground floor but not upstairs, with quoins; the windows are Georgian-glazed, those upstairs considerably narrower than those on the ground floor; chimney-stacks at the gables; the modern doorcase is slightly off-centre, and the upper and lower window openings do not quite correspond. Some of the ceilings have pretty plasterwork. The difference between the storeys might indicate that this is a case of a single-storey house "new riz and slated"; but the owner says that, on the contrary, tradition has it that the house was originally three-storey, was found to be too large for convenience, and so was lowered by a storey. In its present form the house looks as if it dates from the 1830s or 1840s; but there may well have been an earlier house on the site.

The present owner's grandfather bought the house, with 66 acres, from one Thomas Bailie in 1914 for £2100, and subsequently succeeded in acquiring also the house and farm standing between it and the main road. Both are surrounded by clumps of mature trees, with old-fashioned gardens; the garden gateway beside Annaghanoon House bears the date 1873.

Photograph: A C W Merrick.
Situation: 123 Banbridge Road, Waringstown; td, Annaghanoon; District Council, Craigavon; Grid ref. J 111 529.
References: Listed B (14/6/32).

Springfield, Magheralin

118. From the road, behind lawn and trees, a five-bay two-storey house, stuccoed and cream-painted, with ver-miculated quoins; Regency-style glazing-bars; porch with pilasters; and high hipped roof with very tall chimney-stacks. Behind this, the older house, with Georgian glaz-ing-pattern, two storey, stuccoed and painted to conform. Behind that, further outbuildings. All in very good order.

Atkinson, following his visit in 1817, says " Springfield, the seat of Messrs R. and T. Richardson, eminent linen and muslin merchants, in this province; and equally emi-nent factors in the linen hall of Dublin, is situated on the see lands of Dromore - It is distinguished in this county (to which it makes no great contribution of the picturesque) solely by its trade ... Springfield comprehends a plain dwelling house, 85 Irish acres of demesne, and an estab-lishment in the muslin manufacturing and bleaching departments; and in the days of Ireland's prosperity, near-ly 1000 hands were employed here, and 15,000 pieces fin-ished and sold in the Dublin market. - This latter number, however, was reduced to 1,500, one tenth of its former business. In point of prospect, the view from the rear of this house, over its own bleach yard, the river Lagan, and a few neat villas in its vicinity, to the Mountains of Mourne, is, upon the whole, interesting. But this is the only view approaching to the picturesque that this seat can boast of ".

Green reports that "To the rear of a stuccoed early Victorian house is a large walled yard, the upper end of which is occupied by a range of two-storey buildings, near-ly 80 ft. in length and about 21 ft. wide, constructed of basalt masonry with brick window dressings. The roof of this building has recently" (1963) "collapsed ... Springfield must once have been one of the most imposing manufac-turer's premises in Co. Down,". The Valuation book of the 1830s notes Mr John Richardson's house and offices, in category A+, valued at £40 19 3; the Griffith valuation of 1861 says that Charles Richardson holds Springfield from the Ecclesiastical Commissioners, house and offices val-ued first at £36, then at £42.

"An older house on the site which was revamped as yet another Neo-classical house of the Richardson family ... c1850" (Dean). The listers say "Two storey dwelling. The front has been added to an earlier building at right angles. Present appearance dates from late 19th C renovation. Good early Georgian stairway, unusual apse feature cen-tral on the return". Recently extensively restored by the present owner.

Photograph: A C W Merrick.
Situation:15 Springfield Road, Magheralin; td, Ballymacateer; District Council, Craigavon; Grid ref. J 116 577.
References: Listed B (14/7/3).VAL 1B/ 346, p 40, VAL 2B/3/46B, p 74, in PRONI; Atkinson, 'Ireland exhibited', 1823, I, pp 174-175; Green, 'Industrial archaeology', 1963, p 25; Oram, 'Craigavon', UAHS, 1971, Pt II, p 8; Pierce and Coey, 'Taken for granted', 1984, p 123; Dean, 'Gate lodges', UAHS, 1994, p 96.

Duneight House, Blaris

119. This is a mill-owner's house; the remains of the mill are down in the valley by the river. Mr Ward of the Ordnance Survey writes, under "Mills", "Duneight, proprietor Marquis of Downshire, tenant William Hunter, erected 1833; water wheel 26 feet diameter, breadth 5 feet, breast wheel, 3 feet fall of water, machinery wood and iron, 3 pairs of beetles". Rodney Green describes "A derelict bleachworks of fairly modern date", but makes no mention of the house. "The Hunters of Dunmurry built a beetling mill here in 1833, driven by a great breast wheel, 26 ft. in diameter and 5 ft. wide. The Valuation books" (of the 1830s) "describe a wash and boiling house 78 ft. long and an engine house and drying loft 73 ft.long. There was also a dilapidated corn mill. Duneight bleachworks were advertised to be let or sold in 1845 at which time they were said to be capable of bleaching 25,000 pieces a year. Alexander Hunter of Dunmurry still owned Duneight in 1854, although the works were temporarily idle".

The listers say "3-bay symmetrical front with plaster classical detailing. A re-modelling of an earlier house". At the date of visiting, scaffolded and undergoing very major work for the eradication of dry rot, and re-roofing, only the back part of the house habitable. This looks to be the original, probably mid-18th century, house; the front part, two-storey and three-bay, at right angles, would seem to date from the late 1830s or 1840s - stuccoed, with quoins, complicated architraves round the windows with Greek key pattern mouldings, and Regency-style glazing bars.

Photograph: A C W Merrick.
Situation: 34 Green Road, Blaris; td, Duneight; District Council, Lisburn; Grid ref. J 280 607.
References: Listed B2 (19/6/19). VAL 1B/324, p 21, in PRONI; J R Ward, OSM, 1837, Down, III, 1833, p 36; Northern Whig, 13/12/1845; Green, 'Industrial archaeology', 1963, p 26.

Lamb's Island, Waringstown

120. " ... a pleasant Regency farmer's villa" (Dean). That describes it nicely, except that the dating is a bit doubtful. The house appears on Taylor and Skinner's road map of 1777; but that could relate to an older house on the same site, or to part only of the present building. A classic, three-bay, two-storey-and-attic, Georgian gent's farm-house; glazing-bars complete in the windows; radial fan-light at pillared doorcase; white-painted roughcast, black quoins and trim; its distinguishing feature being the setting of the windows in segmental-headed recesses of some elegance and sophistication. There is a straight drive up the hillside from the vernacular gate-posts to the front door; and a very fine monkey-puzzler to one side.

The Archaeological Survey of County Down says "built here in the late 18th or early 19th century and was incorporated in a larger house, c. 1840-50, to which it now forms a rearward return ... The main elevation faces E. and is three windows wide; the central door, contained in a semi-elliptical arched recess, is flanked by columns with moulded capitals supporting an entablature, with a fan-light filling the head of the recess. The windows are flat-arched and sashed, the flanking windows at ground and first floor being set within segmental arched recesses which rise through both storeys". Oram says "The group includes a good range of outbuildings. The drive is headed by a a pair of gargantuan traditional gate standards".

Apparently the house owes its unusual name to Moylan's Fort, "the fine fort situated on a knoll of high ground rising amidst the encircling 'moss', now known as 'Lamb's Island' "(ED Atkinson - Ulster Parish).

Writing of his visit in 1817, A Atkinson says, that Lamb's Island was the seat of the Rev. John Sherrard. Mr Sherrard was described in his obituary as "a man of studious habits, of extensive reading, literary attainments, and unbending integrity". But in his lifetime, his congregation was somewhat less complimentary: in 1811, 114 persons in Tullylish, of which he was Presbyterian Minister, signed a memorial to the synod for his removal; not that they had anything against his morals; but "his usefulness, they thought, was over" at the age of 83! He obligingly retired to Lamb's Island, where he lived on until his death aged 92 in 1829; the History of Congregations describes him as "a peppery old gentleman", but also as "an attractive character, public-spirited, independent, and perhaps not as sagacious as he imagined".

He was followed by the Rev. James Moorhead, Minister of Donaghcloney Presbyterian congregation from 1830 until 1880: he treated it as his manse, but it seems to have been his own property, for on his death in 1880 his successor did not move in, and a new manse was built for him soon thereafter. In 1881, the house, valued at £11, passed to one John Cairns. It was to remain in the occupation of the Cairns family for many years; in 1909 Thomas Cairns bought out the freehold of the farm under the Land Acts; in 1918 Annie Cairns inherited it; in 1928, Joseph Cairns. After the last of the Cairns family, it passed to Rogers, but unfortunately was allowed to lie vacant for fifteen years. In consequence, when it was acquired by the present owner in 1988, it required extensive rebuilding. The façade is original; so is the terrific ceiling rose in the drawing-room; but most of the rest, though quite appropriate, is in fact new: and in consequence, the house has been de-listed.

Photograph: A C W Merrick.
Situation: 147 Banbridge Road, Waringstown; td, Annaghanoon; District Council, Craigavon; Grid ref. J 115 525.
References: No longer listed. VAL 12B/21/9 A-F, in PRONI; Taylor and Skinner, 'Roads', 1778, p 45; Atkinson, 'Ireland exhibited', 1823, I, p 325; Atkinson, 'Ulster Parish', 1898, p 78; Magill and McCafferty, 'Donaclony Meeting', 1950, p 56; ASCD, 1966, p 369 and pl 175; Oram, 'Craigavon', UAHS, 1971, Pt II, p 3; 'History of Congregations', 1982, pp 380, 789.

Kilmore House, Kilmore Road, Lurgan

121. A neat, if surprisingly late, three-bay two-storey house built only in 1853. It is said to stand on the site of an earlier rectory, built about 1750, though to what parish it was annexed is unclear: some of the outbuildings appear to be of this earlier date. The old house lost its roof in the Big Wind of 1839, and the present one was built to replace it. It is of brick, painted a fruity red; nice doorcase, with delicate fanlight, and sidelights, picked out with painted long-and-short work in white; Georgian glazing-bars. It has an excellent garden with fine trees, including a magnificent cedar.

The house was built by George Langtry, a Lurgan man by origin who became a prominent Belfast merchant and Harbour Commissioner, owner and developer of Fortwilliam Park, Belfast. Owen describes him as "one of the pioneers of steam navigation, having between 1820 and 1826 placed several steamers to ply between Belfast and Liverpool and other cross-channel ports with goods and passengers"; however, "He as well as many other shipowners at that time had no faith in the idea of the propulsion of vessels by means of steam, and firmly believed that the new method was not capable of any great development". His fears were justified when he lost his money through the misfortune of the loss of the paddle-steamer *Reindeer* in Belfast Lough (her resting place, half-way between Grey Point and Carrickfergus, is shown on R L Patterson's chart at the front of his admirable Birds, Fishes and Cetacea of Belfast Lough: the wreck was one of Patterson's favourite spots for fishing). George Benn had a high opinion of Langtry - "He is known as the great improver and promoter of our commercial marine, and as the owner of a little fleet of vessels which, before steam navigation was

introduced, conveyed the linens and other goods of Belfast to London, Liverpool, or Chester Fair, with as much regularity as the winds permitted ... The name of George Langtry should, and will, we trust, ever remain honoured and respected in Belfast". (I am pleased to repeat this encomium).

As a result of his losses, Langtry found himself obliged to offer his Kilmore property for sale in 1862 through the Landed Estates Court; the particulars say "The mansion House has been built within the last few years by the Owner, at an expense, as the Owner alleges, of about £600 or £700 ... The House and Demesne Lands (containing 157a. 3r. 23p., statute measure) are in the hands of the Owner" (as quoted in Fitzpatrick). The place was bought by one George Brush from Dromore, but it seems that he and his family never lived there but rented it first to one John M Reed, with 160 acres; the house was valued in 1861 at £20. From 1892 Brush leased to one George McKitterick, JP, who seems to have moved out in 1913, leaving the house vacant for three years. In 1915 the Misses Brush put it on the market, when it was bought by James Fitzpatrick, whose descendants live there still.

Photograph: Anthony C W Merrick.
Situation: 112 Kilmore Road, Lurgan; td, Kilmore; District Council, Craigavon; Grid ref. J 109 608.
References: Listed B (14/8/2). VAL 2B/3/46A, p 2, VAL 12B/21/5A-D, in PRONI; Benn, 'History of Belfast', II, 1880, pp 215-216; Patterson, 'Birds, fishes and Cetacea', 1880, p 213; Owen, 'Port of Belfast', 1917, p 59; Oram, 'Craigavon', UAHS, 1971, Pt II, p 10; Helen Fitzpatrick, in 'Journal of Craigavon Historical Society', V, 3, 1986-7, pp 16-17; information from owner.

Farmhill, Cultra, Holywood

122. "Farmhill House, ... developed in two stages, the original farm, now a mews cottage, reputedly belonging to the early seventeenth century; the main house, a rather substantial two-storey affair, has many features which suggest a date of about 1730-40" (Merrick). The listers say - "c 1740 with alterations of c 1870. A 2-storey symmetrically designed mid-Georgian farmhouse with some late 19th century alterations, however, much of the earlier material remains intact. The building replaces a 17th century house, the shell of which survives on an adjoining site". As Merrick remarks, it is "rather grandly proportioned", perhaps too much so ever to have been just a farmhouse. "There can be little doubt that Farmhill was the first dwelling of any consequence in the Cultra area. The original building was what is now the mews cottage immediately to the rear ... This is a yeoman-type house and there is a strong tradition in the neighbourhood that it dates from the early part of the seventeenth century" (Merrick).

At the head of a fairly steep slope running down to the Victorian Clanbrassil Terrace and Belfast Lough, with splendid views, a five-bay two-storey-and-attic - the original cellar has been filled in - cream-painted stuccoed house in a good garden, with a particularly fine ash-tree in it. An unusual house, in that the front is Victorian, the back Georgian, the interior mostly modernised Georgian, with some good detailing, such as Georgian panelled doors. The front has 19th-century plate-glass glazing, and twin windows in projecting ground-floor bays flanking the similar porch, but all very restrained and in good taste. The rear elevation retains its original Georgian glazing-pattern, including a tall round-headed window at the turn of the stairs, and a lunette above and below it. There are nicely-moulded chimney-stacks, kept properly painted. In the Griffith valuation of 1862, valued at £25; occupied by Henry N Smyth, attorney, under lease from the Kennedy estate; with a note "in wretched repair". Matters had improved by 1864, when the valuation rose to £32, Alex Mitchell, occupier, paying rent to John Greenfield who held under the Kennedys. In 1880, Henry M Charley succeeded Alex Mitchell, and in 1887 Thomas Greenfield seems to have resumed possession. Tony Merrick's grandparents lived here from 1909 to 1914. The, acceptable, extension to the side built by a Mr Eves before 1966. Considerably restored in the 1990s by Dr Nixon, it has changed hands three times since then. Today, an unusual and attractive survival, and apparently in very good shape.

Photograph: A C W Merrick.
Situation: 41 Farmhill Road, Cultra; td, Ballycultra; Parish, Holywood; District Council, North Down; Grid ref. J 408 800.
References: Listed B (23/18/27). VAL 2B/3/182, p 28, VAL 12B/17/10B, and VAL 12B/17/10C, p 7, in PRONI; OS map, 1834; A C W Merrick, in 'Holywood Advertiser', Christmas, 1986; Merrick, 'Buildings of Holywood', 1986, p 19.

27. Kilmore Hose, Cornakinnegar Road, Lurgan (114)
28. Seamount, Cultra, Holywood (124)

29. Berwick Hall, Moira (81)
30. Arthur Street, Hillsborough (138)

Opposite: 31. 160 and 162 Ballygowan Road, Hillsborough (83)
32. Shamrock Vale, Blaris (130)
33. Sexton's lodge, Eglantine (134)
34. Inn's Court, Hillsborough (140)

35. Donaghadee harbour (167), 1834. Watercolour by D Kennedy, private collection
36. Banoge Bridge, Donaghcloney (164)

37.   Harbour and lightkeepers' houses, New Quay, Slanes (169)

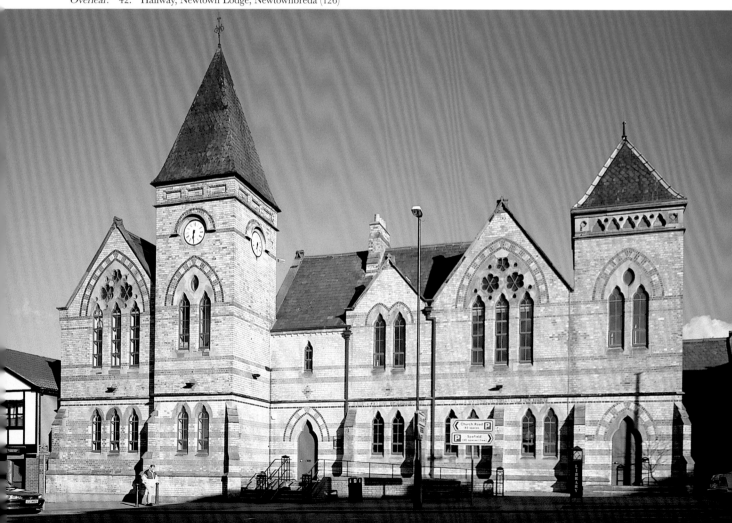

Charleville House, Knockbreda, Castlereagh

123. The present foursquare house appears to date from 1890, when the property was bought by John Robb, junior, of the prosperous Robb family of nearby Lisnabreeny (100), and the value of the house at Charleville shot up from £25 to £48. (Family tradition of the present owners says that when the heavy old embossed wallpaper was stripped from the dining room walls, the pencilled signature of the paper-hanger, and the date 1875, were disclosed; could this have been a misreading for 1895? The evidence of the Valuation books for a later date is quite unambiguous). It is said that the house was built as a golden wedding present from the younger generation to the older: this I somewhat doubt, but it is not impossible. According to the Blackwood papers in the Linen Hall Library, John Robb senior lived from 1828 until 1896; John Robb junior "of Charleville" died in 1926. It is a very old-fashioned house for 1890: five-bay, two-storey frontage, four bays deep, with a nice Corinthian porch of cast-iron fluted columns; plate glass windows; stucco walls painted pale yellow, heavy architraves painted blue-grey; hipped slate roof with four tall square chimney-stacks. It is set amidst mature trees in a delightful garden, through which runs the stream that feeds the Castlereagh glen. The walled garden, outbuildings, farm, and one side of the glen itself, go with the property.

The rooms are extraordinarily tall and spacious; the detailing is of consistently high quality; the house is sunny and, for a late Victorian dwelling, unusually light and airy. The only flies in the ointment are the high-speed Lisnabreeny Road along the top of the Castlereagh hills, and the enormous electricity station across the road, with its obtrusive attendant pylons. Otherwise, this is a marvellous rustic retreat astonishingly close to the centre of Belfast. The freehold was bought out under the Land Purchase Acts in 1908 by the second John Robb. The Robbs sold to Henry Walker in 1923, and he in turn sold to Thomas Morrow in 1926. House and farm were subsequently acquired by one Cecil McBride; and in 1947 were bought by the

father of the present owner. The place is in excellent order.

My great-great-great-grandfather, Charles Brett, after whom the place is named, found it a most convenient country retreat when he took a long lease from his patron, Lord Downshire, and built himself a summer home here in 1790. The lease is recorded in Lord Downshire's Castlereagh rental book of 1801: it was of 16 acres 3 roods and 30 perches, for three lives, at a yearly rent of £15 18 6. The old house must have been quite substantial, able to accommodate his wife and five children in comfort, along with an upright piano by Stodart and a Broadwood grand, as well as a round room: "Mr Gillis returned from France and has brought from thence the most beautiful room paper I ever saw, it is a view of the Isle of Elba, representing on one side sea, shipping, and docks, on the other, old castles, planting and people ... when you are sitting in it you almost think you are in the open air". Here his infant son Wills was taken out by his nursemaid in 1798 and hidden under a hedge in case the United Irishmen might come that way; here his friend Edward Bunting, and his protégés the Irish harpers, were bidden to celebrate his birthdays. Charles Brett retired from business as a wine merchant in High Street, Belfast, in 1827, and made Charleville his home all year round; he died there aged seventy-seven in 1829.

In the first valuation (carried out on Friday 10th May 1833), the house, in category 1B, is shown as the residence of "Rev. Mr Britt", measuring 35 feet six inches by 21 feet six inches by 14 feet 6 inches high, return and out-houses, the valuation "settled at £19 7 0. Not long afterwards, the place was sold by Charles Brett's son, the Reverend Wills Hill Brett, rector of Greyabbey (see 75), to one David McConnell. In the Griffith valuation of 1860, it is described as "a very neat concern but too close to the road - House stone finished and painted". Measurements, 12 yards by 7 yards by one and two-thirds storeys; valuation, £25. David McConnell remained there until 1880, when the occupier is shown as Eliza Miller; John Robb junior acquired the place from her in 1890, and would appear then to have knocked the old house down. From the Ordnance Survey maps it would seem to have been on pretty much the same site as the present one, though no traces of an older building are to be discerned in the new one: only the stables (home to my forbear's black mare, Bess, and her foal, both mentioned in his loquacious will) look to be relics of the original Charleville.

Photograph: A C W Merrick.
Situation: 39 Manse Road, Castlereagh; td, Cregagh; District Council, Castlereagh; Grid ref. J 371 705.
References: Not listed.. D 671/R4/1, D 3303/7/A/39, D 3303/7/B 2, VAL 1B/332, p 17, VAL 2B/3/18D, p 59, VAL 12B/17/7A - F, all in PRONI; R Blackwood, genealogical notes in Linen Hall Library, Belfast; Brett, 'Long shadows cast before', 1978, pp 48 - 59.

Seamount, Cultra, Holywood

124. An unusually attractive, compact and practical house for its date (the listers say it is of the 1920s, though the architect's daughter thinks it may be rather later); designed for a colleague by the distinguished chief-architect-to-be to the Ministry of Finance, T F O Rippingham. He was a very reserved and retiring Englishman who had come to Northern Ireland, along with R Ingleby Smith and R S Wilshere, in 1922, in the case of the first two in order to set up the Chief Architect's branch of the Department of Finance, on the model of the Board of Works in London, from which Rippingham was recruited. Initially he served under Ingleby Smith, who exercised his right to sign every drawing emanating from the office: in consequence, many buildings actually designed by Rippingham have been incorrectly attributed to his boss (or so his daughter has told me). He was the author of many notable public buildings between the 1920s and the 1950s, including numerous police stations and post offices, Stranmillis College, and public housing estates at Antrim and Cregagh, the last of which earned him a Ministry of Housing Bronze Medal. His last public building before retirement was the Petty Sessions Court House in Chichester Street, Belfast. He was very sympathetic to historic buildings, and worked frequently with the Ancient Monuments branch of the Ministry of Finance: one of his first tasks was the conversion of Hillsborough Castle (51) from private dwelling to Government House; one of his last, the restoration of Carrickfergus Castle.

Hugh Dixon writes, of his police stations, "As an instance of official design respecting the character of the province, it set an example which its successors have all too frequently failed to follow". David Evans says "Rippingham was a major figure in Ulster architecture in the period before and after the war and his work had a wide expressive range and consistent high quality". He retired in 1956. It appears that Rippingham ("Thomas" to some; "Rip" to others) built only a very few private houses - one at The Warren, Donaghadee for another colleague; one at Drumbo for his daughter (since demolished); and Seamount. He would have liked to build a house for his own occupation, but never did so; I am told that he and his wife never could agree whether to have separate living-room and dining-room (as she wished) or a dual-purpose room (as he preferred). In consequence, he spent all his working life in rented houses, removing every three years or so!

This is an L-shaped building, with a tall Dutch gable terminating each arm of the L, and each containing a

generous round-headed window upstairs; mostly one-and-a-half-storey, but a square two-storey block containing hall and staircase at the junction of the two arms. Tiled roof, and tall plain chimneys; Georgian glazing-pattern, but the larger windows with eight-pane sashes instead of the more usual six-pane; simplified drip-stones, horizontal or curved. The walls of stucco, painted a pleasant pale yellow, with white trim. Internally, a neat plan, some good fireplaces, and some excellent reeding in the doors. There is an external screen, with an arched opening, dividing the front door and garden from the back door and garage. Only a little way above the shoreline, set in a good mature garden looking out over Belfast Lough.

The listers say, and I concur, "This is a very attractive and comparatively rare example of domestic architecture by one of the leading architects of the time in Northern Ireland who is more usually associated with buildings of a more public or institutional nature, and it retains all its original windows and exterior features". In good order, inside and out, apart from the removal of one of Rippingham's original chimney-pieces, and an inappropriate replacement.

Photograph: A C W Merrick (see also colour illus. 28).
Situation: 19 Circular Road East, Cultra; td, Ballycultra; District Council, North Down; Grid ref. J 414 808.
References: Listed B1 (23/18/55). R McKinstry and A Neill in 'Architects' journal', 31 May, 1951; Dixon, 'Introduction', UAHS, 1975, pp 79-80; Evans, 'Introduction', UAHS, 1977, p 6; information from H Wightman, Mrs Edna Scott, and Mrs Eileen Mills.

Ballydorn Hill, Whiterock, Killinchy

125. In 1933, the present owner, then aged 23 and a law student at Trinity College Dublin, scraped up the money to buy the old single-storey farm-house on Ballydorn Hill, facing Sketrick Castle, with some 18 acres, for £850. He had occupied a cottage in this, then almost uninhabited, corner of County Down since 1929. During the next few years, in close collaboration with his sailing friend, the young architect, Philip Bell, he concocted the plans for a new, ultra-modern, house, on the top of the hill, with marvellous views all round to Scrabo, over the Inner Bay, and across to the Ards peninsula. The plans (still in the owner's possession) were finalised in January 1935; the proud young bachelor owner moved in, in December 1936. The house cost him, then a young and rising barrister, around £1,800. There was absolutely nothing else like it for miles around.

Of white-painted roughcast, with some wooden and some early cast-iron windows - two of them curved - a flat roof, and inconspicuous chimney-stacks, it hugs the hilltop: externally, this has rendered it remarkably inconspicuous (unlike so many hill-top buildings); internally, it has resulted in a great many steps and changes of level. The house employed many novelties. There are single anodised aluminium columns at the porch, and between dining-room and sitting-room. There are many ingenious internal fittings and gadgets: in this respect, the house stands comparison with the Penprase house at Ballintoy, County Antrim. But Ballydorn Hill was modelled on a yacht, where space is at a premium: stairs, cupboards, bunks, fixed seating, drawers that run through from kitchen to dining-room so as to be accessible from either, nautical plywood-panelled walls, bedroom and bathroom fittings, are all ultra-modern (for the date), concise, compact, and still unaltered: though it might be remarked that there was not left much flexible space for future developments such as washing machines, dish-washers, spin-driers, and deep freezes, none of them available when the house was built.

A large and attractive law library, with curved window, was added in 1950; the dining-room was extended in 1951; again, all to the designs of Philip Bell, in close consultation with the owner, now a family man with a need to entertain many guests. The library is unusual in that, at the express demand of the owner, it incorporates a fireplace fronted with blue-and-white Dutch tiles brought back by him from Delft at the end of the war; and, above it, a sheet of mirror-glass which conveys disturbing and misleading reflections of the views from outside the window. It was in this library that the new Northern Ireland local government boundaries of 1972 were worked out by the owner.

This house caused much interest when it was built; the owner recalls that it was noticed by the architectural press in London, though neither he nor I have succeeded in tracking down the reference; and is now greatly admired by historians of the period. The listers say, "A single-storey" (wrong: though low-profile, it is two-storey) "asymmetrical house in International Modern Style designed by Philip Bell ... and subsequently extended by him. Built with plain white walls, some curved corners, flat roofs and metal framed windows ... The house also contains the first use in Northern Ireland of anodised metal stanchions which appear at the internal steps between the living room and the dining room, and as a canopy support outside the front door. The oversailing concrete beam connecting the garage with the main house is also a typical element of the International Modern Style". Cartin, in his thesis on Philip Bell's work, remarks "This was to be his most innovative house to date, incorporating developments in Britain with uncompromising resolve ... The multi roof levels, as seen from the east, give the building a nautical flavour, suggesting decks with the two-storey section, punctuating the skyline, echoing a" (ship's) "bridge ... In planning terms the architect may not have achieved Le Corbusier's 'plan libre', but his new approach to design was much freer than in any other conventional house of the period".

Still occupied by its original owner and progenitor, who runs an excellent daffodil nursery (and fruit farm); in pretty good order; and, as the listers say, "exceptional in that it is an entirely unaltered example of its architect's domestic work in this style."

Photograph: A C W Merrick.
Situation: 63 Ballydorn Road, Whiterock, Killinchy; td, Ballydorn; District Council, Ards; Grid ref. J 522 626.
References: Listed B1 (24/17/86); downgraded, November 1999, to B2 (why?). R McKinstry, in 'RSUA yearbook', 1983, p 20; K J Cartin, The work of George Philip Bell in the international style, unpublished thesis, QUB, 1986, p 41; plans and drawings in owner's possession; information from owner.

CHAPTER SIX

SMALL HOUSES
AND COTTAGES

A damask handloom weaver, Waringstown. Photograph: W A Green, UFTM, WAG 288

SMALL HOUSES
AND COTTAGES

Small houses and cottages vary greatly in character. A few, though not many in north County Down, were quite grand: the elegant columnar hallway of Newtown Lodge (126) is at the top of the scale, with perhaps Erin Lodge (131), Shamrock Vale (130), and Gulladuff (128) a little down the way, but in the same league - cottages for the gentry, somewhat in the Anglo-Indian tradition of the bungalow, as first brought to these shores. At the bottom end of the scale were the miserable rural cottages, with pretty thatched roofs but internally no more than hovels, with their mud floors and mud walls, and no running water or sewage (now almost entirely disappeared, and no great loss); and the crowded terrace housing of mill-workers in town and village (now too almost gone, save for a few refurbished and modernised examples, as at Donagh-cloney (139). In between, there is (or was) a great variety of modest homesteads: almshouses, gate-lodges, estate houses, the simple homes to be found in countryside, village and town: of which a certain number survive, mostly modernised, some sympathetically to their original character, others not.

In north County Down, and particularly in its north-west corner - around Lisburn, Lurgan, Moira, and Waringstown - the greatest loss has been the total disappearance of the weaver's cottage. Spinning and weaving were genuine 'cottage' industries, which contributed greatly to prosperity, and to comfort, for nearly two centuries, and only disappeared just before the span of living memory. Samuel Lewis, writing of Waringstown, says in 1837 "Samuel Waring, a descendant of the same spirited individual to whom the place owes its existence and its name, was the founder of its manufacturing prosperity, in the reign of Queen Anne. Having acquired a knowledge of the processes for making diaper during his travels in Holland and Belgium, he introduced them into his own country, and the first piece of cloth of this description made in Ireland was the produce of his estate. He also, when abroad, procured drawings of wheels and reels in Holland, and with his own hand made the first of the wheels and reels now in general use, before which all the flax made in the country was spun by the rock and spindle. The linen manufacture thus introduced and patronised became the staple of the district and is now carried on to a very great extent in all its branches, there being scarcely a family in the town and neighbourhood which is not more or less employed in some branch of it"[1].

Much earlier, in 1744, Walter Harris had noted that "*Waringstown* ... is a neat well planted and improved Village ... In this Town and the Neighbourhood of it the Linen Manufacture is carried on to great Advantage, where it was introduced and cherished by the late *Samuel Waring* Esq;, well known for the great Services he has done his Country in this Trade; which has spread so considerably here since that Time, that a Colony of fine Diaper Weavers were transplanted lately from hence to *Dundalk*"[2]. Gilbert Camblin, in 1951, illustrated the cottages in Waringstown Main Street, with their thatched roofs, white-washed walls, Georgian-glazed windows, simple sheeted doors, with grass and trees outside; remarking "The weaving of linen continued on a domestic basis until after the famine and indeed might almost be regarded as a branch of agriculture, for the yarn was bought and the finished cloth sold in the local market in the same way as agricultural produce"[3]. Rodney Green wrote in 1963, "As late as 1898 the author of a history of Donaghcloney parish could write that 'the damask weavers of Waringstown still hold their own, scarcely a house in the village being without its weaving shop'. The single long wide street of Waringstown was until recently lined on each side with thatched weavers' cottages which have now been pulled down to make way for improved housing" ... and comments: "The combination of cheap hand-loom labour and concentration on the finer branches of the trade made the transition to power-loom weaving a lengthy one"[4].

These were much better-than-average cottages, for the nature of the work demanded adequate space, height, and above all, light. Gailey refers to "a need for a roof-space unencumbered by tie beams and collar beams to accommodate the height of linen looms after damask weaving was introduced in the early nineteenth century. Plain linen looms are about 2m. high, but addition of the jacquard machine on top to achieve the woven pattern in double damask increased the height substantially"; and refers also to "outshots ... on the rear perhaps to provide added space for a linen loom in a few cases in Waringstown in north-west Down". And: "In the linen-weaving areas of west Down, Armagh, south-east Tyrone, south Antrim and north Monaghan, two- and three-unit houses often had a loom 'shop' added at one end. Sometimes the shop had a fireplace, and often there was internal access from the dwelling, but others had a separate door from outside. Always there was better provision of light from windows for work at the looms than was provided for the dwelling"[5].

So far as I know, the only example of a weaver's cottage, with loft, loom, and all, is in the Ulster Folk Museum at Cultra, and, having been removed from its original site, is ineligible for inclusion in this book; though there are loom and weaver in the Ulster Linen Museum in Lisburn, County Antrim. The total disappearance from the countryside of so important and individual a dwelling type is, I think, much to be regretted. I fear that the Northern Ireland Housing Executive, of which I was once chairman, with its inflexible regulations on modernisation and replacement, must share part of the blame.

References: 1. Lewis, TD, 1837, II, p 674. 2. Harris, 'County of Down', 1744, pp 104-105. 3. Camblin, 'Town in Ulster', 1951, pl 59; p 104. 4. Green, 'Industrial archaeology', 1963, p 12. 5. Gailey, 'Rural houses', 1984, pp 90, 170.

Newtown Lodge (formerly Fair View), Newtownbreda

126. According to the researches of Dr Hunter, a previous owner, built around 1740 as dower house for Belvoir: if so, the future Duke of Wellington may have come here to visit his granny, an endearing thought. Unfortunately, Dr Hunter's detailed notes seem to have been lost, or at any rate temporarily mislaid. Neither Dr Anthony Malcomson nor I have succeeded in identifying any eligible dowager amongst the families of the successive owners of Belvoir; and, in any case, he tells me that he doubts the existence of more than a handful of dower-houses in Ireland: most noble widows longed to leave a lonely life in the country, and to congregate with others of their kind in Dublin, London, or Bath, to indulge in the delights of whist and gossip.

But, as Molly Keane remarks, "Obscure and often forgotten are the little, scrupulously classical, dower houses of Ireland, once married to the great estates ... for where else were widows and unmarried daughters to live out their allotted spans, when sons married and inherited? There were no jobs which might support the able widow or the daughter of the Ascendancy. Their busyness, or their idleness, were housed with proper dignity. Families were responsible for their mothers and aunts and sisters, and the ladies felt no dishonour in their dependance ... The ladies who were housed, perhaps more cosily than their relations, in the Grace and Favours exercised for the most part a stringent and uncomplaining economy ..." Gordon Wheeler thinks the house Regency, and suggests that it might have been built by Robert Bateson soon after he inherited Belvoir in 1818, and newly wed, perhaps to house his mama. He may well be right; certainly the house does not appear in Atkinson's list of the seats of the county Down gentry, compiled apparently in 1817. But for my part, I still favour an earlier date, largely because the fine-

ly-carved detailing is all of painted wood, not stucco.

Whatever its date, this is one of the most delightful small Irish Georgian houses known to me, by reason of the quite exceptional elegance of its interior. Indeed, it is an astonishing survival to find, secretly tucked away in a two-acre wooded garden in the midst of the outer suburbia of South Belfast; exceptionally hard to find, at the end of a long, unmarked, unmade-up, lane: and rightly so. It has a loving owner who does not welcome intruders, and who shall blame him? Shown on the 1834 Ordnance Survey map as 'Fairview'; presumably the translation into English of 'Belvoir'; and 'Fairview' is also referred to as a "mansion or villa", though in the adjoining parish of Drumbo, in the Parliamentary Gazetteer of 1846; but in the Valuation book of 1833, as 'Newton Lodge'.

Externally, a five-bay cottage, with white-painted roughcast walls, tall Georgian-glazed windows on either side of an exceptionally fine elliptically-arched doorcase, with reeded Ionic columns, cobweb fanlight, geometrical side-lights, and fluted scallops in the recess; half-hipped roof, with two square chimney-stacks, each accommodating four chimney-pots; and two returns, one, facing south, incorporating kitchen and dairy with tripartite 'Wyatt' windows, the other the former stabling, between them embracing a central courtyard; an attic storey with pretty round-headed windows in the gables.

Internally, a marvel. The front door opens into a long, stone-flagged, central hall, 38 feet long, with pairs of carved wooden Ionic columns framing the elegant doorcases at each side: there are twenty-two Ionic columns in all. All the details are of the utmost delicacy and excellence: the bunches of grapes in the cornices of the rooms are of carved wood, not stucco; the shutters are all intact and in working order, and there are even narrow shutters to the side-lights in the doorcase. The detailing in each room is different, with carved cable mouldings here, elegant chair-rails everywhere, clustered columns there. The layout is singularly neat and economical: at the rear of the hall, to the left, a beautiful little staircase winds its way up, via a slanted passageway, to a pair of bedrooms in the attic.

How it has survived so little spoiled in such a vulnerable environment is hard to guess. It has more than once fallen into considerable disrepair, but is now well on the way back to good health. The 19th-century history of the house is better documented than most by the valuation books. In 1833, it was classified 1A; the front part measured 49 feet by 31 feet 6 inches by 16 feet 6 inches; was valued at £25 8 11; and was occupied by a Mr Garr (or Gar). In the Griffith valuation of 1861, it is shown as occupied by Alexander Martin; then reverted to the possession of Sir Robert Bateson, Bart. "House has been lately repaired - Nice situation on hill - offs. very bad in front - ho: and land to be let. Expects £5 per Cunningham acre, at will, including the Bogs: £23". It was indeed let, to many tenants, in dizzy succession: John Ferguson, James Meneely, Robert Best, Samuel Moore, William McComb, William McCourt, Mary Montgomery in 1890, "rent said to be £36" - Henry Montgomery, David Esdale: then, in 1916, still valued at £23, to Elma J West; she and her sister seem to have lived on here at least until 1929; it is said that both died in the house. In the 1970s, it belonged to the Westhead family; then to Dr Oliver Hunter; it suffered sadly in the enormous bomb that devastated the nearby Forensic Science Laboratory, and many other buildings, in 1992. Suburbia is slowly creeping up on it, but this delightful little house still retains its integrity: long may it do so.

Photographs: A C W Merrick (see also colour illus. 42).
Situation: 86 Beechhill Road, Newtownbreda; td, Ballylenaghan; District Council, Castlereagh; Grid ref. J 347 688.
References: Listed B (25/15/1). (Not even B1? In my view, the quality of the interior should accord it an A). VAL 1B/321, p 33, VAL 1B/ 332, p 339, VAL 2B/3/29, p 19, VAL 12B/20/7A - F, in PRONI; OS map, 1834; PG, II, 1846, p 81; Pierce and Coey, 'Taken for granted', 1984, p 144; M Keane, in 'In an Irish house', 1988, p 11; information from owner.

Bloomvale House, Bleary, Lurgan

127. An attractive one-and-a-half storey thatched yeoman-farmer-cum-weaver's house, of 1785. It is built, in a somewhat un-Irish style, of random rubble with galleting, the rear and gable walls roughcast and painted; Georgian-glazed windows, with brick heads to the openings, the glazing-bars presently white, the dressed stone surrounds blue; yellow-painted stucco (later, but not too much) plinths and quoins; faintly Gothick fanlight; three chimney-stacks, unevenly spaced; very well restored and rethatched using English wheat straw. As the map of 1826 shows, there was originally a second doorway in the façade, now a window, which led to the small office or shop from which the owners conducted their linen trade with customers as far afield as New York.

Probably built, or at any rate owned from 1815 onwards, by George Gaskin (*sc.* Gascoyne; *sc.* Gascon; a Huguenot incomer); from him it seems to have passed first to one Robert Gaskin, then to his son-in-law William Dobson; then to George Dobson, who ran a substantial linen business from the house as well as farming the land - a weaver's cottage from this property is to be seen at the Ulster Folk Museum. The Valuation book of 1833 shows Robert Gaskin as occupier of the house, in category B+, measurements 19 feet 6 inches by 23 feet by 11 feet six inches, valued at £6 18 2; in 1861 under William Dobson, the value had risen to £8. In 1912, the value had risen to £10 5 0. In 1916, George Dobson bought in the freehold under the Land Purchase Acts; soon after, he moved to Belfast, with his six children, and advertised the place, with its substantial farm, for sale in 1916. (It must have been pretty crowded: his aged uncle retired here from the Moy, where he was known as 'Top Hat Dobson' from his addiction to this headgear). It was bought by a Mr Blane, for £3100, though the sale was not completed until 1921. In the 1970s, the house fell into dereliction, and stood vacant for nine years: it has been laboriously restored and rethatched in 1995, by the present owner who uses it, and its extensive outbuildings, as Ballydougan Pottery and Pottery Shop.

A descendant of the Dobson family, Mr George Dobson Hunter, who lives in London, retains copious documentation for this little estate and its history: in particular, a most attractive map of May 1826, by one John Wells: 'A Map and Survey of Bloomvale in Bleary. Let by Alexr. Stewart Esqr. to Mr. Robert Gaskin in the County of Down'.

Photograph: A C W Merrick. Map: J Wells, courtesy of G D Hunter.
Situation:171 Plantation Road, Bleary, Lurgan; td, Bleary; District Council, Craigavon; Grid ref. J 076 535.
References: Listed B+ (14/5/1). VAL 1B/350, p 68, VAL 2B/3/48B, VAL 12B/21/8A - E, in PRONI; map and papers in possession of Mr George Dobson Hunter; copy documents from that collection on display in the porch; Oram, 'Craigavon', UAHS, 1971, Pt II, p 3; Pierce and Coey, 'Taken for granted', 1984, p 69; information from owner, and from Mrs Norma Boyd, grand-daughter of George Dobson.

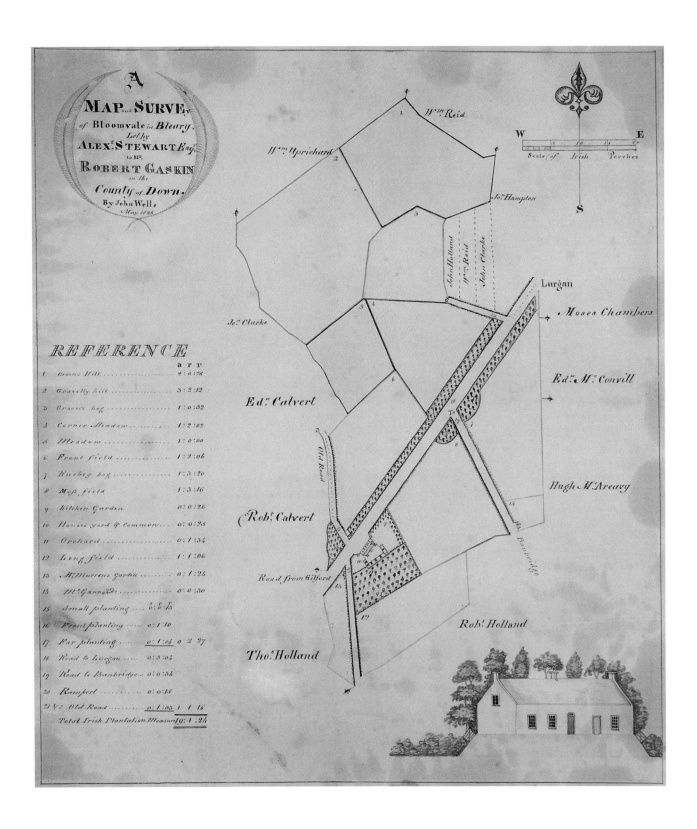

A
MAP and SURVEY
of Bloomvale in Bleary,
Let by
ALEXᴿ STEWART Esqʳ
to Mʳ
ROBERT GASKIN
in the
County of Down,
By John Wells
May 1826

REFERENCE

		a	r	p
1	Greens Hill	2	0	28
2	Gravelly Hill	3	2	12
3	Graves bog	1	0	32
4	Corner Meadow	1	2	02
5	Meadow	1	0	00
6	Front field	1	2	06
7	Rushey bog	1	3	20
8	Moss field	1	3	16
9	Kitchen Garden	0	0	26
10	Houses yard & Common	0	0	25
11	Orchard	0	1	34
12	Long field	1	1	06
13	Mᶜ Murrens Garden	0	1	24
14	Mᶜ Gannen Dᵒ	0	0	30
15	Small planting	0	5	13
16	Front planting	0	1	10
17	Far planting	0	1	04	0 2 27
18	Road to Lurgan	0	3	04
19	Road to Banbridge	0	0	34
20	Rampert	0	0	15
21 &ᶜ	Old Road	0	1	03	1 1 16
	Total Irish Plantation Measure	19	1	24

Gulladuff (formerly Sarahfield), Ballyrobert, Crawfordsburn

128. A pleasant five-bay single-storey-and-dormers late Georgian cottage, with radial fanlight, black-painted Tuscan columns flanking the front door, and four large, deep, Georgian-glazed windows. Nicely sited amidst trees on the hillside overlooking the little group of roadside buildings at Ballyrobert. Oram describes it as "a relatively unaltered mid-Georgian farm house of which very few remain in this part of the province, and considered to have sufficient historical and architectural merit to warrant listing": no over-statement of the case. It is shown on the 1834 and 1858 Ordnance Survey maps, on the latter labelled 'Sarahfield'. Dean, who calls this "a pretty Regency cottage", suggests that it was probably named for its occupant in 1863, Mrs Sarah McDowell; but this seems not right - see below. From the plantings shown on the later map, and from the large windows, this would appear to me more probably to have been originally a gentleman's cottage orné, rather than a farmhouse. It is a pity that the two dormers (apparently not original, though

there was probably always at least one attic room) are clumsier and more obtrusive than they should be.

The Rev. Abraham Liggat, of Ballygilbert Presbyterian church, in 1844 married Miss Sarah Wardlaw, niece of John McDowell of Sarahfield; perhaps the lady in question; "after his marriage he settled in Ballydavey, first in a rented house whose dampness he endured for two years, and finally in Sarahfield, now known as Gulladuff", so the house served as manse from about 1846 until 1858 (McConaghy). The present owner thinks that the house was known as 'Sarahville' rather than 'Sarahfield'.

Photograph; A C W Merrick.
Situation: 573 Belfast Road, Ballyrobert; td, Ballyrobert; District Council, North Down; Grid ref. J 447 808.
References: Listed B2 (23/16/24). OS maps 1834, 1858; notes by R Oram in MBR, 1988; J W and E M McConaghy, 'Light for the road', 1991, p 19; Dean, 'Gate lodges', UAHS, 1994, p 93.

The Cottage, Glen Road, Cultra, Holywood

129. A pretty little one-storey-and-dormers T-shaped house, standing in a good garden with fine trees running down to the railway cutting. Four-bay, painted stucco, the listers call it "Gothic Revival style reconstructed late 19th century". It appears on the 1834 Ordnance Survey map, but was certainly embellished later: in its present form, it looks to me to date from around 1850. Undoubtedly, its porch is ever so Gothic; its dormers are very sharply pitched; but its character depends on the ornate cast-iron crestings and finials, echoed by similar ornate iron barge-boards, and ornate iron gutters, unfortunately, no longer quite complete. Five chimney-stacks to the front with two pots each. Pleasantly enough decorated, but how it would

sparkle if the ornamental ironwork could be restored, and the whole building then repainted in livelier colours !

There is a note in the Monuments and Buildings Record which suggests that this was originally the seaside holiday cottage of one of the Workmans of Workman, Clark; "who may have prettied up its original vernacular style". If so, it constitutes quite a contrast with the other Workman house, Craigdarragh (60).

Photograph: A C W Merrick.
Situation: 10 Glen Road, Cultra; td, Craigavad; District Council, North Down; Grid ref. J 422 806.
References: Listed B (23/18/14). OS map, 1834; file in MBR.

Shamrock Vale (or Shamrock Vale Lodge, or Shamrock Ville), Blaris

130. The listers just say: "Single-storey Georgian style house with basement. Roof hipped and slated. Walls rendered and pointed. Decorative arched doorway". Lieutenant Bordes, of the Ordnance Survey, in 1833, described Lieutenant Clark's "very handsome dwelling"... "recently built ... one of the most beautiful cottages in the north". J R Ward, also of the Ordnance Survey, did not, in 1837, note it as amongst the "Gentlemen's Residences" of the parish; but his colleague, Thomas Fagan, does record that Blaris schoolhouse, dating from 1828 and now gone, "was built by subscriptions from noblemen gentlemen and farmers, cost 250 pounds including furniture and other appendages. The funds were raised at the suggestions of Lieutenant Clarke of Shamrockvale Lodge, Lisburn, who not only bestowed the site for the school and liberally contributed to the erection of the house, but also, at much fatigue and trouble, raised the funds and directed the entire affairs of the school with taste and economy and annually contributes to its support". Samuel Lewis in the same year lists Shamrock Vale as the seat of Lieut. Clarke, RN, amongst the residences of the gentry. Perhaps he was a half-pay Lieutenant left over from the Napoleonic Wars?

In the previous year, 1836, the house appeared in the first Valuation book in category 1A, measuring 54 feet by 17 feet by 10 feet 6 inches: valuation, £19 18 5; held from Lord Downshire by Lt. James Clarke; his name struck out soon afterwards in favour of "Saunders". In 1861, described as "Very neat cottage with basements", with 97 acres of land; occupied by Mary Ann Saunders; valued first at £14, then £16, then £24, which argues that it was enlarged at this period; an additional note, "Lease £72 from Marquis of Downshire and purchased for £1000 or more". She and her son Richard Saunders appear to have remained here until 1904, when one Frank Robertson took the land, but the house is shown as "vacant". In 1909, briefly occupied by a Captain Caldwell; in 1911 by Thomas Lecky. In 1924, the present family acquired the farm in fee - the lease had been bought out under the Land Acts - from one Thomas Thornton: throughout this entire period, still valued at £24, so presumably unaltered.

The front, facing the main Belfast - Dublin dual carriageway, is not very exciting: a single-storey four-bay cottage of lined stucco, the walls light brown, the plinth, quoins and window sills darker brown, under a hipped roof; the old painted doorcase has been replaced by a, not wholly insensitive, modern mahogany reproduction, with elliptical fanlight and sidelights; two tall Georgian-glazed windows to the left, one to the right. The south-facing, two-storey, front is much more interesting, and very much resembles a typical Dublin town-house of the period: a curved bay to each side, with tripartite windows above and below, and two bays with single windows in between, again all Georgian-glazed. Good trees and lawn; extensive farm buildings at the rear, connected to the main house by an underground passage.

The compilers of the Archaeological Survey of County Down took this house seriously, provided admirable plan and section, a photograph, and a lengthy description: "Single storey house with basement, early 19th century, apparently of brick with stone quoins, cement-rendered and lime-washed; the roofs are slate-covered. The house is of U-plan, with rear returns of equal projection on the N. and entrance on the W., towards the county road ... The entrance floor contains the main reception rooms and bedrooms, the basement the kitchens and offices".

Photograph: A C W Merrick (see also colour illus. 32).
Situation: 33 Sprucefield Road, Blaris; td, Magherageery; District Council, Lisburn; Grid ref. J 254 616.
References: Listed B1 (19/4/4). VAL 1B/339, p 24, VAL 2B/3/43, p 28, VAL 12B/20/16A-D, VAL/12B/20/5D, in PRONI; G F W Bordes, OSM, 1833, J R Ward, 1837, and T Fagan, 1837, Down, III, pp 32, 34, 36; Lewis, TD, 1837, II, p 4; ASCD, 1966, pp 388-389, pl 187; Pierce and Coey, 'Taken for granted', 1984, p 73.

Erin Lodge, Donaghadee

131. Tucked away in the middle of a modern high-density housing development, and quite invisible from the Killaughey Road, "A charming Regency cottage-villa of one storey but on a high basement", dating from 1824 according to the Ker estate records. Dixon's description continues: "Typically the two principal facades are at right angles and a shallow bay is used to merge them at the south-east corner. On the four-bay south elevation a flight of six sandstone steps leads to the off-centre front door, with attractive cobweb fanlight and sidelights. Elsewhere the windows adopt a Regency pattern, not over-common in Ulster, of two sashes set as though conventional ones had been turned through right angles and thus giving a strong horizontal emphasis. The walls are rough harled, and there are sandstone window sills and plinth string. Above the deep eaves and low-pitched slate roof chimneys are sprinkled in groups of three and solo along the skyline.

Despite various remodellings the informal interior retains some original cornices and woodwork, including window reveals with fan-finishes as at the Manor House"(Donaghadee, 49). "The building is currently" (1977) "undergoing a sensible programme of conservation". The listers' only comment is "former porch removed".

For many years the home of Mrs Anna Jessie Ker, widow of David Ker of Portavo (65). The house used to stand in an agreeable wooded park, but the houses built after her death are much too closely crowded to leave proper breathing-space for Erin Lodge.

Photograph: Neill Marshall, MBR.
Situation: Off Killaughey Road, Donaghadee; td, Carryreagh; District Council, Ards. Grid ref. J 588 793.
References: Listed B1 (24/7/32). OS map, 1834; former owner's records; Dixon, 'Donaghadee and Portpatrick', UAHS, 1977, p 32.

Burn Lodge, Crawfordsburn House

132. "A unique design, two storey, presenting a symmetrical elevation to the public road. The ground floor plan of one main square living room ... is flanked by two small single storey pedimented wings one advancing to the avenue as the hallway, the other balancing it a small kitchen. The double leaf front door semicircular headed with a spoked fanlight which is in a moulded surround to a stringcourse at spring level. To the side elevations semicircular-headed niches similarly treated ... On the living room elevation a breakfront containing a simple flat-arched window in a recess, arched and treated as before. The ground floor is surmounted by an entablature on which rests an octagonal first floor ... The bedroom approached by stairs from the living room is lit back and front by an oeil-de-boeuf window. Each external corner is emphasised by a Tuscan colonnette carrying the entablature of an octahedral roof which rises to a central finial. All now roughcast and well tended" (Dean, who very confidently attributes this

sophisticated little building to John Nash).

This attribution is based on a drawing at Brighton by George Stanley Repton, one of Nash's assistants, closely resembling this little lodge as built, except for the urns. There is no documentary evidence that Nash or Repton worked for the Crawford Estate. "So how", asks Dean, "did this 'building of extreme individual distinction' come to be here? The answer" he says "is genealogical." Temple says "Apart from some minor details, Burn Lodge is identical to PNB 9. Nash was working for Du Pre Alexander (1777-1839), 2nd Earl of Caledon, Co Tyrone, 1808-13. James Alexander (1730-1802), the first earl, married Anne Crawford, daughter of James Crawford of Crawfordsburn. This connection probably accounts for drawings in the Caledon Papers that record a further variation on the theme which shows a design much as PNB 9, but with the attic storey square in plan". Temple acknowledges help received from William Garner, Hugh Dixon, and Dixie Dean, who adds "The architect would have met Crawford on one of his visits to Co Tyrone and he was never one to forgo the opportunity of another commission, no matter how small". The resemblance to the Brighton drawing is certainly striking, and all concerned deserve much credit for this discovery; but I am not wholly persuaded, in the total absence of documentary evidence, that this little building is really by Nash: there is evidence that George Repton was more than just an assistant in Nash's office. In a letter of 1810 quoted by Temple, Nash says "Mr George Repton who you know was brought up with me is to receive a Moiety of all Cottages farm houses & picturesque buildings ... he also has commenced general Architect but his connexion with me at present extends only to these sort of buildings". Does this not suggest that Burn Lodge was by Repton rather than by Nash?

Having said that, it is certainly very attractive, very well painted with cream and ochre trim (though the renewal of the original smooth creamy stucco favoured by Nash would have been much preferable to the roughcast; and one must agree with Dean that it demands "the urn decoration as the architect intended, return of its squared glazing bars and reinstatement of its gate pillars"). One must also agree with him that, thankfully, the extension of c 1910 is "inconspicuously positioned". Patton unquestioningly accepts Deans's attribution. It is certainly a charming little building, whatever its authorship; it is far from impossible that Dixie Dean is quite right, and that I err on the side of scepticism; but once bitten in a matter of attribution (by Dr Maurice Craig, no less), twice shy.

Photograph: A C W Merrick. Water-colour: G S Repton.
Situation: Burn Lodge, 200 Crawfordsburn Road, Bangor; td, Ballymullan; District Council, North Down; Grid ref. J 471 815.
References: Incredibly, apparently not listed . Temple, 'George Repton's Pavilion notebook,' 1993, p 31, pl PNB 9; Dean, 'Gate lodges', UAHS, 1994, p 71; Patton, 'Bangor', UAHS, 1999, p 61.

Country Gate Lodge, Portaferry House

133. A particularly charming two-room gate-lodge, with harled white walls and central paired diagonal chimney-stacks; ornamental barge-boards at the over-sailing gable ends. There is a nice canted bay window at the end away from the road; and a recessed porch (or as Dean calls it, "sitting out verandah") behind three metal columns supporting the overhang of the roof. One of three gate-lodges at Portaferry House (48) which was remodelled by William Farrell between 1818 and 1820: Dean says "all three in a mild-mannered Picturesque style but none showing the characteristics of Farrell's work", and dates all three to "c 1830", and adds "Simple outer pillars with ball finials flank a cast iron gate screen continuing the ball motif with a repeating crisscross pattern. Inner iron carriage posts".

Photograph: A C W Merrick.
Situation: 4 Kircubbin Road, Portaferry; td, Ballymurphy; District Council, Ards; Grid ref. J 597 517.
References: Listed B (24/1/104). Bell, 'Portaferry & Strangford', UAHS, 1969, p 13; Dean, 'Gate lodges', UAHS, 1994, p 89.

Sexton's Lodge, Eglantine, Hillsborough

134. An uncommonly pretty small L-shaped two-storey house, set beside the lane leading to Eglantine Church (42), and contemporary with it: almost certainly, also by Thomas Drew. Inscribed in Tudor lettering on a stone panel in the front wall 'Sexton's House 1875'. The ground floor is of coursed blackstone, with pinkish ashlar quoins and trim; the upper floor is of soft red brick; the apexes of the gables are red-tiled, and the eaves broadly over-sailing. The tiled roof and chimney-stack look to be more recent. There is a curious green-painted pseudo-porch in the elbow of the L, very churchy-looking, but a porch on closer inspection it is not. Downstairs, there are triple windows, with little green-painted rosettes below them; upstairs, slight projections like shallow oriels frame further trios of windows, but painted white, presumably of wood.

The modestly ornate barge-boards are painted green. Very much the self-conscious creation of an architect, in a mildly humorous semi-ecclesiastical vein, and exactly right for its rural setting. Built by the Mulholland family of Eglantine House, together with rectory, schoolhouse and schoolmaster's house, all at around the same time as the church: they were generous indeed to this country parish, and uncommonly well served by their architect.

Photograph: A C W Merrick (see also colour illus. 33).
Situation: Off Eglantine Road, Hillsborough; td, Carnbane; District Council, Lisburn; Grid ref. J 243 612.
References: Not listed (surely it should be?). 'Short history of All Saints', Eglantine,' n d.

Former Almshouses, Annahilt

135. A striking eleven-bay range of single-storey white-painted housing, slated, with a pedimented gable breaking forward in the centre between two arched recesses (originally open passageways); iron lattice windows; all doors and window-frames, railings, and gates painted a bright and cheerful rustic red. It is a pity that the appearance of these buildings from the Hillsborough road is spoiled by a, no doubt necessary but very obtrusive, road sign.

Lewis says "Robert Sharland, Esq., a native of Barnstaple, Devon, who died on the 6th May 1833, bequeathed from £2000 to £3000 in trust to the clergy of the parish and the proprietor of one or two townlands, for the erection of ten almshouses ... the buildings were about to be commenced in the spring of 1835".

Patton says: "In his will dated May 1833, one Robert Sharland left the balance of his estate, after giving £25 to his sister Sarah and five guineas to be distributed amongst his servants, for the erection of 'ten Almshouses for ten old men and ten old women, all belonging to the Parish of Annahilt'. Each beneficiary was to receive £5 per annum, and the Almshouses were to include a house for 'a housekeeper to inspect the houses and keep them clean'". (How

twenty individuals, and a housekeeper, were to be squeezed into nine tiny houses is unclear). "Sharland actually died during 1833, and it appears that the Almshouses were built shortly after that ... The portion closest to the crossroads was built first, including a larger central block that may have been intended for the housekeeper, and when nos. 191 - 197 were added, the resulting nine houses became a symmetrical design. Over the years the original fund had dwindled, and the Sharland Charity was wound up".

The premises were ultimately acquired for restoration by the Hearth Housing Association in 1987, to provide three modern houses - two one-bedroom, and one two-bedroom - instead of the former nine tiny almshouses, under the supervision of Marcus Patton, whose account of the buildings I have borrowed.

Photograph: A C W Merrick.
Situation: 181 - 197 Magheraconluce Road, Annahilt; td., Ballycrune; District Council, Lisburn; Grid ref. J 296 561.
References: Listed B (19/7/5). Lewis, TD, 1837, I, p 26; Knox, 'County Down', 1875, p 384; Hearth, 'Review of projects', 1999, pp 24 - 25.

36 Ballynagarrick Road, Newmills, Gilford

136 A single-storey white-washed traditional thatched cottage, standing just by the roadside: before 1834, since it is shown on the Ordnance Survey map of that year. It contains three rooms, each with a small square Victorian-glazed window, with a tiny projection housing the front door. The back elevation is somewhat altered - a modest return has been added, and the window-openings enlarged. There are two low, square chimney-stacks. It seems that each of the three rooms is of a different date, for, under the thatch, that to the left has a rough under-thatch of twigs and brush; that in the middle has a tree-trunk; that to the right has a squared beam, and is substantially higher, probably to accommodate a weaver's loom. Very similar to Crabtree Cottage, north of Portadown in County Armagh, which was possibly also a weaver's house.

The cottage was last thatched twelve years ago: it looks in good order, but looks can be deceptive. Acquired by the present owner in 1979 from Flynns; before that, inhabited by the Sergeant family.

Photograph; A C W Merrick.

Situation: 36 Ballynagarrick Road, Newmills; td, Ballynagarrick; District Council, Craigavon; Grid ref. J 055 515.

References: Listed B1/Q (14/5/3). OS map, 1834; Pierce and Coey, 'Taken for granted', 1984, pp 68,69; Brett, 'Buildings of County Armagh', UAHS, 1996, p 212.

113 and 115 Hillhall Road, Lisburn

137. Right on the road frontage, a pre-1833 single-storey thatched cottage, engulfed in the outer reaches of the town of Lisburn: an astonishing survival. Two hundred years ago, Lisburn, and no doubt Belfast, must have had hundreds of little houses like this; it is remarkable not for any particular architectural merit, but for the feat of surviving unspoiled for so long.

Probably originally two tiny cottages: there are two, sheeted, doors, three crude chimney-stacks without pots, and four small Georgian-glazed windows, unevenly spaced. The cottage was rethatched in 1996; but the walls are, at the time of writing, badly in need of whitewashing. This little building must now be almost unique: it could be ruined by over-restoration, but it seems to stand in need of some loving care.

Photograph: A C W Merrick.
Situation: 113 and 115, Hillhall Road, Lisburn; td, Lisnatrunk; District Council, Lisburn; Grid ref. J 279 640.
References: Listed B1 (19/9/4). OS map, 1833; Pierce and Coey, 'Taken for granted', 1984, p 74.

5 - 7 and 20 - 24 Arthur Street, Hillsborough

138. Perhaps the best-preserved pairs of little houses in this intriguing cul-de-sac: at any rate, Number 5 seems to me to be the only one to retain its original lattice windows, though a number of others have modern (or even plastic) latticing. But the street deserves to be considered as an entity, despite the fact that the former smithy at Number 1, although listed in category B1, is now (why?) roofless and boarded up; and the two houses opposite, now Number 4, (likewise listed B1) have been mercilessly pebble-dashed, knocked into one, and modernised. (Why, oh why?).

The enclave comprises Numbers 4 to 24 on the left hand side of Arthur Street, Numbers 3 to 21 on the right-hand side: there is at least one slight break in the roofline half-way down the street, and the listers attribute those nearest Ballynahinch Street to "pre 1833", those farther away to "Mid 19th century". The earlier group at least is certainly shown on the Ordnance Survey map of 1833; but the Valuation book of the same year refers to 25 houses exempt, for being of less than £5 annual rateable value, in "East Lane", surely the same; and my own guess today is that, although neither street is mentioned in the 1837 Ordnance Survey memoir, the houses all date from the late 1820s, built as low-cost housing for workers on the Downshires' Hillsborough estate; though in 1974 I assigned them to the 1850s, a view I have now revised. With their Tudorbethan label mouldings, they remind me of the Seaforde Almshouses built by Colonel Forde in 1828.

Canon Barry has suggested that Arthur Street "came later in the time of Lord Arthur Hill", but this surely cannot be right, for 'Lord Arter' (as the Canon asserts he was known locally) did not take over the management of the Downshire estate until the death of the sixth Marquis, aged only 30, in 1874, when Lord Arthur acted on behalf of his infant nephew until the latter came of age. The name 'Arthur' seems to have been endemic in the Hill family: each of the second and third Marquesses (who died respectively in 1801 and 1845) was named Arthur Hill; and three younger brothers of the latter, Arthur William, Arthur Marcus, and Arthur Augustus, bore the same name, according to Dr W A Maguire's invaluable family tree in his edition of the third Marquess's letters; not to mention the four successive Arthurs in four successive generations of the Hill-Trevor cousins. So it seems to me likely that Canon Barry is mistaken, and that Arthur Street got its name long before 1874.

All the houses are, rightly in my view, listed in category B1. But there have been a surprising number of unfortunate alterations, many of them (but I suspect not all) no doubt antedating the listing: dormers, window-openings, doors, and other details. It would be marvellous if the whole street could be up-graded in an integrated way: such things have happened elsewhere.

Each house, and they are very small, is one-storey plus dormer, two-bay, with an arched and vaulted open passage (used nowadays for bins, coal, and drying washing) between each pair, giving access to their exiguous backyards. Alternate houses have an additional dormer-lit bedroom above the archway: in 1862 the larger and smaller houses were valued at £2 10 0 and £2 15 0 respectively, figures which remained unchanged for a century (the smithy at the end of the street was valued at £9). The front walls are of squared blackstone, random laid, with red-brick dressings to window and door openings, and rosy sandstone detailing around the arched passages. The over-sailing dripstones or label mouldings seem originally to have been of sandstone, but are now in most instances apparently of cement; I suspect that originally there were no gutters or downspouts, and when these came to be inserted, the stonework had to be cut through, with damaging results. The roofs are of slate, with slim brick chimney-stacks, for the most part by now rebuilt. The street, terminated by a view of the church spire and its surrounding trees, is still charming, though it would be even more so if some other lairage could but be found for the motor-cars of the residents.

Photograph: A C W Merrick (see also colour illus. 30).
Situation: Arthur Street, off Ballynahinch Street, Hillsborough; td, Hillsborough; District Council, Lisburn; Grid ref. J 244 588.
References: 1, 3-11, and 13-21; 4-12 and 14-24 Arthur Street, listed B1, (19/5/50); in conservation area. VAL 1B/ 344B, p 50, VAL 2B/3/45C, pp 24-5, in PRONI; OS map, 1833; J R Ward, T C McIlroy, and J C Innes, OSM, 1837, Down, III, p 91; Brett, 'Mid Down', UAHS, 1974, p 23; Downshire, 'Letters', 1974, p 11; Barry, 'Hillsborough', 1982, pp 28, 39.

Mill - workers' Houses, William Street, Donaghcloney

139. Numbers 1 to 31, and 2 to 32, William Street, Donaghcloney, constitute a rare and little-spoiled example of late 19th-century mill-workers' houses. They were built around 1890 by the Liddells of Donaghcloney Mill (156), at a time of comparative prosperity in the industry; and by an employer of comparative liberalism. Classic two-up two-down, red-brick, slated-roof, terraces, they were yet a little larger and more comfortable than many of those built in Belfast or other Ulster linen towns in the second half of the 19th century. In 1977, these houses, with another sixty workers' houses, allotments, playground, roadways and services were bought from the Liddell family for £15,000 by the newly-incorporated Donacloney Housing Association. The houses were modernised in three phases between 1982 and 1985: modern bathrooms and indoor lavatories were installed; the old chimney-stacks taken down and rebuilt while the roofs were 'enveloped'; and the layout was fundamentally altered so that the houses front onto pedestrian areas of garden, paving, and planters, while service access is available from the rear. This has been a highly successful venture, both socially and environmentally; other houses in Main Street and Lagan Terrace have

been similarly modernised; roads and services have all been renewed; and nine mobility bungalows have been built on patches of disused land. Up to the date of writing, 46 of the total of 92 houses originally acquired have been sold, mostly to sitting tenants. As always, this has had its upside and its downside: the purchasers have benefited in many ways; but the harmony and coherence of the streetscape have somewhat suffered, with differing paint colours, doors, window sashes, and so forth.

On balance, however, this scheme must be considered an undoubted success, and one reflecting much credit on the local residents, the Liddell family, and Thelma Armstrong and Erskine Holmes of the N I Federation of Housing Associations, who between them master-minded the scheme.

Photograph: A C W Merrick.
Situation: Parallel to Main Street, Donaghcloney; td, Donaghcloney; District Council, Craigavon; Grid ref. J 131 535.
References: Not listed. Atkinson, 'Ulster parish', 1898, p 80; William Liddell, unpublished ms history; information from Donacloney Housing Association.

Inn's Court, Park Lane, Hillsborough

140. A little dog-legged cobbled courtyard, of a kind very common a century ago in Irish towns and villages, but now extremely rare; with, on one side, the tall stone wall of the Shambles, pierced by a railed gateway; on the other, four modest two-storey two-bay houses of random blackstone with brick dressings, Victorian sashes, and a fine upstairs (modern) studio window in the gable-end of the first house. The group is only spoiled by an intrusive up-and-over garage door, inserted in the back wall of one of the big houses fronting the Square, without the knowledge or consent of the owners of Inn's Court, and so, probably, illegally; though it is to be feared that the effluxion of time may have remedied the breach. Still, the owner of the garage should have a very guilty conscience, and should make amends for his (or his predecessor's) misdeed.

According to the Ordnance Survey memoir of 1837, the Shambles (otherwise cattle-yard, abbatoir, or slaughterhouse) was built by the third Marquess of Downshire in 1829: this little courtyard of modest houses was almost certainly built at the same time. Local tradition has it that here the Downshire estate tenants, unable to find cash to pay their rent, could pay instead in kind; and that Lord Downshire's agent would, on stated dates, sit under the archway of the Shambles to count and value the livestock so delivered.

The Valuation book of 1833 values the "Public Shambles, sheds and yard" at £5 4 0; and the houses next to it, exempt, as being below the minimum rateable value of £5: Park Lane is here called West Lane, by contrast to Arthur Street (138), then called East Lane. By 1862, this little enclave had become Barrack Court off Inn's Lane: with four houses valued at £2 each. I know of no Barrack to justify the title, but so it seems to be. The local residents conjecture that the officers of the North Down Militia were quartered in the two large houses fronting the Square; their stables, grooms and batmen may well have lived in these humbler quarters. As to Inn's Court, there seems to have been an inn, burned down in 1943, on the site of the present Council offices.

Neither description, nor valuation, changed over the next century. But the tenants' names, as shown in the Valuation book, changed with quite exceptional frequency all through those years; perhaps the proximity of the Shambles was found insalubrious; indeed, it is surprising that the Marquess chose to build so offensive an amenity so close to his own mansion (51). However, its original use has long been discontinued. As I described them in 1974, the Shambles comprise "A grassy square, part enclosed with fleur-de-lys railings, part with an interesting and attractive L-shaped range of buildings: formerly used as a pen for cattle travelling the Dublin Road. Most of the range is of rubble, but part of white-painted brick, and part constitutes a slate-roofed arcade on cast-iron columns. The brick-dressed entrance archway is inset in a central pavilion. The weighbridge is of about 1830 - probably the date of the buildings themselves - by H. Pooley & Son. Well-converted to its new use" (as Art Centre) "and tidied up, in 1970, by R. McKinstry and Partner". However, no doubt because of the Troubles, the Art Centre, brainchild of the late Patric Stevenson, Dickie Wilson and Terry Flanagan, has not really flourished; and apart from a thin scattering of outdoor sculptures too heavy to be conveniently stolen, has been converted into offices, and the projected print workshop, which did not flourish either, has been converted by Robert McKinstry into a very pleasant small art gallery, with a large cobbled yard at the rear; whilst the remaining houses provide homes and studios for other artists: so that this corner of Hillsborough has become the artistic quarter, as it were, the Place du Tertre of Ulster's Montmartre!

Photograph: A C W Merrick (see also colour illus. 34).

Situation: Courtyard off Park Lane, Hillsborough; td, Hillsborough; District Council, Lisburn; Grid ref. J 242 585.

References: The houses are not listed, though the Shambles are listed B, and No 1 Park Lane (a stucco house, in my view of much less interest than the surrounding stone buildings) is listed B1; all in conservation area. VAL 1B/344/B p 49, VAL 2B/3/45C, p 39, VAL 12B/20/14/B,C,D, in PRONI; J R Ward, T C McIlroy, and J C Innes, OSM, 1837, Down, III, pp 91, 102; Brett, 'Mid Down', UAHS, 1974, p 17; information from Terence and Sheila Flanagan and Neil Shawcross.

11 Main Street, Hillsborough

141. An interesting example of improvement. In 1974, I wrote "stucco, two-storey and basement, Victorian-glazed, with a fine wide three-light doorcase with fan, and good railings". Since then, the stucco has all been hacked off - a highly risky proceeding: but in this instance, successful, for the work has been sensitively done and the modest façade disclosed is quite charming, perhaps the prettiest of all the pretty buildings (now sometimes even a little cloying) in Hillsborough Main Street. The walls are of random stone, but nicely laid and pointed, with well-cleaned red-brick dressings to all the openings; three bays wide, with all the Georgian glazing-bars restored, and the doorcase, fanlight, sidelights, and railings, most judiciously painted. A 1995 report in the Monuments and Buildings Record states that the render was stripped by hand from the front wall, and that the joints were cleaned out by hand, and repointed using lime mortar - to admirable effect. The Georgian sash-boxes and sashes were replaced in 1998. An outstanding example of what can be done in an Irish street, for all to admire. It would be nice if No 9 could be similarly restored, for plainly, as Gordon Wheeler has pointed out to me, the two houses were designed as a single seven-bay unit with a shared coach-arch in the centre.

Photograph: A C W Merrick.
Situation: 11 Main Street, Hillsborough; td, Hillsborough; District Council, Lisburn; Grid ref. J 243 587.
References: Listed B (9/5/19); in conservation area. Brett, 'Mid Down', UAHS, 1974, p 22; Pierce and Coey, 'Taken for granted', 1984, p 96; notes in MBR.

37 - 39 Court Street, Newtownards

142. An attractive, and attractively restored, five-bay pair of stuccoed two-storey terrace houses, linked by a central coach-arch which is flanked on either side by a stone round-headed door-case with fanlight. Formerly part of a much longer, coherent, terrace, its integrity now much prejudiced by injudicious alterations, and even illegal demolitions. Almost all the houses on this side of the street from No 21 to No 57, No 63 to 71, and Nos 75 and 77, were originally listed: it is to the discredit of the planners that this street, though not yet quite beyond salvation, has been so debased. The listers just describe them as "two-storey dwellings conforming in detail but varying in size. Terraced of Rubble Scrabo Stone with fully-dressed Gibbsian architraves to windows and doors - in many cases modern fittings have been substituted". But that was written 25 years ago.

The two houses here noticed do not in fact have the Gibbsian door-surround, often described as an "Ards doorway", though in fact commonly found throughout the towns and villages of North County Down. The authors of the Hearth Review remark that a tall random stone wall at the rear could well be the last surviving remnant of the seventeenth-century bawn wall of Sir Hugh Montgomery's Newtown House. "Early street directories and valuation records indicate that the street was inhabited by skilled workers, together with a few corn merchants and weaving agents. The houses became empty in the mid-1980s by which time they were owned by the N I Housing Executive, which had ear-marked them for demolition. Hearth was able to acquire them and obtain housing association funding for the restoration of the two houses and conversion of the rear stable block into flats" in 1993-4. "The houses were provided with new kitchen returns and the roof structures were strengthened, but they were otherwise little altered. The stable block required extensive structural work, and some old door and window openings were retained externally but blocked up inside; the old external staircase to the stable now serves as the entrance to the upper flat". Georgian glazing-pattern and cobweb fanlights intact; very nicely painted; a considerable ornament to the town.

Photograph; A C W Merrick.
Situation: 37- 39 Court Street, Newtownards; td, Corporation North; District Council, Ards; Grid ref. J 492 738.
References: Listed B (24/13/21). Not on Londonderry estate map of 1841, but shown on estate map of 1848; Hearth, 'Review of projects', 1999, p 47.

139 Whiterock Bay, Killinchy

143. Described by the listers as "A two-storey house in the 'International Modern' style of white rendered walls, flat roofs with projecting eaves, corner windows and 'porthole' window by the architect Philip Bell. Despite the alterations to the window frames and glazing patterns this remains a good example of its type and mirrors the architecture of Philip Bell's contemporary Strangford Lough Yacht Club on the opposite side of the road". Unhappily, the new front door is singularly out of keeping with the design.

His club-house has by now been demolished and replaced, though the club still flourishes. Philip Bell's widow recalls this as one of a group of houses built for the club, and thinks this one was to provide accommodation for Mr Clarke the boatman. I remember, as a boy, being taken sailing, with my parents, by Philip and Alison Bell, from Whiterock. He was a most enthusiastic yachtsman, who built his own yachts in his dining-room at Lurgan; in his younger days, a ceaseless smoker of cigarettes; when he had reluctantly given them up, a ceaseless chewer of toffees; and, my successor as chairman of the Ulster Architectural Heritage Society.

Photograph: A C W Merrick.
Situation : 139 Whiterock Bay, Killinchy; td, Killinakin; District Council, Ards; Grid ref. J 524 618.
References: Listed B2 (24/17/84). Information from Mrs Alison Bell.

Schoolhouse Brae, Donaghadee

144. In 1977, Hugh Dixon, helpfully, wrote: "Shore Cottages, Nos. 6 -14 Shore Street: - Dating from the late 18th century, the last stretch of early houses on the sea front. Single but occasionally double storey with cement rendered fronts and tiled roofs, several of which retain the traditional seaside roof reinforcement of the Ards; concrete swept over the tiles. Many of the houses are derelict and in extremely bad condition but any redevelopment should respect their scale, texture and planning, especially noting the continuity of the terraces and their relation to what is behind (for example the attractively haphazard layout of Schoolhouse Brae)".

Not long after, the block was declared a Redevelopment Area; and I count its rebuilding, in 1981, to provide nine houses, four bungalows, and twelve flats - a total of twenty-nine dwellings, on a constricted site - as the first real success of my membership of the Board of the Northern Ireland Housing Executive. We had, earlier, received some praise from conservationists for the reconstruction of some long Georgian terraces in Banbridge; but I was not well satisfied with the detailing of these; the former subtle curves had been replaced by crude angles; and I disliked the blank gable-ends. I had been somewhat more successful with the redevelopment of Shore Street, Portaferry: the houses I thought fine, but I had been vastly irritated to be told by our in-house architects that it would be too

expensive to replace attractive old curving curtilage walls of random stone, and that they must be replaced with right-angled walls of roughcast breeze blocks. It was in this Donaghadee scheme that, at long last - after nine years on the Board! - I got my way; and the irregularly curved wall that bounds the steep planted bank between Shore Street, and Schoolhouse Brae, was the result. The architects were McAdam Design partnership.

I was not pleased in quite all respects with this scheme: the two-storey blocks of flats would have looked better with chimney-stacks, and the random protrusion of rocks from rendered walls was dated and artificial; but on the whole, I judged it pretty creditable, and still take pride and pleasure in revisiting it.

Photographs: A C W Merrick; NI Housing Executive.
Situation: Shore Street / Union Street / Schoolhouse Brae, Donaghadee; td, Townparks; District Council, Ards; Grid ref. J 589 801.
References: Not listed; in conservation area. Dixon, 'Donaghadee and Portpatrick', UAHS, 1977, p 25; NIHE, 'Twelfth annual report', 1983.

Crane at Donaghadee harbour (167). Photograph: A C W Merrick

CHAPTER SEVEN

PUBLIC BUILDINGS, COMMERCIAL, ETC.

The most significant public buildings in north County Down are, certainly, the former Newtownards Market House of 1771 (147); the former Hillsborough Market and Court House of the 1760s and 1810 (146); and Helen's Bay Railway Station, of 1863 (172). There are quite a number of impressive bridges, especially over the River Lagan, though, as Rodney Green has said, "Most bridges in the county have been reconstructed and repaired to such an extent that there is no possibility of discovering their original date." There are also important maritime buildings at Donaghadee (167) and the Copeland Islands (168).

As to industrial buildings, the western part of the county is richer than the more agricultural eastern part; though a great deal of its industrial heritage has by now disappeared. In 1823, Atkinson could write: "The woollen manufacture may be considered as a local benefit, employing a certain number of the poor, in a certain spot, but the linen industry is not confined to a factory here and there; the process of sowing, steeping, drying, dressing, spinning, weaving, and bleaching, through which the flax passes, employs a whole country, and unites its entire population in one bond of reciprocal communication and common interest". (Would that it were still so!) ... "The gentry of the country, to a certain extent, being thus engaged in the linen business, have continual communication with the manufacturer in the markets, - their interests become identified, and a chain of communication is kept up between all the ranks of society in a linen district, which does more towards tranquillising the country, consolidating its interests, promoting mutual affection, and exciting an honourable ambition to acquire independence, than can be accomplished by sanguinary laws, military establishments, absentee landlords, an aristocracy which holds no intercourse with the people, and a petty subaltern despotism, to which a system of this description never fails to consign mankind."[2] (Loud cries of, "Hear, Hear!"). The best surviving example of a linen mill, though much of it now of quite late date, is at Donaghcloney (156).

There are also, as will be seen, a considerable, if dwindling, number of lesser buildings: the rare windmill, lime kilns, schools, railway stations, coastguard stations, and banks; but area surveyed can no longer be considered rich in such buildings. Such worthy examples as remain, I have endeavoured to record.

References: 1. Green, 'Industrial archaeology', 1963, p 63. 2. Atkinson, 'Ireland exhibited', 1823, I, p 365.

Crane at Donaghadee harbour (167). Portion of water-colour: D Kennedy, 1834, private collection

Former Market House, Portaferry

145. A plain but charming two-storey building, rendered but with cutstone quoins; hipped roof topped by bell and sailing-ship wind-vane; the end walls blank; the two fronts each topped by a central pediment with inset clock. The principal front has four Georgian-glazed windows above, two partly-blocked round-headed arches, and a plain rectangular doorway at each end below. Built in 1752 by Andrew Savage, builder also of Portaferry House (48). According to the family historian, he was "an officer in the Spanish Army, and was a Roman Catholic. He became a Protestant, and claimed and obtained the Portaferry estate. He conformed 20th July 1738 ... According to local tradition he was 'walking on the Quay in Spain' when the news of his brother John's death was brought to him. He at once left for Ireland ..." His commission is preserved in the Public Record Office of Northern Ireland: named as "Andrea Savage" he was appointed Captain in the first battalion of the "Regimento de Infantrerie de Hibernia"; it is signed in person by no less than King Philip V of Spain, in a sprawling hand, "Yo el Rey": no monarchical plural there. His family, however, "regarded his sojourn in Spain as having rather unfitted him for the life and responsibilities of an Irish country-gentleman". Their letters "are profuse in gentle chidings and mild remonstrances. For example, his father-in-law writes in July 1739: - 'I am told you purpose suddenly building a Market-House at Portaferry. I think you ought to postpone it a while' ... Subsequently Andrew Savage did build the Market-House, in AD 1752" (Savage-Armstrong).

On 10th June 1798, the market house and square were successfully defended against the local United Irishmen, with the aid of the guns of a revenue cutter, the Buckingham, commanded by Captain Hopkins. "He sent guns ashore, and had them placed at each end of the Market-House, with feather beds and other things for protection. There were several men-of war's men at Portaferry at the time, who assisted in working the guns. The Rebels came down High Street first, but a shot from the Market House turned them ... another shot killed the foremost man amongst them, and the rest fled in disorder" (Savage-Armstrong).

G Scott, of the Ordnance Survey, says (around 1835) "Erected in 1752 at the expense of Andrew Savage Esquire; it is an extremely plain building with the Savages' arms outside, dimensions of the building 44 feet by 21 feet in the clear. The rooms to the right and left in the upper storey are the library rooms for the Literary Society and the Mechanic Institute Library. The centre room serves (but seldom) for a ballroom. In this room the seneschal holds the manor court, where debts to the amount of 40s and under are settled. There is also a court leet held in June (once in the year) for appointing a grand jury, petty constables, plotters and apprizers, laying on cess for the repair of houses, purchasing weights, seals. A temperance society frequently drink tea in this room, upon which occasion they ornament it with green leaves etc." And: "Literary Society. Established in 1786, members only admitted by ballot, admittance formerly 5 pounds but now reduced to 2 pounds and is a subscription. In case of dissolution, members to receive books to the proportion of 5 pounds entrance money. The library is in the market house, length of room 20 feet by 18 feet". And: "Mechanic Institute Library. This library was established in 1828, supported by subscriptions. In order to be admitted it is necessary to pay 2s 6d entrance money and 6 guineas a year. In this library are 258 volumes. It is held in the opposite end of the market house to the library room of

the Literary Society, dimensions of the room 20 feet by 18 feet".

The Archaeological Survey of County Down, for some unstated reason, thinks the market house dates from about 1800, and remarks "at the centre, at first-floor level is a panel bearing an achievement of arms with the inscription 'Erected 1752 by Andrew Savage Esq.' This must refer to an earlier building". But why? I know of no evidence for this, and no other writer on the market house seems to doubt that it really does date from 1752. The bell bears the date 1753.

An ornament to the town; refurbished (at the instance of the late Alec Potter, first Professor of Architecture at Queen's University of Belfast, and the Ulster Architectural Heritage Society), in 1972, as a community centre.

Unfortunately, the restoration effected by North Down Rural Council in 1972 did not prove durable; another and more thorough restoration was required in 1998; but this looks to be more successful. Certainly, the restored market house now provides both a social and a visual asset to Portaferry.

Photographs: A C W Merrick.
Situation: In the centre of The Square, Portaferry; td, Ballyphilip; District Council, Ards; Grid ref. J 594 508.
References: Listed B1 (24/1/1); in conservation area. D552/A/3/2, in PRONI; G Scott, OSM, nd (1835?), Down, II, p 12; Savage-Armstrong, 'Savage family in Ulster', 1906, pp 141, 361; ASCD, 1966, pp 433-434; Bell, 'Portaferry & Strangford', UAHS, 1969, p 10; Brett, 'Court houses and market houses', UAHS, 1973, pp 21, 76; J McCartney, in JUAHS, III, 1979, pp 13-14; local information.

Former Market House and Court House, Hillsborough

146. "A most unusual, and very charming, building, in three blocks arranged pyramidally: on a plinth of granite steps, the ground floor has a frontage of nine bays, and sides of five bays, with round open arches in the central block, and round-headed windows in the subsidiary pyramidal-roofed blocks; the central square block of three bays rises another storey, harled and painted pink; above this is a square clock-tower with urns, cupola, and banner weathervane. The lower part of the building is of granite, the upper part of sandstone, the outer walls being surmounted by ball-shaped knops" (Brett, 1974).

The court house makes a splendid centre-piece to the little town, and neatly links town and 'Castle' (51). But, despite its importance, its history is extremely difficult to unravel. Dudley Waterman, in the Archaeological Survey of County Down of 1966, attributed it to W Forsyth, and

dated it 1780, on the strength of a drawing now in the Public Record Office of Northern Ireland. In 1973, after a fresh study of the numerous alternative drawings there, I attributed it to James McBlain, and dated it to around 1790. In 1974, I revised this view in the light of evidence produced by Dr Edward McParland, in the form of a sketch of 1808 by the Rev. D A Beaufort in his Tour. Further evidence may yet come to light; but, for the present, I think the best view is that the central two-storey core of the building represents the Tholsel which Dr Beaufort first saw and recorded in his Journal in 1765; to which, on 28th February 1772, Smith, Lord Downshire's agent, repaired on an alarm of Hearts of Steel in the vicinity; and which, in October 1795, was threatened by "the Kilwarlin boys", of whom four "were lodged in the Black Hole, but escaped" ... "I got through Lord Doneraile a

sergeant's guard from the camp (the Tholsel being threatened) and the sovereign accompanied me to every public house and forbid the sale of liquor" (Barry). Then, in order to provide a court room: "In about 1810 the N and S wings were added, together with the granite plinth, and sandstone details - cornices, urns and balls. A new clock and bell were installed in 1810" (HMNI). One of the drawings in the Public Record Office, unsigned and undated, shows the building almost exactly as it is now: the style closely resembles that of the drawings signed by James McBlain and annotated by the Marquis: "It therefore seems that McBlain's drawings are to be interpreted as plans for the enlargement, subsequent to 1808, of a smaller and much earlier building" (Brett, 1974).

C R Cockerell (1788-1863; "at once the most fastidious and the least pedantic of English neo-classical architects" - Colvin) visited Hillsborough on 24 October 1823, and drew in his diary a sketch of the court house which he annotated "Market ho: at Hillsboro looks remarkably well - the upper part entirely Palladian with excellent effect - a roof quite square & not excessively large in size to look well, the hip giving a graceful inclination to the roof, & having a simple breadth & impression of squareness".

On 12 July 1837, J R Ward of the Ordnance Survey wrote "The court house is a neat, stone building occupying a space 103 feet long and 64 feet broad. At one end is the sessions court, at the other a market place and between them are the grand jury room and caretaker's apartments." In 1862, the "Court House and Caretaker's appartments" were first valued at £25, then declared exempt; interestingly, the estate carpenter's workshop, as well as the 'reading and band room' were also housed here, and separately valued at £12.

The court house was leased in 1959 by the then Lord Downshire to the Government of Northern Ireland at a rent of two white doves per annum (I should know; I drafted the lease). It then underwent a very slow restoration, not completed for many years. Between 1837 and 1959, the north wing had housed the court room; the south wing had housed the Downshire estate office, whose copious and dusty documents I was privileged to pack up and despatch to the Public Record Office of Northern Ireland; the central block housed an open market-hall; the room above it was used as a band-room, and for occasional meetings and functions. After 1959, the court room was used, during the very worst of the Troubles, for many trials of terrorists. The building is now, below, a Tourist Information Centre and interpretative Heritage Centre, above, a kind of community hall. It has been re-christened Market House rather than Court House, presumably from security considerations: it might have been better to have gone back to its first, very proper, title of Tholsel. The restoration work has been well done, and earned a Civic Trust Award: the building now looks well, though there is a slight superfluity of plate glass in the formerly open archways, and a decided superfluity of publicity and marketing material in the windows of what should, by rights, be an austere, proprietorial, and dignified building.

Photograph: A C W Merrick (see also colour illus. 38).
Situation: In the centre of The Square, Hillsborough; td, Hillsborough; District Council, Lisburn; Grid ref. J 243 586.
References: Strangely, not listed, but Monument in state care; in conservation area. D 607/585, 590, D 671/ 88/ 2,3,9B, 10A, 10B, 12, D 671/ P6/1-9, VAL2B/3/45C, p 34, all in PRONI; D A Beaufort, Ms journal, 1765, K6, 54, and tour, 1807-8, K6, 63, p44, in TCD Library; C R Cockerell, diary, 24 October 1823, in RIBA Library; J R Ward, T C McIlroy and J C Innes, OSM, 1837, Down III, p 90; ASCD, 1966, pp 411-414; Brett, 'Court houses and market houses', UAHS, 1973, pp 67-70; Brett, 'Mid Down', UAHS, 1974, pp 5,13,14; HMNI, 1983, pp 111-112; Colvin, 'Biographical dictionary', 1995, p 257.

Former Market House, Newtownards

147. The finest market house in Ulster, designed in 1765 by Ferdinando Stratford of Bristol for the Stewart family; its completion (except for the cupola) delayed until 1771; the cupola evidently added in 1778. An uncommonly well-documented building, as well as an uncommonly handsome one. Stratford "is known principally as a river and canal engineer and surveyor" ... "who died of an ague in Gloucestershire in 1766" ... "his original plan and elevation, almost exactly as executed save for an extra bay in each wing, are preserved amongst the Londonderry papers, signed and dated" ... "A detailed 'Measurement' - equivalent to a present-day quantity surveyor's estimate - survives, entitled 'Measurement of the cutt stone Front of the Market House, Newtown Ards, 22nd October 1771', for a total figure of £380. 11. 1, including 373 feet of architraves at 8d. a foot; 'the whole work of the Venetian window' for £15; and 3/3 'to mending a piece of cornice that was broke in a storm of wind'. The cupola, in a somewhat elaborated version of Stratford's original design, was added considerably later: a drawing and further estimate for £66. 18. 7 were prepared on 26 June 1778 by Robert Bradshaw: 'The cupola of the Market House in Newtown Ards measured and valued to the best of my judgement'" (Brett).

A correspondent in Walker's Hibernian Magazine for September, 1777, gives an interesting near-contemporary description: "In 1769 a new market square was planned, and several new streets, some of which are already built, particularly a handsome street opposite the center arch of the market house. Another is to be built opposite the center arch at the other side. The market square is capable of holding 10,000 people without crouding, or incommoding each other." (A slight exaggeration, perhaps?) "The new market-house forms one side of this square: It contains in each front 9 arches" (*sic*), "the center arch 22 feet high, and 11 wide, the others, 14 by 7. The work is very neat, and entirely of a white free-stone, over the center arch is a most beautiful room 32 feet long and 22 wide, which serves for a drawing-room to the larger or assembly-room. This room is most elegantly stucco'd, the walls painted a light green, and bordered with gold; a large branch for 20 candles, hangs from the ceiling; the marble chimney piece is hardly to be equalled. Over this room is a handsome clock, belfry and cupola. Over one wing of the market house, is the assembly-room, 50 feet by 24. The walls of this room are painted blue, and bordered with gold; the cieling is beautifully stucco'd, from it hang three brass branches, which hold 20 candles each; the stair-case is elegant: the steps are of white free-stone; the ballustrade of iron gilt, and the hand rail mahogany". And, for good measure: "The inhabitants are mostly Presbyterian, as is the landlord ... The language spoken here is broad Scotch, hardly to be understood by strangers. A few Scotch words are to be heard from the best bred people all over the province, but in this neighbourhood, which is entirely inhabited by Scots, no other language is to be heard".

The market house remains remarkably little changed. G Scott of the Ordnance Survey says, around 1835: "The market house in the town is a handsome building and one of the greatest ornaments to it. It is composed of freestone and situated at the north end of the square. The lower part is used for various purposes. The most eastern side is used as potatoe and grain store, the western side for the sale of fresh meat. The gentlemen of the Down hunt meet and dine in the upper rooms at appointed times. Public meetings are also held in them". Samuel Lewis writes "The town hall, for the transaction of the corporation business, is a handsome structure in the Grecian Doric style,

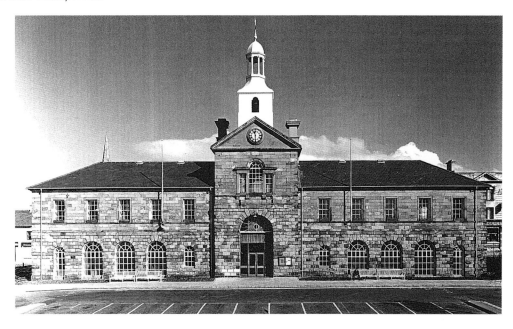

erected in 1770 by the first Marquess of Londonderry: it is surmounted by a cupola, containing a clock, beneath which is the entrance into an area leading through the centre, on one side of which is the flesh market and on the other a weigh-house and other requisite offices and stores; above is an elegant suite of assembly-rooms, with other apartments, in which the members of the Down hunt hold meetings". Surprisingly, the Parliamentary Gazetteer, whilst singing the praises of Newtownards - "one of the most attractive towns of the north of Ireland, as to neatness, regularity, and convenience" - dismisses the building in one curt sentence: "The market house is built of cut stone, and surmounted by a cupola".

A long, two-storey, imposing building, the front to Conway Square of channelled cutstone, the two sides and rear of smooth-rendered rubble-stone with cutstone dressings, with a central cupola on a pedimented advancing bay. The original semi-circular market arches now filled in with glazing, quite tactfully, and the small end windows taken down to ground level; modern central doorway with fanlight and side-lights, a rather unhappy replacement for the handsome doorcase shown in the old photographs; above it, on each frontage, a rather fine Venetian window framed by pilasters. A clock in the pediment; five Georgian-glazed windows above five arches in each wing. The building has a hipped, slated roof, and the rendered and painted cupola is flanked by two tall stone chimney-stacks.

The interior has been very well restored between 1998 and 2000 to provide hospitality rooms upstairs, an exceptionally hospitable Arts Centre downstairs. The original staircase, banisters and whorl survive. The central room on what is now the second floor, with a Venetian window in each front looking out on the geometrically-disposed 18th-century layout of the town centre, is of exceptional charm. There is good plasterwork in the ceiling of the staircase: the Londonderry Room on the first floor, as reconstituted, is rather magnificent, with cornice of dark blue and white arabesques, and chandelier - the original moulds for the plasterwork are still in existence. The fire escapes added at each end of the building in 1991 are as congenial as could be hoped for, with quite delicate modern ironwork. An extraordinary lock-up for malefactors on the ground floor, with a strangely primitive corbelled stone ceiling, has been carefully preserved. Altogether, the refurbishment by Brian Knox, of Knox and Markwell, must be accounted a very considerable success.

Photographs: A C W Merrick; MBR. Drawing: F Stratford, PRONI.
Situation: Conway Square, Newtownards; td, Corporation North; District Council, Ards; Grid ref. J 489 741.
References: Listed B1 (24/13/1). D 654/M70/16, VAL 1B/34, both in PRONI; 'Walker's Hibernian magazine', September 1777, p 619; G Scott, OSM, nd (?1835), Down, II, p 106; Lewis, TD, 1837, II, p 435; P G, III, 1846, p 41; ASCD, 1966, p 431; Brett, 'Court houses and market houses', UAHS, 1973, p 73; McCavery, 'Newtown', 1994, pp 87-89; Ards Arts Centre leaflet, 2000.

Former Florida Manor Court House, Kilmood

148. In 1973, I described this as follows: " A charmingly eccentric little Manor Court House, deceitfully inscribed 'Florida Manor Court House Date of Patent 1638', was in fact built in 1822 for David Gordon, lord of the manor. It continued in use as a court house until 1922, and is now a dwelling. Of one storey to the road, it has a sort of undercroft originally designed to contain a coach-house and stabling for two horses. The pointed front door, in a crudely Gibbsian doorcase, is reached by a pathway carried above basement level on arches; on either side of the central projection are two simple pointed windows. The roof is hipped. The central bay, above the door, rises to form an extraordinary crow-stepped pagoda-cum-pinnacle in a vaguely Chinese taste. In the gable is the inscription, inset in a quatrefoil-in-circle. The building is partly stuccoed, partly roughcast".

Since then, the building served for a number of years as Nick Price's restaurant, predecessor of 'Nick's Warehouse' in Hill Street, Belfast; then reverted to residential use. At present, looking well, cream-painted; but its listing unhappily down-graded in October 1999 from B1 to B2 status. (Incredibly, the professional staff of the Historic Buildings Branch had recommended de-listing, because of the alterations to the interior, ignoring the signal importance of the building to a group of exceptional significance in the

landscape. In 1973, I had recommended an A, as I still should: the more so, as I believe it to be one of only two surviving purpose-built manor court houses in Northern Ireland, the other that for the manor of Armagh in County Fermanagh).

Florida Manor itself is a rather mysterious house, probably of 17th-century origin but much altered, with a disconcerting combination of possibly late 18th-century pompous tetrastyle Ionic porch and sprouting polygonal Elizabethan-style chimney-pots. On the basis of the latter, Hugh Dixon has suggested that it may have been rebuilt around 1810, and, on the model of Narrow Water Castle, proposed a possible attribution to Thomas Duff. Dixie Dean dates the Georgian Gothic style gate lodges to about 1840. Now evidently inaccessible and apparently semi-derelict, though the roof is still on.

Photograph: A C W Merrick.

Situation: 18 Church Road, Kilmood; td, Kilmood; District Council, Ards; Grid ref. J 470 629.

References: Listed B1, down-graded to B2 (24/17/36). Lewis, TD, 1837, II, p 190; House of Commons, Select Committee on Manor Courts, Ireland, 'Report', 1837, p 374; Brett, 'Court houses and market houses', UAHS, 1973, pp 14, 69, 71; Brett, 'East Down', UAHS, 1973, p 46; Dean, 'Gate lodges', UAHS, 1994, p 76; H Dixon, undated notes in MBR.

Former Schoolhouse, Drumbo

149. *Drumbo National School 1840* proclaims an inscribed stone panel above the front door of the left-hand portion, originally both schoolroom and the schoolmaster's house. There was another schoolhouse at Purdysburn, erected in 1822 at a cost of £300 of which £200 was paid by Narcissus Batt; there seems sometimes to have been confusion between the two schoolhouses in such close proximity. Mr Scott of the Ordnance Survey mentions yet another school in the townland of Drumbo, erected 1836, cost £97, and the Purdysburn school in the townland of Ballycoan. In 1889 the Drumbo schoolhouse (in Ballylesson) was enlarged (the large double-height part to the right), under the superintendence of W J Watson, architect, of Newry, who was apparently a friend of Robert Narcissus Batt since he was appointed an executor of his will. In 1950 the schoolhouse was transferred to the parish from the Ministry of Education, and over £1300 was spent on converting Watson's schoolroom into the parish hall. Subsequently, when in 1991 a brand new parish hall was built to designs by Richard Pierce, architect, of Enniskillen,

the hall and house next door were sold off and converted into a single private residence.

It is a handsome little building with Jacobean detailing. There is a remarkable pattern of timber quatrefoils in the schoolroom gable; windows, with double or triple lights, Tudor pointed, some with lattice glazing, under label mouldings; and fine tall chimney-stacks rising from the roof of the rear section. It is a pity that the original smooth, creamy stucco should have been replaced with a rather raw grey cement rendering. This rather charming building could look a lot better if sympathetically painted as a single entity.

Photograph: A C W Merrick.
Situation: 76 Ballylesson Road, Drumbo; td, Ballycowan; District Council, Lisburn; Grid ref. J 330 676.
References: Listed B1 (19/23/39). G Scott, OSM, nd (?1837), Down, II, p 57; J F Rankin, 'Heritage of Drumbo', 1981, passim; information from Karen Latimer and J F Rankin.

Former National Schools, Holywood

150. "The first really important school in Holywood was the Sullivan National Schools, completed in April 1862 at a cost of £2,000, the money being donated by the well-known educationalist the philanthropist Dr. Robert Sullivan (1800-1868). He was born in a thatched cottage in High Street ... the clock tower and the adjoining hall ... were built in 1877 in an identical style of architecture and also for £2,000, the money on that occasion being part of a bequest left by Dr. Sullivan ... The architects responsible for the design were Messrs Lanyon, Lynn & Lanyon ... the individual partner most likely being W H Lynn" (Merrick). It seems that Dr Sullivan, with a Presbyterian mother, an Episcopalian father, and a Roman Catholic wife, was a notable proponent of non-sectarian education: himself one of the first Inspectors of Schools.

This very accomplished Ruskinian Venetian building, in polychrome brick (pale yellow, relieved by stripes of red and black), with stone trim, has, stylistically, something in common with Lynn's Diocesan Offices in May Street, Belfast of 1867. The upper floor was for the girls; the lower floor for the boys. 56 pupils could be accommodated on each floor, and, under the three-shift system of working, a total of 168 children could be educated on each floor each day: which sounds rather exhausting for their teachers. The front has an inscription on the sandstone string-course *Holywood National Schools / Built by Robert Sullivan LLD 1862*. There are agreeable fish-scale slates on the roof. First, National School; then, Public Elementary School; then Holywood Technical College; disused by 1982. Made wind- and weather-tight in 1983-4, at a considerable loss, by the ACE workers of Heritage Repairs Ltd, a company set up by the late John Lewis-Crosby: a financial disaster but a conservation triumph. Thoroughly restored in 1995 by the Southern Education and Library Board, under the supervision of its chief architect, S K Savage, as branch public library and further education centre.

Photograph: A C W Merrick (see also colour illus. 39).
Situation: High Street, Holywood.; td, Holywood; District Council, North Down; Grid ref. J 397 789.
References: Listed B (23/20/13). DB, IV, 1862, p 95; 'North Down Spectator', 19/1/1984; Merrick, 'Buildings of Holywood', 1986, pp 67-68; UA, October/November 1993.

Model School, Newtownards

151. The District Model National School at Newtownards, built to the design of Frederick Darley of Dublin at a cost of over £10,000, was evidently designed in or before 1858, but opened only in July 1862. Wylie describes it as "a Jacobean revival mansion consisting of an almost symmetrical principal block representing the main house, to which are annexed two rather plain ranges of accommodation suggesting estate buildings or out-offices": a very acute description of a very handsome and striking building, almost unaltered, and still in use, now as a primary school. To further the new system of National Education established in the mid-19th century, twenty-eight Model Schools were built throughout Ireland. "The objectives of these ... were declared to be the promotion of united (i.e. integrated) education; improved methods of literary and scientific education; and the training of teachers ..." (As rôle-models) "They provided not only exemplary teaching practices, but also residential teacher-training and facilities for scientific, vocational, agricultural and adult education" (Wylie). "After 1870 Model Schools were phased out, but the Newtownards school retained its name and it succeeded as a 'model' school by its own efforts, under the National School scheme" (McCavery).

Frederick Darley, junior (1798-1872), a pupil of Francis Johnston, found his nose evidently put out of joint when he considered that his position in Johnston's office was usurped by William Murray. Nonetheless, Darley enjoyed many public offices during his career, working amongst others for the Ecclesiastical Commissioners, Trinity College Dublin, The King's Inns, and the Royal Dublin Society; architect to the Board of Education (and its successor, the Board of Works), from 1848 until 1858. He was an accomplished individual who was responsible for the neo-classical library at The King's Inns in Dublin, and at least six new Church of Ireland churches.

The two-storey school at Newtownards, with its nine-bay front, is built of the local Scrabo stone "finished with a chiselled texture", or, to my eye, largely of pecked stone. I cannot improve on Robin Wylie's description of the building, and will not try. "The wings and centre of the main façade are projected boldly from the three-bay links, which are themselves further modelled by slight single-bay breakfronts. Shaped gables alternate with semi-circular gablets each pinnacled according to rank. The wings are further emphasised by quoined returns, superimposed pilasters, and larger six-pane windows set in projecting square bays which are crowned with solid parapets carved in low relief in lieu of brattishing work. The centre has been embellished with superimposed Tuscan Doric orders of double pilasters, the lower of which rest on pedestals flanking a curiously plain arched front doorcase and side lights ... As in his design for Belfast, Darley has placed an eyecatcher on the roof high above the centre - a four-square tower on a tall base with diminutive pilasters in tune with those below, but up here supporting their own small order and finally a concave pyramid roof covered with decorative leadwork".

Originally, the three principal schoolrooms were designed to accommodate 150 boys, 120 girls, and 100 infants respectively, as well as a residence for the headmaster, together with a dormitory and rooms for the pupil-teachers. The school is nicely placed below Scrabo Hill, and surrounded by trees, shrubs and grass.

Photograph: A C W Merrick.
Situation: Scrabo Road, Newtownards; td, Ballycullen; District Council, Ards; Grid ref. J 478 738.
References: Listed B+ (24/11/12). McCavery, 'Newtown', 1994, p 152; Wylie, 'Ulster Model Schools', UAHS, 1997, pp ix, 23-27 and back cover; file in IAA.

Former Orphanage, Ballygowan

152. A rather surprising feature in the middle of a little settlement of very moderate charm. In itself, more of a curiosity than a building of architectural merit: a rather grim blackstone edifice of 1866 of four storeys and eleven bays, with crow-stepped gables and central clock-tower, amidst a sea of tarmac. Bassett, in 1886, says, a little enigmatically, "The village consists of about 25 houses, exclusive of the building recently put up by Mr. A. O. Reid in memory of his only son. It is constructed of blue stone, relieved by dressings of freestone. A tower in the centre is surmounted by a square white stone, beneath which, in large letters, it is impressively intimated that THE TIME IS SHORT. Notwithstanding the force of the inscription,

a great deal of time has been spent in controversy concerning the disposition of the building". It seems that Mr Reid's son had been tragically killed in a shooting accident. It soon outlived its original purpose; was used for some years as a school; then a health centre; now as Presbyterian church hall. Extensively restored in 1982, and again in 1995.

Photograph: A C W Merrick.
Situation: Comber Road, Ballygowan; td, Ballygowan; District Council, Ards; Grid ref. J 432 638.
References Listed B (24/16/7). Inscription; Bassett, 'County Down', 1886, p 281; UA, February/March 1996, p 43.

Gilmore's Pub, Kircubbin

153. An attractive old pub-front, apparently of about 1830, in the main street of Kircubbin village, with Georgian-glazed bow windows on either side of the entrance doorway, said to have been brought from Liverpool many years ago; "H Gilmore & Sons" in outstandingly good relief lettering across the fascia-board above. This forms the left-hand part of a two-storey seven-bay range, stuccoed and painted, with ornamented window surrounds; the right-hand section is today the owner's residence from which, unfortunately the elegant fanlight shown in the Green photograph has disappeared; in the middle, a broad coach-arch (now, but apparently not when the Green photograph was taken) gives access to two spacious yards divided by two more two-storey ranges of pleasant stone out-buildings, in turn giving access to the fields at the rear.

Gordon Wheeler suggests that what has happened is, that the block was originally built as two units, of four and three bays respectively - one for the pub, the other for the adjoining shop - "note how, in the Green photograph, the shop door and the grand doorcase share the same step ... What has happened is that the pub frontage has been shortened by the removal of the original entrance to the owner's upstairs accommodation, in order to widen the delivery arch beside it into a larger carriage arch. The original lettering has been admirably redeployed on the present shorter fascia-board. The original small shop next door to the pub has become the unfortunate modern window ... The whole block has obviously been pulled together at some stage by the addition of the ornamental window architraves". (It looks as if this happened in 1926, when the valuation suddenly rose from £11 to £26). These premises served a great number of purposes: public-house, farmhouse, auctioneer, and, according to Bassett in 1886, coal merchant, spirit grocer, timber merchant, and seller of seeds and manures.

The house is said to be one of the oldest in the village, and the family that has occupied house, pub, and farm for six generations acquired it around 1850 from one John Boal who, according to the present owner, "came to grief and emigrated to America". Boal, however, is not amongst the names shown in the Valuation book compiled in December 1836. But - though this is conjecture - this might well be the 'Public House and Carman's Store' occupied by Robert Miller, valued at £6 16 8: "There is a good yard and gateway to this concern and a garden worth 15/- a year. This house is one of the best situations in town and is well established altho an old house". In 1869, the house, offices, yard and garden occupied by Hugh Gilmore (under lease from William Kelly) increased in value from £7 10 0 to £11. The valuation was unchanged in 1878, except that a new weigh-bridge here attracted an additional valuation of £9. So matters remained until 1926, when the weigh-bridge was struck out, and the value of the licensed house, offices and yard occupied by the representatives of Hugh Gilmore, deceased, under lease from Thomas Maxwell, shot up to £26.

According to the family tombstones in Lisbane (17) graveyard, the first to live here was Denis Gilmore (d 1861); then his son Hugh (d 1888); then his son John (d 1922); then his son John (d 1993, aged 83); his son, the present owner, being named John Gerard to distinguish him from his father.

These buildings may well date from the beginning of the 19th century, or even earlier; they certainly appear on the 1834 Ordnance Survey map; though the present stuccoed appearance is presumably much later. The Ordnance Survey memoir (undated, but probably of around 1836) says "In the town there are 88 2-storey houses, 33 1-storey houses and 5 3-storey houses" ... "On some of the oldest houses in the town there is the date of 1769, previous to which there were only a few small cabins" ... "The best houses in the town have been erected within the last 15 years. Others are at present building, both of brick and stone" ... "Grocers and spirit sellers 17, cabinet maker 1, bakers 2, woollen drapers 2, nailer 1" ... "The town is noted for making straw bonnets. The straw is sent from England. When made up they are sent to England, Belfast and Dublin". But Samuel Lewis, in 1837, writes: "The town ... is of very recent origin, having been built since the year 1790, previously to which there were not more than five houses in this place ... The present town contains 117 houses, for the greater part neatly built".

At present, the façade is very nicely painted: cream walls, green quoins, architraves and trim, gilt lettering, brown glazing-bars and sashes, all very much in the early-Victorian tradition, though the previous white-painted glazing-bars in the Georgian manner had something going for them, too. Most unusually, the premises retain, inside and out, the pleasing character of a simple country-town inn: the present owner wisely eschews plastic, garish paint, fruit machines, noise machines, and the other paraphernalia of the modernised pub. Warmly recommended to the passer-by who seeks a quiet drink in traditional surroundings.

Photographs: A C W Merrick; W A Green, UFTM, WAG 1837.
Situation: 46 and 48 Main Street, Kircubbin, td, Kircubbin; District Council, Ards; Grid ref. J 598 627.
References: Surprisingly, not listed, although several of its (to me, less interesting) neighbours are. VAL 1B/311B, p 122, VAL 12B/23/19A-F, in PRONI; OS map, 1834; G Scott, OSM, nd (?1836), Down , II, p 84; Lewis, TD, 1837, II, p 235; Bassett, 'County Down', 1886, p 363; information from owner.

Cunningburn Milltown, Newtownards

154. An intriguing group, comprising an 18th-century water-powered corn mill; a thatched miller's cottage, perhaps of the same date; a corn kiln; a somewhat later steam-powered flax scutching mill, with chimney; steam engine house; and stores.

The corn mill was powered by water from the Cunning Burn, impounded in a mill dam, and had a wooden high breast-shot waterwheel. It is of two storeys, of random Scrabo stone, and originally (but alas, no longer) a roof of graduated Scrabo slates. The building is set into quite a steep slope, so access is available from two levels. In the keystone over the upstairs entrance are inscribed the words A 1776 W HARRIS MILLER; above the lower entrance, 1776 BT BY AS. The mill ceased working about 1932; the present owner of the cottage was born there, his father having been the last miller. The corn mill has now been ingeniously converted into a two-storey house, incorporating as 'features' much of its original machinery, including a remarkable revolving glass table set on top of the mill wheel. Two millstones stand outside; the original roof-timbers are visible in the interior. Whilst this is a very creditable conversion, the effect is rather spoilt by the fussy layout of low walls and plantings between the mill and the road.

G Scott of the Ordnance Survey reports, in about 1835, "In the townland of Cunningburn there is a flax mill belonging to John Cooper. Diameter of wheel 15 feet, breadth 3 feet, fall of water 4 feet, breast wheel. There is a second flax mill, diameter of wheel 12 feet, breadth 4 feet, fall of water 4 feet, breast wheel. Corn mill, in the same townland, diameter of wheel 12 feet, breadth 2 and a half feet, fall of water 5 feet, breast wheel. The 3 mills belong to John Cooper. They are on the same water. There is not a sufficiency of water in the summer season and the little there is is said to be frequently cut off before it reaches the mills". No wonder it was subsequently found convenient to add the steam engine. This is borne out by the copious (indeed, duplicated?) entries in the Valuation books. In 1836 John Cooper alone is shown as owner of flax mill, miller's house, and store, valued at £3 19 6, with the note "water 5 months in the year"; whilst the corn mill, kiln, turf house, and kiln man's house were valued at £8 13 0,

occupied by John Cooper and Thomas Robinson, with the note " pair of stones to this mill, one for grinding, one for shelling, one new and the other old; metal machinery near new, value £20 ... water 9 months in the year. 5 townlands are bound to this mill" - i.e. required to use the mill, under leases from Lord Londonderry. At this date, Cooper and Robinson also had a windmill in the townland: according to Rodney Green, there were two windmills in the townland, one pre-1810, and the other post-1834 but pre-1859. By 1861, the concern was jointly owned, as to two-thirds by Hugh Cooper, one-third by John Robinson; total value, including "Flax steam mill", £37 10 0; "£100 per annum paid for these mills and 24 acres". By 1878 the flax mill had been struck out as "in ruins". Before 1878, the concern had been taken over by John and David Warden, ancestors of the present owner of the cottage, and valued, with the mill pond, at £45.

The miller's cottage is, for the Ards, a great rarity: a single-storey white-washed thatched cottage with original Georgian-glazed windows. The windows are much larger than would have been usual in a simple Georgian cottage, leading to the query whether the cottage might not be a good deal later than the mill; though the owner thinks not.

It is of 8 bays, with two half-doors in the doorways (the cottage was sub-divided on the marriage of the present owner's father, but is now one again). There is a slated stable range alongside. The rear slope of the roof is in fact slated, though you would never know it; the front was last rethatched about 1988. All is very spick and span, and kept blessedly simple.

The present flax scutching mill buildings and chimney are apparently considerably later, probably dating from the 1860s when the linen trade reached its peak of prosperity. The stone and slated mill, kiln, and stores have also been converted, sensitively, into a two-storey dwelling. The very tall, tapering square chimney is of mellow red brick, and in good repair.

Photograph: A C W Merrick.
Situation: Cottage, 10 Cunningburn Road, Newtownards; td, Cunningburn Milltown; District Council, Ards; Grid ref. J 535 713.
References: Corn mill, listed B1, cottage, listed B1/Q, flax mill, engine house and chimney, listed B (24/8/1/A, B and C). Datestones; VAL 1B/34 p 193, VAL 2B/3/6A, p 48, VAL 12B/23/21A-E, in PRONI; G Scott, OSM, nd (?1835) Down, II, p 104; Green, 'Industrial archaeology', 1963, pp 39, 54; F W Hamond, notes in MBR, 1988; information from owners.

Ballycopeland Windmill, Millisle

155. The only working windmill in the whole of Ireland - though it is only worked on exceptional occasions. Acquired in 1935 from Samuel McGilton, the last miller, when "Major structural repairs to the cap and sails were necessary"; after twenty years of disuse, further restored very painstakingly between 1950 and 1959 under the supervision of the eminent conservation architect, Harold Meek; brought back into working order, "involving highly skilled and specialised replacement of iron and wooden parts and refurbishing of the sails" (Hamlin) in the 1980s.

A picturesque whitewashed mill (in some need of repainting at the time of writing), built probably about 1785. Rodney Green says that "as a result of damage by dry rot and wood worm, extensive repairs, involving replacement of all the structural timbers, and some of the lighter wooden machinery, were carried out between 1958 and 1959 by the Ministry of Finance, Northern Ireland ... The walls of Silurian masonry are 2ft. thick. The mill was underdrift, i.e. the spur wheel drove the three pairs of wheels from below. The brake wheel is of wood with iron cogs, ss is the spur wheel, while the stone nuts are wooden cogged". According to a note in the Monuments and Buildings Record, "In 1832 it passed into the hands of the McGilton family who held it for a century before presenting it to the government". The miller's house, office, windmill, corn kiln, two pairs of stones, and machinery were valued at £4 11 8 in 1836; at £11 in 1861.

"Windmills were once common in grain-growing E Down, but all except Ballycopeland are now ruined. Built probably in the 1780s, it was worked by the McGilton family until the 1914-18 war and from the 1950s to 1978 was restored to full working order. The mill is approached past the kiln house ... It is a tower mill, the cap with the sails moving on a 'dead curb' and kept into the eye of the wind by the fantail. The top floor has the hoppers into which the grain was emptied, falling to the stones floors below, where there are three pairs of grind stones. Below again is the drive floor where the drive from the central shaft is transferred to the stones, and finally the ground floor where the grain began and ended its journey. Hulls were collected in and cleared from the dusthouse adjoining the mill" (HMNI).

The interior of the mill is very cramped, with steep wooden ladders from floor to floor, almost all the space being taken up by the noisy and shuddering machinery. "Ballycopeland was a provender mill producing oatmeal and wheatmeal for human consumption, but not flour, and a variety of animal feedstuffs" (HMSO guidebook). The adjoining miller's house, incorporating the kilnhouse, has also been restored most successfully as a display area: externally, it has red-brick dressings and whitewashed walls. The group is most attractive, though rather spoiled by a very ill-placed, ugly and intrusive modern bungalow just across the road - however did the Planning Service come to permit this?

Photograph: from Green, 'Industrial archaeology', pl 20.
Situation: One mile west of Millisle on Newtownards Road; td, Ballycopeland; District Council, Ards; Grid ref. J 579 761
References: Monument in state care (DOW 006:500). VAL 1B/32, p 117, VAL 2B/3/3A, p 49, in PRONI; Green, 'Industrial archaeology',1963, p 53, and fig. 3; HMSO guidebook, 1962; HMNI, 1983, p 109; A Hamlin, DoENI, guidecard, 1985; notes in MBR.

Liddell's Mill, Donaghcloney

the pit of a water wheel. As early as 1742 this property was in the possession of a linen draper, Marmaduke Dempster. It was sold in 1808 by David Dempster and leased by the purchaser to John Brown (1770-1834) who bought it outright four years later. John Brown's son, also John, died at the age of forty in 1837, leaving a brother and a four-teen-year old son, John Shaw Brown. Around this time, the bleachworks were valued at £40 and consisted of two beetling mills, boiling house, wash house and drying loft all worked by three water wheels of about 15 ft. in diameter. The business was 'in full work'. John Brown's executors sold part of the property, Robert G Nicholson of Banoge purchasing the bleachgreen and Donaghcloney House. James Brown continued to carry on his brother's business, and in 1840 he employed 250 damask weavers. When he died in 1851 all his land was sold to Nicholson. In 1855 William Liddell, a cousin of the Nicholsons of Banoge, went into partnership with John Shaw Brown. This lasted until 1866 when Brown withdrew to build the St. Ellen works at Edenderry near Belfast. "A power-loom factory was set up by Robert Nicholson's Moorhead brothers-in-law after his death which William Liddell later" (1871) "acquired as well." This factory was built in 1866, and it is recorded that "there was great anxiety lest the old Donaghcloney bridge would collapse under the weight of the huge boiler which was transported by road from Newry" (Liddell).

Atkinson, in 1898, says " "The atmosphere of the locality is now intensely modern, the large damask factory of Messrs. William Liddell & Sons occupying a site on the original meadow or 'clon' immediately adjoining the churchyard, while close at hand the modern village of Donaghcloney has sprung up and increased rapidly in recent years". (For the well-restored mill-workers' houses, see 139). Inexplicably, neither Bassett nor McCutcheon has much to say about Donaghcloney Mill.

The mill's remains are impressive: above all, the magnificent octagonal, tapered brick chimney, 145 feet high, secured by iron tie-bars all the way up, and painted red - it must have been quite a 'smoak' in its day. The boiler-house has now been demolished to make way for a car-park; but the office block of 1898, three bays wide and five bays deep, still survives with its formal pedimented door-case and oculi; as does the very much earlier range, with an 1813 datestone, originally of 16 bays and three storeys with very tall windows to light the workspace within, now somewhat altered, but not irreparably.

156. One of the very few linen mills in Ulster still, in part at least, serving its original purpose. On 1 December, 1708, John Magill of Gill Hall leased to David Dempster of Donaghcloney, Gentleman, a large site in the townland of Donaghcloney for ever, at a yearly rent of £10 18 stg per half-year "together with the yearly duties of Four days work of man and horse or 4/- stg in lieu thereof & one couple of fat hens one for each smoak upon the prems. or one shilling in lieu". It would be interesting to know how the number of 'smoaks' was in practice counted.

Rodney Green, writing in 1963, says "The oldest part of the present works is a stone masonry block, roughcast, 186 ft. long and 24 ft wide and dated 1813. On the ground level are a series of seven old windows with relieving arches over which are probably original. The mill dam lies just behind the block and drove two turbines, one installed in

Photograph: A C W Merrick.

Situation: 53 Main Street, Donaghcloney; td, Donaghcloney; District Council, Craigavon; Grid ref. J 130 533.

References: Not listed. Copy lease of 1708 in possession of Donacloney Housing Association; datestone; VAL 1B, 340, p 42, in PRONI; Atkinson, 'Ulster parish', 1898, p 80; Green, 'Industrial archaeology', 1963, pp 12, 24; William Liddell, unpublished ms history; information from Donacloney Housing Association.

Lime Kilns, Clare Hill, Moira

157. Samuel Lewis writes that Moira " ... is at the western termination of a ridge of white limestone; there are many kilns always at work, and vast quantities of the stone in its natural state are annually sent away by the canal, and by land carriage, to distant parts". Limestone was used for building; burned lime was used for mortar, for plaster, for colour-washes, and as a fertiliser. According to Scally, over twelve thousand lime kilns were shown on the OS maps of the 1830s in the six counties that are now Northern Ireland; less than a dozen limestone quarries are still in use, though Hamond remarks that powdered lime is still used "in a wide range of products such as paint, putty, cosmetics, linoleum, toothpaste and even flour". It is surprising that neither Green nor McCutcheon discusses the limestone industry, once so very substantial; though McCutcheon does illustrate this group of buildings.

The Clare Hill kilns must be amongst the largest and most impressive to survive. In his description in the Monuments and Buildings Record, Scally says "The kiln block is of monumental proportions ... built of limestone blocks set in regular courses, and is cut into the end of a small hill or ridge, thus allowing access from above ... The four draw-hole arches and pots are of brick and virtually intact. The arches are 3.0 m. wide x 3.3 m. high; these measurements can only give an impression of the size of the kiln block. From the top, one can look down into the brick-lined pots. A huge amount of fuel alternately layered with quarried rock would have been needed to fill each one for firing". The three-storey store next door is also stone; the manager's house, likewise of stone, may be somewhat later, as it is not bonded into the store. These two buildings, presently, have corrugated iron roofs. The official description in the Monuments and Buildings Record runs "Disused lime kilns with high retaining wall in coursed stone with sneck-filled joints and containing four fine semi-circular arches to kilns, which are framed in diminishing arched brick. Adjoining 3-storey stone buildings with rubble and brick walls and corrugated iron roof. Appears to be mid 19th century".

This estimate of date is corroborated by the Valuation books: there is no reference to kilns or buildings in the book for 1834; but by the Griffith valuation of 1862, James Hammond is shown as the lessee of "four kilns, well built, chalk quarry", valued at £150, but (ominously) quickly revalued downwards to £120. Worse was to come: in 1868 they were further devalued to £90; then, in 1876, by which date George Nelson had taken them over, to £60 - with an almost indecipherable note, justifying the reduction, which seems to read "Rent reduced from £140 to £120. The quarry has very deep top upon it - hard to work". It looks as if this was an injudicious investment by Sir Thomas Bateson, who built (or allowed his lessee to build) too ambitious a bank of kilns at a site where the stone was buried under an uneconomically thick overburden of soil. The site changed tenants several times; by 1904 the Valuation book contains a note "limekilns and quarry disused. Buildings vacant. Not worked for 3 years". So far as the valuation records show, they were never again worked thereafter: but they were so well built that they are still in fine order. A proposal to turn the store and manager's house into self-catering holiday accommodation was approved in 1994, but not pursued for reasons of cost. It is greatly to be hoped that some means of restoring this exceptionally fine piece of the industrial heritage can be found.

Photograph: A C W Merrick.

Situation: Clare Hill Road, Moira; td, Clare; District Council, Lisburn; Grid ref. J 158 602.

References: Listed B1 (19/22/45). VAL 1B/347; VAL 2B/3/47A, p 36; VAL 12B/21/7 A-E, in PRONI; Lewis, TD, II, 1837, p 377; OS map, 1858; McCutcheon, 'Industrial archaeology', 1980, pls 138.2, 139.3; Hamond, 'Antrim coast and glens", 1991, p 26; C P Scally, in 'Perspective', November/December 1995, p 59; C P Scally and F W Hamond, notes in MBR, 1996.

Home (or Model) Farm, Crawfordsburn

158. A most uncommon group of buildings, of uncertain origin. Originally, it seems, the ambitious range of farm buildings built around 1890 for Lt Col. Sharman Crawford of Crawfordsburn House, which was the predecessor of the large and ugly new house built for him in 1906; now, due to disproportionate enlargements, even uglier than before. The buildings, none of them apparently originally residential, were arranged round a square central stone-paved courtyard, in a manner rather reminiscent of a French *grange*. They appear to have included a corn-mill as well as barns, byres, stables and tack-rooms. When the big house was sold to become a hospital in 1946, the

model farm and surrounding fields were retained in the Crawford estate and let out to agricultural tenants. Eventually, the buildings were allowed to fall into disrepair; in 1987, the section overlooking the sea was converted into two quite large houses, and in the following year the section fronting the road was converted into two smaller ones. Apart from the insertion of unsuitable plastic window-frames, the conversions have been quite sensitively handled. The water-tank in the tower has been removed, and an extra bedroom with a splendid view over the fields and down to the sea provided instead: it is reached by a spiral iron staircase (by Macfarlanes of Glasgow) which came from the Crown Bar in Belfast.

The former farm buildings now comprise an extensive two-storey quadrangle round the central yard: of sharply-cut red brick, with 'stockbrokers' Tudor' black-and-white geometrical timbered gables; a wide entrance archway, topped by a gable and then a square water-tower, with pyramidal roof, and at the summit weather-vane and two curious pinnacles. The origins, and early uses, of the group are obscure. The old Valuation books are of no help, since presumably all enjoyed the benefit of agricultural de-rating.

Its architectural authorship is a puzzle. Patton, who seems not much impressed by it, says "Home farm: c 1890: Single storey" (*sic*) "red brick building with half-timbered gables forming a formal courtyard in front of outbuildings. Square tower with weathercock and pyramidal roof"; but suggests no attribution, though Crawfordsburn House itself was apparently, according to him, rebuilt by Vincent Craig in 1906, replacing earlier houses of 1780 and 1820. One might have expected the architect of the new house to have been the architect of the slightly earlier farm buildings; and stylistically, this is not impossible, though I do not think the sophisticated Vincent Craig cared much for 'stockbrokers' Tudor'. Hugh Dixon's generally very reliable notes in the Monuments and Buildings Record suggest that the group is by Graeme Watt and Tulloch. Dean, too, says of the Home Farm gate lodge, "c 1900; architects Watt and Tulloch. To an ornamental Edwardian farmyard complex this complementary one and a half storey lodge in similar half timbered Arts-and-Crafts style. From a pyramidal roofed main body projects a 'black and white' gabled upper attic jettying out beyond the red brick ground floor". The whole matter is further complicated by a card in Hugh Dixon's handwriting in the exiguous Graeme Watt and Tulloch file in the Monuments and Buildings Record, referring to "Farm Buildings, Entrance Block, Cattle Byre, Cottage and Agent's House for Lt Col Sharman Crawford" and citing document D 1898/1/32 in the Public Record Office; but that document appears to relate to Belfast Gas Showrooms. My own suggestion is that it might be by Berkeley D Wise, to whom is generally attributed the surprisingly similar, though now demolished, Portrush Railway Station of 1893, but this is conjecture: I know of no documentary evidence to support the attribution.

Anyhow, unfashionable as it may be to do so, I like and admire this enigmatic group of buildings very much.

Photographs: A C W Merrick.
Situation: Sharman Manor, Crawfordsburn Road, Bangor; td, Ballykillaire; District Council, North Down; Grid ref. J 473 817.
References: Not listed. IB, XLVI, 1904, p 772; W D Girvan, 'North Antrim', UAHS, 1972, pp 12-14; Dean, 'Gate lodges', UAHS, 1994, p 71; Patton, 'Bangor', UAHS, 1999, p 59; file in MBR; information from Denis Templeton.

Former Shop, Loan Ends, Dromara

159. The listers say "circa 1770, renovated circa 1820: two storey substantial farmhouse with late Georgian detailing but it is quite possible that this has been the result of modernising an earlier building. The end bay was a shop ... a good example of its type with the added interest of the 19th century shop interior and the unusual windows, divided into four panes in the width as well as the height of each". Oram says "It could easily have been a posting inn but we have no evidence". Piggott says "Smooth painted render to front and sides, with quoins painted on. Slates. Two 16-pane shop windows, otherwise 8-pane sashes ... Last used as a shop 60 or 70 years ago, but most of the original fittings have been left untouched ... The house occupies a very prominent position at the cross roads and is a very attractive building".

A cheerfully straightforward two-storey four-bay house, its stucco presently painted pale grey, with white-painted window surrounds and glazing bars, and (my favourite) beautifully painted *trompe-l'oeil* geometrical quoins in three well-chosen colours. A little let down by the modern un-stuccoed brick chimneys, and by the modern doorway and sidelights; but these are not irreversible.

Photograph: A C W Merrick.
Situation: 189 Ballynahinch Road, Loan Ends; td, Ballykeel; District Council, Lisburn; Grid ref. J 274 529.
References: Listed B1 (19/7/24).OS map, 1833; R Oram and D Piggott, undated notes in MBR.

Former Belfast Bank, Newtownards

160. The most architecturally accomplished building in Newtownards: a very fine Venetian-Gothic ashlar stone building in the centre of the town, by W H Lynn of Lanyon & Lynn, much under the influence of John Ruskin's Stones of Venice. As Hugh Dixon says, "all the windows group together in the middle of the facades just like those of Venetian Palaces along the canal fronts". Almost square, two-storey, with a pyramidal roof rising to a single broad stone chimney-stack; the eaves borne on dentils above a barley-sugar moulding; a row of five linked Gothic cusped and ogee-headed arches in the upper floor, the central one blank but for a rosette, containing the arms of Belfast, motto, and the date 1855. Further rosettes between the pinnacles of the arches, which are topped by bearded heads (bank directors, or perhaps executed bank robbers, Gordon Wheeler suggests); below, a similar three bay arrangement minus the heads; the entrance by a single-storey gabled porch at one side; a set-back bay on the other side; delicious vertical barley-sugar colonettes marking the corners of the principal block, a most elegant way of turning the corners.

Very similar to, but not identical with, the Dungannon, County Tyrone, branch of 1854-5, in squared rubble-stone, the contract drawings for which dated 4 June 1855 "are witnessed by W H Lynn, the contractor being John Lowry". In this case, there are four linked central windows below, three above; but flanked, at a distance, by cusped ogee doorway and smaller window below, single windows above; only one rosette, placed between the storeys; but the same sticks of barley-sugar at the corners and in the coved eaves cornice. Though the detailing may differ, the massing of both banks is the same; each has what Oram and Rankin call a "superbly robust low-built wide central chimney-stack"; and they must be accounted amongst the most important buildings in Northern Ireland from an architectural point of view, and amongst W H Lynn's very best. Whilst the lettering of the present owners is reasonably congruous and unobtrusive, the same cannot be said of their pink and blue logo.

Photograph: A C W Merrick.
Situation: Regent Street, Newtownards; td, Corporation North; District Council, Ards; Grid ref. J 489 742.
References: Listed B1 (24/13/59) - should that not be A? Datestone; Oram and Rankin, 'Dungannon & Cookstown', UAHS, 1971, pp 8, 21; Dixon, 'Introduction', UAHS, 1975, p 61.

Shaw's Bridge, Drumbo

161. It may be assumed that at any rate one-half of Shaw's Bridge, over the River Lagan, is in County Down: a county not, on the whole, noted for bridges of any great significance, perhaps because it boasts not many rivers of any great significance: apart from the Lagan and the Bann, both of which it shares with other counties. The Lagan, however, rises on the slopes of Slieve Croob, above Ballynahinch; not, as the Laganside Commissioners reprehensibly assert in their Lagan Look-out in Central Belfast, in the Mourne Mountains.

"Shaw's Bridge was one of several where the towpath not only did not pass under the arches but also changed to the opposite side of the river. A barge travelling up or downstream had to be unhitched, the horse walked over the bridge, and the barge re-hitched on the other side. This presented no problem as the horse soon learned to do

what was expected of him" (Blair).

This must have been an early fording-point. Timber piles found here, when the adjacent concrete dual carriageway bridge was being built, have been dated by dendrochronology to 1617: and there are some traces of defensive fortifications on either bank. Carleton asserts that, in 1655, Captain Shaw, an artificer in Cromwell's train of artillery, "laid a bridge of bawk oak timbre and palles. A platforme of oak spares" in order to get the army's gun carriages across the river. But alas, his authority for this quotation is the highly dubious Colin Johnston Robb. Yet it is shown as "Shawe's Bridge" on Sir William Petty's Down Survey map of the Barony of Belfast of about 1657. So perhaps, this time, Robb may (cautiously) be trusted.

In 1691, Thomas Burgh, "Third Engineer of Fortification", is said to have rebuilt it in stone. According to

Pakenham-Walsh, Burgh was appointed to the Irish Engineers only in February 1691: if so, this must be the first recorded work of the distinguished Surveyor-General and architect; but it is not mentioned in Rolf Loeber's 1981 biography. However, his bridge was washed away in a flood in 1709. When rebuilt, after this flood, Shaw's Bridge had six arches; so it cannot be the present one, which has five. George Benn, the historian of Belfast, wrote in 1823 "Shaw's Bridge ... crosses the Lagan three miles from Belfast, and is much stronger than those which are commonly found on private roads. This bridge is of some antiquity, and was built with ruins of an old castle in the neighbourhood. There is also a traditional account, that it was carried away by a great flood in the year 1709". The old castle to which Benn refers was in all probability 'Hilsborowe', the early 17th-century fort and house of Sir Moses Hill which had been destroyed in 1641.

Pithily described by the Archaeological Survey of County Down: "This plain, rubble-built structure, spanning the river Lagan above Belfast, may have been built at the end of the 17th century. It is of five semi-elliptical arched spans, built on plank centering, with triangular cutwaters stopped well below road level. The plain parapet has been rebuilt". It has attracted surprisingly little attention from local historians. O'Keeffe and Simington remark that "Before the construction of the Old Long Bridge at the mouth of the Lagan this was the lowest bridge crossing. On the Down Survey 1656 there are no

less than seven bridges shown across the river between Belfast Lough and Magheralin, a length of 15 miles. This concentration no doubt resulted from the funnelling of northbound traffic from a a 50-mile wide band (Armagh - Downpatrick) into the neck of land between Lough Neagh and Belfast" - and add : "Given the scarcity of survivors from this period, it is hoped that all its characteristics will be measured and recorded in the near future". Dr Michael Gould says "It can only be said with certainty that the present bridge, now preserved as part of a pedestrian path, dates from the early 18th century. It is a pleasing example of the early bridge-builder's art". Now an attractive feature of the Lagan Valley Park, though considerably overshadowed by the roaring traffic over the new bridge, nearby, carrying the Belfast Outer Ring Road.

Photographs: MBR, A C W Merrick.
Situation: Milltown Road, Drumbo; td, Ballynavalley; District Council, Castlereagh; Grid ref. J 325 690.
References: Listed B1 (25/17/1). W Petty, Down Survey map, c. 1657, T 2313/1/17, in PRONI; Benn, 'History of Belfast', 1823, p 168; W P Pakenham-Walsh, in 'Royal Engineers' journal', VI, 1907, pp 69-74; ASCD, 1966, p 440; T Carleton, in UJA, 3rd series, XXXIX, 1976, pp 62,64,67; Blair, 'Once upon the Lagan', 1994, pp 9-10; Loeber, 'Biographical dictionary', 1981, pp 31-39; O'Keeffe and Simington,'Irish stone bridges', 1991, p 229; M Gould, in UA, August 1994, p 41.

Newmill Bridge, Moira

162. Present, though unnamed, on Oliver Sloane's manuscript map of 1739, but possibly reconstructed in the later 18th century. Messrs J R Ward and T C McIlroy of the Ordnance Survey write in 1837: "New Mill bridge over the River Lagan is 55 feet long and 23 feet 6 inches broad. It is built of whinstone and freestone and consists of 3 semi-circular arches" - though in fact all three are segmental-headed - with angled cutwaters both upstream and downstream, the parapets with square granite copings.

There are numerous subsidiary streams and watercourses in the vicinity - and, formerly, the Lagan canal - running through a broad flat flood-plain to the Clare Hill kilns and quarry (157) at the foot of the hill upon

which Moira is built. Hamond remarks "With its rubble stonework and lack of embellishment, the bridge has the appearance of having been constructed in the 18th century (the designation 'new' implying later, rather than earlier)". However this may be, it is an attractive element in an otherwise rather featureless landscape.

Photograph: A C W Merrick.
Situation: On Clare Hill Road, Moira; tds, Aughandrumman and Bottier; District Council, Lisburn; Grid ref. J 163 598.
References: Listed B (19/22/46). O Sloane, map of County Down, 1739, in Linen Hall Library; Taylor and Skinner, 'Roads', 1778, p 285; OS map, 1833; J R Ward and T C McIlroy, OSM, 1837, Down, III, p 119; Oram, 'Craigavon', UAHS, 1971, Pt II, p11; F W Hamond, notes in MBR, 1994.

High Bridge and Lock House, Ballyskeagh, Drumbeg

163. Both built by Thomas Omer, canal engineer, between 1759 and 1763, as part of only the second canal in the British Isles, these two structures are inextricably connected: but you might not think it today, when the trees have grown up to conceal their proper relationship, and a new (in some ways very welcome) foot-bridge was in 1995 rather incongruously inserted into the landscape, the canal having, unhappily, been closed in 1956. (Perhaps it may yet be reopened). The symbiosis between the two is well demonstrated in the very accurate drawings by William Wallace Legge in his sketchbook of 1816.

The original road from Belfast to Lisburn here crosses the canal, at a high level, over a curious S-shaped path. There are two semi-circular stone arches, one broad (over the canal), one narrow (over the towpath). The bridge is of squared, reddish, sandstone, with two string-courses. Fred Hamond remarks, "wear marks of the barge tow ropes are

visible along the edges of the central pier", and sums up the significance of the bridge: "Historically it is of interest on account of its mid-eighteenth century construction date ... Architecturally, it is arguably the most impressive canal bridge, in terms of scale and proportion, to survive in the province. Finally, it makes a very significant impact on the landscape hereabouts".

Just above the bridge, on the hill-top, stands the lock-keeper's house, built to serve the eighth lock on the Lagan Navigation. There are 34 steps down to the canal: as Michael Gould remarks, "It is understood that, before the trees grew up, good views were to be had in both directions, thus allowing the keeper time to get from his house to his lock when boats came. Truly a job for a keep fit fanatic!"

It is an exceptionally attractive little two-storey stone building, in Omer's inimitable idiom, to be seen also in the similar lock-keeper's house at nearby Drum Bridge in

County Antrim: "square in plan and of two floors, built of ... rubble with wrought dressings; the roof is slated ... At the centre of each elevation is a recess, with semicircular arched head with key-block, rising from the platband; on the N, the recess contains a door with block architrave and square head formed of stepped and projecting voussoirs, the keystone rising to the level of the platband which is continuous across the recess; the recesses on the other elevations contain windows" (Archaeological Survey of County Down). Under threat of demolition for many years; eventually admirably restored in 1992-3 by Hearth Revolving Fund, rebuilding the original brick end gables in stone; now prettily colour-washed and painted, and a real ornament to the Lagan valley.

Photograph: A C W Merrick. Wood-engraving: from 'Twenty-one views in Belfast', 1836. Drawing: W W Legge, Lisburn Museum.
Situation: On Ballyskeagh Road, Drumbeg; td, Ballyskeagh; District Council, Lisburn; Grid ref. J 288 669.
References: Bridge, listed B (19/9/7), lock-keeper's house, listed B1, 17/9/3); House of Commons, Ireland, 'Journal', XI, p 283, 14 November, 1759; W W Legge, unpublished sketchbook, 1816, photocopies in Lisburn Museum; Green, 'Industrial archaeology', 1963, p 74; ASCD, 1966, p 441; M Gould, in UA, April/May, 1995, p 5; Hearth, 'Review of projects', 1999, pp 15, 41; F W Hamond, notes in MBR.

Banoge Bridge, Donaghcloney

164. Spanning the River Lagan, one of the prettiest bridges in the county, due largely to its setting between wooded banks, just downstream of a horseshoe-shaped weir, and the village of Donaghcloney.

The authoritative and reliable Fred Hamond says "The bridge's appearance suggests an 18th century date. Although neither Harris (1743) nor Taylor & Skinner (1777) depict a road across the Lagan at this point, this may simply reflect an imprecision of survey, rather than a real absence. It is possibly associated with the erection of the nearby Banoge flour mill in the 1760s" (i.e. 1764 - Green) "... The bridge comprises three semi-circular spans, with angled cutwaters on its up and down sides (terminating at arch-top level). It is of rubble basalt throughout, with split stone voussoirs. The central arch is higher than those at either side, giving the carriageway a hump. The parapets are coped with large blocks of squared granite. The extended approach on the left bank accommodates a tailrace from the nearby mill".

Photograph: A C W Merrick (see also colour illus. 36).
Situation: On Hall Road, Donaghcloney; td, Banoge; District Council, Craigavon; Grid ref. J 123 538.
References: Listed B (14/7/7). OS map, 1833; Green, 'Industrial archaeology', 1963, p 46; Oram, 'Craigavon'. UAHS, 1971, Pt II, pp 4, 11; F W Hamond, notes in MBR, 1994.

Wolfenden's Bridge, Drumbeg

165. Hamond calls it "a good example of earlier 18th century bridge architecture. It is particularly impressive on account of its nine spans, and lends considerable character to the riverscape". Five of the segmental-headed arches span the river, four are flood arches on the County Antrim side. The bridge is built of basalt and sandstone rubble, with triangular cutwaters both upstream and downstream. There is no bridge shown here on Mol's map of 1714, but it is present on Oliver Sloane's manuscript map of 1739, although unnamed. The fact that a bridge is marked on Sir William Petty's Down Survey map of 1657 would suggest, in view of the difficulties experienced by King William recorded below, that an earlier wooden structure had collapsed.

Thomas Fagan of the Ordnance Survey, in the autumn of 1837, wrote: " That bridge across the Lagan a short distance north of the village of Lambeg and locally called Wolfenden's bridge, has 9 half-circle arches; span of each arch 15 feet, breadth of the road on the bridge 18 feet; average height of parapets 2 feet 6 inches, thickness of parapets 1 foot 4 inches; length of the bridge 52 yards, length of parapets on either side of the road 120 yards. The bridge and parapets are built of whinstone and seem in permanent condition at present. It is said to be a very old bridge. However, William III, in travelling to Lisburn, 1688, crossed from the county Down into the county Antrim by a ford on the site of the above bridge. It would seem that his carriage sustained some injury in crossing the ford, for in ascending a hill in the road a little to the south of it, his carriage broke down. It is rather singular that one of the Royal Family of Russia, in travelling the same line of road to Lisburn about 20 years ago, had his carriage broken down on the same site where King William's carriage broke down nearly 130 years previous".

A slightly different version of events is given in an unsigned article in 1852 in the Ulster Journal of Archaeology: "As the King passed through the village of Lambeg, near Lisburn, he was addressed in French by Rene Bulmer, a Huguenot, who had fled from France ... and settled in the neighbourhood of this village". Bulmer sought, and obtained, leave to embrace his Majesty; who thereupon, "stooping from his horse towards Bulmer's wife, a pretty Frenchwoman, said 'and thy wife also' and saluted her heartily. The King stopped at Lambeg House" (Chrome Hill House: 90) "then belonging to the Wolfendens ... It was necessary to cross the Lagan at this part by an ancient ford, and here one of the waggons broke down, which caused some delay. It was repaired with timber furnished from the neighbouring manufactory of Mr Wolfenden ... Two persons of this name had, at that time, their works at this part of the river; one, on the county Antrim side, manufacturing blankets, the other, on the county Down side making paper: they were originally Germans". Of the Wolfenden family, Rodney Green says "There is a tombstone in Lambeg churchyard dated 1744 on which a Richard Wolfenden is described as a linen draper" ... "By 1809 Richard Wolfenden & Son had added the manufacturing of calicos and muslins. Apparently the Wolfendens went to Dublin in the end and became muslin factors at the Linen Hall".

Photograph: A C W Merrick.
Situation: On Ballyskeagh Road, Drumbeg; td, Ballyskeagh; District Council, Lisburn; Grid ref. J 284 668.
References: Listed B (19/9/8). W Petty, Down Survey map, c. 1657, T 2313/1/17, in PRONI; O Sloane, map of County Down, 1739, in Linen Hall Library; OS map, 1834; T Fagan, OSM, 1837, Antrim, II, p 140; UJA, 1st series, I, 1852, p 135; Green, 'Industrial archaeology', 1963, p 27; F W Hamond, notes in MBR, 1994.

Spencer's Bridge, Moira

166. An impressive long sinuous blackstone bridge, with lengthy stone-walled approach embankments, carrying the old road from Moira to Hillsborough across a bend in the river Lagan through the townland of Inisloughan in County Antrim. On Oliver Sloane's manuscript map of 1739 it appears as Inisloughan Bridge and on Walter Harris's map of 1743 as Spencer's Bridge: it is unclear whether the present structure is the same, or a rebuilding.

Thomas Fagan of the Ordnance Survey provides an uncommonly full description in 1837. He tells us that the Spincers, or Spencers, had built Trummery House, just up the road, in about 1740 (but Sloane's map already shows it standing in 1739). " Spincer's bridge ... has 3 half-circle arches: span of centre arch 22 feet, span of each of the outside arches 21 feet, average width of the road on the bridge 21 feet 6, average height of parapets 4 feet, thickness of parapets 1 foot 6, length of parapets on either side of the road 355 yards, length of the bridge 30 yards. Detached from the bridge on the county Down side stands 3 arches to accommodate in case of high floods in the river. These arches stand at some distance from one another. The span of the west arch of these is 12 feet, span of each of the other two is 7 feet". (These flood arches are now wholly or partially blocked up). "On the county Antrim side of the bridge also stands 2 arches to serve as above, span of each 10 feet ... The main bridge seems in a permanent state of repair. The other arches and the parapets has suffered partial dilapidation.

"The bridge is said to be old, but no accurate account here of the cost, date of building or who the engineer of it was. It is said to be erected at the expense of the 2 counties of Antrim and Down, in which it is equally situate". It has triangular cutwaters both upstream and downstream; dressed sandstone voussoirs; heavy metal strengthening tie-bars; and an unsightly pipe carried along the downstream face. It also has, at the centre of the upstream parapet, a small granite column carved with a coronet and the letter 'D' (presumably for Downshire) and a date, now very difficult to decipher. Harvey Bicker and I thought it read '1818'. But Fred Hamond reads it as 1843, and comments "The bridge's 1843 datestone is somewhat puzzling, as normally this would be taken to signify the bridge's erection date. However, the Ordnance Survey memoir describes the bridge almost exactly as it is today. Indeed, its rubble stone construction and relative lack of embellishment would be more in keeping with a later 18th or early 19th century date, rather than the mid 19th century." So, perhaps the datestone records a repair rather than the original date of building?

Photograph: A C W Merrick.
Situation: On Hillsborough Road, Moira; tds, Ballyknock, Co Down, Inisloughan, Co Antrim; District Council, Lisburn; Grid ref. J 183 603.
References: Listed B (19/22/62). O Sloane, map of County Down, 1739, in Linen Hall Library; map, 1743, in Harris, 'County of Down', 1744; datestone; OS map, 1834; T Fagan, OSM, 1837, Antrim, VII, p 118; Oram, 'Craigavon', UAHS, 1971, Pt II, p 11; F W Hamond, notes in MBR, 1994.

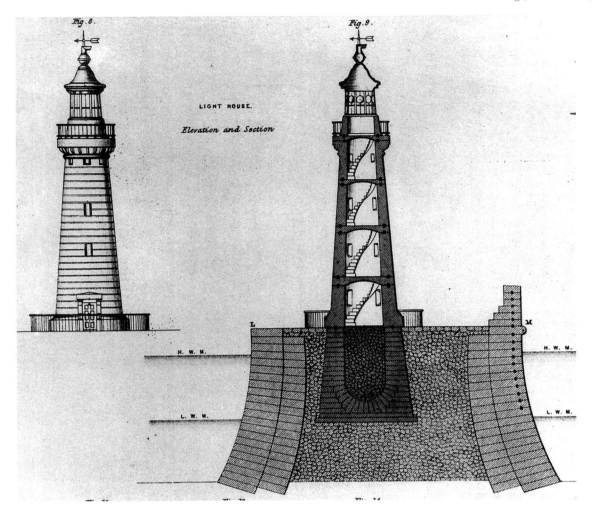

Fig. 8.

LIGHT HOUSE.

Elevation and Section

Fig. 9.

Harbour and Lighthouse, Donaghadee

167. " ... by chance, it has become a rare and important survival, a late Georgian harbour more or less as it was built" (Dixon). It is certainly very attractive and completely unspoiled; the seafront buildings well-scaled and retaining quite a few survivors of merit; any attempt at redevelopment in the contemporary style, marinas, or such-like, should be energetically opposed - and there have been such proposals.

It took from 1821 until 1837 to build the new harbour, which was the port of call of the Portpatrick and Donaghadee mail service until 1849, when Belfast won out, only to be itself superseded in 1867 by the Larne-Stranraer route. An abortive attempt by Government to revive the Portpatrick-Donaghadee service in the 1860s was doomed to failure almost from the start. As Bassett remarks, "For many years the star of Donaghadee was in the ascendant, but it fell when the town ceased to be the landing place for the mails from Scotland. Portpatrick is only 22 miles distant, and at one time it was considered highly improbable that cross-channel mail communication would be found more desirable from any other point. While it was a packet station nearly £300,000 was spent upon harbour works".

In 1814, John Rennie, senior, was commissioned "to make detailed surveys of the coasts on each side of the channel. It was on this work that the younger Rennie, then aged twenty, gained his first experience of surveying ..." John Rennie (senior) "produced a plan ... consisting of two piers, ... and a lighthouse, for an estimated total of £145,000 ... The first stone was laid by the Marquis of

Downshire on 1 August 1821" (Green). "He, however, died within two months of work beginning, and was succeeded by his son John, later Sir John Rennie, who had as his resident engineer a fellow Scot, the seasoned marine builder, David Logan, who had assisted Robert Stevenson at the Bell Rock lighthouse (1807-1810)" (Dixon). The lighthouse was not finished until November 1834. By 1825, the harbour, though incomplete, was usable. "On Saturday, 21st May, 1825, the sea was readmitted to what was identified as the outer basin. The previous evening a celebration was held on the floor of the harbour 'which never after was trodden by the foot of man'". In the same month, "the Dumfries Courier reported that 'On Saturday last [30 April 1825] there arrived at Portpatrick from the Thames, HM steam packets the *Dasher*, Captain Smithett, and the *Arrow*, Captain Pascoe, to be used in the conveyance of the mail between that port and Donaghadee. Both these steam packets are newly and completely fitted out for the service, and afford the most elegant accommodation for passengers'". The two paddle-steamers entered service in May, mainly to provide a daily mail service; cabin passengers being charged a fare of eight shillings, harvestmen and paupers two shillings (MacHaffie).

In March, 1837, M M Kertland of the Ordnance Survey wrote: "The formation of the new harbour has already cost the government 150,000 pounds. It is not yet quite finished, men being at present employed in diving bells, blasting and removing a portion of rock which lies within the harbour at the north pier. It is a very fine one in point of execution and appearance, but fails in giving full satisfaction to nautical men owing to its affording little or no shelter from the northern and north western winds, and being too shallow and confined at low water. A further objection is that it does not afford good anchorage, its bottom being formed of a thin superstratum of mud and sand lying on the bare rock. All the hewn stone used in facing the piers was brought from Wales. It is a kind of limestone and the fragments of it were burned to make lime. The great body of the building is of a stone which is indigenous to the country, but which was, for some reason, deemed unfit for the facing, probably from the difficulty of working it ... A lighthouse is situated on the extremity of the southern pier, showing red lights seaward and lights of the ordinary colour towards land". The Parliamentary Gazetteer, in 1846, ominously comments: "in spite of the recent and exceedingly elaborate and expensive construction of a suitable artificial harbour, [its] importance continues to wane, and possibly may, at a brief date hence, become extinct". So it proved, and for the past 150 years, the harbour has been used only by fishing craft, pleasure boats, and the Donaghadee lifeboat; though the lighthouse has retained its utility.

The descriptions of the harbour provided by Rodney Green and Hugh Dixon are strangely discrepant. Green says: "Donaghadee harbour consists of two piers, the southern being 900 ft. long and the northern, which is wholly detached, 820 ft. long. The outer slopes are of loose graywacke rubble stone dressed off to a flat glacis. The inside walls are of V-jointed dressed limestone masonry ... The entrance to the harbour is 150 ft. wide and is 15 ft. deep at low water spring tides". Dixon says " The North pier, sundered from the shore at high tide is a bluff bulwark of wrought stone, 430 feet long, defended on the outer face by a sloping glacis of giant rubble and at each end by a great grey drum-shaped bastion. With the simple strength and grandeur of slightly earlier Martello fortifications, it is the harbour's shield against angry seas ... The South pier, though of the same size and with similar defences, appears less formidable ... As on the north pier, the top is sheltered by a rampart wall on the seaward side, though here it is punctuated in the middle by a gazebo for the Harbour Master". It seems that, in this instance, Rodney Green was in the right, and Hugh Dixon in the wrong.

At least both seem agreed on the merits of the lighthouse: Green: "The lighthouse stands 50 ft. above high spring tides and is also of V-jointed limestone masonry, painted white. The building was designed by Sir John Rennie and the glazing, railings and wrought-iron door were provided by Deville of London". Dixon: "Completed

November 1834; Sir John Rennie, engineer. The tapering, cylindrical tower, standing on the north bastion of the south pier, shares the v-jointed, Anglesea masonry of the harbour, but stands out serene and white on its black base ... Quite apart from its functional importance to mariners, it provides a characterful focus in views of the harbour and sea from the town, as well as a destination for unhurried holiday strollers". All still true, although the black-and-white paintwork is, at time of writing, in need of renewal. It seems that the stonework was first painted, all white, between 1865 and 1875. Would a return to this colour-scheme be a good idea?

Both Dixon and Green draw attention to the flights of stone steps, which "display special skill in the deep diagonal binding of each solid step, providing a typically robust engineer's response to the wear of seaboots and waves alike" (Dixon); "The construction of the steps is worth noticing, each flight being a solid block of stone set in at an angle" (Green). The latter carried out very extensive researches into all the government papers and authorities, and also reproduces Rennie's master plan, which I forbear to repeat here; but only the former notices that the original crane, shown in a water-colour of 1834 (see pages 224, 225), is still there, and evidently still in use - an exceptionally rare survival, almost comparable to the Great Crane of Gdansk which I have always wanted to see. It is painted a serviceable grey; perhaps black would look better. In 1996 there were proposals to replace it by a modern crane, but happily these were overturned, and instead a removable electric motor and chain hoist can be added when required. Rather unexpectedly, the harbour is a 'Trust Port wholly owned by Department of the Environment, Northern Ireland, with departmental officials serving as Harbour Commis-sioners'. This odd arrangement seems to have worked very well to date: Donaghadee harbour is arguably the best preserved in Northern Ireland. The lighthouse belongs to the Irish Lights Commissioners in Dublin. In 1934, it became the first Irish unmanned lighthouse.

Photograph: A C W Merrick. Engraving: J Rennie. (See also colour illus. 35).

Situation: Grid ref. J 594 802; td, Donaghadee; District Council, Ards.

References: Harbour, listed B (24/7/22), lighthouse, listed B (24/7/23); in conservation area. M M Kertland, OSM, 1837, Down, II, p 47; Lewis, TD, 1837, I, p 465; PG, II, 1846, p 25; plans in Rennie, 'British and foreign harbours', II, 1854; Bassett, 'County Down', 1886, p 307; Green, 'Industrial archaeology', 1963, pp 75-77, and pl 33; Dixon, 'Donaghadee and Portpatrick', UAHS, 1977, pp 21-23; Long, 'Bright light, white water', 1997, pp 186-187; Krauskopf, 'Irish lighthouses', 2001, p 77; MacHaffie, 'Portpatrick to Donaghadee', 2001, passim; correspondence and documents in MBR.

Lighthouse, Mew Island, Copeland Islands

168. Of the three Copeland Islands, shown on the Ordnance Survey map as Light House Island, Mew Island, and Copeland Island, confusingly the present lighthouse stands on Mew Island, the most north-easterly of the group. Its first predecessor seems to have been built about 1715; Harris gives a very full description of it: " ... a *Light-House* ... built of Lime and Stone, which the Island affords in Abundance, of a square Form, 70 Feet high to the Lantern, and the Walls of it seven Feet thick. It

consists of three Stories, of which the lower and second are laid with Beams and boarded; but the third is Arched and covered with large Flag Stones seven or eight Feet in length, of which there are several Quarries in the Island. In the middle of the House is erected a round Tower, on which the Grate is fixed on a thick iron Spindel. *Scotland* supplies it with Coals, of which, in a windy Night, it consumes a Tun and Half, burning from Evening to Day Light both Winter and Summer ... The Light is plainly

seen at *Port-Patrick*, and the Mull of *Galloway*, which last Place stands near ten Leagues distant from it."

The next light, built by Thomas Rogers in 1796 on Lighthouse Island and improved by George Halpin in 1815, was discontinued on the completion of the present lighthouse in November 1884; "As commerce increased and sailing vessels were being replaced by steam driven vessels a better positioned light was looked for and in January 1875 the Belfast Harbour Commissioners were the first to request the removal of the Copeland light to Mew Island" (Irish Lights Commissioners).

Praeger, in 1898, says "Mew Island is a low rock of 26 acres intersected by gullies ... At its eastern end towers the splendid lighthouse - completed in 1884 - which guards the entrance to Belfast Lough. The light stands 121 feet above high water, and is one of the most powerful in the world, its full strength being 177,000 candle power. It shows four short white flashes followed by 38 seconds of darkness, the whole cycle occupying one minute ... Mew Island is a well known haunt of the Tern or Sea Swallow."

The tower, to the design of William Douglass, engineer-in-chief of the Irish Lights, is of rubble masonry, quarried on the island, stuccoed in Portland cement. (Before 1954 it was painted black, but in that year a 27-feet deep band of white was painted roughly half-way up; the official Admiralty description is "black tower, white band"). The appearance of this pleasing group of buildings has not been improved by the addition of an airport-like watch-tower, and a prominent wireless mast. A handsome terrace of houses to provide accommodation for the keepers' families was built at the Warren, Donaghadee, in 1884-5.

In 1997, the lighthouse-keepers themselves were set ashore, and the light was rendered automatic. Just before this sad event occurred, the Commissioners of Irish Lights, headed by their chairman, the then Mr (now Lord) Cooke, invited the members of the Northern Ireland Committee of the National Trust (of whom I was one) to accompany them, on their (then) luxurious and exceptionally well-found tender *Granuaile*, on an inspection of the premises, with a view to a possible handover to the

Trust. Unfortunately, nothing came of this; though perhaps the newly-formed Irish Landmark Trust may be more successful. Not the least of the problems of such an insular property is that, in the absence of the all-year-round presence of burly lighthouse-keepers to keep them cleared, the steps at the landing-places speedily become overgrown and slippery with excess of seaweed: a problem not unknown at other coastal properties.

Photographs: MBR; RJ Welch, UM, W05/37/35.
Situation: Mew Island, Copeland Islands, Donaghadee; td, Copeland; District Council, Ards; Grid ref. J 603 863.
References: Listed B (24/06/34). Harris, 'County of Down', 1744, pp 132-133; Praeger, 'BCDR. Official guide to County Down', 1898, p 90; Dixon, 'Donaghadee and Portpatrick', UAHS, 1977, p 29; McCutcheon, 'Industrial archaeology', 1980, pl 149.3; Long, 'Bright light, white water', 1997, pp 184-186; Krauskopf, 'Irish lighthouses', 2001, pp 73-77; Irish Lights Commissioners, unpublished notes in MBR.

Harbour and Lightkeepers' Houses, New Quay, Slanes

169. The 60-feet high lighthouse on the South Rock, off the Ards coast, one of the earliest offshore lighthouses around the British Isles, was built between 1793 and 1797, to designs by Thomas Rogers, builder of the slightly earlier Howth lighthouse in County Dublin; and the little harbour at Slanes was apparently built to serve both the builders and the keepers of the light. In 1795, the Belfast News-Letter reported that "a pier had been built on the shore opposite to it, for landing the stone from Wales". At first, "the lightkeeper lived in the tower with three children in squalid circumstances, their food being a few potatoes" (Blaney). Then four lightkeepers were appointed, three to be always on the rock and their families ashore; in 1820 the three front cottages at Slanes were built for their accommodation; in 1863 a fourth dwelling was added, the two-storey house at the rear facing inland. In 1877, the light - being considered too far from the submerged South Rock to be effective - was replaced by a lightship: this also was served from the little harbour at Slanes, where the family of the crew continued to live. In 1909 the harbour and cottages were sold off, though the quay continued to be used to service the lightship. In the early 1950s, the lightship was superseded by an unmanned light. The dodecagonal lantern was stolen from the tower in 1972, but the ashlar granite masonry appears still to be in good order. The little harbour is still sporadically used by fishermen; the houses have become holiday homes.

In an undated note, presumably of around 1836, M M Kertland of the Ordnance Survey writes: "There is a lighthouse on the south rock. 3 houses are erected on the shore in the townland of Newcastle as residences for the lightkeepers who are 3 in number, and near them are stores for such commodities as the economy of the lighthouse requires. It" (the store-house?) "was built about five years ago. 2 men are always on the rock". The listers say, "Group of four former lightkeepers' houses and stores"; the houses and stores appear to be listed buildings, but unfortunately the harbour does not.

At the end of a very long, unmade-up, lane, perched just above the shoreline in a situation of great peace and seclusion, the cottages with their modest fanlights and double pitched roofs are of considerable charm, though of no great architectural merit; originally three, they have now been carved up to provide two good single-storey holiday houses, though with some slightly regrettable accretions, including clumsy double glazing in the southern cottage. They were exempt from rates, but the whole group was valued at £20 in 1866 and thereafter.

However, the real interest of the group resides in the little harbour, built of shale-like stones set vertically: an attractive pattern, and a very efficient one for resisting storms; and one not very often to be seen - though there is another, later, example, in the yacht harbour at Old Court, Strangford, not far away; also, I am told, at Knockinelder.

The whole group - cottages, gardens, store-house, boundary walls, foreshore and harbour - were bought by one John Kearon when put up for sale by the Commissioners of Irish Lights in 1909. Then, in the 1920s, the houses were bought by W J Coulter; and in 1944 by the grandfather of the present owner, and a friend. One house was reorganised to plans by the Fermanagh architect Richard Pierce in 1993-4, and recently altered again to his plans; the other part was acquired by its present owners in 1991.

Photograph: A C W Merrick (see also colour illus. 37).

Situation: At the end of a long lane south of Cloghy; td, Newcastle; District Council, Ards; Grid ref. J 647 533.

References: Cottages and stores listed B (24/1/97), harbour not listed. VAL 12B/23/27A-C, in PRONI; BNL, 6/4/1795, 24/2/1797; M M Kertland, OSM, nd (?1836), Down, II, p 121; J S Sloane, Manual for lightkeepers, 1868; Green, 'Industrial archaeology', 1963, pp 78-79, and pl 22; ASCD, 1966, p 441, and pl 206; D Gallagher, in JUAHS, II, 1978, pp 6-7; J Blaney, in JUAHS, XIII, 1989, p 3; J Blaney, in 'Beam: journal of Irish Lights', 1997-8, p 21; information from Mrs Jane McClure.

Former Coastguard Station, Marino, Cultra, Holywood

170. A delightful terrace of five modest brick cottages, which gain greatly from being painted and maintained as a coherent group. Mainly of mellow red brick, but with a yellow brick dog-tooth string-course; the ornamental stone trim around windows and doors is painted white in four of the five houses. At one end the officer's house, with look-out tower and pyramidal slated roof, has two projecting triangular oriels on geometrical supports, with carved stone angled pistol loops; at the other end, the boatswain's house has one similar oriel with loops: the Admiralty must have considered the Fenians of Marino and Cultra to have been a savagely aggressive lot. Built, Merrick says, around 1877 - 8, to designs of Enoch Trevor Owen of the Board of Works in Dublin, one of Sir Charles Lanyon's brothers in law; a variant from his standard design, first built at Dun Laoghaire in 1859, and followed by over sixty others in the course of the next twenty years.

In fact, however, it seems to have been rather earlier; the tracings for plan and elevation dated April 1870 are in the Public Record Office of Northern Ireland, and show the terrace almost exactly as built, pistol loops and all, except, rather surprisingly, that it seems to have been originally intended to build it of squared stone with brick dressings. Very similar to, but rather smaller and prettier than, the group's opposite number across the lough at Whitehead. The siting and orientation of this station are puzzling: it stands a little inland from Farmhill (122), at right angles to the shore, with look-out tower furthest inland. It has no view over the lough or its shoreline today: possibly it might have had if the surroundings had been bare of trees 130 years ago, but I rather doubt it; and, anyway, there must even then have been mature trees around Farmhill House. However, there is a memorandum from William Gray of 1 June 1870 on file: "In the plan of the station, the Watch Tower may be altogether omitted, as all the adjoining land is to be laid out in villa sites, and there will not be any view to sea in process of time. Also the station is a considerable distance from the strand and from the contemplated site of boat house". It looks as though the Admiralty (or Board of Works) had had difficulty in securing a suitable site from the Kennedy estate, which saw the area, especially those plots with sea views, as ripe for development. In the end, as a result no doubt of the inexorable pressures of bureaucracy, the watch tower went up in accordance with the original plans, regardless of its lack of a seaward view.

Photograph: A C W Merrick (see also colour illus. 40).

Situation: 29-37 Farmhill Road (1 - 5 Coast Guard Cottages), Marino, Cultra; td, Ballycultra; District Council, North Down; Grid ref. J 408 800.

References: Listed B1 (23/18/28A - E). FIN 16/5/1, in PRONI (I am indebted to Mr Denis Mayne for this reference); F O'Dwyer, in 'Public works', 1988, p 30; Brett, 'Buildings of County Antrim', UAHS, 1996, p 281.

Railway Station, Moira

171. Just outside County Down, just inside County Antrim; but only by a few feet. Rodney Green includes it in his County Down volume; McCutcheon treats it as in County Antrim. Since it is an interesting building which I omitted from my County Antrim volume on the grounds that Moira was in County Down, it seems only fair to include it here; and I therefore follow the eminent example of Dr Green, cheat, and (in lawyers' parlance) *deem* it to be, for my purposes, in County Down.

As Green says, "Moira Station is only a few yards across the county boundary and probably dates from between August 1839 and November 1841 when the line of the Ulster Railway was extended from Lisburn to Lurgan. The station building is in the same Italianate style used by John Godwin, engineer for the railway from 1836-61, for the Armagh and Belfast terminuses. There is a battered basement storey (formerly reached by a set of stone steps from the main platform) which originally provided

living accommodation for the station-master, but now has its entrances bricked up. Below the part of the station buildings immediately flanking the platform the basement is in stone; in the extension behind this it is in brickwork rendered over with stucco, as is the whole of the block at platform level above. A pumphouse was formerly sited at the rear of these buildings. At platform level there is an office, two waiting-rooms, and a men's lavatory". However, the lower storey has now disappeared: the ground surrounding it has been filled in, tarmacked over, and is now a much-used commuter car-park. The station itself now acts only as a halt: the buildings are closed up and described as 'unattended'. With their paired round-headed recessed windows, and elegant detailing, they are very well kept - well-painted too, not in Northern Ireland Railways' usual rather garish colours, but with cream walls and dark-green trim. The original signal-box remains, intact, at the end of the platform. Just as, today, there is a marked resemblance between airports and bus stations, so at the beginning of the age of steam, in the early 1840s, the first railway stations and the first paddle-steamer harbours were very similar. The surviving crane at Moira station is very similar to the surviving crane at Donaghadee harbour (see 167 - and illustrations on pages 224, 225), though this time the jib is an octagonal baulk of timber. And the names of the first steamships, and of the first railway engines, alike give expression to their fiery force: the first seven engines to visit Moira Station were the *Ajax*, *Achilles*, *Express*, *Etna*, *Firefly*, *Fury*, and *Spitfire*: names not dissimilar from those of the first Donaghadee to Portpatrick paddle-steamers, *Arrow* and *Dasher*.

For once, the condition of these buildings does real credit to Northern Ireland Railways. McCutcheon illustrates the station with two vivid line drawings showing its original two-storey character, but does not discuss it apart from the caption to his Fig. 49: "Track (platform) and side

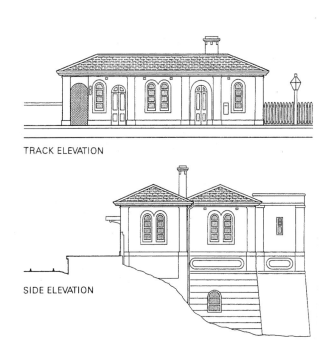

TRACK ELEVATION

SIDE ELEVATION

elevation of the railway station at Moira, County Antrim, which dates from 1841 and is the oldest surviving railway building in the province".

Photographs: A C W Merrick. Drawing: W A McCutcheon, MBR.
Situation: Railway Road, Moira; td, Drumbane; District Council, Lisburn; Grid ref. J 157 618.
References: Not listed? (Odd). Green, 'Industrial archaeology', 1963, p 80, pl 32; McCutcheon, 'Industrial archaeology', 1980, p 107, pl 26.3.

Railway Station, Helen's Bay

172. Referred to on the 1858 Ordnance Survey map as "Clandeboye Station"; at that date, it was only the bay that was Helen's. A marvellous concoction of 1863: "The station at Helen's Bay is one of the most remarkable in Northern Ireland and owes its appearance to specific collaboration between the Baron Dufferin and Clandeboye and his architect Benjamin Ferrey" (McCutcheon). Ferrey (1810-1880) was an English architect, a pupil of the elder Pugin and biographer both of A C Pugin and A W N Pugin. "During construction of the railway from Holywood to Bangor the Baron Dufferin and Clandeboye, on whose estate the station at Helen's Bay was situated, took a personal interest in construction work and had the architect Benjamin Ferrey prepare plans for the new station in an exuberant and playful Scottish baronial style, complete with covered yard, stabling, private waiting accommodation, and a splendid archway beneath the track surmounted by the Dufferin crest and topped with ornamental half-turrets at platform level" (McCutcheon). All this expensive work, and more at Cultra and on the Sharman Crawford estate at Crawfordsburn, had to be carried out at the cost of the unfortunate railway promoters to comply with the conditions laid down by the landowners.

I cannot improve upon McCutcheon's detailed description of this complex, and (by permission) will not try: "it was very much an architectural expression reflecting the cosmopolitan background of a cultured landowner. The main station ... is in an exuberant Scottish baronial style in chunkily coursed Ordovician greywacke, quarried within a stone's throw of the site, with painted freestone (limestone) dressings. Two of the three crow-stepped gables feature inset panels bearing the Dufferin and Ava monogram surmounted by a coronet, and a colonnade incorporating three arches - two round-headed, the third smaller and tudoresque in outline - leads into a small recessed cloister off which opened the main station rooms. On the northwest gable four lancet windows provided light for Lord

Dufferin's private waiting room which was approached by a long, covered stone stairway leading up from a hexagonal courtyard where horse-drawn vehicles plying to and from Clandeboye" (52) " along a tree-lined avenue set down and picked up their passengers or goods. At the north-west corner of the station building stands a circular turret which culminated in a low spire, long since removed". (But for its restoration, see below). "The avenue leading to Clandeboye passes beneath the railway through a fine ornamental archway from which the two projecting turrets on each face rise up through the platform boundary walls. The archway itself is surmounted on each face by massive and finely carved heraldic crests of the Dufferin family, each enclosed within an inverted shield formed by the upward moulding of the two topmost courses of the stepped voussoirs which surmount the arches".

The whole affair was in a sad state in the 1970s; the station proper was then let out as a café by the N I Transport Holding Company; in the late 1970s it was taken over by an enterprising restaurateur. In 1992 it became 'Dean's on the Square', a gourmet restaurant, and, having been listed, was restored by John Lewis-Crosby of Heritage Repairs Ltd in 1994. The glazing of the cloister arches was sympathetically achieved; the restoration of the turret above the waiting room stairs was a great success - in 1993 Dick Oram, with characteristic enthusiasm, minuted "The restored turret is a marvellous asset. I never in my wildest dreams thought this would ever happen. Fantastic !!!". Upgraded by the listers from B to A in 1994: rightly, in my view. Subsequently renamed 'The Carriage Restaurant'; now 'The Carriage Nouveau', without material alterations, and with seating for 34 persons. Today, in pretty good shape, apart from some breeze-block addenda by the oil tanks at the side: surely these never obtained listed building approval? The only, ignominious, shelter nowadays provided for passengers, whether peer or commoner, is one despicable tin rabbit-hutch on each platform. What a come-down!

That admirable author Harold Nicolson - who modestly described himself as "the nephew, if only by marriage, of Lord Dufferin" - described the station so well in such a splendid purple passage of prose in 1937 that I cannot forbear to quote him, almost in full.

"One of the most fantastic" stations "in the United Kingdom ... The station itself did not, at first sight, differ from the other stations of the Belfast and County Down Railway. There were the same long low buildings, the same weather-boarding painted a faint pink, the same 'approach' where the jaunting cars waited for possible passengers, their drivers standing up upon the footboard waving expectant whips. Yet the last door on the left opened upon a little corridor which in its turn led to Lord Dufferin's private waiting-room. This room was, on the whole, the least successful room that I have ever known. It managed to combine the atmosphere of a room which is used too little with the atmosphere of a room which is used too much. It had about it all that sense of the provisional, the transitory and the promiscuous which we associate with public waiting-rooms; its solitary window looked out upon the platform; and its silence was disturbed by the passage of trains, the shuffling of passengers, and the cry of the porter, which (for he was of County Down) was both loud and long. At the same time it exuded the musty depression of something deserted and forlorn: the key with which the station-master opened the door rasped in a rusty lock: dead flies innumerable lined the mantelpiece and the sill; the window, which looked on to the platform and the lives of men was blurred with dust. These contrasts were rendered all the more disturbing by the disparity which existed between the proportions of the room and the furniture which it contained. In construction and design it was nothing more than a little room in a country railway station. Its furniture, however, and ornaments were those of a Victorian parlour. There was a circular table in the centre covered with an Indian cloth. The five chairs which were arranged around it had blue cushions embroidered with a coronet. There was a little red carpet with a criss-cross pattern and vague black flowers in each diamond square. There was a hard sofa in a corner and three cold Spode vases on the mantelpiece. There was an enormous composite

engraving of the House of Lords in 1862 with a key-plan hanging framed below it. There were also (for some unfathomable reason) three billiard balls in a little box with a glass top. And there were four, or it may have been five, Landseer engravings in frames of light-coloured wood.

Yet there were stranger things to come. Having rested in the waiting-room, the visitor was then conducted back into the corridor and down a flight of steep stone steps which led to the level of the avenue. On reaching the bottom he was startled to find himself in a large pentagonal forecourt. The walls of this Propylea were constructed of black granite irregularly morticed together with thick cement. There were a large number of turrets, pinnacles, barbicans, embrasures, machicoulis, ramparts, merlons, battlements and arrow-slits. The avenue passed through this outer ward at right angles to the railway line. To the right there was a high portcullised gateway which led down to the sea. To the left an even more imposing feudal arch disguised the railway bridge. Each of these two arches was decorated with a large coat of arms - dexter, a lion with a tressure flory counterflory or, sinister a heraldic tiger ermine.

Today" (1937) "the avenue, the forecourt, the waiting-room, and indeed the railway station, are seldom used. The tressure of the lion has become more counterflory than ever; some of the balls have dropped from the coronets; and the arrow-slits are hidden in ivy. But on that August morning of 1889" (when the author's uncle came home, covered with honours, from the Vice-Royalty of India and the British Embassy in Rome) "the whole outer ward glistened in welcome. The carriages were waiting at the door of the staircase; the agent and tenants formed a mounted escort; Lord Dufferin, accompanied by ... his impending son-in-law, drove in happy triumph to his home."

Photograph: A C W Merrick. Drawing: B Ferrey, copy in MBR.
Situation: Station Square, Helen's Bay; td, Ballygrot; District Council, North Down; Grid ref. J 458 821.
References: Listed A (23/15/34, 35, 36, 37). B Ferrey, drawings in Dufferin and Ava archive, Clandeboye; Nicolson, 'Helen's Tower', 1937, pp 187, 222-224; Green, 'Industrial archaeology', 1963, p 80; Dixon, 'Ulster architecture', UAHS, 1972, p 28; Dixon, 'Introduction', UAHS, 1975, p 64; McCutcheon, 'Industrial archaeology', 1980, pp 145, 178, 218; H Dixon, notes in MBR, 3 March 1975; R Oram, notes in MBR, 24 September 1993; F W Hamond, notes in MBR, 22 December 1994.

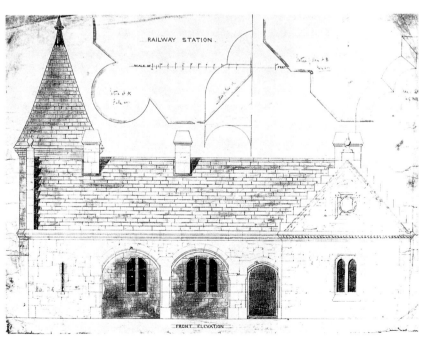

Third Marquess of Downshire's memorial, Hillsborough (177). Engraving: PRONI, T 3793/1/32/9

CHAPTER EIGHT

FOLLIES, MONUMENTS
AND MEMORIALS

As elsewhere, it is hard to place in any kind of logical categories the buildings in this chapter. The charming 18th-century pebble-house at Rubane has been allowed to fall into such a state of dereliction that it is no longer deserving of notice; a great shame. Much the finest survivor, unquestionably, is the Temple of the Winds (173) at Mount Stewart, with its enchantingly sophisticated inlaid floors, acanthus-leaf capitals, and other elegant details. Next, there is the charming Gothick naiveté of the 'Nun's Cottage' (174), at Greyabbey. Then there is that entertaining knock-about pair, Helen's Tower (175), and Scrabo Tower (176); rivalling each other in Victorian quiddity. Next come the grave, indeed perhaps rather pompous, memorials to the Marquesses of Downshire (177, 178); which are, nonetheless, of much higher quality than any of the other statuary in this part of the county. There is (or was?) the remarkable series of mausolea at Knockbreda (180), now sadly decayed, and likely to follow their occupants into final dissolution unless soon attended to. There are the Cleland mausoleum at Dundonald (179), and the Corry mausoleum at Newtownards (181). And finally, there are the enjoyable oddities at Holywood (182) and Ballygilbert (183). Apart from these, there seems to be a disappointing roster of follies and so forth in north County Down.

Parquetry floor by John Ferguson, Temple of the Winds (173), Mount Stewart, Greyabbey. Photograph: Chris Hill, courtesy of the National Trust

Temple of the Winds, Mount Stewart, Greyabbey

173. Commissioned by Robert Stewart, later 1st Marquess of Londonderry, this is, in my judgement, one of the most elegant and beautiful buildings in Ireland, and the only building in the country designed by James 'Athenian' Stuart. For delicacy and clarity it ranks with Francis Johnston's Archbishop's Chapel in Armagh, with Sir William Chambers's Casino Marino outside Dublin, and with the Earl-Bishop's Mussenden Temple in north Derry. The first volume of Stuart and Revett's Antiquities of Athens, from which the model is taken, appeared in 1762; an advertisement for bricklayers appeared in the Belfast News-Letter in June 1781 (although it is not beyond doubt that this was for work at the Temple, where there is much stonework, but no visible brickwork); in June 1783 Stuart was paid £54 3 4 for "Temple at Mount Stewart for cost of the Plan & Designs for furnishing it". It had certainly been completed by 1786 when it is mentioned in the Post-Chaise Companion, but evidently not much earlier, for payments continued until December 1785 to David McBlain (who also worked on the Mussenden Temple) and Michael Campbell, stone masons, John Ferguson, carpenter, William Fitzgerald, plasterer, and William Stewart, smith. The cumulative cost from 1782 until 1803 appears to have been £1307 14 8. It stands on a hilltop amidst mature trees, but "it was not originally surrounded by trees and thus was much more of a landmark than at present" (Casement).

Externally, this is regarded as a very correct and exact interpretation of the octagonal original in Athens, which, however it little resembles except in its details: including notably the beautifully-carved and unusual capitals (the Archaeological Survey of County Down, which contains a very detailed description of the temple, describes the style as "Hellenistic with Egyptian influence in the capital detail"), but with balustrades instead of pediments above each of the porches, and of course substituting tall Georgian-glazed windows, some of them discreetly false, for the carved panels of the original depicting the eight wind-gods. There is a domed circular projection at the rear to contain the staircase. As Jackson-Stops puts it, "The Temple of the Winds was designed as a banqueting house, as well as being a belvedere and (seen from a distance) an eyecatcher. From the vaulted basement runs a passage, with a connecting wine cellar and scullery, leading to a small set of offices hidden from view by the contours of the hill ... It is interesting that when someone suggested turning the Temple into a mausoleum after Castlereagh's death, the 3rd Marquess wrote in answer 'I am entirely against the Idea ... I have no Taste for Turning a Temple built for Mirth and Jollity into a Sepulchre - The place is solely appropriate for a Junketting Retreat in the Grounds". However, oral history has it that, until the arrival of Edith Lady Londonderry in the early 20th century, the lower floor provided somewhat squalid accommodation for at least two families of servants; whilst her husband, the 7th Marquess, used to ride out here on his horse to read the newspapers in the upper room.

The interior is exquisite. The plasterwork in the ceiling of the upper room, and the rosettes and coffering (including the miniature oak-leaves in the central ceiling rose) of the dome above the beautifully constructed spiral stone staircase, were both executed by William Fitzgerald; and the marvellous geometrical parquetry floors by John Ferguson (see illustration on page 263) are of quite exceptional quality. So is the chair-rail (the finest known to me). There is a similar floor in the Music Room of Mount Stewart House (53 - and see illustration on page 75). The marble chimneypiece in the upper room was ordered

from Thomas Scheemakers; that in the lower room was removed to the big house and installed in the drawing room in the 1920s reorganisation; it is interesting that the the two fireplaces in this tiny building were placed on opposite walls, the flues being reunited under the roof in the central chimney-stack. The colour-scheme is that propounded, after much study of scrapes, by John Fowler in 1962: and in this instance seems to me wholly appropriate, though my tastes do not always accord with his.

Lieutenant Tucker of the Ordnance Survey, writing in about 1834, says "In the south part of the demesne there is a small circular stone building having columns of the Ionic order, surrounded by wood which shuts out the views except to the north west, but by making judicious openings, good views may be obtained over Lough Strangford". Samuel Lewis is much more enthusiastic: "On the summit of an eminence in the grounds is an elegant building, a model of the Temple of the Winds at Athens, erected under the personal superintendence of J. Stewart [sic], Esq., whose skill and taste in Grecian architecture have procured for him the appellation of Athenian Stewart [sic]; it is built of stone from the quarries of Scrabo, and the floors, which are of bog-fir found in the peat-moss on the estate, are, for beauty of material and elegance of design, unequalled by anything of the kind in the country". As

Anne Casement points out, "three accounts of the demesne mention a spire in connection with the Temple": Atkinson in 1823 describes a temple dedicated to Neptune 'lifting its lofty spire above the land and water'; the Parliamentary Gazetteer also mentions a spire; and so does J B Doyle. But it seems most unlikely that this ever existed. Perhaps they were just describing the pyramidal roof? Montgomery-Massingberd considers it "the finest garden building in Ireland": and so do I.

Engraving: from J Stuart, 'Antiquities of Athens', I, 1762. Photographs: A C W Merrick (see also colour illus. 1); D Lindsay, 1987, NT.
Situation: On a hill overlooking Strangford Lough, within the Mount Stewart demesne wall; td, Mount Stewart; District Council, Ards; Grid ref. J 558 692.
References: Listed A (24/4/51). D 654/H 1/1, pp 33 - 82, H 1/6, H2/3, p 6, D 1088/100/30/1, in PRONI; BNL, 19-22/6/1781; Wilson, 'Post-chaise companion', 1786, p 24; Atkinson, 'Ireland exhibited', 1823, I, p 222; H Tucker, OSM, nd, (?1834), Down, II, p 68; Lewis, TD, 1837, I, p 674; PG, II, 1846, p 808; Doyle, 'Tours in Ulster', 1854, p 91; ASCD, 1966, p 376; Knight of Glin, NT guidebook to Temple of the Winds, 1966, passim; Howley, 'Follies and garden buildings', 1993, pp 155-160; A Casement, Mount Stewart landscape study, (unpublished), 1995, p 19, and appendices, passim (copy in MBR); G Jackson-Stops, in NT guidebook to Mount Stewart, 1997, pp 25-29; Montgomery-Massingberd and Sykes, 'Great houses of Ireland', 1999, p 205.

Cottage Hill (or 'The Nuns' Cottage'), Greyabbey

174. A romantic folly-house on the summit of the hill opposite the church, abbey, and Rosemount House (4), at the end of a long, dog-legged lane, amidst fine mature trees. Mr and Mrs Hall, in 1843, say "The vicinity of these ruins" (of Grey Abbey) "is beautiful and picturesque; the residence of the heir of the Montgomeries immediately adjoins them; and a pretty little temple has been erected on the grounds, in order to afford accommodation to visitors; the place being, as it ought to be, in high favour with the townspeople of Belfast, who occasionally luxuriate in the delicious neighbourhood"; though it must be said that the building is far too modest to afford much in the way of accommodation: however, Doyle provides an explanation: " ... The number " (of visitors) " is much increased. A beautiful little temple has been erected in the grounds for their accommodation, by which visitors have an agreeable retreat from the vicissitudes of the weather" - perhaps they could here be provided with Ulster fries, as I was in my childhood at Scrabo, a favourite outing?

It consists, in original essence, of a pair of pinnacles, divided by a crow-stepped gable, with an ornamental stuccoed façade incorporating cross-slits, a quatrefoil, and a keystone bearing the date 1807, and contains an octagonal room with a ribbed and domed ceiling, corner niches for china ornaments, and below them cleverly contrived corner folding writing- or sketching-niches; with, at the rear, a small and simple two-storey cottage, very plain, providing accommodation for a servant to supply tea, claret, and picnics to the visitors who walked up from Rosemount House. Its function seems originally to have been not dissimilar from that of the earlier Mount Stewart Temple of the Winds (173), or indeed the later Helen's Tower (175). It was built for Charlotte Montgomery, eldest of the unmarried daughters of Rosemount.

There are splendid views over the abbey, Strangford Lough, on clear days the distant Mourne Mountains, and the village of Greyabbey, though the trees now conceal all but the chimney-pots of Rosemount: why will they so perversely keep growing? At some time in the 19th century the cottage was slightly enlarged by the addition of another couple of rooms at the rear, with stone outhouse, invisible from below behind the screen of trees originally planted to frame the view of the folly from below. The outhouse contained cobbled wash-house, earthen-floored store, and privy with stone-slabbed floor, and recess to hold a candle - for it lacks a window. In the early 20th century, the house seems to have been inhabited by a witch-like old lady, though I can find no trace of her in the Valuation books;

then it seems to have been used as a tea-room, to which charabanc parties walked up the steep hill path from Church Street to admire the view and enjoy refreshments. It was somewhat altered and 'modernised' in the 1950s; then fell into disrepair and vandalism, suffering a serious fire in 1988. In 1990, it was acquired from the Montgomery estate by the present owner, who is in the process of restoring it to a high standard, whilst arranging, inconspicuously, to enlarge it and render it rather more comfortable a family home.

Maurice Craig and the Knight of Glin call this "a charming late-eighteenth-century Gothick eye-catcher". Jeremy Musson says "A Gothic sketching house - presumably the 'pretty little temple' referred to in Hall's 'Ireland: its scenery and character' (1843) was ... built about 1780 on the hill that overlooks the ruins and church towards the house". Bence-Jones says, "On the hill opposite the house, there is a charming little c18 Gothic 'eye-catcher'".

(My editor enquires, cogently, "Why do so many of the 'authorities' go for 'late 18th century' despite the 1807 keystone?" I can only assume, because so few of them took the pains to go up to the top of the hill). The listers report "Single-storey cottage in form of mock Gothic and set on hill among trees. Porch added later". Unfortunately, the trees have grown up so that it is now invisible from most

angles. Barbara Jones observes " ... pale and rightly grey, it is very pretty indeed from a distance ... The most cut-out cardboard façade of all". Howley says "Although ... a simple rendered structure, it is a relatively refined composition and well enough proportioned to suggest that an architect or at least a good amateur conceived it".

A commonplace-book at Rosemount, formerly kept in the cottage, is inscribed on the title-page: "To the Passing Visitor this Album is dedicated by the Abbess of the Nunnery" - Emilia Montgomery. This may perhaps have been a reflection of the late-Georgian predilection for romantick monks and nuns. The first entry is dated 1807, the date in the keystone; the latest, 1821; it seems that the young, or, later, middle-aged, ladies went there to sketch almost daily; also, that it was the scene of "drunken aristocratic picnic parties on the lawn". A delightful oddity.

Photograph: A C W Merrick.
Situation: 7 Cottage Hill (off Cardy Road), Greyabbey; td, Ballynester; District Council, Ards; Grid ref. J 585 685.
References: Listed B1 (24/4/15). Manuscript commonplace book at Rosemount, Greyabbey; Hall, 'Ireland', III, 1843, p 19; Craig and Knight of Glin, 'Ireland observed', 1970, p 60; Jones, 'Follies and grottoes', 1974, p 429; Bence-Jones, 'Burke's guide', 1978, p 147; Howley, 'Follies and garden buildings', 1993, p 119; J Musson, in CL, 10 October, 1997, p 50; information from W H C Montgomery.

Helen's Tower, Clandeboye, Bangor

175. "On a hill-top about a mile from Clandeboye towards Newtownards stands this most famous of the first Marquess' architectural achievements. a square-plan tower in basalt" (Patton). The tower was first designed by William Burn (for whom, see Bangor Castle, 64) as a 'Gamekeeper's Tower' in 1848, the year after Lord Dufferin came of age. Burn's original sepia drawing is in the RIBA Library. As Gavin Stamp says, "It was possibly built as part of the expensive improvements to the Clandeboye estate undertaken by Lord Dufferin after he attained his majority in 1847 to relieve the unemployment and the destitution caused by the Famine". But work on the tower seems to have gone on very slowly, for, although it was named 'Helen's Tower' in 1850, it seems not then to have been completed internally; it was not until 23 October, 1861 that Helen McDonnell and Hariott Hamilton were able to hoist the flag over it for the first time. Lord Dufferin's mother, Helen, in whose honour the tower was named, was still alive and, indeed, lived on until 1867: as Patton puts it, "the Tower is a celebration rather than a funereal tribute". The walls of the upper room are panelled with specially solicited poems by Lord Tennyson, Robert Browning, Thomas Carlisle, Sir Edwin Arnold, Rudyard Kipling, Richard Garnett, and W S Blunt - among others.

As Stamp says, it is "a revival of the typical Ulster (and Scottish) fortified tower of the 16th and 17th centuries, with a projecting spiral staircase surmounted by a gabled turret. It is a product of twin mid-Victorian obsessions: with the revival of Romantic and historical building traditions and with the raising of towers". It is built on a rocky

Corrigendum - page 269

The photograph, purporting to illustrate Helen's Tower, is in fact of the main tower of Ballymena Castle, County Antrim (built in the 1870s to a design by W H Lynn; demolished, after a fire, in the 1950s).

Unfortunately, when this section of the book was in preparation, foot-and-mouth disease restrictions made it impossible for Anthony Merrick to take an up-to-date photograph of the building. The author then recalled having seen in the list of photographs by W A Green in the Ulster Folk and Transport Museum one described as being of Helen's Tower, and ordered a print, which is that reproduced on page 269. But, regrettably, the photograph of Ballymena Castle had at some time been recorded as being of Helen's Tower.

The new photograph of Helen's Tower was specially taken in June 2002 by Anthony Merrick; and the printing and circulation of this correction sheet have been paid for out of a generous contribution, received too late to be acknowledged in the book, from North Down Borough Council.

C E B B
June, 2002

knoll, upon which the earliest Ordnance Survey map indicates "Nelson's Monument": nothing is now known of this, but there is no inherent improbability, for Sir Henry Blackwood ("the Admiral") was one of Nelson's captains, commanding the 34-gun frigate *Penelope* in a notable action on 30 March 1800 with the French *Guillaume Tell* of no less than 80 guns. The tower is built of random blackstone, with granite quoins, sandstone trim to the arrow-slit windows, and odd bits of rendering. The porch has coronet, "D & A", and the date 1850 above the doorway: also a convenient iron ring for tethering one's mount after the two-mile ride uphill from the house. Thoroughly restored in 1989 under the supervision of Colin Deane, it is presently in good order, inside and out, and, with the benefit of mod. cons. habitable if hardly luxurious: would suit a modern hermit.

As to the interior, Patton describes it as follows: "Inside there are indeed a couple of rooms where a gamekeeper might live, but the room on the second floor has a heavily coffered ceiling emblazoned with heraldic devices, and the third floor is richly panelled with timber Gothic tracery including rib vaulting and barley sugar columns. There is a further small turret room on the parapets, from which a stunning view of the surrounding countryside can be seen ..." As he says, the view is quite magnificent, and well worth the slightly breathless climb. Stamp suggests that possibly the interior "was partly the work of Ferrey" - (see Helen's Bay Railway Station, 172) "who was working for Lord Dufferin in the 1850s, or of Lynn, for while the Tower itself has round-headed windows, some of the interiors are Gothic in style". The drawings for the interior of the Gothic room, preserved in Clandeboye House, certainly look like Ferrey's work; and the intricate elegance of the interior furnishing seems much more like Ferrey than Burn or Lynn.

After the death of Lord Dufferin, the building fell into a degree of decay. Harold Nicolson, Lord Dufferin's nephew by marriage, wrote a charming biography of Lord Dufferin, rather misleadingly entitled Helen's Tower, in 1937: it contains only four pages on the subject of the tower, but they are not without interest. "A stone turret

stairway leads from the ground floor where the caretaker has his kitchen and from which the smell of rabbit-stew and potato-cakes creeps into the upper chambers, mingling the living savour of an Irish bothy with the dead scent of closed rooms, of Victorian woodwork, of camphor and of decaying brocades ..."

Helen's Tower is built on the highest point of the Clandeboye demesne; "more than just a Victorian conceit, a picturesque folly on a country estate. Standing at the top of a hill above the surrounding trees, it is visible for miles around and has become a symbol not just for Clandeboye but for all Ulster" (Stamp). Its pre-eminence, trumpeted by Tennyson, has been considerably reduced by the growth to maturity of the pine trees by which it is surrounded. It was trumped, moreover, by the Stewarts of Mount Stewart when, in 1856, they commissioned Scrabo Tower (176) - which the present Lady Dufferin refers to as "the copycat tower" - on the rocky outcrop above Newtownards, after an acrimonious competition between Charles Lanyon and W J Barre, won - by means of foul play? - by the former. But, in the end, the Dufferins out-trumped the Stewarts: for, in 1921, a considerably enlarged reproduction of Helen's Tower was built on the ridge at Thiepval, to commemorate the men of the Ulster Division, killed at the Somme in 1916, who had encamped at Clandeboye for their training before they embarked.

A bit unkindly described by Barbara Jones: "This is a famous tower, marked in its own right on quite small maps for no reason that I can see, for it is distinguished only by a smug air of piety and privilege". Oh dear!

Drawing: W Burn, RIBA Library, copy in MBR. Photograph: W A Green, UFTM, WAG 3137.

Situation: In Clandeboye demesne, on the outskirts of Bangor; td, Ballyleidy; District Council, North Down; Grid ref. J 489 773.

References: Listed A (23/6/9). W Burn, drawing in RIBA Library; drawings in Dufferin and Ava archive, Clandeboye; Nicolson, 'Helen's Tower', 1937, p 138; Brett, 'Buildings of Belfast', 1967, p 31; Jones, 'Follies and grottoes', 1974, p 429; G Stamp, in 'Clandeboye', UAHS, 1985, p 29; Patton, 'Bangor', UAHS, 1999, p 49; information from Mrs Lola Armstrong, Clandeboye.

Scrabo Tower, Newtownards

176. As Jeremy Williams puts it: "The Scrabo memorial is a multi-storied Scottish Baronial tower with four corner-turrets, three corbelled, and a spiral stairs; more curious than beautiful". "Erected in memory of Charles William Vane 3rd Marquess of Londonderry by his tenantry and friends. Fame belongs to history, remembrance to us", according to the plaque in the wall. As R L Praeger crisply puts it, with evident distaste, "This nobleman had a varied career. Born in 1778, he entered the army, and was lieutenant-colonel of the 5th dragoons when that regiment was disbanded for insubordination. He was adjutant-general to Sir Arthur Wellesley's army from 1809 to 1812; subsequently envoy-extraordinary to Berlin and ambassador to Vienna; built a harbour at Seaham at a cost of £250,000; fought a duel with Henry Grattan; published a Narrative of the Peninsular War, and an 8-volume Life of

Lord Castlereagh; and died in 1854, leaving vast estates in England and Ireland. Disraeli has portrayed him in Vivian Grey under the name of Col. von Trumpetson".

He died, having "been the proprietor of the town and parish since 1822, ... and it was thought fitting that some permanent memorial should be made to him ... 450 of the 600 subscribers were connected with the estate. However, there were about 1200 tenant farmers on the estate and an urban population of many thousands in Newtownards and Comber so that 450 was not a large proportion of the whole tenantry ... Two thirds of the cost was raised by 98 individuals (the list headed by the Emperor Napoleon III of France), most of whom were fellow gentry from Antrim and Down, and personal friends of the Marquess". And McCavery goes on "If the Tower is a symbol of anything, it is surely a symbol of landlord power ... whenever the

tenant farmer looked up, the Tower would be there, a gracious but stoney reminder of who was in charge".

The commission was put out to competition, to cost not more than £2,000, and gave rise to shenanigans of uncommon bitterness. "Mr Barre's design - an obelisk on a pedestal - was awarded first prize; a Mr Boyd came second; drawings by Messrs Lanyon were placed third and fourth. But Lanyon got the job. It is worth quoting Dunlop" (biographer of W J Barre) "at length: 'Mark the scandalous artifice resorted to - the flagrant injustice practised. While Mr Barre was tied down to have his design constructed of Scrabo freestone, *no such condition was imposed* as regards the third-rate competitor whose design was to be favoured! *He was not required to build with freestone at all!* Whinstone, rubble, surface scrapings, or anything he pleased, might be used by him, and was used! What was to cost only £2,000, actually cost £3,010, and even then it was not properly constructed or finished,

though the unfortunate contractor was ruined! With the same material, Mr Barre's design could have been built for £1,600!'" (Brett).

The building of the tower was fraught with difficulties. It was reduced by a storey to save costs. The design seems to have been by W H Lynn, then working for Lanyon; perhaps not one of his greatest successes. The pro-Lanyon account in the Dublin Builder of 1865 says that it "forms a conspicuous object, seen from a circle of country for 80 miles round. The cost was about £2,300, and the total height 195 feet. The Scotch baronial style was selected as being more capable of adapting the materials on the site, and applying the debris of freestone lying about. It was also conceived that it had a special suitability as a style for a monument to a Stewart. In its lofty and isolated position, size and mass were the chief objects to be attained at a comparatively small cost, and any monument in the form of an obelisk would not have been effective on such a bold

rugged site. So far as the accomplishment of these objects go, this has been a success. The materials used are the stones of which the mountain is composed, a green whinstone and a hard laminated freestone. The excavations for the foundations disclosed a vast quantity of wild boars' tusks and bones, suggesting that this elevated position had been formerly the scene of Druidical sacrifices or of prehistoric picnics. There are apartments for a caretaker within, and a large chamber for the use of visitors intended to be fitted up as an armoury, and a winding staircase to the battlements, which command fine views of an extensive tract of country".

The Archaeological Survey of County Down says, crisply, "The summit of this prominent hilltop, at 540 ft. O.D., is enclosed by a bank of piled stone and earth, now about 3 ft. high, forming an oval hill-fort about 300 ft. long by 120 ft. In places, especially on the S., the rock outcrop seems to have been scarped to create a ditch. It is not clear where the entrance lay ... There are a number of hut groups on the rough ground (now used as a golf course) just below this outcrop".

This is an extraordinarily prominent landmark, visible for miles around, and now regarded with general affection. Praeger says "the sandstones of Scrabo have been protected from the ravages of denudation by the thick mass of hardened lava above them, and, still crowned by their volcanic cap, they stand out as a high bold hill over the surrounding plain. In the quarries, striking evidence of the ancient history of the hill may be seen. If we split up the blocks of sandstone that are everywhere strewn about, we shall find their surfaces ripple-marked exactly as our present sands are when the tide leaves them. Elsewhere they are sun-cracked, just like the bottom of a sunny pond that is drained and exposed to the heat of the day. Again, we may find the unmistakable prints of rain-drops, left by some old-time shower on the then soft material. In those ancient times the waves danced and the rain fell and the sun shone just like today".

It must, however, be said, that whilst its prominence and profile far exceed those of Helen's Tower (175), the architectural merits of Scrabo Tower are inferior. It was one of W H Lynn's earlier ventures, and not by any means his most successful. However, its popularity remains undimmed. It was struck by lightning, but mended, in 1925. Having fallen into considerable disrepair, it was taken into public ownership, and £20,000 was spent on its restoration, in 1992. The Millin family were its caretakers for over 100 years: it was one of the great school-holiday treats of my childhood to be taken to Scrabo for one of their generous fries. And it was on Scrabo Hill, when I was aged about eleven, that my parents took me to play my first, and only, game of golf. I decided swiftly, and conclusively, that this was a boring and time-wasting exercise in which I had no interest: and I have ever since adhered to that view.

Engraving: DB, VII, 1865. Photograph: A C W Merrick.
Situation: On Scrabo Hill, Newtownards; td, Scrabo; District Council, Ards; Grid ref. J 477 726.
References: Listed B+ (24/1/31). DB, VII 1865, pp 124-125; Dunlop, 'W J Barre', 1868, pp15-16; Praeger, 'BCDR. Official guide to County Down', 1898, pp 83-84; ASCD, 1966, pp 147,179,180; Brett, 'Buildings of Belfast', 1985, pp 37-38; 'Newtownards Chronicle', 25/1/1973; McCavery, 'Newtown', 1994, p 140; Williams, 'Architecture in Ireland', 1994, pp 112-113; C Monro and R Oram, notes in MBR.

Third Marquess of Downshire's Memorial, Hillsborough

177. Outside Hillsborough, in the Monument Field (no longer, it seems, used either for grazing or cropping; now just an open space for the walking of suburban dogs), a highly impressive pillar-with-figure-atop, comparable to Nelson's column in London's Trafalgar Square, a landmark for miles around. The field is now surrounded by post-war housing of no architectural relevance.

Listed in category A, no less; described by the listers as "Tall Greek Doric column on square podium and stylobate possibly 130 feet high, with statue of 3rd Marquis of Downshire atop". Described by me in 1974: "a very tall imposing fluted Doric column of dressed stone, with a square base, on a podium of three tall raked steps; perhaps by Sands; possibly by Thomas Duff. The more-than-life-size-statue is masked by its platform from any vantage-point near at hand, so it is hard to judge its quality: the name of the sculptor does not seem to be known, and would be hard to guess without an uncommonly tall ladder. Inset in the base to the north are the Downshire arms, with their immoral motto - 'per deum et ferrum obtinui'. In the south face, a long and verbose testimonial to the 3rd Marquis who fell off his horse in an apoplectic fit in 1845".

There have been complaints for years about the condition of this important memorial, whose merits can be known in detail only to the pilots of, and passengers in, helicopters landing at or taking off from Hillsborough Castle. The Government has been prepared to offer a degree of grant aid, but not (so far) to take the monument into state ownership. The Hill family has been prepared to bear a part, but not all, of the cost of a memorial which it has regarded as more public than private in character. In 1988, a condition report from Leighton Johnston, architects, recommended expenditure of £13,934 to put it in order; but it proved impossible to reach agreement on funding. Nothing has been done; the Hillsborough Concerned Residents Group protests sporadically; the florid inscription, lately indecipherable in parts, seems at the date of writing to have been taken away - let us hope, to have the lettering recut. Otherwise, the monument seems at present in fairly good order.

Since the inscription at the base is presently unavailable, it seems worth while to record the transcription provided by Mr Robin Hill (now, the 8th Marquess), which runs as follows:

To commemorate
The public and private virtues of the most Honorable
Arthur Wills Blundell Sands Trumbull Hill
Third Marquis of Downshire
Lieutenant of the County of Down, Colonel of the Royal South
Down Regiment of Militia, and Knight of the Most Illustrious
Order of Saint Patrick
Alike distinguished for patriotism, rectitude of principle,
of honesty, of purpose
Upholding his station with becoming dignity
He was also mindful of the wants of others
And practised its duties with benevolence and humility
Which won the regard of every virtuous mind
Adding lustre to his exalted rank
Those who knew his work and admired the uprightness of his
character and conduct
In the several relations of life
Have erected this Monumental Column
As a token of their friendship and esteem
1848

There the poor old boy still stands, like a Stylite on his pillar: will nobody come to his rescue? Surely, as the incumbent of one of the very few A-listed buildings in the province, he deserves better than this?

Photographs: A C W Merrick. Engraving: (see page 262).
Situation: Off Monument Road, Hillsborough; td, Hillsborough; District Council, Lisburn; Grid ref. J 237 582.
References: Listed A (19/5/114). Inscription; Maguire, 'Downshire estates', 1972, pp 8, 26; Brett, 'Mid Down', UAHS, 1974, p 16; correspondence file in MBR.

Fourth Marquess of Downshire's Memorial, Hillsborough

178. In 1974 I wrote, and I do not think I can improve on it: "In a small and dusty garden, on the site of the former brewery (apparently a Gothick building to match the church opposite) stands a statue of 'Arthur 4th Marquis of Downshire born 8th August 1812 died 6th August 1868, erected by his friends and tenants', on a high stone plinth: the bronze statue was modelled in 1873 by Samuel Ferres Lynn (brother of W H Lynn the architect) and was cast by Prince & Co. of Southwark. The Marquis is more than lifesize, though he seems to have been a more-than-lifesize man: he is portrayed as a bull of a country gent, with high gum boots, a formidably knobbly blackthorn, and an enormous shawl over his arm; his corduroy trousers are rendered with a masterly clarity which recalls the ridge-and-furrow treatment of Nigerian bronze masks".

Nothing about him has changed in the quarter-century since I wrote that description.

Photographs: A C W Merrick.
Situation: In a small public park at the foot of Main Street, Hillsborough; td, Hillsborough; District Council, Lisburn; Grid ref. J 243 588.
References: Listed B+ (9/5/15); in conservation area. Inscription on plinth; Brett, 'Mid Down', UAHS, 1974, p 22.

Cleland Mausoleum, Dundonald

179. Curl says, with accuracy: "One of the largest mausolea in Ulster, and one that commands a spectacular site, is found in the churchyard of Dundonald parish church. The combination of church, tower, mausoleum and vast motte is an unforgettably dramatic composition. The mausoleum ... is that of the Cleland family, erected by Eliza Cleland in memory of her husband, Samuel Cleland of Stormount, who died in 1842 ... This vast neoclassical mausoleum consists of an underground vault over which is a cubic superstructure that acts as the pedestal for the cupola with its peristyle of classical columns".

The Archaeological Survey of County Down describes it as a "square Greek Doric structure of V-grooved wrought granite on stepped base, engaged angle columns supporting entablature, with triangular pediment bearing acroterial ornaments to each face; blocking course, with pedestals supporting draped vases at angles; above is a drum supporting sarcophagus enclosed by six Ionic columns with entablature and dome". It adds, however, of the motte, that "The castle here was taken by King John in 1210 and the Irish Pipe Roll 1211-12 records the erection of a new bridge, grange and pig-sty". The old church, built in 1771, and dedicated for some reason to St Elizabeth of Hungary, was deconsecrated in 1967, but happily not demolished: it now stands, a boarded-up silhouette, on the skyline close to the motte. The new church

nearby, consecrated in 1966, is by Hobart & Heron, architects, and with its strange helmet-like spire appears somewhat incongruous.

The Cleland family seem to have been amongst the most (deservedly) unpopular in Ulster. In 1805 John Cleland, "scourge of the United Irishmen and one of the most hated men in County Down" (Carr), married Esther Jackson of Mount Pleasant, now Stormont. He combined his position as rector of Newtownards with the agency for Lord Castlereagh: and one way or another built up substantial wealth. He died aged 80 in 1834; he was succeeded by his son Samuel, who was crushed to death by falling masonry while demolishing with his own hands the house formerly occupied by his head groom, who had been caught defrauding him. Samuel's 25-year-old widow built the mausoleum, said to have been built high to be visible from Stormont and to have cost £2000.

Photograph: A C W Merrick.
Situation: Off Church Green, Dundonald; td, Church Quarter; District Council, Castlereagh; Grid ref. J 418 739.
References: Listed A (25/5/2). Inscription; Leslie. 'Clergy of Diocese of Down', 1936, p 158; 'ASCD', 1966, pp 193, 327; Curl, 'Mausolea in Ulster', UAHS, 1978, p 14; Carr, 'Most unpretending of places', 1987, pp 110-113; J F Rankin in 'Clergy of Down and Dromore', 1996, p110.

Greg Mausoleum, Knockbreda Churchyard, Newtownbreda

180. Curl says "There is ... an astounding array of funerary monuments in the parish churchyard of Knockbreda. Four large mausolea were built there in the last two decades of the eighteenth century by worthies of Belfast and the surrounding area. These mausolea are all square on plan and have elegant Adamesque arrangements of classical columns, pilasters, and entablatures. Above the crowning cornices are inventive superstructures of domes, pyramids, obelisks, and urns. These mausolea comprise the oddest and finest of buildings in the genre in Ulster, and cannot be surpassed architecturally as a group of mausolea.

"The most ornate of the Knockbreda mausolea is the Greg tomb of the last decade of the eighteenth century, although the contemporary Waddell Cunningham Douglas tomb, with its superstructure of urns, pyramids, and other classical elements, is almost as elaborate. These mausolea are sumptuous, yet refined; ostentatious, yet delicate. The smaller Rainey tomb is topped by four elongated pyramids, by an octagonal cap with concave sides, and by a crowning urn. All these mausolea are undoubtedly by the same hand, and may have had their origins in the pattern-books of tombs that were current at the time. It is tempting to associate the Rococo genius of an architect of the stature of Mulholland with these glorious mausolea.

There is no evidence for such speculations, however, and we must be content to see these wonderfully inventive mausolea as part of a pattern that had emerged in burial fashions in the European cemeteries in India. Indeed, the nearest models for the elaborate tombs in Knockbreda, to the best of my knowledge, are the memorials in Surat and in the South Parks cemetery in Calcutta".

Maurice and Michael Craig pursue the same theme in their Mausolea Hibernica: "The Belfast-Bengal axis is one of the curiosities of the subject. The small group of mausolea at Knockbreda, which is now on the edge of Belfast, would not excite remark in the South Park Street Cemetery in Calcutta ... some trading link may be suspected. The mausolea at Knockbreda have a strong family resemblance, and, unlike those at Kilbride, are largely made of compo and have suffered in consequence ... The Cave Hill may be seen in the background, while overhead are evidences of the present discontents" - Michael Craig's illustration is a-buzz with helicopters.

In 1966, the compilers of the Archaeological Survey of County Down thought this tomb, and four others (out of the vast number in this overflowing graveyard) worthy of notice, detailed description, and illustration: the latter show the mausoleum to have been in pretty good order at that date. (The description is too long to quote here, which demonstrates the importance attached to the structure). Some ten years later, the listers say "large square monument with ogee section dome; coupled Tuscan columns angle-set at each corner; surmounting urns; finely carved neo-classical decorations": implying that all was still reasonably well. In 1978, Curl recorded his judgement and contributed his photograph, and it seems that all was still pretty well.

The Greg monument, erected in memory of Thomas Greg, who died in 1796, is however not of compo, but is faced in dressed sandstone; and its present state, like that of its companions, is quite lamentable: three of the corner urns fallen, stone panels fallen off, other stonework cracked, ivy and other vegetation creeping over all. Greg was a merchant, speculator, and ship-owner; perhaps this might supply the missing Indian link. He is reputed to have refused a baronetcy, and had thirteen children, of whom at least two are buried here with him. In partnership with his neighbour-in-death Waddell Cunningham, he had in 1764 opened the sulphuric acid factory on Vitriol Island at Lisburn (now luxurious seat of the Lisburn District Council). The first vessel to navigate the new Lagan Navigation, on 9 September 1763, was Greg's 60-ton lighter the *Lord Hertford*. The Belfast News-Letter, and Dr McCutcheon, report:

"Mr. and Mrs. Greg had upon this occasion invited a numerous company of ladies and gentlemen to make the voyage and dine on board. The day was indeed a happy one, the weather was fair, the prospect diversified with bleach greens breaking in upon every reach of the river, together with the woodlawn and meadow and the happiness and jollity of the reapers in nearly every field cutting down their harvest, all diffused joy and pleasure. The party were met at Drum Bridge by the principal gentlemen of the town of Lisburn who came on board and the whole company were entertained by Mr. Greg and his family in the most elegant and polite manner with a cold collation and wines of all sorts. A band of music played the whole way to a crowd of over one thousand persons who accompanied the lighter on the banks of the waterway as far as Lisburn where the inhabitants expressed their unfeigned satisfaction at the completion of this great and truly useful work up to their town, and at the near prospect of its being rendered much more advantageous by having the passage by water opened to Lough Neagh". What a splendid party that must have been!

The others in the group are, for the most part, in even worse case than Mr Greg's: the tomb of his colleague, that notable Belfast citizen Waddell Cunningham, of 1797, is in quite terrible order. This sorry state of affairs reflects credit neither on the parish - though it is understandable that it should prefer to spend its money on its distinguished place of worship (18) rather than on its graveyard - nor on the Historic Buildings system. In November 1986 there was even a crass proposal by the vestry to bulldoze the lot: acting with uncharacteristic alacrity, the authorities managed to list the four mausolea by January 1987. Ever since there has been deadlock: the memorials have not been demolished, but neither have they been repaired. Is it too late? Can nothing be done to arrest this disgraceful decay? Could the National Heritage Lottery Fund not, perhaps, step in?

Photographs: A C W Merrick; MBR.
Situation: Knockbreda churchyard, Church Road, Newtownbreda; td, Breda; District Council, Castlereagh; Grid ref. J 351 702.
References: Listed B+ (25/16/5d). Inscriptions; BNL, 9/9/1763; ASCD, 1966, p 334, pl 122; Curl, 'Mausolea in Ulster', UAHS, 1978, pp 7, 10, pl 5; McCutcheon, 'Industrial archaeology', 1980, p 89; Curl, 'Celebration of death', 1993, pp 170-176; Craig, 'Mausolea hibernica', 1999, pp 48-49; file in MBR.

Corry Mausoleum, Movilla Graveyard, Newtownards

181. A very fine miniature classical temple, elegant and well detailed, antefixae and acroteria all complete: one wonders whether its author, very un-Victorian, had been to Greece? "In the centre of the oldest part of this" (Movilla) "graveyard, the burying-place of the late Robert Corry is conspicuously marked by a beautiful monument, after the style of a Grecian temple: it bears the date 1860, and was designed by Mr. John Corry of London" (Dewar). The listers say only "Erected in the form of a miniature Greek Doric temple. Includes 1708 grave of John Corry". In the centre of the monument is a slab inscribed *Under this stone lieth the body of John Corry, late Provost of Newtown, who died the 8 day of January, 1708, in ye 70 year of his age.* Inset into the underside of the roof, there are four more slabs commemorating other members of the family, one of them to "Robert Corry of Belfast who erected this monument", and died in 1869. Since then, many other members of the family have been buried and commemorated here: can there be much room left?

The mausoleum was actually designed by Robert Corry's son, John Corry, "of London", whose "highly cultured taste as an architect is exemplified in his design of Elmwood Church, which is a beautiful specimen of ecclesiastical architecture. Its handsome belfry and graceful spire command especial admiration. It is considered one of the finest Presbyterian Churches in Ulster ... He was also the architect of the graceful-looking Presbyterian Church at Dunmurry" (Dewar): all this despite the fact that he managed the shipping fleet of the family firm, and had no architectural qualifications whatever! In pretty good shape, in a very large, very old, graveyard; somewhat crowded-in by the adjacent triple memorial to the Robbs of Charleville (123). The white marble chippings on the floor are no doubt practical, but not stylistically wholly congruous - Scrabo-stone slabs might have seemed preferable.

Photograph: A C W Merrick.
Situation: In Movilla graveyard, Newtownards; td, Bootown; District Council, Ards; Grid ref. J 503 744.
References: Listed B1 (24/8/5). Datestone in pediment; Dewar, 'History of Elmwood Church', 1900, pp 41, 47, 65.

The Maypole, Holywood

182. Holywood's Maypole, the heart and soul of north Down - pagan or Christian? who can tell? - is reputed to be the only one surviving in Ireland; and its ancestry apparently antedates Thomas Raven's map of 1625, on which it appears to be shown with a flag at the mast-head. It seems however to have had a somewhat discontinuous existence. The observant Harris does not notice it, though he does, endearingly, remark that "On the Shores about *Hollywood* are found vast Quantities of Muscles, (but not of the sort that breed Pearls) on which the poor Inhabitants feed much without feeling any Inconvenience, dressing

them when shelled with Butter, Pepper and Onions". It is not mentioned by Dubourdieu, by the Ordnance Survey memoir compilers or their map-making colleagues, by Lewis, by the Parliamentary Gazetteer, or even by Father O'Laverty, priest of the parish. So one might have concluded it to be a figment of the folk revival of the late 19th century, but for energetic oral tradition, supported by its appearance in prints of 1842 and 1854, and a Lawrence photograph of about 1878.

The average life of a maypole seems to have been around thirty years. The present one was erected in 1977 by the Borough Council, in deference to strong local feeling, at a cost to the ratepayers of, I am told by Tony Merrick, £10,000. It is around 70 feet high, painted white, plain and stumpy, with rudimentary cross trees and compass-point-letters (but no weather-cock) above the truck (or bun). It is ornamented with weather-cock, and circlet of sailing-boats. Dancing takes place around it on May Day, and on other occasions of celebration. A predecessor came to grief in 1955 when a lorry crashed into it at rush-hour, snapping off the pole, which fell harmlessly down the centre of the Shore Road, damaging neither person nor vehicle. In 1957 and 1949 previous poles were erected at the expense of the Dunn family of Tudor Hall (56). The 1936 pole, the highest on record, at eighty feet, and the most graceful, was erected by the then Holywood Urban District Council, but blew down in a gale at noon on 12 February 1943, narrowly missing a bus standing at the nearby stop: I recall the public dismay, and the impossibility of replacing it in war-time. Earlier maypoles seem to have been paid for by the Harrison family of Mertoun Hall (demolished). Successive maypoles, and the citizens of Holywood, appear to have lived charmed lives.

Today, "the base of the Maypole is slotted into a hinged metal sleeve, in turn secured to a ten feet deep concrete foundation, so enabling the pole to be lowered for maintenance work etc. Even more importantly, this arrangement almost totally eliminates the possibility of rot occurring" (information from Tony Merrick). The sleeve is clumsy and ugly, painted black, but leaves no doubt that, in another collision between vehicle and maypole, the maypole would, this time, come off best. The pole, which is not repainted as often as it might be, is bedecked with bunting, light-bulbs, and other ornaments on feast-days. By long-standing custom, the flag is flown at half-mast on the death of a notable individual either born in Holywood, or else resident for at least fifty years. I think I qualify under the former heading, though not the latter; but whether I shall receive this honour, on my way to join my great-grandfather in the old Priory graveyard, I shall not live to learn!

Photograph: A C W Merrick. Lithograph: from J B Doyle, 'Tours in Ulster'.

Situation: Junction of High Street and Shore Road, Holywood; td, Demesne; District Council, North Down; Grid ref. J 397 791.

References: Not listed (why not?). Raven, map, 1625; Harris, 'County of Down', 1744, p 70; Marcus Ward, print, 1842; Doyle, 'Tours in Ulster', 1854; Merrick, 'Buildings of Holywood', 1986, pp 13-16.

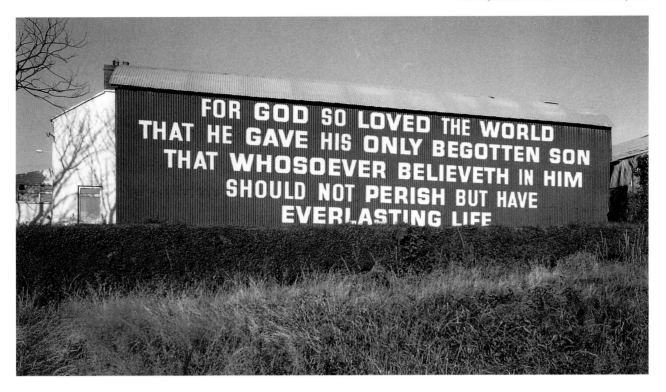

Pious Barn, Coach Hill, Ballygilbert, Clandeboye, Bangor

183. Neither a folly, nor a monument, nor a memorial; but where else to classify it? Painted, very neatly, in enormous three-foot-high white sans-serif letters on the corrugated iron barn, verse 16 from St John's Gospel, chapter 4.

It seems that, about 1930, the farmer, one Samuel Graham, set about erecting his fine new barn. A passing Methodist minister from Bangor, the Rev. Mr Armstrong, pointed out that its side wall would provide a magnificent site for a biblical text (as indeed, it was to prove), and, with the willing consent of Mr Graham, commissioned the painting. Originally, the barn was painted red; it is not remembered who laid out and executed the lettering in white, but there it remained, through rain and storm, for many years. The lettering was renewed in the late 1950s, and again in 1979, in each case by a professional sign-painter. Then, in 1994, the barn wall was battered down by a gale. Samuel Graham's grandsons, with exemplary piety, resheeted it in corrugated iron, even though it was no longer needed for agricultural purposes, and its structure was otherwise in poor order; and called in a sign-painter from Dundonald who, using old photographs, very creditably laid out the text again, and with masking-tape put it back as good as new, this time white on brown: no mean feat, and it required a considerable expenditure of masking-tape.

Patton says "On the gable of a more permanent barn facing the road is the name of the farm in white pebbles set in the render. On the hill up behind is a large ring of trees, named by Lord Dufferin *Jan Mayen Clump*". The farmhouse at Coach Hill was, according to local tradition, a half-way stopping point for the mail coaches driving from Belfast to Donaghadee.

One of the icons of my childhood; in fact, the only one to survive quite unspoiled and almost unaltered, except for the change from red to brown. The other icons were: the great rock, on the shore beside the road from Newtown-ards to Portaferry, which used to ask the unanswerable

question ETERNITY WHERE? until, comparatively recently, defaced and vandalised; R L Praeger, no less, describes this as "the Butterlump Stone, a huge block of black basalt lying tilted on bright red beds of Triassic sandstone. This block is estimated to contain about 1,720 cubic feet, and to weigh about 130 tons. It is a relic of the Great Ice Age, carried here from some spot further north, where such rock occurs - possibly from Scrabo Hill".

And then, the successive stencilled exhortations, paint-ed on walls and fences in the late 1930s by two old gentle-men who followed each other around, a few weeks apart, the first writing up GUINNESS IS GOOD FOR YOU, and the second writing up BOOZE IS BAD FOR YOU: one hopes, and supposes, that never the twain did meet.

And lastly, the Kircubbin Pig, painted a different colour every year to match the wall upon which he perched at the entrance to the village, brutally and iconoclastically slaughtered by a new owner some dozen years ago, to my dismay, because every time I passed this way I used to enjoy looking to see what colour the pig was this year.

The barn, I am happy to say, is almost exactly as I have always remembered it. If I had a barn facing a main high-way, which alas I have not, I would have painted on it my favourite pseudo-scriptural text, which is from the Notebooks of Samuel Butler, and would read: "When the virtuous man turneth away from the virtue which he hath committed, and doeth that which is unlawful and nice, it shall sometimes be a good deal better both for him and everyone else". It would, however, have to be a good-sized barn!

Photograph: A C W Merrick (see also colour illus. 41).

Situation: 360 Belfast Road, Clandeboye; td, Ballygilbert; District Council, North Down; Grid ref. J 461 802.

References: Not listed (unsurprisingly). Butler, 'Notebooks', 1934, p 164; Praeger, 'BCDR. Official Guide to County Down,' 1898, p 94; Patton, 'Bangor', UAHS, 1999, pp 22, 210; information from family of the present owner and from A C W Merrick.

BIBLIOGRAPHY

This bibliography relates only to printed books. Citations from newspapers and journals; particulars of maps, guides to individual buildings, deeds, documents, letters, private papers and unpublished material, will be found in the references appended to the entries for the buildings concerned. Where no such particulars are given, it may be assumed that the authority in question is in private hands and unavailable for public access.

Anderson, Amy and Lyttle, Joy *Portaferry Presbyterian Church 1642-1992,* [Portaferry, ?1993]

An archaeological survey of County Down Ed. by E.M.Jope, Belfast, 1966

The architecture of Richard Morrison and William Vitruvius Morrison. Ed. by A.M.Rowan, Dublin, 1989

Atkinson, A *Ireland exhibited to England in a political and moral survey of her population,* 2 vols, London, 1823

Atkinson, E.D. *Dromore: an Ulster diocese,* Dundalk, 1925

Atkinson, E.D. *An Ulster parish: being a history of Donaghcloney (Waringstown),* Dublin, 1898

Baillie M.G.L. *Tree-ring dating and archaeology,* London, 1982

Ballywalter Park. Ed. by Peter Rankin, UAHS, Belfast, 1985

Barry, John *Hillsborough: a parish in the Ulster Plantation,* 3rd ed., Belfast, 1982

Bassett, G.H. *County Down guide and directory,* Dublin 1886

Bell, Philip, Brett, C.E.B. and Matthew, Robert *Portaferry & Strangford,* UAHS, Belfast, 1969

Bence-Jones, Mark *Burke's guide to country houses,* Vol. 1: *Ireland,* London, 1978; 1988

Benn, George *The history of the town of Belfast ... and a description of some remarkable antiquities in its neighbourhood,* Belfast, 1823

Benn, George *A history of the town of Belfast from the earliest times to ... 1810 ,* London, 1877-1880

Blair, May *Once upon the Lagan: the story of the Lagan canal,* Belfast, 1981 (with corrections, 1994)

Borlase, William *Dolmens of Ireland,* 3 vols, London, 1897

Boswell, James *Boswell in search of a wife, 1766-9.* Ed. by F.Brady and F.A. Pottle, London, 1957 (Yale edition of the private papers)

Brett, C.E.B. *Buildings of Belfast,1700-1914,* London, 1967; Belfast, 1985

Brett, C.E.B. *Buildings of County Antrim,* UAHS, Belfast, 1996

Brett, C.E.B. *Buildings of County Armagh,* UAHS, Belfast, 1999

Brett, C.E.B. *Court houses and market houses of the province of Ulster,* UAHS, Belfast, 1973

Brett, C.E.B. *East Down, including Ardglass, Killough, Dundrum, Clough, Seaforde, Loughinisland, Killyleagh, Killinchy and Crossgar,* UAHS, Belfast, 1973

Brett, C.E.B. *Five big houses of Cushendun,* Belfast, 1997

Brett, C.E.B. *Long shadows cast before: nine lives in Ulster, 1625-1977,* Edinburgh, 1978

Brett, C.E.B. *Mid Down: Hillsborough, Dromore, Dromara, Ballynahinch, The Spa, Drumaness and Saintfield,* UAHS, Belfast, 1974

Buildings at risk: a catalogue of historic buildings at risk in Northern Ireland, UAHS, Belfast, 1- , 1993-

Burke, Bernard *A genealogical and heraldic history of the landed gentry of Ireland,* new ed., London, 1912

Burke's peerage and baronetage, 106th ed., 2 vols, Chicago, 1999

Butler, Samuel *Further extracts from the notebooks.* Ed by A.T. Bartholomew, London, 1934

Calendar of State papers relating to Ireland, 11 vols, London, 1860-1912

Camblin, Gilbert *The town in Ulster: an account of the origin and building of the towns of the Province and the development of their rural setting,* Belfast, 1951

Carey, J.A. *Historical notes on the abbey and parish of Bangor,* Belfast, 1963

Carr, Peter, 'The most unpretending of places': a history of Dundonald, County Down,* Dundonald 1987 (with corrections 1990)

Childe-Pemberton, W.S. *The Earl Bishop: the life of Frederick Hervey, Bishop of Derry, Earl of Bristol,* 2 vols, London, 1924

Clandeboye. Ed. By Peter Rankin, UAHS, Belfast, 1985

Clergy of Down and Dromore. Ed. and with brief parish histories by Fred Rankin, Belfast, 1996

Colvin, *Sir* Howard, *A biographical dictionary of British architects, 1600-1840,* 3rd ed., London, 1995

The compleat Irish traveller: containing a general description of the most noted cities, towns, seats, buildings, loughs, &c in the kingdom of Ireland, 2 vols, London, 1788

Craig, Maurice *The architecture of Ireland from the earliest times to 1880,* London, 1982

Craig, Maurice and Craig, Michael *Mausolea hibernica,* Dublin, 1999

Craig, Maurice and The Knight of Glin *Ireland observed: a handbook to the buildings and antiquities,* Cork, 1970

Curl, J.S. *A celebration of death: an introduction to some of the buildings, monuments and settings of funerary architecture in the western European tradition,* rev. ed., London, 1993

Curl, J.S. *Classical churches in Ulster,* UAHS, Belfast, 1980

Curl, J.S. *Mausolea in Ulster,* UAHS, Belfast, 1978

DoENI *Hillsborough conservation area,* Belfast, 1976

Dean, J.A.K. *The gate lodges of Ulster: a gazetteer,* UAHS, Belfast, 1994

Delany, Mary, *Letters from Georgian Ireland: the correspondence, 1731-68.* Ed. by Angélique Day, Belfast, 1991

Dewar, James *History of Elmwood Church with biographical sketches of its pastors and founders 1859-1899,* Belfast, 1900

The dictionary of architecture. Ed. by Wyatt Papworth for the Architectural Publication Society, 8 vols, London, 1852-1892

Dictionary of national biography . Ed. by Sir Leslie Stephen [and others], 79 vols, London, 1885-1996

Dixon, Hugh, Kenmuir, Kenneth and Kennett, Jill *Donaghadee and Portpatrick,* UAHS, Belfast, 1977

Dixon, Hugh *An introduction to Ulster architecture,* UAHS, Belfast, 1975

Dixon, Hugh *Soane and the Belfast Academical Institution,* Ballycotton, 1976

Dixon, Hugh *Ulster architecture 1800-1900,* UAHS, Belfast, 1972

Down and Connor Church Accommodation Society *Fourth and final report ... together with a detailed account of the different churches towards the building of which the Committee have given assistance,* Belfast, 1843

Downshire A.B.S.T.H. 3rd marquess of *Letters of a great Irish landlord: a selection from the estate correspondence ... 1809-45.* Ed. by W.A. Maguire, Belfast, 1974

Doyle, J.B. *Tours in Ulster: a handbook to the antiquities and scenery of the north of Ireland,* Dublin, 1854

Dubourdieu, John *Statistical survey of the county of Down, with observations on the means of improvement,* Dublin, 1802

Dunlop, Durham *Life of W.J. Barre,* Belfast, 1868

Edwardian architecture and its origins. Ed. by Alastair Service, London, 1975

Encyclopaedia Britannica, 11th ed., 29 vols, London, 1910-1911

Evans, David *An introduction to modern Ulster architecture,* UAHS, Belfast, 1977

Ewart, L.M. *Handbook of the United Diocese of Down & Connor & Dromore,* Belfast, [1886]

Further glimpses of the Ards, Ards Historical Society, Newtownards, 1980

Gailey, Alan *Rural houses of the north of Ireland,* Edinburgh, 1984

Gallagher, Lyn and Rogers, Dick *Castle, coast and cottage: the National Trust in Northern Ireland,* Belfast, 1986; 1992

Girouard, Mark *The Victorian country house,* rev. ed., London, 1979

Girvan, W.D. *North Antrim,* UAHS, Belfast, 1972

Gomme, Andor and Walker, David *Architecture of Glasgow,* 2nd ed., London, 1987

Gravestone inscriptions Ed. by R.S.J. Clarke. County Down II, III, V (Comp. by R.S.J. Clarke), XVII (Comp. by A.C.W. Merrick), Belfast, 1988,1969,1984,1978.

Green, E.R.R. *The industrial archaeology of County Down,* Belfast, 1963

Gwynn, Aubrey and Hadcock, R.N. *Medieval religious houses: Ireland,* London, 1970

Hall, S.C. and Hall, A.M. *Ireland: its scenery, character,* 3 vols, London, 1841-1843

Hammond, N.G.L. *A history of Greece to 322 B.C.,* 3rd ed., Oxford, 1986

Hamond, F.W. *Antrim coast & glens: industrial heritage,* Belfast, 1991

[Harris, Walter and Smith, Charles] *The antient and present state of the County of Down, containing a chorographical description, with the natural and civil history of the same,* Dublin, 1744

Hearth, *A review of projects 1999,* Belfast, 1999

Hillsborough Castle. Ed. by Peter Rankin, UAHS, Belfast, 1993

Historic monuments of Northern Ireland. Ed. by Ann Hamlin, Belfast, 1983

A history of congregations in the Presbyterian Church in Ireland 1610-1982, Belfast, 1982

Hitchcock, H.- R. *Architecture: nineteenth and twentieth centuries,* 4th ed., New Haven, 1987

House of Commons, Select Committee on Manor Courts in Ireland, *Report,* 1837, London, 1838 [HC 1837(494) xv]

Howley, James *Follies and garden buildings of Ireland,* New Haven, 1993

In an Irish garden. Ed. by Sibyl Connolly and Helen Dillon, London, 1986

In an Irish house. Ed. by Sibyl Connolly, London, 1988

An introduction to the Abercorn letters (as relating to Ireland 1736-1816). Selected and ed. by J.H. Gebbie, Omagh, 1972

Jones, Barbara *Follies and grottoes,* 2nd ed., London, 1974

Jupp, Belinda, *Heritage gardens inventory 1992,* Belfast, 1992

Kelly, T.T. *History of Holywood: the advantages which it affords as a summer retreat,* Belfast, 1850

Killen, John *A history of the Linen Hall Library 1788-1988,* Belfast, 1990

Knox, Alexander *History of the County Down,* Dublin, 1875

Krauskopf, Sharma *Irish lighthouses,* Belfast, 2001

Lawlor, H.C. *The Monastery of St Mochaoi of Nendrum,* Belfast, 1925

Lawson, J.P. *The gazetteer of Ireland,* 1842

Leslie, J.B. *Biographical succession lists of the clergy of Diocese of Down,* Enniskillen, 1936

Lewis, Samuel *A topographical dictionary of Ireland,* 3 vols, London, 1837; 1840; 1847

Linen houses of Banbridge: a historical and architectural study of the houses of the linen merchants of Banbridge by Banbridge Heritage Development. [Ed. by] Catherine Cahill, Jack Diamond, Banbridge, 1995

Little, James *Castlereagh Presbyterian Church 1658-1935: the story of an historic church,* Belfast, 1935

Loeber, Rolf *A biographical dictionary of architects in Ireland 1600-1720,* London, 1981

Long, Bill *Bright light, white water: the lighthouses of Ireland,* 2nd ed., Dublin, 1997

Lyttle, W.G. *The Bangor season: what's to be seen and how to see it,* Bangor, 1885

McCavery, Trevor *Newtown: a history of Newtownards,* Dundonald, 1994

McConaghy, J.W. and McConaghy, E.M. *A light for the road: Ballygilbert Presbyterian Church 1841-1991,* Holywood, 1991

McCutcheon, W.A. *The industrial archaeology of Northern Ireland,* Belfast, 1980

McDonald, K.C. *City of Dunedin,* Dunedin, 1965

MacHaffie, F.G. *Portpatrick to Donaghadee: the original short sea route,* Stranraer, 2002

McParland, Edward *Francis Johnston, architect, 1760-1829,* Celbridge, 1969 (Quarterly bulletin of the IGS, XII, Nos 3/4)

McWilliam, Colin *Lothian, except Edinburgh,* Harmondsworth, 1978 (Buildings of Scotland)

Magill, Joseph and McCafferty, *Donacloney Meeting: an historical survey,* Lurgan, 1950

Maguire, W.A. *The Downshire estates in Ireland, 1801-1845: the management of Irish landed estates in the early nineteenth century,* Oxford, 1972

Malins, Edward and Bowe, Patrick *Irish gardens and demesnes from 1830,* London, 1980

Mallory, J.P. and McNeill, T.E. *The archaeology of Ulster from colonization to Plantation,* Belfast, 1991

Marshal, H.C. *The parish of Lambeg,* Lisburn, 1933

Mason, W.S. *A statistical account, or parochial survey of Ireland,* 3 vols, Dublin, 1814, 1816, 1819

Mayo, Janet *A history of ecclesiastical dress,* London, 1984

Merrick, A.C.W. *Buildings of Holywood,* Holywood, 1986

Montgomery, William *The Montgomery manuscripts,* Belfast, 1830; Ed. by George Hill, Belfast, 1869

Montgomery-Massingberd, Hugh and Sykes, Simon *Great houses of Ireland,* London, 1999

Nicolson, Harold, *Helen's Tower,* London, 1937

O'Donovan, John *Letters containing information relative to the antiquities of the county of Down collected during the progress of the Ordnance Survey in 1834.* Ed ... by Michael Herity, Dublin, 2001 (Ordnance Survey letters. Down)

O'Keefe, Peter and Simington, Tom *Irish stone bridges: history and heritage,* Blackrock, 1991

O'Laverty, James *A historical account of the Diocese of Down and Connor,* 5 vols, Dublin, 1878, 1880, 1884, 1887, 1895

Oram, Richard *Craigavon,* UAHS, Belfast, 1971

Oram, Richard and Rankin, P.J. *Dungannon & Cookstown; Coalisland, Stewartstown, Tullyhogue, Newmills, Donaghmore, Castlecaulfield and Pomeroy,* UAHS, Belfast, 1971

Oram, Richard *Expressions of faith: Ulster's church heritage,* Newtownards, 2001

Ordnance Survey memoirs of Ireland. Ed. by Angélique Day, 40 vols, Belfast, 1990-1998

Owen, D.J. *A short history of the port of Belfast,* Belfast, 1917

Pack-Beresford, S.E. *Christ Church, Carrowdore,* [Carrowdore], 1994

The parliamentary gazetteer of Ireland, 3 vols, Dublin, 1845-1846

Parissien, Steven *The Georgian Group book of the Georgian house,* London, 1995

Patterson, R.L. *Birds, fishes and Cetacea commonly frequenting Belfast Lough,* London, 1880

Patton, Marcus *Bangor: an historical gazetteer including Carnalea, Conlig , the Copeland Islands, Crawfordsburn, Groomsport and Six Road Ends,* UAHS, Belfast, 1999

Pevsner, Nikolaus *London [Vol. I]: the Cities of London and Westminster,* 3rd ed., Harmondsworth, 1973 (Buildings of England)

Pierce, Richard and Coey, Alastair, *Taken for granted*, Belfast, 1984

Potterton, Homan *Irish church monuments 1570-1880*, UAHS, Belfast, 1975

Praeger, R.L. *Belfast and County Down Railway Company. Official guide to County Down and the Mourne Mountains*, Belfast, 1898

Prehistoric ritual and religion: essays in honour of Aubrey Burl. Ed. by Alex Gibson & Derek Simpson, Stroud, 1998

A preliminary survey of the ancient monuments of Northern Ireland. Ed. by D.A. Chart, Belfast, 1940

Public works: the architecture of the Office of Public Works, 1831-1987. Ed. by C. O'Connor and J. O'Regan, Dublin, 1988

Rankin, J.F. *The heritage of Drumbo*, [Drumbo], 1981

Rankin, P.J. *Irish building ventures of the Earl Bishop of Derry 1730-1803*, UAHS, Belfast, 1972

Reeves, William, *Ecclesiastical antiquities of Down, Connor and Dromore*, Dublin, 1847

Reilly, E.G.S. *A genealogical history of the family of Montgomery, comprising the lines of Eglinton and Braidstane in Scotland and Mount-Alexander and Grey-Abbey in Ireland*, London, 1842

Rennie, John *The theory, formation and construction of British and foreign harbours*, 2 vols, London, 1851-1854

Rice, J. *The Giant's Ring: a BELB booklet for teachers*, Belfast, 1996

Richardson, D.S. *Gothic revival architecture in Ireland*, 2 vols, New York, 1983

St. Andrew's Inishargy, Balligan. Ed. by Frances Jackson, [Belfast, 1966]

Savage-Armstrong, G.F. *A genealogical history of the Savage family in Ulster*, London, 1906

Scott, E.V. *Churches of the Diocese of Connor: an illustrated history*, [Newtownabbey?, 1997]

Seven Victorian architects ... Ed. by Jane Fawcett, London, 1976

Smith, Elizabeth *The Irish journals, 1840-1850: a selection.* Ed. by David Thomson and McGusty, Oxford, 1980

Stalley, Roger *The Cistercian monasteries of Ireland: an account of the history, art and architecture of the white monks in Ireland 1142-1540*, London, 1987

Stanford, W.B. *Ireland and the classical tradition*, Dublin, 1976

Strickland, W.G. *A dictionary of Irish artists*, 2 vols, Dublin, 1913

Stuart, James and Revett, Nicholas *The antiquities of Athens, measured and delineated*, 4 vols, London, 1762-1816

Swanzy, H.B. *Succession lists of the Diocese of Dromore*, Belfast, 1933

Taylor, George and Skinner, Andrew *Maps of the roads of Ireland*, London, 1778; 1783

Temple, Nigel *George Repton's Pavilion notebook: a catalogue raisonné*, Aldershot, 1993

Twentieth century architecture, Ireland. Ed. by Annette Bekker [and others], Munich, 1997

Twenty-one views in Belfast and its neighbourhood [Ed. by P.D.Hardy], Dublin, 1836 [1837]

The Upper Ards Historical Society guide to Portaferry and district, [rev. ed.] Compiled by Amy Anderson, Banbridge, [1997]

Walker, Simon *Historic Ulster churches*, Belfast, 2000

Ware, Dora *A short dictionary of British architects*, London, 1967

Williams, Jeremy *Architecture in Ireland, 1837-1921*, Dublin, 1994

Wilson, Ian *Bangor: historic photographs of the County Down town 1870-1914*, Belfast, 1992

Wilson, William *The post-chaise companion ... through Ireland*, Dublin, 1784; 1786; 1803; 1813

Wylie, Robin *Ulster Model Schools: the architecture and fittings of Model National Schools built in Ulster in the nineteenth century*, UAHS, Belfast, 1997

Young, R.M. *Belfast and the province of Ulster in the twentieth century*, Brighton, 1909

The Battle Garden, Kilwarlin (26). Photograph: MBR

INDEX
(to page numbers)

Cleland mausoleum (179), old church, and motte, Dundonald. Photograph: A C W Merrick

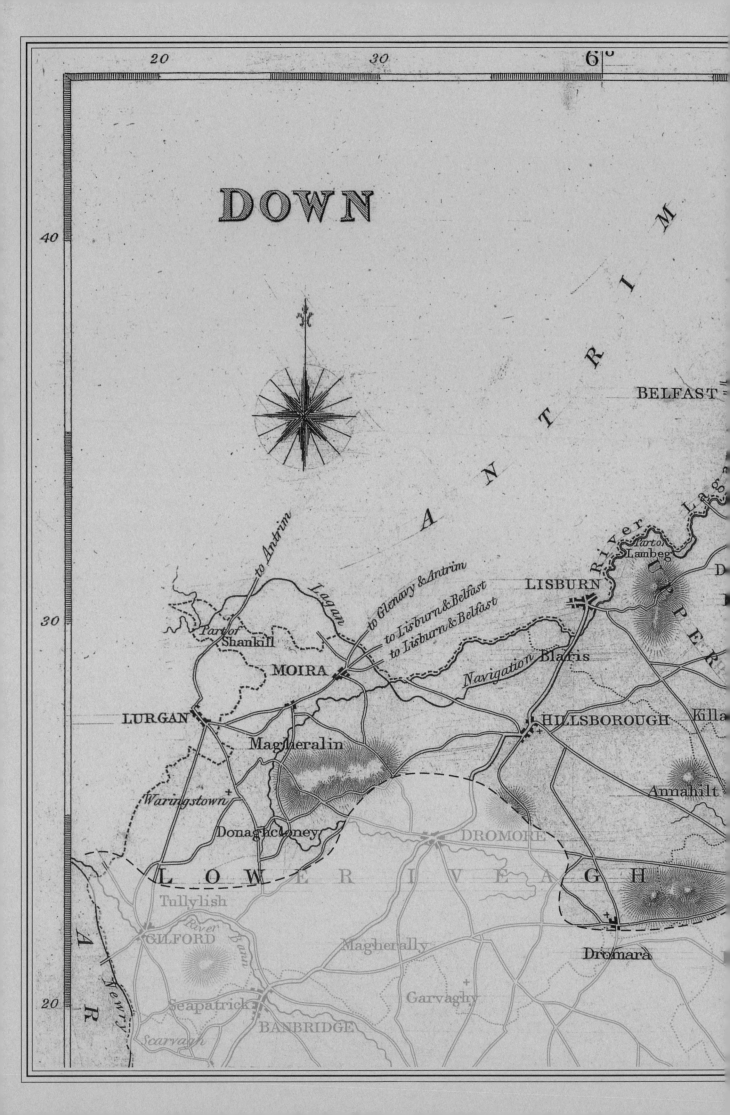